America's
TEST KITCHEN

Also by the Editors of *Cook's Illustrated*

The America's Test Kitchen Family Cookbook

The Best Recipe Series:
The Best 30-Minute Recipe
The Best Light Recipe
The Cook's Illustrated Guide to Grilling and Barbecue
Best American Side Dishes
The New Best Recipe
Cover & Bake
Steaks, Chops, Roasts, and Ribs
Baking Illustrated
Restaurant Favorites at Home
Perfect Vegetables
Italian Classics
The Best American Classics
The Best Soups & Stews

The TV Companion Series:
Cooking at Home with America's Test Kitchen
America's Test Kitchen Live!
Inside America's Test Kitchen
Here in America's Test Kitchen
The America's Test Kitchen Cookbook

834 Kitchen Quick Tips

For a full listing of all our books or to order titles:
http://www.cooksillustrated.com
http://www.americastestkitchen.com
or call 800-611-0759

The cast of *America's Test Kitchen,* from left to right: Jack Bishop, Erika Bruce, Rebecca Hays, Julia Collin Davison, Christopher Kimball, Bridget Lancaster, and Adam Ried.

test kitchen favorites

test kitchen favorites

BY THE EDITORS AT
AMERICA'S TEST KITCHEN

ILLUSTRATIONS
John Burgoyne

PHOTOGRAPHY
Daniel J. van Ackere
Carl Tremblay

America's
TEST KITCHEN

AMERICA'S TEST KITCHEN
BROOKLINE, MASSACHUSETTS

America's Test Kitchen
17 Station Street
Brookline, MA 02445

Library of Congress Cataloging-in-Publication Data
The Editors at America's Test Kitchen

Test Kitchen Favorites
1st Edition

ISBN-13: 978-1-933615-04-2
ISBN-10: 1-933615-04-4
(hardback): $34.95 U.S./$43.95 CAN
1. Cooking. 1. Title
2006

Manufactured in the United States of America

10 9 8 7 6 5 4 3 2 1

Distributed by America's Test Kitchen
17 Station Street, Brookline, MA 02445

Senior Editor: Lori Galvin
Assistant Editor: Elizabeth Wray Emery
Series Designer: Amy Klee
Art Director: Carolynn DeCillo
Designer: Matthew Warnick
Photographers: Daniel J. van Ackere and Carl Tremblay
Jacket Photographs: Daniel J. van Ackere
Food Stylists: Marie Piraino and Mary Jane Sawyer
Line Illustrations: John Burgoyne
Science Illustrations: Sean McNaughton
Senior Production Manager: Jessica Lindheimer Quirk
Copyeditor: Debra Hudak
Proofreader: Jeffrey Schier
Indexer: Elizabeth Parson

CONTENTS

PREFACE

I HAVE BEEN AROUND HORSES ALL MY LIFE AND HAVE learned, the hard way, that for every horse expert there is yet another theory about training, healing, or riding. One neighbor, Tom, had a horse that kept violently throwing his head. Instead of using a tie-down (a half-halter with a strap that connects to the breastplate, keeping the horse's head from rising up), he just grabbed a small piece of two-by-four. On the next ride, when his horse threw his head, well, Tom gave him a good rap and that was that. The horse learned his lesson.

Yes, a firm hand is a good thing around any large animal, but, rather than use the two-by-four, I am more in the camp that tries to understand why a horse does what it does. Having read a number of "horse whisperer" books, I've discovered that horses are driven by fear and an over-riding concern for safety. But every author has a different theory about what to do next. I've ridden horses that will spook at the sight of a stick, a chipmunk, a chicken, even a fern blowing in the breeze. I've even found myself at a full gallop on a horse that saw a small puddle and managed to make a full lateral move to the other side of the road without breaking stride.

Once in a while, however, I come across someone who really knows what she is doing. One of our horses, Chip, has navicular disease, which affects tendons and cartilage in the leg and results in lameness. We had Chip X-rayed and treated with drugs, and even considered expensive surgery. Then Geena showed up—all five feet and 95 pounds of her—and immediately diagnosed the problem as being the horseshoes. They force a horse to step toe first (instead of heel first, which is more natural) and do not allow the feet to spread and develop properly. The shoes were removed, the hooves were trimmed for shoeless walking, and a month later, Chip is almost 100 percent recovered. There was a problem, and Geena had the answer.

In this day and age of media experts, mega-celebrities, and instant stars, there is something comforting about really knowing what works and what doesn't. Those of us who are lucky enough to be on the set of *America's Test Kitchen* know very well that it isn't our looks or breezy personalities that make ours the most watched cooking show on public television. It's that we have, over many years, put in the time and effort to test every conceivable culinary theory we've come across. It can be said, without fear of argument, that there are culinary rights and wrongs. There is a right way to cook a pot roast. Cornstarch, flour, and tapioca are all thickeners, but each has its pros and cons. High heat is great for some things but lousy for others. Some knives sharpen well and others don't. There is a lot to learn on the way to becoming a good cook.

After seven years of filming *America's Test Kitchen*, however, we have all learned one totally unexpected lesson: We really love to cook, even after a full day of it in the test kitchen. We like to "stand facing the stove," as Irma Rombauer instructed in the *Joy of Cooking*. We love working together, performing for the film crew, and teaching what we have learned in the test kitchen; and, of course, we love to eat our own food.

Sure, cooking is a trade—there is a wealth of information that is key to becoming proficient—but, as with horses, it should ultimately be about having fun. When you start a recipe or swing your leg over the saddle, you ought to be excited at the prospect of spending time doing what you love most. The skills that took time and effort to master are now second nature, and the pure joy of doing something well is one of life's great rewards. (One of the few joys of having reached the half-century mark is that I can now write about "life's rewards.")

So take these recipes and watch *America's Test Kitchen* knowing that, at the end of the day, you are going to become a very good cook (if you aren't already) and that this simple skill will be a source of great pleasure every time you walk into the kitchen, grab your chef's knife, and stand facing the stove.

Christopher Kimball
Founder and editor, *Cook's Illustrated* and *Cook's Country*
Host, *America's Test Kitchen*
Brookline, Massachusetts, 2006

WELCOME TO AMERICA'S TEST KITCHEN

AMERICA'S TEST KITCHEN IS A VERY REAL 2,500-SQUARE-foot kitchen located just outside of Boston. It is the home of *Cook's Illustrated* and *Cook's Country* magazines and is the Monday through Friday destination of more than two dozen test cooks, editors, food scientists, tasters, photographers, and cookware specialists. Our mission is to test recipes over and over again until we understand how and why they work and until we arrive at the best version.

Our television show highlights the best recipes developed in the test kitchen during the past year—those recipes that our test kitchen staff makes at home time and time again. These recipes are accompanied by our most exhaustive equipment tests and our most interesting food tastings.

Christopher Kimball, the founder and editor of *Cook's Illustrated* magazine, is host of the show and asks the questions you might ask. It's the job of our chefs, Julia Collin Davison, Bridget Lancaster, Rebecca Hays, and Erika Bruce to demonstrate our recipes. The chefs show Chris what works and what doesn't, and they explain why. In the process, they discuss (and show us) the best and worst examples from our development process: tough beef stew, greasy fish and chips, and light cheesecakes no one wanted to eat.

Adam Ried, our equipment guru, shares the highlights from our detailed testing process in Equipment Corner segments. He brings with him our favorite (and least favorite) gadgets and tools. He tells you which standing mixers performed best in a dozen kitchen tests and shows why you should put together your own knife set instead of buying a packaged set.

Jack Bishop is our ingredient expert. He has Chris taste our favorite (and least favorite) brands of common food products—everything from filet mignon and breakfast sausage to sandwich bread and bottled salad dressing. Chris may not always enjoy these exercises (cider vinegar and canned refried beans aren't a whole lot of fun to taste), but he usually learns something as Jack explains what makes one brand superior to another.

Although there are just seven cooks and editors who appear on the television show, another 50 people worked to make the show a reality. Melissa Baldino helped coordinate many aspects of filming to ensure that taping would run smoothly. Meg Ragland conducted all the historical recipe research. Along with the on-air crew, executive chefs Erin McMurrer and Dawn Yanagihara planned and organized the 26 television episodes shot in May 2006. Erin, with the help of Keith Dresser, ran the "back kitchen," where all the food that appeared on camera originated. Garth Clingingsmith organized the tasting and equipment segments with the assistance of Elizabeth Bomze.

During filming, chefs Erika Bruce, Meredith Butcher, Katie Henderson, Matt Herron, Cali Rich, Jeremy Sauer, Diane Unger, and Sandra Wu were in the kitchen from early in the morning to late at night helping Erin and Keith cook all the food needed on set. Nadia Domeq was charged with the Herculean task of making sure all the ingredients we needed were on hand. Kitchen assistants Billy Otis, Christine Morrison, Melody McLoud, Maria Elena Delgado, and Ena Guidel also worked long hours. Charles Kelsey, David

Pazmiño, Rachel Toomey, Megan Wycoff, and Andrew Loy helped coordinate the efforts of the kitchen with the television set by readying props, equipment, and food.

The staff of A La Carte Communications turned our recipes, tastings, testings, and science experiments into a lively television show. Special thanks to executive producers Geoffrey Drummond and Nat Katzman; director and editor Herb Sevush; supervising producer Richard Dooley; director of photography Jan Maliszewski.

We also appreciate the hard work of the video production team, including Stephen Hussar, Michael McEachern, Peter Dingle, Ken Fraser, Patrick Kelly, Gilles Morin, Brenda Coffey, Patrick Ruth, Jack McPhee, Aaron Frutman, Elena Battista, Catherine Uyenoyama, Virginia Quigley, and Rachel Burgio.

We also would like to thank Hope Reed, who handles station relations, and the team at American Public Television that presents the show: Cynthia Fenniman, Chris Funkhauser, Judy Barlow, and Tom Davison. Thanks also for production support from DGA Productions, Boston; Paul Swensen Productions, Santa Rosa, California; and Zebra Productions, New York. Thermador, Kohler, Woodbridge Wines, Viva Towels, and Cooking.com helped underwrite the show and we thank them for their support. Fresh produce was supplied for the show by Olgo Russo at A. Russo & Sons of Watertown, Massachusetts. Live plants and garden items for the show were supplied by Mark Cutler at Mahoney's Garden Center of Brighton, Massachusetts. Aprons for Christopher Kimball by Nicole Romano and staff aprons by Crooked Brook.

We hope this book gives you an inside look at America's Test Kitchen. We are passionate about our work, and we hope you enjoy our recipes as well as reading about the process by which they were created. Our mission is pretty simple. We want to help make you a better cook. We believe that our television show and this book will do just that. If you have comments or questions about the show or the book, contact us at www.americastestkitchen.com.

TEST KITCHEN FAVORITES

Julia and Chris dig into a juicy, all-beef meat loaf made with ground chuck and ground sirloin (and a pinch of gelatin to keep the loaf tender) and on the side—crispy skillet-roasted potatoes.

MEAT LOAF
dinner

CHAPTER 1

Meat loaf is as synonymous with good old-fashioned American cooking as apple pie. While some may prefer meat loaf made with meat loaf mix, a combination of beef, pork, and veal, there's something to be said for an all-beef loaf. An all-beef loaf can have terrific meaty flavor and it's convenient to boot, especially when you can't find meat loaf mix, or just don't want to fuss with buying three kinds of meat. However, a meat loaf made with all beef does require some special handling so that it doesn't taste like a dry, loaf-shaped hamburger. We set out to make a loaf with well-seasoned meat and just enough binder to give the loaf a tender, not tough, texture.

In choosing a side dish to partner with our meat loaf, we turned to another old-fashioned dish—skillet-roasted potatoes. Skillet-roasted potatoes are cooked on the stovetop, thus allowing the cook to free up the oven for the main course. We wanted potatoes that are creamy on the inside and crusty on the outside. Some skillet-roasted potatoes can be soggy and greasy—a pitfall we'd need to avoid in developing our recipe.

ALL-BEEF MEAT LOAF

WHAT WE WANTED: A well-seasoned all-beef meat loaf with a moist and tender texture.

All-beef meat loaf is an American classic that has as many variations as the Heinz ketchup that traditionally glazes it. But this humble approach has taken a backseat to loaves made from meat loaf mix—a combination of beef, pork, and veal. The reason for using a combination of meats was made abundantly clear as soon as we tasted an all-beef version. The texture was chewy, and the flavor was less interesting than the loaf made with three types of meat—more of a hamburger in the shape of a log. But when you can't find meat loaf mix or don't have it on hand for a quick, last-minute dinner, can an all-beef loaf make the grade?

We thought choosing the beef would be simple, but with the number of choices at the supermarket, we were stymied. Not only did ground beef come in several lean/fat percentage variations, but it was also often labeled according to the part of the animal it came from (see page 7 for tips on buying ground beef).

Knowing that meat loaf turns dry and tough without fat, we focused first on the 80 percent lean/20 percent fat ground beef, our choice for hamburgers. Taking samples from three supermarkets, we proceeded to build a simple working recipe. Despite having the same lean/fat percentages, each sample produced a different meat loaf. Some were moist and tender, while others were gristly, with fibrous curds. When we turned to ground beef from specific cuts—chuck, round, and sirloin—a clearer picture began to emerge. The chuck (20 percent fat) produced a moist but chewy loaf, with pieces of gristle. Ground round (15 percent fat) yielded more desirable results, but the flavor needed a boost. More pronounced and natural beef flavor came through with the ground sirloin (10 percent fat), but to the detriment of the texture, which was dry, chalky, and chewy. The solution? A combination. After several tests, tasters agreed that equal parts ground chuck and sirloin (1 pound of each) provided just the right balance of juicy, tender meat and assertive beefy flavor.

We needed to choose a liquid component that would both add moisture and tone down beef's naturally livery flavor. While milk is the traditional choice, after sampling milk and other dairy products (buttermilk and yogurt), tasters agreed that none of them did much to mitigate off-notes. Beef broth was even worse, contributing an additional (metallic) off-taste. Chicken broth was the surprise winner, transforming the loaf from livery to savory.

Taking cues from other meat loaf recipes, we added cheese for its welcome flavor, moisture, and binding qualities. After testing eight kinds, we settled on Monterey Jack for its moderate moisture content and neutral cheese flavor (this was meat loaf, after all, not cheese loaf). Surprisingly, the method we used to break down the cheese proved critical. Dicing and shredding left visible "hot pockets" of cheese that oozed unappealing liquid once the loaf was cut. Grated cheese proved superior, and freezing the grated cheese kept it crumbly.

Many recipes forgo starchy binders, but a battery of tests made their advantages clear: lightening the texture, retaining moisture, and improving sliceability. We decided from the outset to pass on rice and potatoes (too much trouble) and focused instead on bread crumbs (dry and fresh), crackers, oats, croutons, cereal, and stuffing mix. The last three were quickly discarded for their overwhelming flavors. Saltines emerged as the clear favorite, delivering a well-seasoned, tender loaf with good moisture.

We had now cooked 110 loaves, but the texture still seemed a bit tough. The solution came to us in reviewing our testing notes. In early tests, we had success with reduced veal stock, a gelatinous ingredient chefs rely on to give savory recipes an unctuous texture. The problem is, the majority of home cooks don't typically keep veal stock on hand. But what if we added powdered gelatin to the loaf to replicate the gelatinous qualities of the veal stock? We began adding unflavored powdered gelatin to the chicken broth before mixing it into the meat loaf. We tried a full packet, and, indeed, the texture was radically different—bouncy, like Jell-O. More tests revealed that a mere half-teaspoon was ideal, making the texture luxuriously smooth rather than gelatinously weird.

After sampling raw, sautéed, and caramelized onions, tasters agreed that sautéed onions produced the best flavor profile. Celery and garlic added a more complex savory flavor. Fresh thyme, paprika, soy sauce, and prepared mustard delivered an assertive flavor that married well with the beef. We cooked these seasonings along with the onions, celery, and garlic and deglazed the pan with tomato juice to create an intense, aromatic flavor.

The almost-finished meat loaf needed its crowning glory—a glaze. After experimenting with mustard, Worcestershire, and steak sauce, we settled on meat loaf's trusty and traditional sidekick: ketchup. Applied at the beginning of cooking, the glaze mixed unappealingly with the liquids seeping out of the loaf. Finishing with the glaze produced better results, especially when we placed the loaf briefly under the broiler.

As a final test, we tried the recipe using the ground beef variations we had previously discarded, but tasters weren't fooled: They overwhelmingly preferred the mixture of 80/20 chuck and 90/10 sirloin. (A loaf made entirely with 85/15 round was an acceptable but distant second.) But in any case, all-beef meat loaf had finally graduated from a compromise of convenience to truly luxuriant comfort food.

WHAT WE LEARNED: A combination of half ground chuck and half ground sirloin yields a juicy, tender loaf with great beef flavor. Chicken broth, not beef broth or dairy, tames the beef's livery notes. Partially frozen shredded Monterey Jack cheese provides binding and flavor. And a surprise ingredient—powdered gelatin—gives our meatloaf a smooth, light texture that most all-beef meat loaves lack.

TESTING NOTES:

Troubleshooting Meat Loaf

Here are two problems we encountered with making meat loaf— and the steps we now take to avoid them.

Gray	**Greasy**
Problem: Sides of meat loaf remain crustless.	**Problem:** Meat loaf sits in an unappealing pool of grease.
Solution: Loaf pans expose only one side of the meat loaf to browning heat. By opting for a free-form loaf, we achieved an all-over browned crust.	**Solution:** Baking directly on a sheet pan provides no outlet for exuded grease. A foil base, poked with holes and set on a cooling rack, lets juices drain as the loaf cooks.

GLAZED ALL-BEEF MEAT LOAF

Serves 6 to 8

If you can't find chuck and/or sirloin, substitute 85 percent lean ground beef.

meat loaf

- 3 ounces Monterey Jack cheese, grated on the small holes of a box grater (about 1 cup)
- 1 tablespoon unsalted butter
- 1 medium onion, chopped fine (about 1 cup)
- 1 medium celery rib, chopped fine (about ½ cup)
- 1 medium garlic clove, minced or pressed through a garlic press (about 1 teaspoon)
- 2 teaspoons minced fresh thyme leaves
- 1 teaspoon paprika
- ¼ cup tomato juice
- ½ cup low-sodium chicken broth
- 2 large eggs
- ½ teaspoon unflavored powdered gelatin
- 1 tablespoon soy sauce
- 1 teaspoon Dijon mustard
- ⅔ cup crushed saltines
- 2 tablespoons minced fresh parsley leaves
- ¾ teaspoon salt
- ½ teaspoon ground black pepper
- 1 pound ground sirloin
- 1 pound ground chuck

glaze

- ½ cup ketchup
- 1 teaspoon hot pepper sauce
- ½ teaspoon ground coriander
- ¼ cup cider vinegar
- 3 tablespoons light brown sugar

1. FOR THE MEAT LOAF: Adjust an oven rack to the middle position and heat the oven to 375 degrees. Spread the cheese on a plate and place in the freezer until ready to use. To prepare the baking sheet, set a metal cooling rack over a rimmed baking sheet. Fold a sheet of heavy-duty aluminum foil to form a 10 by 6-inch rectangle. Center the foil on the cooling rack and poke holes in the foil with a skewer (about half an inch apart). Spray the foil with non-stick cooking spray.

2. Heat the butter in a 10-inch skillet over medium-high heat until foaming; add the onion and celery and cook, stirring occasionally, until beginning to brown, 6 to 8 minutes. Add the garlic, thyme, and paprika and cook, stirring, until fragrant, about 1 minute. Reduce the heat to low and add the tomato juice. Cook, stirring to scrape up the browned bits from the pan, until thickened, about 1 minute. Transfer the mixture to a small bowl and set aside to cool.

3. Whisk the broth and eggs in a large bowl until combined. Sprinkle the gelatin over the liquid and let stand 5 minutes. Stir in the soy sauce, mustard, saltines, parsley, salt, pepper, and onion mixture. Crumble the frozen cheese into a coarse powder and sprinkle over the mixture. Add the ground beef; mix gently with your hands until thoroughly combined, about 1 minute. Transfer the meat to the foil rectangle and shape into a 10 by 6-inch oval about 2 inches high. Smooth the top and edges of the meat loaf with a moistened spatula. Bake until an instant-read thermometer inserted into the center of the loaf reads 135 to 140 degrees, 55 to 65 minutes. Remove the meat loaf from the oven and turn on the broiler.

4. FOR THE GLAZE: While the meat loaf cooks, combine the ingredients for the glaze in a small saucepan; bring to a simmer over medium heat and cook, stirring, until thick and syrupy, about 5 minutes. Spread half of the glaze evenly over the cooked meat loaf with a rubber spatula; place under the broiler and cook until the glaze bubbles and begins to brown at the edges, about 5 minutes. Remove the meat loaf from the oven and spread evenly with the remaining glaze; place back under the broiler and cook until the glaze is again bubbling and beginning to brown, about 5 minutes more. Let the meat loaf cool about 20 minutes before slicing.

SHOPPING NOTES: Ground Beef

OUR GLAZED ALL-BEEF MEAT LOAF GETS ITS GREAT TEXTURE from two types of ground beef: lean sirloin and fattier chuck. Easy enough, except that many supermarkets sell ground beef labeled not by primal cut (chuck, round, sirloin, and so on) but by lean/fat percentage. When we tried substituting the appropriate percentages (80/20 for chuck, 90/10 for sirloin), the resulting loaves had remarkably inconsistent textures; some turned out tender, while others were gristly.

Puzzled, we contacted a meat specialist at Texas A&M University, who explained that supermarkets have two choices when it comes to offering ground beef by lean/fat percentage. They can buy it ground and individually packaged at an off-site facility, or they can buy large amounts from a wholesaler in "chub packs," grinding them further in the store while adding some of their own "shop trim" to the mix. Unlike large off-site packing facilities, supermarket butchers don't usually have the expensive equipment required to measure fat content accurately, so their product is less consistent than beef that's ground off-site.

How much less? To find out, we bought 30 packages of ground beef from different grocery stores in the same chain: 10 labeled chuck, which naturally has about 20 percent fat; 10 labeled 80/20, packed and processed in-store; and 10 labeled 80/20, packed and processed off-site. Off they went to the lab for fat analysis.

The results? The packages of chuck were within 2 percent of the expected fat content. The 80/20 beef packed off-site fell within the same range. But the 80/20 packed in-store was off by as much as 7 percent! No wonder our loaves were all over the map: For a recipe designed around 80/20 ground beef, "87/13" just didn't cut it. (That's like using regular milk in a recipe that calls for half-and-half.)

So for recipes that call for ground beef with specific fat percentages, we recommend buying packages labeled by primal cut or packaged by an off-site distributor. Look for the designation "Packed in [name of city]" on the label.

SCIENCE DESK: How Gelatin Mimics Veal

MANY MEAT LOAF RECIPES CALL FOR THREE DIFFERENT meats (beef, pork, and veal), and each one has a core function. Beef contributes assertive beefiness, while pork adds dimension with flavor and extra fattiness. With veal, it's mostly about the gelatin—a viscous substance with natural water-retaining qualities that help keep a meat loaf moist and unctuous. Gelatin is formed when collagen, the protein in a cow's connective tissue, breaks down during cooking. The collagen in calves (the source of veal) is more loosely structured—and therefore converts to gelatin more easily—than the collagen in an adult cow. In our all-beef meat loaf, we successfully replicated the gelatinous qualities of veal by adding powdered gelatin.

So how does it work? Gelatin is a pure protein that suspends water in a meshlike, semisolid matrix. By slowing down the movement of liquids, gelatin has a stabilizing effect, making it harder for water and other liquids to be forced out, essentially fencing them in. In meat loaf, then, gelatin helps by (1) decreasing the amount of liquid leaking from the meat as the other proteins coagulate and (2) improving the textural feel by making the liquids more viscous even when very hot. That viscosity translates to a luxuriant texture in the mouth—much like reduced stock, or demi-glace—and the perception of greater richness.

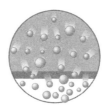 

Meat Loaf Without Gelatin
Moisture leaks out of meat loaf, giving it a coarser, grainier texture.

Meat Loaf With Gelatin
Moisture is suspended in a semisolid matrix, keeping the meat loaf juicy.

TASTING LAB: Ground Beef

MOST RECIPES SIMPLY CALL FOR "GROUND BEEF," BUT AS any supermarket shopper knows the choices are much more varied. The U.S. Department of Agriculture defines "ground beef" as ground fresh and/or frozen beef from primal cuts and trimmings containing no more than 30 percent fat. But that doesn't really help anyone understand the difference between ground round, ground chuck, and ground sirloin. And what about fat content, which can range as low as 7 percent?

To find out if the cut matters, we prepared hamburgers, Bolognese sauce, and meat loaf using each type of ground beef and held a blind tasting, asking tasters to comment on the taste and texture of each sample. The results were clear; differences between the cuts were obvious and noted across the board.

Ground round and ground beef consistently ranked last in our tests, with ground round described as "tough" and "chewy"; less polite tasters deemed the ground beef "livery" and "gross." Tasters preferred ground chuck and sirloin; the ultra-lean sirloin was favored for dishes in which other ingredients added much-needed fat, whereas chuck was preferred in hamburgers.

Rating Ground Beef

ELEVEN MEMBERS OF THE AMERICA'S TEST KITCHEN staff tasted four kinds of ground beef in hamburgers, Bolognese sauce, and meat loaf. The types of ground beef are listed below in order of preference based on their combined scores in the three tastings. For more information about shopping for ground beef, see page 7.

RECOMMENDED
Ground Chuck
Cut from the shoulder, ground chuck ranges from 15 to 20 percent fat and was favored by our tasters for its "rich" flavor and "tender," "moist" texture. The best choice for burgers.

RECOMMENDED
Ground Sirloin
Tasters praised the ground sirloin as "tender and tasty," especially in the meat loaf and Bolognese sauce, but found it a bit "dry" in hamburgers, though it did have "good beef flavor." Cut from the midsection of the animal near the hip, ground sirloin usually ranges in fat content from 7 to 10 percent.

NOT RECOMMENDED
Ground Round
Lean and tough, ground round comes from the rear upper leg and rump of the cow. Tasters rejected the round as "gristly" and "lacking beef flavor." The fat content is similar to that of ground chuck, usually ranging from 10 to 20 percent.

NOT RECOMMENDED
Ground Beef
Any cut or combination of cuts can be labeled "ground beef," so consistency is a problem. Because ground beef may have as much as 30 percent fat, greasiness can also be an issue. Our tasters dismissed the ground beef in all applications as "mushy," with an "old boiled beef taste."

CRISPY SKILLET-ROASTED POTATOES

WHAT WE WANTED: Evenly browned, crusty potatoes that are moist and creamy—and never greasy.

Before ovens were common in home kitchens, potatoes were roasted in a heavy skillet on the stovetop. The promise of this time-honored but old-fashioned method is extraordinarily crisp texture, something that is not always easily achieved in an oven. Thinking that this classic method deserved to be resurrected, we prepared a handful of recipes, most of them found in French cookbooks. Some required peeling and cutting, while others left the skin on and/or used whole potatoes. Olive oil, vegetable oil, butter, and clarified butter were all suggested, as were a variety of methods to facilitate crisping and cooking. The result? Six batches of stovetop-roasted potatoes that failed to impress. Uneven cooking, browned but soft exteriors, pale exteriors, dry insides, and greasy outsides were just a few of the problems. So why bother?

When done right, skillet-roasted potatoes are truly outstanding: extra-crisp on the outside and moist and creamy on the inside. And, the notion of preparing potatoes on the stovetop—freeing up the oven and saving time—was also appealing. So back into the test kitchen we went to discover what had gone wrong with our half-dozen plates of disappointing spuds.

Initial tests convinced us that if the potatoes were to brown evenly, they would have to cook in a single layer without being crowded. We also noted that the best browning occurred when the potatoes were left undisturbed before turning. Without making any final decisions about potato type, we started with Red Bliss—a low-starch, high-moisture variety that we use for oven-roasting. We wanted to cook as many potatoes as possible, so we chose a hefty 12-inch skillet, the largest in most households.

Tasters preferred the appearance, texture, and flavor of potatoes cooked with the skin on. Potato size and cut became an obsession. It was obvious that the pieces had to be uniform for even cooking. Ten test batches later, we came to the conclusion that quartered medium potatoes (lemon-sized) were best, as they offered two cut sides for crisping and one beautifully rounded side. Halved small potatoes were another good option.

Up until now, we had been using a traditional skillet, but occasionally a potato would stick. We switched to non-stick and were pleased that this rare problem disappeared completely and that the roasting results were equally good. In terms of fat for browning, butter proved problematic given its tendency to burn. We ruled out clarified butter (less prone to burning, but too much effort to make). Next we pitted vegetable oil against olive oil, and the latter won for extra flavor. As for the amount, 1 tablespoon was serviceable, while 2 tablespoons produced a much crispier crust; 3 tablespoons were too much, making for greasy spuds.

Our biggest remaining challenge was getting the interiors to cook through completely within the time it took for the exteriors to crisp and brown. We wondered if precooking

the potatoes might help. We scrubbed and cut a batch, placed them in a saucepan with cold water, and brought them to a boil. Immediately, we drained the potatoes and put them in a hot skillet. The insides were cooked but mushy, and the outsides did not brown well. Much like precooking, adding some water to the pan failed. We then thought maybe the cover could trap moisture and help solve this problem. We browned both cut sides of the potatoes uncovered over medium-high heat and then covered the skillet and finished cooking over medium-low. This technique, combined with the rinsing and drying of the cut potatoes before cooking (a common step when frying potatoes that removes surface starch), turned out crisp skillet potatoes that were also cooked through.

Now it was time to revisit potato type. We had been using the dense, high-moisture Red Bliss, the type of "waxy" potato one might use in a typical potato salad. At the other end of the spectrum are russets. These dry, low-starch potatoes turn out light and fluffy when baked but were a poor choice for this recipe: Dry interiors and poor browning were their downfall. Yukon Golds sit in the middle of the potato scale—neither dense and moist nor light and dry—but when skillet-roasted, they were judged on the dry side as well. So Red Bliss it was.

A sprinkle of pepper was most welcome, and table salt lost out to kosher salt and sea salt (added just before serving), which provided bigger, more interesting hits of flavor. With a great crust, a moist interior, and a nicely salted and peppered outer layer, these were hands down the best skillet-roasted potatoes we had ever eaten.

WHAT WE LEARNED: Red Bliss potatoes are the best choice because their high-moisture content yields evenly browned potatoes with a creamy, moist interior. Cut and rinse the potatoes to remove surface starch, which would otherwise cause the potatoes to stick to the pan and inhibit browning. Cook the potatoes in a single layer so that they brown evenly. And after browning both sides of the potatoes, cover the skillet to cook the potatoes through.

Recycled clementine crates make great storage containers for potatoes or other foods.

SKILLET-ROASTED POTATOES

Serves 3 to 4

For even cooking and proper browning, the potatoes must be cooked in a single layer and should not be crowded in the pan.

1½	pounds small or medium Red Bliss potatoes, scrubbed and unpeeled
2	tablespoons olive oil
¾	teaspoon kosher salt (or sea salt)
¾	teaspoon ground black pepper

1. If using small potatoes (1½- to 2-inch diameter), halve each potato. If using medium potatoes (2- to 3-inch diameter), quarter each potato to create ¾- to 1-inch chunks. Rinse the potatoes in cold water and drain well; spread on a clean kitchen towel and thoroughly pat dry.

2. Heat the oil in a heavy-bottomed 12-inch nonstick skillet over medium-high heat until shimmering. Add the potatoes cut side down in a single layer. Cook, without stirring, until the potatoes are golden brown (the oil should sizzle but not smoke), 5 to 7 minutes. Using tongs, turn the potatoes skin side down if using halved small potatoes or second cut side down if using quartered medium potatoes. Again, cook, without stirring, until the potatoes are deep golden brown, 5 to 6 minutes longer. Stir the potatoes, then redistribute in a single layer. Reduce the heat to medium-low, cover, and cook until the potatoes are tender (a paring knife can be inserted into the potatoes with no resistance), 6 to 9 minutes.

3. When the potatoes are tender, sprinkle with salt and pepper and toss or stir gently to combine; serve immediately.

SKILLET-ROASTED POTATOES WITH GARLIC AND ROSEMARY

Fresh rosemary is a must in this fragrant variation; do not substitute dried.

Combine 1½ teaspoons minced or pressed garlic and 2 teaspoons minced fresh rosemary in a small bowl. Follow the recipe for Skillet-Roasted Potatoes; after seasoning the potatoes with salt and pepper in step 3, clear the center of the skillet and add the garlic and rosemary mixture. Cook over medium-low heat, mashing with a heatproof rubber spatula, until fragrant, about 45 seconds, then stir the mixture into the potatoes.

SKILLET-ROASTED POTATOES WITH LEMON AND CHIVES

When grating the lemon zest, take care in avoiding the bitter white pith beneath the yellow peel.

Combine 2 teaspoons grated lemon zest and 2 tablespoons minced fresh chives in a small bowl. Follow the recipe for Skillet-Roasted Potatoes; after seasoning the potatoes with salt and pepper in step 3, stir the lemon zest and chives into the potatoes.

SPICY SKILLET-ROASTED POTATOES WITH CHILI AND CUMIN

Take care in not overcooking the spices or they will impart a bitter flavor to the potatoes. Note that the heat level of chili powder varies by brand, so you may want to increase or decrease the amount used in this recipe accordingly.

Stir together 1 teaspoon chili powder, 1 teaspoon sweet paprika, ½ teaspoon ground cumin, and ¼ teaspoon cayenne in a small bowl. Follow the recipe for Skillet-Roasted Potatoes, substituting the chili mixture for the black pepper and cooking the seasoned potatoes over medium-low heat until the spices are fragrant, about 30 seconds.

GETTING IT RIGHT:
The Right Cut for the Right Potato

Small and medium potatoes can be used in our recipe, but they must be cut differently. Large potatoes are a poor choice: the cut pieces will be uneven and won't cook at the same rate.

Small

Small potatoes (1½ to 2 inches in diameter) should be cut in half.

Medium

Medium potatoes (2 to 3 inches in diameter) should be cut into quarters.

TESTING NOTES: Skillet Potatoes

We uncovered several recurring problems when testing other recipes for skillet potatoes.

Wrong Cut
Thinly sliced potatoes cook unevenly. Some are browned, some are pale.

Too Much Fat
Potatoes roasted with 1½ sticks of butter taste fried and fatty.

Added Liquid
Adding broth to the skillet makes the potatoes soggy.

EQUIPMENT CORNER: Kitchen Tongs

BELIEVE IT OR NOT, TONGS ARE NO LONGER THE straightforward affair they once were. Of course, you can still buy a basic model—two plain metal arms connected by a spring, with scalloped pincers for gripping—but you are just as likely to find tongs that fold in half, telescope, or pull double-duty as a spatula. Arms come cushioned or curved, and pincers can be nonstick-friendly and have various degrees of scalloping around the edges. With so many innovations, our question here was simple: Are these newfangled tongs any better than basic, old-school models?

The business end of a pair of tongs, the pincers, can be smooth or scalloped, and we found that those with scalloped edges get a better grip on food. But that's not the end of the story. The shape of the scalloping can vary. Our tests showed that edges with deep, sharp scalloping were more likely to break through the delicate breading on a chicken cutlet or shred meat fibers on a pot roast than edges with wide, shallow scalloping. Pronounced scalloping did not necessarily spell disaster, but we preferred the gentler touch of wide, shallow scalloping.

Pincers that were slightly concave, or cupped, did a good job of grasping hard, irregularly shaped, and large objects. The nearly flat pincers of the KitchenAid tongs, for instance, had a tenuous hold on lobsters, ramekins, and pot roasts. Imagine shooting a basketball while wearing a stiff oven mitt that limits the flex of your hand. Using your palm and fingers to cup the ball improves control; the same proved true with the pincers—the concavity helped tongs cradle the curved sides of the ramekins and lobsters.

Two of our contestants featured nonstick-friendly pincers, made of nylon on the Oxo (and heatsafe up to 400 degrees) and silicone on the Chef'n. The nylon Oxo really surprised testers, matching the aim and precision of the regular Oxo move for move until hard, slick lobsters slipped right out of the pincers. Because of their wide-body design and bulk, the silicone pincers on the Chef'n suffered the

TECHNIQUE: Cooking Caddy for Tongs

The splay of tongs makes them unsuitable for placing on a spoon rest while cooking. We like this space-saving alternative for catching drips and spills: Place the tongs in a heavy beer mug or coffee mug to keep your stovetop or counter clean.

opposite problem—they were clumsy and imprecise for fine work such as moving a scallop or a spear of asparagus.

The Kuhn Rikon tongs had unique pincers, shaped like spatulas and made of wire. Unfortunately, unique does not equal effective. The flexible wire tines offered a poor grip on hard, large, and heavy items, and they were too wide to position small items accurately. What's the moral of the pincer story? Whether you go nonstick-friendly or not, look for pincers with gentle concavity and wide, shallow scalloping.

The arms of several contenders featured unusual designs that, by and large, made little sense to our testers. We failed to see any advantage to the curved arms of the Chantal tongs, or the 10- to 14-inch telescoping arms of the Amco tongs (which could not be set to 12 inches, our preferred length). Worse yet, the G&S Design tongs, which fold up along the length of the tongs for easy storage, infuriated us by ratcheting downward under strain—bad news during the pot roast trials. The good news is that the soft cushioning on the arms of both the Oxo and the Chef'n models kept hands comfortable, firmly planted, and cool in case the tongs heated up during use. (Flipping frying chicken can make all-metal tongs unbearably hot.)

After all the testing was done, the Oxo tongs—both nonstick-friendly and regular—proved to be the best of show. If you wield your tongs with wild abandon (and worry about scratching your nonstick cookware), Oxo's nylon-tipped tongs ($9.95) may be the way to go. But if you really want just one pair that will do it all and are willing to use them gingerly when using nonstick cookware, you can't beat Oxo's regular, metal-tipped tongs ($9.95).

Rating Kitchen Tongs

WE TESTED 11 PAIRS OF 12-INCH TONGS (OR AS CLOSE TO THAT SIZE AS POSSIBLE FROM SOME MANUFACTURERS) and evaluated them according to construction, design, performance, and handle comfort. A range of testers (large- and small-handed) participated in the performance tests and evaluations of overall handle comfort, ease of use, and design. Tongs are listed in order of preference. See www.americastestkitchen.com for up-to-date prices and mail-order sources for top-rated products.

RECOMMENDED
Oxo Good Grips 12-Inch Locking Tongs
$9.95

Missed a perfect score only because one picky tester thought the pincers bruised cooked asparagus—a minor complaint. Class valedictorian in every other respect.

RECOMMENDED
Oxo Good Grips 12-Inch Tongs (Nylon Tips)
$9.95

Nonstick-friendly and effective with everything but hard objects. We could get a (tenuous) grip on ramekins, but lobster was a no-go.

RECOMMENDED
Edlund 12-Inch Locking Tongs
$9.25

Described as light and natural; one tester remarked, "They just belong in your hand." Sharp, deeply defined scalloping can tear delicate foods.

RECOMMENDED WITH RESERVATIONS
Vollrath 12-Inch One-Piece Utility Tongs
$7.65

Performance equaled (surpassed, in fact) that of many of the locking tongs, but storage is less convenient. Some testers found the tension a bit too stiff.

RECOMMENDED WITH RESERVATIONS
Chantal Contoured Kitchen Tongs
$14.99

Several testers noted that the pincers shredded fibers on the surface of tender meat and the crust of chicken cutlets. The curved handles left testers more puzzled than impressed.

RECOMMENDED WITH RESERVATIONS
Amco Houseworks 10-Inch and 14-Inch Telescoping Tongs
$12.95

Many testers disliked both lengths these tongs offer, finding that "the long is too long and the short is too short."

RECOMMENDED WITH RESERVATIONS
KitchenAid Utility Tongs
$9.99

The nearly flat pincers made for a compromised grip on large, hard, and soft objects alike.

NOT RECOMMENDED
Chef'n Tongo 12-Inch Silicone Tongs
$14.99

These tongs had bulky pincers that were too flexible to be precise and arms that had a proclivity for pinching unsuspecting fingers.

NOT RECOMMENDED
Kuhn Rikon Easy-Lock Wire Tongs
$19.99

Hybrid spatula/pincers slid under asparagus and breaded cutlets easily but could neither fit around nor lift lobsters and pot roast.

NOT RECOMMENDED
G&S Design Compactables Locking Tongs
$16.99

The folding arms collapsed under the weight of the pot roast, causing a tidal wave of hot braising liquid when the meat dropped into the pot. Testers found the handles awkward.

NOT RECOMMENDED
Progressive Multi-Purpose (10-Inch) Kitchen Tongs
$1.99

When it comes to these hardware store standards, one word says it all: flimsy. More words? How about "misaligned, uncomfortable, and loose"?

Chris finds that you don't have to rely on multiple pans to produce good chicken and rice.

STREAMLINED
CHAPTER 2

chicken skillet
suppers

Dinners prepared entirely in one skillet are perfect for weeknight cooking. Less cleanup is one obvious benefit. A skillet also gives the cook a bit more control over cooking multiple elements. In the oven, dishes such as chicken and rice—ingredients with disparate cooking times—can cook unevenly, so that when the dish comes out of the oven, you end up with mixed results, such as tender rice and dry chicken—or conversely, crunchy rice and moist chicken. A skillet gives you the freedom to move items in and out of the skillet accordingly so that everything comes out perfectly cooked.

We have also discovered that a skillet comes in handy in some pasta dishes. Take the restaurant favorite chicken, broccoli, and ziti. Typically, the pasta is boiled in one pot and then one or sometimes two more pans are required to cook the chicken, broccoli, and sauce. We condensed all the elements into a skillet—even the pasta, which cooks right in the sauce, soaking up maximum flavor for an exemplary version of this favorite dish.

SKILLET CHICKEN AND RICE

WHAT WE WANTED: A skillet version of the classic casserole with moist, tender meat and creamy rice.

Most recipes for chicken and rice rely on boneless chicken breasts, instant rice, and canned soup. Everything—the chicken, the rice, and the soup—goes into a casserole and bakes in the oven. The result? The chicken comes out dry, the rice mushy, and the sauce tastes, well, canned. We knew we could do better on all fronts.

First, we made a decision to trade in our casserole for a skillet. That way we'd have more control over cooking the chicken and rice—two foods with distinctly different cooking times. We started with the chicken. There's no denying

that chicken breasts are convenient and they're quick cooking—a boon for the weeknight cook, so we saw no reason to use anything else. We would, however, need to make some modifications to prevent this lean meat from drying out.

First, we used a nonstick skillet to prevent the chicken (and the rice) from sticking. A nonstick skillet also means easy cleanup. From prior testing, we'd found that dredging the chicken breasts in flour protected their exterior, giving the chicken a golden brown crust, which ensures juicy meat. We began by sautéing the chicken until browned on one side, then removed the chicken to a plate while we turned to the rice.

We melted butter in the skillet and sautéed minced onion, garlic, and red pepper flakes. Next, we added rice to the skillet, stirring to coat the rice with the butter and aromatics. Toasting the grains of rice prior to adding liquid is a method used in pilafs and risotto—it gives the rice a deeper flavor and ensures distinct, not mushy, grains. For bright flavor, we added white wine—again just like a risotto. Once the wine evaporated, chicken broth is poured into the skillet and then the chicken is returned to the skillet, browned side up, to finish cooking and impart more of its meaty flavor to the rice. Once the chicken was done, we removed it to a plate and covered with foil to keep warm. Meanwhile, the rice finished cooking through, becoming tender and creamy. Cooking the peas couldn't have been easier—they're sprinkled over the rice and covered for just 2 minutes to heat through. To finish and boost the fresh flavors in this dish even further, we stirred lemon juice and scallions into the rice before serving.

WHAT WE LEARNED: Flour the chicken prior to sautéing to help protect the meat from drying out. Toast the rice in butter and aromatics before adding the liquid to ensure distinct, creamy grains of rice. White wine, lemon juice, and scallions add a fresh brightness missing from the usual chicken and rice dish.

SKILLET CHICKEN AND RICE WITH PEAS AND SCALLIONS

Serves 4

Be sure to use chicken breasts that are roughly the same size to ensure even cooking.

4   boneless, skinless chicken breasts (6 to 8 ounces each)
    Salt and ground black pepper
½   cup unbleached all-purpose flour
2   tablespoons vegetable oil
2   tablespoons unsalted butter
1   medium onion, minced
3   medium garlic cloves, minced or pressed through a garlic press (about 1 tablespoon)
    Pinch red pepper flakes
1½ cups long-grain white rice
½   cup dry white wine
4½ cups low-sodium chicken broth
1   cup frozen peas
5   scallions, sliced thin
2   tablespoons juice from 1 lemon
1   lemon, cut into wedges, for serving

1. Pat the chicken dry with paper towels and season with salt and pepper. Dredge the chicken in flour to coat and shake off any excess. Heat the oil in a 12-inch nonstick skillet over medium-high heat just until smoking. Brown the chicken well on one side, about 5 minutes. Transfer the chicken to a plate and set aside.

2. Off the heat, add the butter to the skillet, and swirl to melt. Add the onion and ½ teaspoon salt, and return to medium-high heat until softened, 2 to 5 minutes. Stir in the garlic and pepper flakes and cook until fragrant, about 30 seconds. Stir in the rice thoroughly and let toast for about 30 seconds.

3. Stir in the wine and let the rice absorb it completely, about 1 minute. Stir in the broth, scraping up any browned bits. Nestle the chicken into the rice, browned side facing up, including any accumulated juices. Cover and cook over medium heat until the thickest part of the chicken registers 160 degrees on an instant-read thermometer, about 10 minutes.

4. Transfer the chicken to a clean plate. Gently brush off and discard any rice clinging to the chicken, then tent the chicken with foil and set aside. Return the skillet of rice to medium-low heat, cover, and continue to cook, stirring occasionally, until the liquid is absorbed and the rice is tender, 8 to 12 minutes longer.

5. Off the heat, sprinkle the peas over the rice, cover, and let warm through, about 2 minutes. Add the scallions and lemon juice to the rice. Season with salt and pepper to taste and serve with the chicken and lemon wedges.

TASTING LAB: White Wines for Cooking

WHEN A RECIPE CALLS FOR "DRY WHITE WINE," IT'S tempting to grab whatever open bottle is in the fridge, regardless of grape varietal. Are we doing our dishes a disservice? Sure, Chardonnay and Pinot Grigio may taste different straight from the glass, but how much do those distinctive flavor profiles really come through once the wines get cooked down with other ingredients?

To find out, we tried four different varietals and a supermarket "cooking wine" in five recipes: braised fennel, risotto, a basic pan sauce, a beurre blanc, and chicken chasseur. In our tests, only Sauvignon Blanc consistently boiled down to a "clean" yet sufficiently acidic flavor—one that played nicely with the rest of the ingredients. Differences between the wines were most dramatic in gently flavored dishes, such as the risotto and beurre blanc. Chardonnay turned our risotto and beurre blanc bitter. Riesling gave those same dishes an out-of-place sweet flavor. Pinot Grigio didn't ruin any dishes, but didn't brighten or improve them either—its flavor is simply too subtle in cooking. Not surprisingly, "cooking wine," which is very high in salt, performed poorly.

In contrast, all five wines produced similar (and fine) results when used in chicken chasseur, no doubt because of all the other strong flavors in this dish.

But what's a cook without leftover Sauvignon Blanc to do? Is there a more convenient option than opening a fresh bottle? To find out, we ran the same cooking tests with sherry and vermouth, wines fortified with alcohol to increase their shelf life. Sherry was too distinct and didn't fare well in these tests, but vermouth was surprisingly good. In fact, its clean, bright flavor bested all but one of the drinking wines. And at $5 a bottle (for Gallo, our top-rated brand of vermouth), you can't argue with the price.

Rating White Wines for Cooking

TEN MEMBERS OF THE AMERICA'S TEST KITCHEN staff tasted seven different white wines for cooking in five applications: braised fennel, risotto, a basic pan sauce, a beurre blanc, and chicken chasseur. The wines are listed in order of preference based on their combined scores from these five tastings. The wines can be purchased nationwide.

HIGHLY RECOMMENDED
Sauvignon Blanc
Crisp, clean, and bright, this wine was strong enough to share the spotlight with other ingredients but refused to steal the show.

HIGHLY RECOMMENDED
Dry Vermouth
A pleasing sweet/tart balance made this fortified wine a close second. And, after being opened, it can sit on the shelf for months.

RECOMMENDED WITH RESERVATIONS
Chardonnay
Most inexpensive Chardonnays are simply too oaky from barrel aging for most recipes. When cooked, "oaky" became bitter, not woody.

RECOMMENDED WITH RESERVATIONS
Riesling
This wine's fruity sweetness paired well with a few recipes but was out of place in other dishes. Too sweet.

RECOMMENDED WITH RESERVATIONS
Pinot Grigio
While this slightly acidic, mild wine won't ruin a recipe, it won't improve it much either, adding only a "generic wine-iness" that fades quickly into the background. Too shy.

NOT RECOMMENDED
Cooking Wine
The salt used to preserve inexpensive cooking wine makes it unpotable.

NOT RECOMMENDED
Sherry
Complex sherry worked well with the robust flavors in chasseur, but its "earthy" notes dominated the simple beurre blanc and risotto. Not a team player.

CHICKEN, BROCCOLI, AND ZITI

WHAT WE WANTED: A streamlined, fresher flavored version of the restaurant classic with moist and tender chicken, crisp broccoli, and a light cream sauce.

This pasta chain classic rarely tastes as good as it sounds. Usually it's just mediocre—so-so pieces of chicken and a stingy amount of broccoli tossed with pasta in a slick oil- or cream-based sauce that suffers from an overdose of garlic. And at its worst, all of the elements are overcooked so the result is mushy pasta and broccoli with dry, chewy pieces of chicken. We wanted to revamp this dish into what it should be: a well-seasoned combination of pasta, tender chicken, and crisp broccoli in a light and silky fresh-flavored sauce. In addition, we wanted to streamline its prep for easy weeknight cooking.

From prior testing, we knew we could streamline the dish's preparation by cooking the entire dish (including the pasta) in a skillet. This method not only gets rid of an extra pot to wash, it allows the pasta to absorb maximum flavor—because it cooks right in the sauce.

We started by lightly browning small pieces of boneless, skinless chicken breasts in oil, then removed the chicken to a dish while we turned to the other elements. Later we'd return the chicken to the mixture to heat and cook through—this way we'd avoid overcooked meat. Next, we started the sauce by sautéing onion in the skillet, then garlic, dried oregano, and red pepper flakes. We then added the ziti, chicken broth, and water to the pan and brought the mixture to a simmer. The pasta absorbed the flavorful liquid and became tender, and the liquid thickened to a saucy consistency. At this point, we turned to the broccoli, which we added to the skillet along with more water and chopped sun-dried tomatoes, which provided some depth to the dish. We then covered the skillet, lowered the heat, and cooked the broccoli just until it turned bright green.

To complete this dish we simply added the chicken back to the skillet to finish cooking and heat through. We finished the sauce with just ½ cup of heavy cream—any more would obscure the fresh flavors of the broccoli. And the final touch to this quick and easy dinner was some grated Asiago cheese for richness and a little lemon juice for brightness.

WHAT WE LEARNED: Lightly brown the chicken and then cook it through in the sauce just before serving to keep it moist and tender. Instead of boiling the pasta separately, cook it in the same skillet as the rest of the dish in a combination of chicken broth and water, to absorb maximum flavor. Cook the broccoli just until it turns bright green and it is almost tender—it will continue to cook with residual heat.

SKILLET CHICKEN, BROCCOLI, AND ZITI

Serves 4

This recipe also works well with 8 ounces of penne. Parmesan cheese can be substituted for the Asiago. Using a nonstick skillet here makes cleanup a breeze.

1	pound boneless, skinless chicken breasts, cut into 1-inch squares following the illustrations on page 112
	Salt and ground black pepper
2	tablespoons vegetable or olive oil
1	medium onion, minced (about 1 cup)
3	medium garlic cloves, minced or pressed through a garlic press (about 1 tablespoon)
¼	teaspoon dried oregano leaves
⅛	teaspoon red pepper flakes
8	ounces ziti (2½ cups)
2¾	cups water
1⅔	cups low-sodium chicken broth
12	ounces broccoli florets (4 cups)
¼	cup oil-packed sun-dried tomatoes, rinsed and chopped coarse
½	cup heavy cream
1	ounce Asiago cheese, grated (½ cup), plus extra for serving
1	tablespoon juice from 1 lemon

1. Season the chicken with salt and pepper. Heat 1 tablespoon of the oil in a 12-inch nonstick skillet over medium-high heat until just smoking. Add the chicken in a single layer and cook for 1 minute without stirring. Stir the chicken and continue to cook until most, but not all, of the pink color has disappeared and the chicken is lightly browned around the edges, 1 to 2 minutes longer. Transfer the chicken to a clean bowl and set aside.

2. Add the remaining tablespoon of oil, onion, and ½ teaspoon salt to the skillet. Return the skillet to medium-high heat and cook, stirring often, until the onion is softened, 2 to 5 minutes. Stir in the garlic, oregano, and pepper flakes, and cook until fragrant, about 30 seconds.

3. Add the ziti, 2 cups of the water, and the broth. Bring to a boil over high heat and cook until the liquid is very thick and syrupy and almost completely absorbed, 12 to 15 minutes.

4. Add the broccoli, sun-dried tomatoes, and the remaining ¾ cup water. Cover, reduce the heat to medium, and cook until the broccoli turns bright green and is almost tender, 3 to 5 minutes.

5. Uncover and return the heat to high. Stir in the cream, Asiago, and reserved chicken with any accumulated juices and continue to simmer, uncovered, until the sauce is thickened and the chicken is cooked and heated through, 1 to 2 minutes. Off the heat, stir in the lemon juice and season with salt and pepper to taste. Serve, passing more grated Asiago at the table, if desired.

TECHNIQUE:
Cutting Broccoli Florets

To quickly remove the florets from a bunch of broccoli, break off the stalks and place upside down on a cutting board. Using a large knife, trim off the florets very close to their heads, reserving the stalks for another use.

EQUIPMENT CORNER: Inexpensive Knife Sets

IN THE TEST KITCHEN, WE'VE ALWAYS ADVOCATED purchasing knives individually rather than in sets. That's because many sets include knives you'll never use—why pay for something you don't need? But is this still the case? To find out, we tested relatively modest sets (with 7 to 10 pieces) that focused on kitchen knives rather than steak knives—all for $100 or less.

First we focused on the construction of the knives. Knives are either stamped (cut from a sheet of metal) or forged (molded from molten metal). Forged knives are generally heavier and more expensive and were for many years the standard of quality. In the past decade, however, stamped knives have gotten so much better that the test kitchen doesn't exclusively recommend forged over stamped. Five of the seven sets we tested—including the top-rated set—were stamped; the forged sets finished second and fourth.

We wanted to narrow down our knife testing to those knives we consider the most useful and, thus, the most important. With a chef's knife, paring knife, and bread knife, you can accomplish almost any kitchen task, so that's where we concentrated our testing. Starting with chef's knives, we selected sets that contained 8-inch chef's knives, knowing from experience that anything shorter will not handle heavy jobs. The best chef's knives also have very sharp and gently curved blades that allow for good rocking and pivoting motions. We had testers with various hand sizes and levels of kitchen skills chop carrots, mince parsley, and quarter butternut squash with each chef's knife.

The test kitchen prefers 3½ to 4-inch paring knives, which offer the most dexterity and can cut, peel, and pare with great precision. A good paring knife should be razor sharp, and its blade should have enough flex to navigate rounded objects. Our testers peeled apples and peeled and minced ginger with the paring knives.

Bread knives should be long enough (ideally, 10 inches) to get through big loaves, and their serrated edge should glide through bread, making it almost effortless to cut thin slices. Our testers cut through both soft and crusty bread and also sliced tomatoes.

We also looked at the sets' overall package. The elements common to every set we tested were the block itself, along with a chef's knife and at least one paring knife. Most sets included a slicing (also called carving) knife and kitchen shears, and every set (except one) came with a sharpening steel.

Remarkably, three sets did not include a bread knife—one of the three knives on which we concentrated our testing. (For the bread and tomato tests with those sets, we chose the next closest thing, a slicer or a serrated utility knife.) Many sets included a utility knife (basically an oversized paring knife, sometimes with serrations); we didn't find this knife very useful, except for slicing tomatoes.

As for the quality of the knives, they ranged from mediocre to just plain awful. Flimsy blades, clumsy handles, and dull edges were recurring complaints from testers. We did find a few good knives residing in the slots of these blocks, but each one came from a different set. In the end, we don't recommend any of these knife sets. Instead, we suggest putting together your own set based on knives that have earned test kitchen recommendations.

BEST INEXPENSIVE KNIFE SET

If you want to put together an inexpensive knife set, we suggest that you buy an empty block and then add the following knives—all test kitchen favorites that are reasonably priced. These knives are available at cutleryandmore.com, where you can pick up an empty knife block for another $20 to $30. Total cost for three very good knives, a steel, and block? Just about $100. Now that's a gift we'd be proud to give—and happy to receive.

Chef's Knife: Forschner Fibrox 8-inch, $22.95
Paring Knife: Forschner Fibrox 4-inch, $4.95
Bread Knife: Forschner Fibrox 10-inch, $22.95
Sharpening Steel: Forschner Fibrox 12-inch, $22.95

Top blade steak—with its beefy, buttery flavor—is a terrific match to malty beer and sweet onions in a Belgian-style stew.

BEST BEEF *stew*

CHAPTER 3

A basic beef stew can be altered in dozens of ways, usually by adding more ingredients to the pot. But can you go the other way and strip beef stew down to its bare bones (or, to be more precise, to its beef)? If you trade the carrots and potatoes for a mess of onions and add a good dose of beer (instead of red wine) as part of the braising liquid, you've created a simple Belgian beef stew called carbonnade à la flamande. Beef, beer, and onions have a natural affinity—think burger, onion rings, and a beer. In a carbonnade, the heartiness of beef melds with the soft sweetness of sliced onions in a lightly thickened broth that is rich, deep, and satisfying, with the malty flavor of beer. We aimed to create the very best version of this cold-weather favorite.

Sweet acorn squash makes a worthy partner alongside carbonnade or with many other dishes during the cold weather season, but too often this squash turns out dry and stringy. We wanted to devise a method that ensured sweet, tender squash, without a lot of hassle.

Join us as we uncover the secrets behind a favorite beef stew and streamline a hearty side dish.

IN THIS CHAPTER

THE RECIPES

Carbonnade à la Flamande (Belgian Beef, Beer, and Onion Stew)

Quick Roasted Acorn Squash with Brown Sugar
Quick Roasted Acorn Squash with Rosemary–Dried Fig Compote

EQUIPMENT CORNER

Paring Knives

TASTING LAB

Beer for Carbonnade

SCIENCE DESK

Are All Microwaves Created Equal?

BEEF CARBONNADE

WHAT WE WANTED: Tender chunks of beef and sweet onions in a rich broth seasoned with the malty flavor of beer.

Belgian-style beef stew, called carbonnade à la fla-mande, may not be as familiar as its French cousin, boeuf bourguignonne, but it's just as rich and deli-cious. Beef, beer, and onions form the base of the stew. We made several versions of carbonnade and discovered that making a poor one is easy. Some stews were so gussied up that it was hard to notice all but the most serious flaws. But

stews stripped down to the three main ingredients were primed for failure—any mistake really stood out. After sev-eral trials, we wound up with batches of tasteless beef and onions in a pale, one-dimensional broth.

We decided on a basic method that would serve as a springboard for arriving at an improved recipe. Beef is browned and set aside, onions are sautéed in the empty pot, flour is sprinkled over the onions, liquid is added, the beef is returned to the pot, and the pot simmers in the oven. Now we had to figure out the best cut of beef, the best way to cook the onions, and the right type of beer.

Nearly every recipe we consulted recommended cubed chuck roast. To check this recommendation, we tested a dozen cuts of beef and hit upon an unusual winner. Blade steaks (also called top blade or flatiron steaks) are small, long, narrow steaks cut from the shoulder (or chuck) area of the cow. Most blade steaks have a decent amount of fat marbling, which gives them good flavor as well as a tender texture. A perfect choice, we thought, for carbonnade. One taster described the blade steak in carbonnade as "buttery," a quality that is well suited to this stew. If you cannot find a blade steak, however, any chuck roast will do. Just be sure to avoid the round, the portion of the rear leg from the knee to the hip. It has less fat than the chuck (the forequarter of the animal), and our tasters weren't wild about the flavor.

Onions—and lots of them—go into a traditional car-bonnade. Two pounds was the right amount for a generous pot of stew (made with 3½ pounds of beef). We tried white and red onions, but both were cloyingly sweet. Thinly sliced yellow onions tasted the best. The onions are lightly browned before being incorporated into the stew—if they are overcaramelized, they disintegrate after two hours of stewing.

To deepen their gentle sweetness, we thought to add a spoonful of tomato paste while sautéing the onions, a trick we had used in other recipes. This simple (if untraditional) ingredient dramatically improved the flavor. (We also tried brown sugar but found it too sweet.) A sprinkling of salt helped the onions release their moisture, which kept the flavorful fond (browned bits) from burning and helped to loosen the bits from the pot during deglazing. Garlic is not an ingredient in all carbonnade recipes, but we liked it, adding two minced cloves to the onions only after the onions had cooked to make sure the garlic didn't burn.

Key to the cuisine of Belgium is beer, its national drink. Belgians routinely pour beer into dishes at times when other cooks might uncork a bottle of wine. Cooking with wine is fairly straightforward; most reasonable choices work just fine in a stew. Cooking with beer is a different story. Beers of the light, lager persuasion, popular in America but not traditional in carbonnade, lack potency and result in pale, watery-tasting stews. We tried a number of dark beers and found that reasonably dark ales, very dark ales, and stouts made the richest and best-tasting carbonnades (for individual flavor profiles of a variety of beers, see "Beer for Carbonnade" on page 27).

While the braising liquid for carbonnade is typically beer, beef stock is sometimes added. We made carbonnades with beer as the only liquid, but they lacked backbone and were sometimes overwhelmingly bitter, depending on the type of beer used. Canned beef broth made for a tinny taste, whereas chicken broth didn't provide enough depth. Equal parts chicken and beef broth plus beer, however, created a stew with solid, complex flavor. Fresh thyme and bay leaves were natural additions, and cider vinegar perked things up with sweet-and-sour tones.

With a blade steak, plenty of yellow onions, and a rich dark beer, we made the simplest of all stews, carbonnade, finally come to life.

WHAT WE LEARNED: Use top blade steak for meat with buttery flavor. Yellow onions are preferred over white and red onions, as they aren't quite as sweet. Don't overcaramelize the onions or they'll disintegrate into the stew. A rich dark beer—not a pale lager—in combination with chicken and beef broth, make for a stew with deep, complex flavors.

CARBONNADE À LA FLAMANDE
(Belgian Beef, Beer, and Onion Stew)
Serves 6

Top blade steaks (also called blade or flatiron steaks) are our first choice, but any boneless roast from the chuck will work. If you end up using a chuck roast, look for the chuck eye roast, an especially flavorful cut that can easily be trimmed and cut into 1-inch pieces. Buttered egg noodles or mashed potatoes make excellent accompaniments to carbonnade.

3½ pounds top blade steaks, 1 inch thick, trimmed of gristle and fat and cut into 1-inch pieces (see the illustrations on page 26)
    Salt and ground black pepper
3   tablespoons vegetable oil
2   pounds yellow onions (about 3 medium), halved and sliced ¼ inch thick (about 8 cups)
1   tablespoon tomato paste
2   medium garlic cloves, minced or pressed through a garlic press (about 2 teaspoons)
3   tablespoons all-purpose flour
¾   cup low-sodium chicken broth
¾   cup low-sodium beef broth
1½ cups (12-ounce bottle or can) beer (see "Beer for Carbonnade" on page 27)
4   sprigs fresh thyme, tied with kitchen twine
2   bay leaves
1   tablespoon cider vinegar

1. Adjust an oven rack to the lower-middle position and heat the oven to 300 degrees. Dry the beef thoroughly with paper towels, then season generously with salt and pepper. Heat 2 teaspoons of the oil in a large heavy-bottomed Dutch oven over medium-high heat until beginning to smoke; add about one-third of the beef to the pot. Cook without moving the pieces until well browned, 2 to 3 minutes; using tongs, turn each piece and continue cooking until the second side is well browned, about 5 minutes longer. Transfer the browned beef to a medium bowl. Repeat with additional 2 teaspoons oil and half of the remaining beef. (If drippings in bottom of pot are very dark, add about ½ cup of the chicken or beef broth and scrape the pan bottom with a wooden spoon to loosen the browned bits; pour the liquid into the bowl with the browned beef, then proceed.) Repeat once more with 2 teaspoons oil and the remaining beef.

2. Add remaining 1 tablespoon oil to the now-empty Dutch oven; reduce the heat to medium-low. Add the onions, ½ teaspoon salt, and tomato paste; cook, scraping the bottom of the pot with a wooden spoon to loosen the browned bits, until the onions have released some moisture, about 5 minutes. Increase the heat to medium and continue to cook, stirring occasionally, until the onions are lightly browned, 12 to 14 minutes. Stir in the garlic and cook until fragrant,

about 30 seconds. Add the flour and stir until the onions are evenly coated and the flour is lightly browned, about 2 minutes. Stir in the broths, scraping the pan bottom to loosen any browned bits; stir in the beer, thyme, bay leaves, vinegar, browned beef with any accumulated juices, and salt and pepper to taste. Increase the heat to medium-high and bring to a full simmer, stirring occasionally; cover partially, then place the pot in the oven. Cook until a fork inserted into the beef meets little resistance, 2 to 2½ hours.

3. Discard the thyme and bay leaves. Adjust the seasonings with salt and pepper to taste and serve. (The stew can be cooled and refrigerated in an airtight container for up to 4 days; reheat over medium-low heat.)

TASTING LAB: Beer for Carbonnade

WHEN MAKING CARBONNADE À LA FLAMANDE, PURISTS will settle for nothing less than a traditional copper-colored Belgian ale with fruity, spicy aromas and a pleasant hoppy bitterness. But is it the only choice? To find out, we pulled together nine different styles of beer, ranging from a dark, full-bodied stout to a nonalcoholic brew. We even included some good old Bud Light (after all, it was already in the fridge).

After a few hours in the oven, the flavors you taste straight from the bottle (or can) are concentrated and easily recognized in this stew. Our tasters preferred beers that possessed plenty of sweetness matched with moderate bitterness. Light-bodied beers, like Bud Light, were noted for a mild sweetness but lacked the contrasting bitterness to make a balanced, full-flavored stew. On the other hand, brews with a high degree of bitterness often did not have enough sweetness. This was the case with Sierra Nevada's Pale Ale, which came across as singularly bitter.

While we found that only the bitterest of beers can completely ruin a carbonnade, choosing a well-balanced, medium-bodied brew will improve this dish significantly.

TECHNIQUE:
Trimming Blade Steaks

1. Halve each steak lengthwise, leaving the gristle on one half.

2. Cut away the gristle from the half to which it is still attached.

3. Cut the trimmed meat crosswise into 1-inch pieces.

Rating Beers for Carbonnade

ELEVEN MEMBERS OF THE AMERICA'S TEST KITCHEN STAFF TASTED NINE BEERS IN OUR CARBONNADE RECIPE. THE beers are listed in order of preference based on their scores in this tasting. The beers can be purchased nationwide.

RECOMMENDED

Chimay Pères Trappistes Ale-Première

$9.49 for 25.4-ounce bottle

The Belgians have had this right the whole time. This traditional Trappist ale was "rich and robust" and brought out a "very deep flavor" with a "dark chocolate finish."

RECOMMENDED WITH RESERVATIONS

Anchor Steam

$8.69 for six-pack

"Grassy, barley" notes made a very "hearty" stew, but this beer pushed the bitter limits.

RECOMMENDED WITH RESERVATIONS

Sierra Nevada Porter

$7.99 for six-pack

This beer's flavor profile was very similar to that of the stout's, but it lacked enough contrasting sweetness. Several tasters likened this stew to "espresso."

RECOMMENDED

Newcastle Brown Ale

$7.49 for six-pack

This English ale was noted for its relatively low sweetness and bitterness, which allowed for "lots of malt" flavor.

RECOMMENDED WITH RESERVATIONS

Samuel Adams Boston Lager

$7.29 for six-pack

"Black pepper" and "sweet spices" dominate this premium lager, alternately described as "burnt" or "molasses-sweet."

RECOMMENDED WITH RESERVATIONS

Bud Light

$5.29 for six-pack

"Boring," not bitter, not sweet, and not very flavorful. Stew was "flat."

RECOMMENDED

O'Doul's Amber (Nonalcoholic)

$4.99 for six-pack

This nonalcoholic beer was the dark-horse favorite. A fruity sweetness brought out some "rich beefiness." Do not confuse this beer with regular O'Doul's.

RECOMMENDED WITH RESERVATIONS

Guinness Extra Stout

$7.29 for six-pack

The archetypal stout bordered on "bitter and burnt," but a high degree of sweetness countered for a vigorously flavored carbonnade.

NOT RECOMMENDED

Sierra Nevada Pale Ale

$7.99 for six-pack

This beer is good straight from the bottle but made a stew that was overwhelmingly "bitter" and "sour."

ACORN SQUASH

WHAT WE WANTED: The flavor of slow-roasted acorn squash in a fraction of the time.

After what seems like eons in the oven, acorn squash usually lands on the table with little flavor and a dry, grainy texture. Yet acorn squash can be quite good, if not outright delicious, when prepared properly. At its rare best, it is characterized by a sweet, almost nutty taste and moist, smooth flesh. Could we solve this culinary challenge and do so relatively quickly?

Most cookbook authors recommend baking acorn squash in a covered dish, while a few suggest somewhat unconventional methods, including steaming, boiling, and braising. Steamed and boiled chunks of peeled squash cooked quickly but turned out mushy and waterlogged. Braising resulted in a soggy, stringy texture that was all the more disappointing given the arduous task of peeling the squash before cooking it. And as for the baked squash, it turned out just as we'd expected: dry, very dry.

We were running out of hope until a test cook came across a recipe on the Internet that suggested microwaving, a cooking method we avoid at all costs here in the test kitchen because of its finicky nature and its poor powers of flavor enhancement. Still, we gave the microwave a try. And after tasting the microwaved squash, we were sold. It was tender and silky smooth, with nary a trace of dryness or stringiness. We were so surprised with the results that we repeated the test once, and then again. When subsequent tries produced identical outcomes, we seemed to have no choice but to use the microwave to cook the squash.

Hammering out the details was easy: Microwave on high power for 20 minutes (give or take a few, depending on the model used—see "Are All Microwaves Created Equal?" on page 31), and the squash is perfectly cooked. It was best to halve and seed the squash before cooking; whole pierced squash cooked unevenly. Last, we learned that when added before cooking, salt seemed to better permeate the squash.

Now we had a 20-minute recipe and vastly improved results!

Why was the microwave such a success? Our science editor explained that as microwaves (which, like radio waves, are electromagnetic) enter food, water molecules in the food begin to vibrate, and this activity generates heat evenly and efficiently, for quick cooking. In effect, the microwave was steaming the squash in its own juices. In contrast, a conventional oven uses dry, hot air to slowly heat food from the outside in, causing dehydration and a less desirable texture.

The one important issue we had left to tackle was the topping, or flavoring, for the squash. Tasters were loud and clear about what they wanted: a classic butter and sugar glaze. Dark brown sugar is the most common choice and was named the best sweetener, with maple syrup a runner-up. Other options (honey, granulated sugar, and light brown sugar) were either not sweet enough or didn't provide the familiar flavor that we wanted. We limited the amount of brown sugar to 3 tablespoons—enough to provide ample sweetness but not so much that we'd be tempted to serve the squash with a scoop of vanilla ice cream. An equal amount of butter made the best complement.

One problem remained. The squash was still lacking the sticky, caramelized glaze that forms when it is baked. Passing the buttered and sugared squash under the broiler for a few minutes after microwaving was the way to go. Many recipes simply call for placing a pat of butter in the cavity of the squash and then adding a coating of sugar. A better method, we found, was to melt the two ingredients, along with a pinch of salt, on the stovetop for a smooth, cohesive mixture. By using the microwave and broiler, we were now able to produce squash with great texture and flavor. Not bad for 20 minutes' work.

WHAT WE LEARNED: Starting the squash in the microwave yielded moist and tender squash. Finishing the squash under the broiler gave the squash a welcome roasted texture and great caramelized flavor.

SHOPPING NOTES:
How to Buy and Store Acorn Squash

As we halved, seeded, and cooked more than 50 squash for this recipe, we noted significant differences in quality, depending on where we purchased the squash, how we stored it, and how long we kept it. Some were richly flavored, with deep, golden orange flesh, while others were spongy and pale. Here's what we learned.

Season: Acorn squash is domestically in season from July through November. When purchased in the off-season, the squash, which during those months is usually imported from Mexico, is likely to be more expensive. Squash that had spent weeks in transit cooked up dehydrated, fibrous, and pasty in the test kitchen.

Weight: Squash should be hard and heavy for its size, an indication that it contains a lot of moisture and has not been sitting on the supermarket produce shelf for weeks.

Color: The most popular variety of acorn squash is green, though gold and white varieties are spottily available. Gold or orange tinges on the rind of green squash are not indicators of ripeness but rather a mark of where the fruit touched the ground during growing (and was therefore untouched by sunlight).

Storage: Acorn squash should be stored at cool room temperature, not in the refrigerator. When we stored squash for a few weeks in the refrigerator, chill damage set in, causing the flavor and texture to deteriorate.

GETTING IT RIGHT:
Prepping Squash for the Microwave

If your microwave is spacious enough to accommodate it, a 13 by 9-inch microwave-safe baking dish works well for containing the squash halves. Otherwise, a large, wide microwave-safe bowl can be used. If using a bowl, position the squash with the cut sides facing out.

QUICK ROASTED ACORN SQUASH WITH BROWN SUGAR

Serves 4

This half-and-half method relies on the microwave oven and broiler and was developed using acorn squash. Squash smaller than 1½ pounds will likely cook a little faster than the recipe indicates, so begin checking for doneness a few minutes early. Likewise, larger squash will take slightly longer to cook. However, keep in mind that the cooking time is largely dependent on the microwave. If microwaving the squash in Pyrex, the manufacturer recommends adding water to the dish (or bowl) prior to cooking. To avoid a steam burn when uncovering the cooked squash, peel back the plastic wrap very carefully, starting from the side that is farthest away from you.

> 2 acorn squash (about 1½ pounds each), halved pole to pole and seeded (see the illustrations on page 30)
>   Salt
> 3 tablespoons unsalted butter
> 3 tablespoons dark brown sugar

1. Sprinkle the squash halves with salt and place the halves cut side down in a 13 by 9-inch microwave-safe baking dish or arrange the halves in a large (about 4-quart) microwave-safe bowl so that the cut sides face out. If using Pyrex, add ¼ cup water to the dish or bowl. Cover tightly with plastic wrap, using multiple sheets, if necessary; with a paring knife, poke about 4 steam vents in the wrap. Microwave on high power until the squash is very tender and offers no resistance when pierced with a paring knife, 15 to 25 minutes. Using potholders, remove the baking dish or bowl from the oven and set on a clean, dry surface (avoid damp or cold surfaces).

2. While the squash is cooking, adjust an oven rack to the uppermost position (about 6 inches from the heating element); heat the broiler. On the stovetop, melt the butter, brown sugar, and ⅛ teaspoon salt in a small saucepan over low heat, whisking occasionally, until combined.

3. When the squash is cooked, carefully pull back the plastic wrap from the side farthest from you. Using tongs, transfer the cooked squash cut side up to a rimmed baking sheet. Spoon a portion of the butter-sugar mixture onto each squash half. Broil until brown and caramelized, 5 to 8 minutes, rotating the baking sheet as necessary and removing the squash halves as they are done. Set the squash halves on individual plates and serve immediately.

VARIATION

QUICK ROASTED ACORN SQUASH WITH ROSEMARY–DRIED FIG COMPOTE
This slightly more involved variation is perfect for company.

1. Follow the recipe for Quick Roasted Acorn Squash with Brown Sugar, omitting the brown sugar–butter mixture. While the squash is cooking, combine 1 cup orange juice, 4 dried black figs, chopped medium (scant ½ cup), ½ teaspoon minced fresh rosemary, 1 tablespoon dark brown sugar, ¼ teaspoon ground black pepper, and ⅛ teaspoon salt in a small saucepan. Simmer rapidly over medium–high heat, stirring occasionally, until syrupy and the liquid is reduced to about 3 tablespoons, 15 to 20 minutes. Stir in 1 tablespoon butter.

2. Continue with the recipe to fill and broil the squash halves, substituting the fig compote for the brown sugar–butter mixture.

TECHNIQUE:
Two Ways to Cut Acorn Squash Safely

Metal Bench Scraper and Hammer

1. Set the squash on a damp kitchen towel to hold it in place. Position the bench scraper on the rind.

2. Strike the handle of the bench scraper with a hammer to drive the blade into the squash. Continue to hit the bench scraper with the hammer until the blade cuts through the squash.

Knife and Rubber Mallet

1. Set the squash on a damp kitchen towel to hold it in place. Position the knife on the rind.

2. Strike the back of the knife with a rubber mallet to drive it into the squash. Continue to hit the knife with the mallet until the knife cuts through the squash.

SCIENCE DESK:
Are All Microwaves Created Equal?

BECAUSE EVERY COOK'S MICROWAVE OVEN VARIES IN SIZE, wattage, type, and age, we were concerned about writing a recipe using equipment whose power is difficult to quantify. Would microwaving on "high" power produce consistent results among different machines? We were doubtful.

The amount of microwave energy absorbed by a food is a function of the cooking time, power (watts), portion size, and the amount of water in the food to be cooked (the energy produced by the microwave is absorbed primarily by water). Roughly speaking, the more watts, the faster food will cook. Theoretically, a microwave with 1,000 watts of power would cook the same volume of food twice as quickly as a machine with 500 watts.

To gauge real-life differences, we sent armfuls of acorn squash and bags of microwave popcorn (an easy gauge of cooking power) home with our colleagues to cook in their microwaves. When they reported back, we found that differences in cooking times correlated roughly—though not

reliably—to the power of the microwave used. For example, popcorn took three minutes and 45 seconds in the only 700-watt microwave tested, while the same brand of popcorn was ready in just two minutes in several 1,100-watt models. The same thing held true for squash, with cooking times running from a low of 15 minutes in several powerful microwaves to a high of 27 minutes in the same weak 700-watt microwave.

What to do, then, when cooking the squash in your microwave? Check the label inside the machine (or your owner's manual) to determine its wattage. If your microwave runs on fewer than 900 watts of power, you will likely need to increase the cooking time by a few minutes. If you own a high-wattage machine (more than 1,100 watts), you may need to decrease the cooking time. That said, it always pays to use your senses, not a timer, to judge when food is ready.

EQUIPMENT CORNER: Paring Knives

IF YOU OWN A KNIFE SET, WE'RE WILLING TO BARGAIN that there are really only three that you use on a regular basis—a chef's knife, a bread knife, and a paring knife. Paring knives are particularly useful. You can use a paring knife not only for "paring" tasks—peeling an apple or turnip, carving the rind off an orange, coring a tomato—but also for jobs suited to a mini chef's knife or a boning knife—dicing a shallot or slipping the blade into the nooks and crannies of a chicken thigh.

In the test kitchen, we find that 3.5–4-inch blades are the best size for most paring tasks, so for our testing we chose knives with blades as close to that size as possible within each brand, with a price limit of $30. We then asked six testers of varying hand size and levels of knife skill to peel and core apples, core tomatoes, dice shallots, and remove the silver skin (a tough, thin membrane) from a pork tenderloin.

First to consider were the types of blades used in knives: forged or stamped. Forged blades are made of molded steel, while stamped blades are simply cut out of a larger piece of metal. Because the forging process can be so time-consuming, forged knives are usually expensive. But testers didn't necessarily find them to be any better. The top-rated Forschner features a stamped blade.

We next examined the thinness of the blade. Only a thin blade will slide under an apple peel or a length of silver skin without removing too much of the flesh beneath. The best knives had blades that were no more than a millimeter thick. Thin blades were also more flexible, which was important for peeling round apples and cutting around a tomato core. The Forschner had a very thin and flexible blade, whereas the Farberware and Calphalon had blades that were stiff and thick. In addition, testers rejected wide blades as clumsy, especially on the tomato test, where a narrow blade is key to cutting a tight circle around the core.

A knife is only as good as it is sharp. All the knives tested were sharp right out of the package, but some (such as the Farberware and Chicago Cutlery) dulled so quickly during testing they would require constant sharpening to be of any use.

Handling, too, is important. Despite a wide range of shapes, sizes, and materials, most of the knife handles fit comfortably in the hand. There were, however, some uncomfortable standouts. The rough wooden handle of the Chicago Cutlery knife was dismissed as irritating, while the Messermeister's large molded plastic handle was uncomfortable in all but the largest of hands.

Overall, what did we find? The cheapest knife, the lightweight Forschner Fibrox, turned out to be the best, beating models that cost six times as much. For cooks looking for a little more heft, the KitchenAid finished a close second and is a great performer at a good price.

Rating Paring Knives

WE TESTED TEN PARING KNIVES IN A VARIETY OF TASKS: PEELING AND CORING AN APPLE, CORING A TOMATO, removing the silver skin from a pork tenderloin, and dicing a shallot. Knives were rated for sharpness, blade thinness and flexibility, and handle comfort. Knives are listed in order of preference. See www.americastestkitchen.com for up-to-date prices and mail-order sources for top-rated products.

HIGHLY RECOMMENDED
Forschner Fibrox 4-Inch Paring Knife
$4.95

Testers loved the "great flexibility" of this knife, which slid under silver skin easily and turned the curve of an apple nicely. Though some testers complained that this lightest of all the knives lacked "heft," most agreed that the super-thin, razor-sharp edge more than made up for it.

RECOMMENDED
KitchenAid Cook's Series 3.5-Inch Paring Knife
$9.99

With the thinnest of all blades and an extremely narrow pointed tip, this knife was a standout in the tenderloin and apple tests. Some testers complained about the heavy handle, but most praised the "smooth" cuts from the "nice sharp blade."

RECOMMENDED
Wüsthof Classic 3.5-Inch Paring Knife
$29.95

Testers praised the "incredibly sharp" blade that made slicing an apple "like cutting butter." Though the "stiff" blade came in handy in the shallot test, most testers agreed that they would prefer a bit more flexibility.

RECOMMENDED WITH RESERVATIONS
Calphalon Contemporary 3.5-Inch Paring Knife
$14.95

Testers with smaller hands found the molded handle uncomfortable, and all testers found the weight excessive. Though quite sharp, the thick blade was very inflexible.

RECOMMENDED WITH RESERVATIONS
Oxo Good Grips Professional 3.5-Inch Paring Knife
$14.99

Testers liked the "comfy" no-slip rubber handle but were put off by the thick blade that was "not super-sharp." Though the blade had some bend, most agreed that it "could be more flexible."

RECOMMENDED WITH RESERVATIONS
Mac Knives 4-Inch Paring Knife
$17.95

Though the blade was "very sharp and thin," it was also deemed "too long" by most testers, who were uncomfortable with the fact that the cutting edge came so close to the handle.

RECOMMENDED WITH RESERVATIONS
Henckels Classic 4-Inch Paring Knife
$19.95

The long narrow blade was perfect for removing silver skin but good for little else. Even small-handed testers found the handle too narrow, though the "not-so-flexible" blade was "sharp."

NOT RECOMMENDED
Messermeister 4-Inch Four Seasons Paring Knife
$5.95

The thin, narrow blade won points for flexibility but was "not sharp enough," and its length gave testers little control, making this knife "hard to use." The large plastic handle was too bulky for all but the biggest hands.

NOT RECOMMENDED
Chicago Cutlery Walnut Signature 3.5-Inch Paring Knife
$9.95

Testers universally panned the "boxy" wooden handle that felt "like sandpaper." Though the thin blade was fairly flexible, it was simply "not sharp enough" and failed to perform well on any task.

NOT RECOMMENDED
Farberware Pro 3.75-Inch Paring Knife
$7.99

With a blade more than twice as thick as those on our top-rated knives, the Farberware lost points across the board. Deemed "so dull" that it smashed rather than sliced shallots, and considered "too stiff" for all other tasks.

To ensure that there's plenty of chicken to go around, Bridget starts with a large bird that weighs 5 to 6 pounds.

SUNDAY ROAST

CHAPTER 4

chicken and stuffing

The idea of roast chicken and stuffing is very appealing—moist, well-seasoned meat and plenty of flavorful stuffing to satisfy everyone at the table. But in reality, a chicken, even one upward of 5 pounds (serving 4 to 6 people), doesn't contain a cavity large enough to accommodate the amount of stuffing you'd need to serve everyone. Sure, you can bake the stuffing separately in a baking dish, but you miss out on all the flavorful juices imparted from the chicken. Our aim, therefore, would be to develop a recipe for roast chicken and stuffing where we could somehow still mimic the flavorful benefits of cooking the stuffing inside the bird.

A quick sauté of spinach, especially one with garlic and lemon, goes well alongside roast chicken (in addition to many other dishes). But this simple approach can often go wrong—overcooked spinach, burnt garlic, too much oil—the list goes on. We would focus on avoiding these pitfalls to turn out a tasty side dish you can rely on again and again.

ROAST CHICKEN WITH STUFFING

WHAT WE WANTED: A streamlined version of roast chicken with plenty of stuffing to go around—and to solve the problem of cooking the stuffing to a safe temperature without drying out the delicate breast meat of the chicken.

Stuffed roast chicken should be the culinary equivalent of a power couple. Each partner brings a lot to the table, and this marriage represents the ultimate symbiotic relationship—at least in theory. The stuffing elevates the roast chicken beyond common everyday fare, while the chicken lends flavor and moisture to what would otherwise be dry bread crumbs. And, unlike roast turkey, its bigger and more complicated cousin, stuffed roast chicken should be simple. But stuffed roast chicken often doesn't deliver. What you get instead is either a perfectly cooked bird filled with lukewarm stuffing (hello, salmonella!) or safe-to-eat stuffing packed in parched poultry. We also wanted more than a few tablespoons of stuffing per person, a problem given the small cavity of a roasting chicken, even one weighing in at more than 5 pounds. No wonder most home cooks ask for a trial separation when it comes to this everyday recipe.

We've roasted literally thousands of chickens in the test kitchen and made more than our fair share of stuffing. It will come as no surprise, then, that we immediately decided to brine the bird before stuffing and roasting it. This was the only way to ensure moist, flavorful white meat. Next we were on to the stuffing, and our initial tests revolved around the traditional stuff-'n'-truss method used in turkey preparation. This technique was an abject failure. When we packed the chicken loosely with stuffing, we ended up with a miserly 1½ cups. We then packed the chicken until it nearly burst (about 3 cups), first heating the stuffing to 145 degrees in a microwave to give it a head start. But the stuffing still did not reach the safe temperature of 165 degrees by the time the meat was done. Apparently, fully cooked stuffing meant overcooked breast meat.

A few years back, the test kitchen developed a method for high-roast chicken that started with a butterflied bird. (The backbone is removed and the bird is flattened and then roasted at 500 degrees.) We figured it was worth a try. We began with a flattened, brined bird and placed it on top of a broiler pan with 3 cups of stuffing directly beneath the chicken and another 5 cups in the bottom of the pan. After an hour, the skin on the chicken was crisp and evenly browned and the meat mostly moist. Finally, we had enough stuffing (at a safe 165 degrees) to feed a crowd, but now it suffered from a dual identity. The stuffing underneath the cavity was cohesive, while its counterpart in the bottom of the pan was dry and crunchy. When we tried placing all of the stuffing in the bottom of the pan (not directly beneath the chicken), it became greasy.

For our next test, we replaced the broiler pan with a traditional roasting pan and piled a mound of stuffing into it before placing a splayed butterflied chicken on top. After about an hour at 500 degrees, the chicken was slightly dry and the stuffing had many burnt bits. At 425 degrees, the chicken skin browned less evenly, but the stuffing was moist and cohesive. Tasters agreed that 450 degrees yielded the best results, although the stuffing was still charred in some areas and was greasy from the rendered fat.

To solve these two problems, we began a series of tests that eventually culminated in a strange version of culinary origami. First, we placed the stuffing inside an 8-inch square baking dish upon which the butterflied chicken perched; the whole thing then went into a roasting pan. Because the splayed chicken extended partially over the top of the baking dish, we hoped most of the fat from the skin would drip into the roasting pan rather than into the stuffing, but this was not the case. Next, we turned to aluminum foil, creating a packet around the stuffing that we poked with holes so the chicken juices could irrigate the dry contents. Sure, this stuffing was moist, but it lacked color and texture because it was shielded from the oven's dry heat. Finally, we

made an aluminum foil bowl, mounded the stuffing into it, and placed the chicken on top, snugly encasing the stuffing. After about an hour of roasting, with a single pan rotation in between, the stuffing was browned and chewy on the bottom as well as moist and flavorful throughout from the juices. The fat from the skin was deposited directly into the roasting pan, never even touching the stuffing. Even though the roasting pan was hot, we could easily grab the foil bowl with bare hands and dump the stuffing in one fell swoop into a serving bowl. Good technique and cleanup, all in one!

With our cooking technique established, we could now focus on the stuffing specifics. An informal poll in the test kitchen revealed that most people wanted a jazzed-up version of a traditional bread stuffing. We obliged by replacing the typical onion with thinly sliced leek, adding the requisite celery, and throwing in some chopped mushrooms for additional texture and substance. A dose of minced garlic, fresh sage and parsley, and chicken broth finished our recipe. (In addition we came up with two flavor variations on our traditional stuffing.) With a roasting technique and stuffing recipes now in place, we had finally managed to turn stuffed roast chicken into a successful marriage.

WHAT WE LEARNED: Brine the chicken for moist, well-seasoned meat. Butterfly and flatten the chicken to reduce cooking time. Pile the stuffing into a foil "bowl" (set in a roasting pan) and place the butterflied chicken on top to roast. This allows the stuffing to cook to a safe temperature and soak up the flavorful juices from the chicken without becoming greasy, as the rendered fat drips into the roasting pan—not onto the stuffing.

STUFFED ROAST BUTTERFLIED CHICKEN

Serves 4

Use a traditional (not nonstick) roasting pan to prepare this recipe; the dark finish of a nonstick pan may cause the stuffing to overbrown. If using a kosher chicken, skip step 1.

1 cup Diamond Crystal Kosher Salt, ¾ cup Morton Kosher salt, or ½ cup table salt
1 whole chicken (5 to 6 pounds), trimmed of excess fat, giblets discarded
1 teaspoon vegetable or olive oil
  Ground black pepper
1 recipe stuffing (recipes follow)

1. Dissolve the salt in 2 quarts cold water in a large container. Immerse the chicken and refrigerate until fully seasoned, about 1 hour.

2. Adjust an oven rack to the lower-middle position and heat the oven to 450 degrees. Remove the chicken from the brine and rinse under cold running water; pat dry with paper towels. Butterfly the chicken, flatten the breastbone, and tuck the wings behind the back. Rub the skin with oil and sprinkle with pepper.

3. Prepare a foil bowl for the stuffing by stacking two 12-inch-square pieces of heavy-duty foil on top of each other. Fold the edges to construct an 8 by 6-inch bowl. Coat the inside of the foil bowl with nonstick cooking spray and place the bowl in the roasting pan. Gently mound and pack the stuffing into the foil bowl and position the chicken over the stuffing (the chicken should extend past the edges of the bowl so that most of the fat renders into the roasting pan, not into the foil bowl). Roast the chicken until just beginning to brown, about 30 minutes. Rotate the pan and continue to roast until the skin is crisped and deep golden brown and an instant-read thermometer registers 160 degrees in the thickest part of the breast, 175 degrees in the thickest part of the thigh, and 165 degrees in the

TECHNIQUE: Butterflying a Chicken

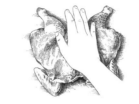

1. Cut through the bones on either side of the backbone, then remove and discard the backbone.

2. Flip the chicken over and use the heel of your hand to flatten the breastbone. Tuck the tips of the wings behind the back.

stuffing, 25 to 35 minutes longer. Using tongs, transfer the chicken to a cutting board; let rest 10 minutes.

4. While the chicken rests, transfer the stuffing from the foil bowl to a serving bowl; fluff the stuffing with a spoon. Cover the stuffing with foil to keep warm. Carve the chicken and serve with the stuffing.

MUSHROOM-LEEK BREAD STUFFING WITH HERBS

Serves 4

6 ounces white sandwich bread (about 6 slices), cut into ¼-inch cubes (about 5 cups)
2 tablespoons unsalted butter
1 small leek, halved lengthwise, rinsed thoroughly, white and light green parts cut crosswise into ⅛-inch slices (about 1 cup)
1 small celery rib, chopped fine
8 ounces white button mushrooms, cleaned and chopped medium (about 2½ cups)

vegetables begin to brown, 2 to 3 minutes. Stir in the sage, thyme, and parsley and cook until fragrant, about 1 minute.

3. Whisk the egg, broth, salt, and pepper in a large bowl until combined. Add the bread cubes and mushroom-leek mixture; toss gently until evenly moistened and combined. Set aside until ready to roast the chicken.

1   large garlic clove, minced or pressed through a garlic press (about 1½ teaspoons)

½   teaspoon minced fresh sage leaves (or ¼ teaspoon dried)

½   teaspoon minced fresh thyme leaves (or ¼ teaspoon dried)

¼   cup minced fresh parsley leaves

1   large egg

½   cup plus 2 tablespoons low-sodium chicken broth

½   teaspoon salt

¼   teaspoon ground black pepper

1. Adjust an oven rack to the middle position and heat the oven to 250 degrees. Spread the bread cubes in a single layer on a baking sheet; bake until thoroughly dried but not browned, about 30 minutes, stirring once halfway through the baking time.

2. Meanwhile, heat the butter in a 12-inch skillet over medium-high heat; when the foam subsides, add the leek, celery, and mushrooms and cook, stirring occasionally, until the vegetables begin to soften, about 4 minutes. Add the garlic and continue to cook, stirring frequently, until the

---

TECHNIQUE: Cleaning Leeks

Leeks can be especially gritty, so it's important to clean them thoroughly.

1. Start by trimming and discarding the roots and dark green leaves with a sharp knife. Slice the leeks as directed.

2. Place the cut leeks into a large bowl, fill with cold water, and swish the leeks with your hands to loosen any dirt and sand. Let stand for a few minutes to allow the dirt to settle to the bottom of the bowl and, using your hands, lift the clean leeks out from the water.

CURRANT-PECAN BREAD STUFFING

Serves 4

6	ounces white sandwich bread (about 6 slices), cut into ¼-inch cubes (about 5 cups)
½	cup sweet Marsala
⅓	cup dried currants
2	tablespoons unsalted butter
4	large shallots, chopped fine (about 1 cup)
1	large celery rib, chopped fine
½	teaspoon minced fresh sage leaves (or ¼ teaspoon dried)
½	teaspoon minced fresh thyme leaves (or ¼ teaspoon dried)
¼	cup minced fresh parsley leaves
1	large egg
½	cup plus 2 tablespoons low-sodium chicken broth
½	teaspoon salt
½	teaspoon ground black pepper
½	cup chopped pecans, toasted

1. Adjust an oven rack to the middle position and heat the oven to 250 degrees. Spread the bread cubes in a single layer on a baking sheet; bake until thoroughly dried but not browned, about 30 minutes, stirring once halfway through the baking time.

2. Meanwhile, bring the Marsala and currants to a boil in a small saucepan over medium-high heat; once boiling, cover and set aside off the heat until the currants have plumped, about 5 minutes. Drain, reserving the Marsala.

3. Heat the butter in a 12-inch skillet over medium-high heat; when the foam subsides, add the shallots and celery and cook, stirring occasionally, until softened, about 5 minutes. Stir in the sage, thyme, parsley, and reserved Marsala and cook until the moisture has evaporated, about 1 minute; set skillet aside off heat.

4. Whisk the egg, broth, salt, and pepper in a large bowl until combined. Add the bread cubes, currants, and shallot-celery mixture; toss gently until evenly moistened and combined. Set aside until ready to roast the chicken. Just before serving, stir in the pecans.

COUSCOUS STUFFING WITH FENNEL, DRIED APRICOTS, AND CASHEWS

Serves 4

2	tablespoons unsalted butter
½	medium bulb of fennel, chopped fine (about 1 cup)
1	medium garlic clove, minced or pressed through a garlic press (about 1 teaspoon)
⅓	cup finely chopped dried apricots
⅛	teaspoon ground cinnamon
¼	teaspoon ground cumin
½	teaspoon salt
¼	teaspoon ground black pepper
2	cups low-sodium chicken broth
10	ounces plain couscous (1 box or 1½ cups plus 2 tablespoons)
1	medium scallion, sliced thin
¼	cup chopped fresh parsley leaves
¼	cup chopped unsalted raw cashews, toasted

1. Heat the butter in a 12-inch skillet over medium-high heat; when the foam subsides, add the fennel and cook, stirring occasionally, until it begins to soften, about 2 minutes. Add the garlic, apricots, cinnamon, cumin, salt, and pepper and cook, stirring frequently, until fragrant, about 2 minutes. Add the broth and bring to a boil; stir in the couscous, cover the pan, and let it stand off the heat until the liquid is absorbed, about 5 minutes. Set aside until ready to roast the chicken.

2. Just before serving, stir in the scallion, parsley, and toasted cashews.

TECHNIQUE: Preparing Fennel

1. Cut off the stems and feathery fronds. (The fronds can be minced and used for a garnish, if desired.) Trim a very thin slice from the base and remove any tough or blemished outer layers from the bulb.

2. Cut the bulb in half through the base. Use a small, sharp knife to remove the pyramid-shaped core.

3. Place the cored fennel on a work surface and, with the knife parallel to the cutting board, cut the fennel in half crosswise. Then, cut the fennel pieces lengthwise into thin strips.

EQUIPMENT CORNER: Kitchen Shears

WITH KITCHEN SHEARS THAT COME APART FOR CLEANING, you don't have to worry about what's growing in between the blades. We tested seven pairs of "take-apart" kitchen shears, focusing on core tasks—snipping chives, cutting lengths of butcher's twine and rounds of parchment paper, trimming pie pastry, and butterflying chicken. We excluded poultry shears, with their characteristic bulky, curved blades, because a good pair of kitchen shears can handle poultry with ease, while poultry shears are awkward and unwieldy for other tasks. Built like poultry shears, Anolon's Forged Kitchen Shears ($49.95) and Chef's Choice Professional Kitchen Shears ($31.95) didn't surprise us when they failed all but the chicken test.

We disliked models with short blades, such as Mundial's 2½-inch Take-A-Part Kitchen Shears ($20), which made jobs harder by requiring extra cuts. Short blades can seem even shorter when they have a notch for crushing bones, and the Mundial loses half an inch of cutting surface to its notch.

Our favorite shears, Messermeister's Take-Apart Shears ($23.99), have a curved cutting edge on one blade that acts like a notch without giving up valuable length. The long (almost 3-inch) blades are precise and supersharp. A slip-resistant handle and slim blades make these shears agile without sacrificing their brute force. The only downside is a definite right-hand bias. For lefties, Wüsthof's Come-Apart Kitchen Shears ($19.95) performed well, with greater comfort.

BEST KITCHEN SHEARS

Messermeister's Take-Apart Shears ($23.99) were a cut above the rest.

SPINACH WITH GARLIC AND LEMON

WHAT WE WANTED: Tender sautéed spinach, seasoned with a perfect balance of garlic and lemon so that their flavors complement, not overwhelm, the delicate greens.

This classic Italian preparation for spinach has been known to win over even the most stubborn of the anti-spinach set. Sautéed spinach, tossed with lemon and garlic, becomes glossy and tender, and the supporting flavors define rather than camouflage the leafy greens' sweet mineral tang. This dish, however, has been known to miss the mark, resulting in overcooked spinach, bitter burnt garlic, and pallid lemon flavor. We wanted to figure out just what is the best method for cooking the spinach and how to handle the garlic and lemon successfully.

The first step was to choose the most suitable variety of spinach. Most markets sell two types: flat leaf (more delicate in texture though stronger in flavor) and crinkle leaf (crumpled-looking leaves grown for sturdiness). Flat-leaf spinach is sold as either "baby" spinach (generally prewashed and bagged) or more mature spinach (in bunches with stems and roots still attached), with leaves three to four times larger than the baby variety. Because the bagged varieties are undeniably convenient and are carried more regularly than the bunched version, we decided to pursue our testing with them.

We began with the baby spinach, but the delicate leaves couldn't withstand the pan's high heat. It wilted to astonishingly little when cooked, floating in a puddle of murky looking liquid. The texture was even more shocking; one taster described it as "chewing on wet tissue." Crinkle-leaf spinach fared much better, retaining a pleasant resiliency and mineral-rich flavor, and though it didn't exude as much liquid as the flat leaf, the liquid was still a problem.

Most recipes we researched relied on evaporation to eliminate the "juice," but more often than not this method overcooked the spinach and destroyed its sweet flavor and tender texture. Other recipes cooled the spinach down after wilting and squeezed it dry before seasoning. While we thought this technique had promise, we were dissuaded by the additional time it required. Could we somehow squeeze the spinach while it was still hot so that it could be seasoned and served immediately?

Clearly, hands weren't an option, and the wooden spoon we had been using to stir the leaves was awkward.

What about tongs? We grabbed a set and worked the wilted leaves into a bunch, gently squeezing it. The juices flowed free and we were left with tender, flavorful greens ready for seasoning. The tongs proved such an agile tool that we pressed them into service for the rest of the recipe.

With the spinach perfectly cooked, we concentrated on the seasonings. For a cooking medium, we tried both regular and extra-virgin olive oil, and tasters favored the fruitier flavor of the extra-virgin oil. Garlic proved a little harder to handle, as its flavor varied considerably according to the cooking method. Briefly sautéed minced garlic tasted too strong and looked unappealing; garlic poached in oil (a favorite technique of the test kitchen for pasta) tasted odd in conjunction with the mineral bite of the spinach; and raw garlic overwhelmed the dish. Lightly browned, slivered garlic (sautéed before the spinach is added) was the tasters' favorite. Its sweet nuttiness paired well with the spinach.

Lemon juice proved finicky as well, either dominating the spinach with a brassy bite or fading altogether. Spritzing the spinach with juice early on made for a faint lemon flavor; the juice disappeared down the drain with the exuded liquid. Adding the citrus "post-squeeze" proved a better option, as the juice stayed with the spinach and saw just enough heat to marry with the other flavors. A little zest rounded out the lemon flavor without increasing the acidity, and a pinch of red pepper flakes added some gentle heat.

The coup de grace, as with most Italian vegetable dishes, was a drizzle of raw extra-virgin olive oil to reinforce the fruitiness and lend the dish a luxurious texture. In only five minutes of cooking, we were able to produce a paragon of spinach dishes.

WHAT WE LEARNED: Crinkle-leaf spinach is tasty, convenient, and holds up to heat better than flat-leaf baby spinach. Sautéed slivered garlic gives the spinach a sweet nuttiness. Once the spinach is cooked, use tongs to squeeze the spinach of excess juices then return it to the pan and add fresh lemon juice for a bright refreshing note.

SAUTÉED GARLIC-LEMON SPINACH

Serves 4

The amount of spinach may seem excessive, but the spinach wilts considerably with cooking. We like to use a salad spinner to wash and dry the spinach. If you have kosher or coarsely ground sea salt on hand, use one for the final sprinkling just before serving. This spinach dish makes an excellent accompaniment to almost any main course from chicken and fish to steak and pork.

- 2 tablespoons extra-virgin olive oil, plus 1 teaspoon for drizzling
- 4 medium garlic cloves, cut crosswise into very thin (1/16-inch) slices (about 2 tablespoons)
- 3 10-ounce bags crinkle-leaf spinach, stems removed, leaves washed and dried
  Salt
  Pinch red pepper flakes
- ½ teaspoon grated zest plus 2 teaspoons juice from 1 lemon

1. Heat 2 tablespoons of the oil and garlic in a Dutch oven over medium-high heat; cook until the garlic is light golden brown, shaking the pan back and forth when the garlic begins to sizzle, about 3 minutes (stirring with a spoon will cause the garlic to clump). Add the spinach by the handful, using tongs to stir and coat the spinach with the oil.

2. Once all the spinach is added, sprinkle ¼ teaspoon salt, pepper flakes, and lemon zest over the top and continue stirring with tongs until the spinach is uniformly wilted and glossy green, about 2 minutes. Using tongs, transfer the spinach to a colander set in a sink and gently squeeze spinach with tongs to release excess juices. Return the spinach to the Dutch oven; sprinkle with lemon juice and stir to coat. Drizzle with the remaining 1 teaspoon olive oil and sprinkle with additional salt to taste. Serve immediately.

Once the glaze is simmering, the seared pork chops should be returned to the pan to finish cooking through.

TWO WAYS
with pork

When it comes to cuts of pork, there are two choices you'll almost always find at the supermarket: boneless chops and tenderloin. Boneless chops are lean and quick-cooking, making them ideal for weeknight meals. Pan-searing is our preferred method for cooking pork chops, but when pan-seared, boneless pork chops can easily dry out by the time the exterior has developed a flavorful browned crust. Many boneless pork chop recipes feature a glaze—a terrific idea for both flavor and moisture, but glazes can be fussy—some can turn out thin and flavorless, while others can be overly sweet and gloppy. We wanted a streamlined method for pan-searing glazed chops with tender meat and deep flavor.

Pork tenderloin, which is also lean, has a somewhat fussy reputation, perhaps due to the fact that this cut is often more familiar at the restaurant table than in the home kitchen. But that doesn't mean you need to be a chef to cook tenderloin properly. The tenderloin, however, is not without its problems. Its oblong, tapered shape, makes it difficult to get even slices. And, the hallmark of tenderloin is its tender texture, but its flavor is often described as weak or boring. Typical recipes take such flavor-enhancing measures as long marinating times or a pan-sear/oven-roast approach, but we wanted a simple weeknight option with a few no-fuss, savory pan sauces.

With these easy and tasty recipes, you'll find that boneless pork chops and tenderloin are great choices for tonight's supper.

GREAT GLAZED PORK CHOPS

WHAT WE WANTED: The convenience and speed of thin, boneless pork chops with the flavor and moist, juicy interior of their thicker, bone-in counterparts.

We've grilled, seared, pan-roasted, and barbecued our way through plenty of pork in the test kitchen, and, through all this testing, we've developed some pretty solid opinions. Specifically, we like pork chops big, brined, and bone-in: The size makes them hard to overcook and good candidates for brining, which keeps them moist; cooking on the bone promotes meaty flavor.

That said, we wondered if we'd been too hasty in turning a blind eye to the thin boneless pork chop. After all, these chops are always available straight from the supermarket meat case (no attentive butcher required), they cook up quickly, and they're inexpensive. So what's the problem? A few hours of cooking reminded us. Most of the thin chops we cooked curled up unattractively in the pan as they surrendered their last ounce of moisture. The ones that remained juicy did so at the expense of good browning and, by extension, good flavor.

Our goal was to find a way to take advantage of the convenience of thin boneless pork chops yet still have both a pronounced sear and a moist, juicy interior. Most important, we wanted the chops on the table in about 30 minutes. So out went brining, grilling, and pan-roasting; in went pan-searing, using only the stovetop. This would open up the opportunity to make a pan sauce, as we would likely end up with a nice fond (the browned bits left behind by the cooked meat on the surface of the skillet, which enhance the flavor of any sauce).

From prior testing, we'd found that to cook pork chops completely on the stovetop (without brining and without finishing in the oven), it's best to stick with chops ¾ inch thick or thinner. So far, so good. But the foolproof cooking method we developed—starting the chops in a cold pan

and gently bringing them up to heat—wasn't so foolproof here. The difference? For that recipe, we used bone-in chops, which took on a lightly browned exterior just as the interior turned juicy and tender. The leaner boneless chops we were using cooked more quickly, and it was impossible to get adequate color within that time frame. What's more, back then we took pains to call for natural pork chops rather than enhanced chops (pork injected with a saline solution to keep it moist), which release excess juices during cooking and, thus, inhibit quick browning. We wanted our recipe to work well no matter what was available at the supermarket.

Consequently, we turned to our traditional searing method: high heat, smoking pan, even color on both sides of the meat. Unfortunately, the meat failed to stay flat and in direct contact with the pan. Instead, it curled up and took on a spotty, light golden sear by the time it was cooked through. The first problem was easily solved when we slashed through the fat and the silver skin, which creates the bowing effect as it contracts. The second problem—lack of a dark, rich sear—was not so easy. We had thought we could get away with searing one side of the chop pretty heavily and putting a quick sear on the second side once the pan was nice and hot. The presentation side, after all, was what really counted. Although this method worked, the cooking time was critical: A few extra seconds were all the pan's high heat needed to take the chops from perfectly tender to dry and tough. Too close for comfort, but we were out of ideas. We decided to put the cooking method on hold for a bit while we experimented with the sauce.

Exploring some options for pan sauces, we thought we would try a glaze. We whipped up a few simple ones, but they were too thick, sweet, and one-dimensional. While honey added a distinct depth of flavor, it tended to crystallize and become grainy. Instead, we settled on brown sugar. We tempered this sweet base with soy sauce, vinegar, Dijon mustard, and cayenne and then added apple cider

for depth of flavor. Adding the juices from the resting pork was the final touch. As good as this sweet and savory glaze tasted, the texture was inconsistent—at times too thick, at other times too thin. By adjusting the cooking time, we finally arrived at the point where the glaze both adhered well to the chops and was plentiful enough to spoon over them once they were plated.

The recipe now called for searing the chops on the first side until well browned, turning them over, finishing on the other side, then removing them from the pan while we made the glaze. When we used thicker chops, however, we had to give them more time to sear on the "nonpresentation" side to get them up to the right temperature. A few times, we charred the pan and ruined the fond we needed for the glaze. Ah—the glaze! Perhaps if we added it to the pan earlier and turned down the heat, we could get a head start on its reduction, save time, and keep the fond from burning.

Not only did this trick work, but it gave us the insurance we'd been missing in our cooking method. Finishing the chops over moderate heat (rather than high heat) slowed things down just enough to give us a better chance of getting them out of the pan while they were still juicy. The precise cooking time became much less critical. What's more, unlike the high, relatively dry heat of searing, gently simmering the chops in the wet glaze over moderate heat seemed to help them retain their moisture, almost as though we were poaching them. Once the meat reached 140 degrees, a five-minute rest off the heat on a platter let the temperature rise a bit more and let the juices redistribute throughout the meat.

At last, we had produced foolproof glazed pork chops that could make it from the supermarket to weeknight dinner table in record time.

WHAT WE LEARNED: Prior to cooking, cut through the sides of the pork chops to prevent the chops from curling. Sear the chops, remove them from the pan, add the glaze mixture, and then return the chops to the pan to finish cooking them through.

CIDER-GLAZED PORK CHOPS

Serves 4

If your chops are closer to 1 inch thick, you may need to increase the simmering time in step 2.

glaze
½	cup distilled white vinegar or cider vinegar
⅓	cup light brown sugar
⅓	cup apple cider or apple juice
2	tablespoons Dijon mustard
1	tablespoon soy sauce
	Pinch cayenne

chops
4	boneless center-cut or loin pork chops, 5 to 7 ounces each, ½ to ¾ inch thick
	Salt and ground black pepper
1	tablespoon vegetable oil

1. Combine all the glaze ingredients in a medium bowl; mix thoroughly and set aside. For each pork chop, slash through the fat and silver skin with sharp knife, making 2 cuts about 2 inches apart in each one (do not cut into the meat of the chops). Pat the chops dry with paper towels and season with salt and pepper.

2. Heat the oil in heavy-bottomed 12-inch skillet over medium-high heat until smoking. Add the pork to the skillet and cook until well browned, 4 to 6 minutes. Turn the chops and cook 1 minute longer; transfer the chops to a platter and pour off any oil in the skillet. (Check the internal temperature of the thinner chops; see the note above.) Return the chops to the skillet, browned side up, and add the glaze mixture; cook over medium heat until the center of the chops registers 140 degrees on an instant-read thermometer, 5 to 8 minutes. Remove the skillet from the heat; transfer the chops to a clean platter, tent with foil, and let rest until the temperature reaches 150 degrees (about 5 minutes).

3. When the chops have rested, add any accumulated juices to the skillet and set over medium heat. Simmer, whisking constantly, until the glaze is thick and the color of dark caramel (a heatproof spatula should leave a wide trail when dragged through the glaze), 2 to 6 minutes. Return the chops to the skillet; turn to coat both sides with the glaze. Transfer the chops back to the plate, browned side up, and spread the remaining glaze over the chops. Serve immediately.

GLAZED PORK CHOPS WITH GERMAN FLAVORS

Any beer can be used here except a dark beer like porter or stout.

Toast ¾ teaspoon caraway seeds in a small dry skillet over medium heat, stirring frequently, until fragrant, 3 to 5 minutes. Roughly chop the seeds and set aside in a small bowl. Follow the recipe for Cider-Glazed Pork Chops, replacing the cider or juice with ⅓ cup beer, reducing the soy sauce to 2 teaspoons, and adding 3 tablespoons whole grain mustard (along with the Dijon mustard), 1 tablespoon minced fresh thyme leaves, and reserved caraway seeds to the glaze ingredients. Omit the cayenne.

GLAZED PORK CHOPS WITH ASIAN FLAVORS

Toast 1 teaspoon sesame seeds in a small dry skillet over medium heat, stirring frequently, until lightly browned and fragrant, 3 to 5 minutes; set aside in a small bowl. Follow the recipe for Cider-Glazed Pork Chops, replacing the white or cider vinegar with ½ cup rice vinegar, omitting the cider or juice, and adding 3 tablespoons each orange juice and mirin and 1 teaspoon finely grated fresh ginger to the glaze ingredients. In step 3, stir another 2 teaspoons rice vinegar and 1 teaspoon toasted sesame oil into the glaze before returning the chops to the skillet. Before serving, garnish the chops with the reserved sesame seeds.

TASTING LAB: Cider Vinegar

EVEN THOUGH CIDER VINEGAR IS NOW USED MORE FOR brightening sauces and salad dressings than staving off spoilage (as it was once used before the advent of refrigeration), most cooks (including us) still opt for the most generic brand possible. As supermarkets have begun to offer a more varied selection—some in the vinegar aisle, some in the "natural foods" section—we wondered if it was time to change our tune. How much does cider vinegar brand matter? To find out, we purchased ten brands available in supermarkets or by mail—six produced domestically, three from France, and one from Canada. We tasted them four ways: plain, in a Carolina-style barbecue sauce, in a pan sauce, and on romaine lettuce in a simple vinaigrette.

Right off the bat, it was plain that these were not identical products. Some vinegars were pale yellow, others deep gold, a few caramel colored. They also ranged from very cloudy to sparkling clear; one contained distinct reddish particles. Their tastes were varied, too, from slightly sweet and mellow to harsh and not sweet at all. The aroma and taste of apple were forthright in some, oddly missing in others.

Any hopes of a clear-cut victory along national lines were dashed as soon as the results were tallied. Of the two favorites, one was French (Maille), the other American (Spectrum Naturals Unfiltered). Could cloudiness or clarity be the winning factor? Cloudiness is a sign of unfiltered, unpasteurized vinegar, which still contains the "mother of vinegar," a gelatinous substance consisting of cellulose (plant fibers) and acetic bacteria (which ultimately produce vinegar). Clear vinegars are filtered. Again, tasters were split: One winner was clear, the other cloudy. Color? Wrong again: One was deep caramel, the other pale yellow.

Investigations into the manufacturing process proved similarly fruitless. Nine of the ten vinegars are mass-produced in an acetator, a machine that can create thousands of gallons of vinegar in a matter of hours. Only the Quebec vinegar (Verger Pierre Gingras) was made in the traditional way, with cider left in wooden barrels for months to ferment first into alcohol, then into vinegar. While a small but vocal minority of tasters sang the praises of the distinctive

---

GETTING IT RIGHT: Great Glaze

Getting the glaze right takes some finessing—a few extra seconds can mean the difference between luxurious texture and gooey mess. Our solution? Monitor the size of the bubbles, the color of the glaze, and the amount of exposed pan surface.

Not Yet
Pan surface has just a few small bubbles, and a spatula makes no trails.

Just Right
Increased bubbles, caramel color, and a spatula just starts to make trails.

Too Long
Many large bubbles, ultra-dark glaze, and plenty of exposed pan surface.

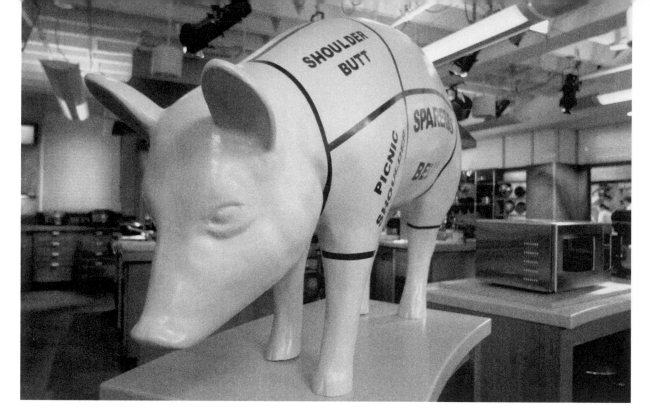

complexity lent by barrel fermentation, most were put off by this artisanal vinegar's astringent, "musty" qualities. It finished toward the bottom of the pack along with two French vinegars that had similar flavor profiles. (Of course, this may say more about the American palate than the vinegars.)

Our first important clue came not from the labels but from tasters' positive comments. Praise abounded for the "sweet honey and caramel" notes of first-place Maille and the "appley sweetness" of second-place Spectrum Naturals Unfiltered. From the top brand to the bottom, sweetness—or lack thereof—was clearly an overriding concern for tasters. On a hunch, we sent all ten vinegars to a laboratory to be analyzed for sugar content.

The results from the lab reports cleared things up considerably. High sugar content correlated directly with taster preference. Maille and Spectrum Naturals Unfiltered—our two winning vinegars—were the sweetest of the group, with 1.31 and 1.56 grams of sugar (per 100-milliliter sample), respectively. The next three vinegars, in descending chart order, were White House (1.13 grams), Eden (0.75 grams), and Bragg (0.69 grams). The last-place Delouis (0.53 grams) had the lowest sugar level of the entire group—about one-third the amount of the winners.

The one exception to the "sweeter is better" rule was the sixth-place Spectrum Naturals Filtered, sibling to our runner-up, which had plenty of sugar but did not fare so well. A call to an industry insider, Roger Fairchild, proprietor of Golden Valley Vinegars of Fruitland, Idaho, revealed one trick of the trade. "Vinegar making is as much an art as a science," Fairchild said. "Some days you make great vinegar, some days good vinegar, and other days it's not good at all." While he throws away the vinegars that don't make the grade, he says vinegar makers filter mediocre vinegar to make it taste better. Filtering also makes the vinegar more appealing to consumers who associate a clear product with a pure one. But filtering, which removes apple solids and the mother of vinegar, also strips out much of the apple flavor.

So sweetness counts when it comes to apple cider vinegar, but even generous sugar levels can't make up for a lack of apple flavor, a by-product of filtering. For vinegars that performed well in every test, the tasting results point to the rich, smooth Maille and the sweet and tangy Spectrum Naturals Unfiltered. For those intrigued by the complexity of a French-style cider vinegar, the Verger Pierre Gingras (from Quebec) had several enthusiastic fans. But bear in mind that the majority of tasters found this vinegar unpleasantly "medicinal" (landing it in an unremarkable ninth place) and that its $19 price tag makes it a fairly high-priced gamble.

Rating Apple Cider Vinegars

TEN APPLE CIDER VINEGARS WERE SAMPLED BY 24 MEMBERS OF THE TEST KITCHEN. THE VINEGARS WERE TASTED FOUR WAYS: plain; in a Carolina-style vinegar-based barbecue sauce; in a pan sauce made with butter, cream, and shallots; and in a vinaigrette made with olive oil, salt, and pepper and served on romaine lettuce. Tasters judged the vinegars on their fruity, appley flavor, their balance of sweetness to tartness, and their complexity. Scores for the four tastings were combined to obtain overall rankings. The vinegars are available nationwide in supermarkets and natural foods stores.

RECOMMENDED
Maille Apple Cider Vinegar
$4.00 for 16.9 ounces (about 24 cents per ounce)
Tasters raved about this French vinegar's "deep, warm" flavor profile and complex notes of honey, caramel, and sweet, "definite apple" taste. In the cream sauce, tasters liked this vinegar's "mellow, smooth cider flavor."

RECOMMENDED
Spectrum Naturals Organic Apple Cider Vinegar, Unfiltered
$2.89 for 16 ounces (18 cents per ounce)
Tasters liked the California-made Spectrum's sweetness. In addition, its "distinct apple flavor," "floral" aroma, and "assertive, tangy" qualities also gave it an edge. Cooked in the cream sauce, Spectrum's strong apple taste came through as well.

RECOMMENDED WITH RESERVATIONS
White House Apple Cider Vinegar
$1.99 for 32 ounces (6 cents per ounce)
American-made White House performed in the middle of the pack until the vinaigrette tasting, where it suddenly took top honors with a "good balance of acidity." But it was also downgraded for having "not much apple" flavor.

RECOMMENDED WITH RESERVATIONS
Eden Organic Apple Cider Vinegar
$2.06 for 16 ounces (13 cents per ounce)
While some tasters liked Eden's "pronounced apple cider profile" and light, mild, "pleasantly fruity flavor," most deemed it "mundane," "flat," and "a little too subtle."

RECOMMENDED WITH RESERVATIONS
Bragg Organic Apple Cider Vinegar
$2.59 for 16 ounces (16 cents per ounce)
A few tasters responded to this California vinegar's "good apple flavor" and "cidery" qualities, enjoying its "bright and vibrant" effect on the pan sauce. But uncooked, those strong notes came across as "harsh, medicinal."

RECOMMENDED WITH RESERVATIONS
Spectrum Naturals Organic Apple Cider Vinegar, Filtered
$3.09 for 16 ounces (19 cents per ounce)
In each of the four tastings, the filtered Spectrum fared distinctly worse than its unfiltered sibling, with tasters complaining, "Where's the apple?"

RECOMMENDED WITH RESERVATIONS
Vilux Apple Cider Vinegar
$4.50 for 25.4 ounces (18 cents per ounce)
"Ick," wrote one succinct panelist. This French vinegar really riled up tasters, eliciting comments about its "Chloraseptic throat spray" qualities and "sour, moldy," "stale, musty," off-notes. In the pan sauce, it was "very bland."

RECOMMENDED WITH RESERVATIONS
Heinz Apple Cider Vinegar
$2.19 for 32 ounces (7 cents per ounce)
The best panelists could muster for this ubiquitous American vinegar was to call it simple and mild: "No harm, no foul." Several decried it as "very acidic without much apple" flavor.

RECOMMENDED WITH RESERVATIONS
Verger Pierre Gingras Apple Cider Vinegar
$19.00 for 16 ounces ($1.19 per ounce)
A few raved that this wood-aged artisanal vinegar from Quebec was "the best one yet; flavor is full, tasty!" But most complained that it smelled "awful," was "stinky," and imparted "burnt, ashy flavors" to the pan sauce.

RECOMMENDED WITH RESERVATIONS
Delouis Organic Apple Cider Vinegar
$3.15 for 16.9 ounces (19 cents per ounce)
Rated as "odd and clinical tasting" and "quite strong, maybe too much," this French vinegar had an "off, sour flavor" that was described as "gross" and "musty."

SAUTÉED PORK TENDERLOIN

WHAT WE WANTED: An easy, weeknight method for cooking pork tenderloin medallions with great flavor.

With no bones, minimal fat, and wide availability, pork tenderloin has plenty going for it. When cooked properly, its tenderness rivals that of beef tenderloin, the deluxe roast that gives us filet mignon. On the downside, this ultra-lean cut has an ultra-mild flavor that needs a major boost. Long marinades and hybrid searing/roasting techniques (the latter providing flavorful browning) help remedy such deficiencies, but they also take the home cook a long way from the realm of the no-fuss meal.

We wanted a recipe for a fast weeknight dinner, so we were left with only a small arsenal of tools at our disposal to enhance flavor and ensure juiciness. Skillets and quick pan sauces were in; brining, marinating, and heating a grill or oven were out.

The first problem was the tenderloin's oblong, tapered shape. Vacuum-sealed individually or in sets of two, the loins looked like neatly packed, identically sized sausages. Once we opened the packages, we found that they varied greatly in length (from 9 inches to 14 inches) and shape. And when packed in pairs, the two loins were almost guaranteed to be substantially different in weight, making it tricky to portion them out into equal servings. Tucking the tail end under the thicker section, then tying it into an evenly shaped roast, fixed that problem. But cooking the tenderloin whole (either pan-roasting or sautéing) took more than 30 minutes.

Slicing the tenderloin into thin medallions made for uniform thickness, but some pieces were nearly 3 inches wide while others were barely an inch. Attempts to cheat nature with creative bias slicing proved unreliable. What about cutting the smaller parts thicker and pounding them to equal width? More consistent, yes, but thanks to the expanded surface area, they required sautéing in several batches.

Overcooking was an even bigger problem with these sliced medallions. We wanted to get as much browning on the exterior as possible to provide textural contrast with the tender interior and to improve flavor. But with such thin slices, we had only two choices: overcooked medallions with a pronounced, flavorful sear or wan, gray disks. Neither was an acceptable compromise.

To get adequate browning without overcooking the interior, we next tried increasing the thickness of the medallions by increments—first ½ inch, then ¾ inch, 1 inch, and so on—until they began to resemble miniature versions of beef tenderloin filets. At 2 inches thick, the "pork mignons" were developing a dark brown sear before the interiors had cooked through. At 1½ inches, the interior was cooked through but still juicy and the top and bottom surfaces were beautifully browned. These rounds also offered the advantage of fitting into a 12-inch skillet in one batch. Treating pork tenderloin like beef tenderloin was really doing the trick. Several tasters objected to leaving the sides unbrowned, so we made a point to stand the medallions on their sides (using tongs) during searing.

Cutting the pork into 1½-inch pieces left odd bits from both ends of the tenderloin, and even the slices from the central section were problematic, making for oblong pieces that would flop over and "flatten" awkwardly during cooking. To limit the number of odd pieces, we scored the section near the tail, creating a small flap of meat that folded underneath the larger half to yield the right-sized medallion (see illustrations on page 55). To prevent the pork from flopping over, we took another cue from beef tenderloin and tied the meat with twine, which gave it much better structure. (Blanched bacon, wrapped around the thick medallions and fastened with toothpicks, was another effective method that also gave the dish a smoky flavor.)

At this point, our pork tenderloin medallions were juicy and nicely browned—and they could all be cooked in

just one batch. But we wanted to boost the flavor even more. Unwilling to revisit the notion of a marinade, we decided to take advantage of the deep fond (the browned bits) left in the skillet by coming up with a few easy pan sauces to make while the medallions rested off the heat.

Following the test kitchen's usual method for pan sauces, we cooked aromatics in the hot skillet until fragrant, deglazed the skillet with broth, then reduced the broth along with other flavorful ingredients. Given how mild pork tenderloin can be, we gravitated toward bold flavors. Raiding the pantry for staple items, we balanced the sweetness of maple syrup with balsamic vinegar and spicy whole grain mustard. For a more exotic—but still easy—spin on this sweet and sour theme, we combined orange juice, hoisin sauce, ginger, and sesame oil, sprinkling chopped scallions over the medallions at the end for color and contrast. Both these sauces were ready in minutes.

Our final sauce—a more complex mix of diced apples, apple cider, apple brandy, cinnamon, shallots, and thyme—wasn't thickening as much as we wanted during the pork's five-minute resting period. The solution was to cook most of the ingredients in a saucepan beforehand, then pour the reduced liquid into the skillet to finish.

WHAT WE LEARNED: For medallions with a browned flavorful crust and juicy interior, cut the pork crosswise into 1½-inch pieces and tie them—this helps retain their shape. Fold over the thinner end pieces so they're of equal thickness and tie them, too. Sear the sides of the meat as well as the tops and bottoms for optimal flavor. For pan sauces with rich flavor in short order, use bold ingredients like whole grain mustard and balsamic vinegar.

THICK-CUT PORK TENDERLOIN MEDALLIONS

Serves 4 to 6

Serve with a pan sauce (recipes follow). We prefer natural to enhanced pork (pork that has been injected with a salt solution to increase moistness and flavor), though both will work in this recipe. Begin checking the doneness of smaller medallions 1 or 2 minutes early; they may need to be taken out of the pan a little sooner. See page 56 for Bacon-Wrapped Pork Tenderloin Medallions.

2   pork tenderloins (1 to 1¼ pounds each), trimmed of fat and silver skin, cut crosswise into 1½-inch pieces, and tied (see photo, page 56); thinner end pieces removed and tied together according to the illustrations on page 55
    Kosher salt and ground black pepper
2   tablespoons vegetable oil

1. Season the pork with salt and pepper.

2. Heat the oil in a 12-inch skillet over medium-high heat until shimmering. Add the pork cut side down and cook, without moving the pieces, until well browned, 3 to 5 minutes. Turn the pork and brown on the second side, 3 to 5 minutes more. Reduce the heat to medium. Using tongs, stand each piece on its side and cook, turning the pieces as necessary, until the sides are well browned and the internal temperature registers 145 to 150 degrees on an instant-read thermometer, 8 to 12 minutes. Transfer the pork to a platter and tent lightly with foil; let rest while making a pan sauce (recipes follow), then serve.

MAPLE-MUSTARD SAUCE

Makes enough to sauce 2 pork tenderloins

2   teaspoons vegetable oil
1   medium onion, halved and sliced thin (about 1 cup)
1   cup low-sodium chicken broth
⅓   cup maple syrup
3   tablespoons balsamic vinegar
3   tablespoons whole grain mustard
    Salt and ground black pepper

Pour off any fat from the skillet in which the pork was cooked. Add the oil and heat the skillet over medium heat until shimmering. Add the onion and cook, stirring occasionally, until softened and beginning to brown, 3 to 4 minutes. Increase the heat to medium-high and add the broth; bring to a simmer, scraping the bottom of the skillet with a wooden spoon to loosen any browned bits. Simmer until the liquid is reduced to ½ cup, 3 to 4 minutes. Add the maple syrup, vinegar, mustard, and any juices from the resting meat and cook until thickened and reduced to 1 cup, 3 to 4 minutes longer. Adjust seasonings with salt and pepper to taste, pour the sauce over pork, and serve immediately.

HOISIN-SESAME SAUCE

Makes enough to sauce 2 pork tenderloins

- 1 teaspoon vegetable oil
- 2 teaspoons minced fresh ginger
- ¼ cup hoisin sauce
- ½ cup orange juice from 2 oranges
- ½ cup low-sodium chicken broth
- 1 teaspoon toasted sesame oil
- 2 scallions, sliced ⅛ inch thick on the bias
  Salt and ground black pepper

Pour off any fat from the skillet in which the pork was cooked. Add the oil to the skillet and heat over medium heat until shimmering. Add the ginger and cook, stirring constantly, until fragrant, about 15 seconds. Add the hoisin sauce, orange juice, broth, and any juices from the resting meat and bring to a simmer, scraping the bottom of the skillet with a wooden spoon to loosen any browned bits. Simmer until the liquid is reduced to 1 cup, 2 to 3 minutes. Stir in the sesame oil and scallions. Adjust the seasonings with salt and pepper to taste, pour the sauce over the pork, and serve immediately.

APPLE CIDER SAUCE

Makes enough to sauce 2 pork tenderloins

Complete step I of this recipe either before or during the cooking of the pork, then finish the sauce while the pork rests.

- 1½ cups apple cider
- 1 cup low-sodium chicken broth
- 2 teaspoons cider vinegar
- 1 cinnamon stick
- 4 tablespoons unsalted butter, cut into 4 pieces
- 2 large shallots, minced (about ½ cup)
- 1 tart apple, such as Granny Smith, cored, peeled, and diced small
- ¼ cup Calvados or apple-flavored brandy
- 1 teaspoon minced fresh thyme leaves
  Salt and ground black pepper

1. Combine the cider, broth, vinegar, and cinnamon stick in a medium saucepan; simmer over medium-high heat until the liquid is reduced to 1 cup, 10 to 12 minutes. Remove the cinnamon stick and discard. Set the sauce aside until the pork is cooked.

TECHNIQUE: Turning the Tailpiece into a Medallion

1. Score the last 1½ inches of the tenderloin's tapered tail end.

2. Fold in half at the incision. (For two very small pieces, fold together.)

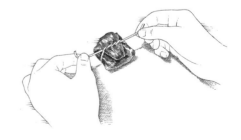

3. Tie the medallion with butcher's twine, making sure the outer surfaces are flat.

browned bits. Add the reduced cider mixture, any juices from the resting meat, and the thyme; increase the heat to medium-high and simmer until thickened and reduced to 1¼ cups, 3 to 4 minutes. Off the heat, whisk in the remaining butter and adjust the seasonings with salt and pepper to taste. Pour the sauce over the pork and serve immediately.

BACON-WRAPPED PORK TENDERLOIN MEDALLIONS

Place 12 to 14 slices bacon (1 slice for each pork medallion), slightly overlapping, in a microwave-safe pie plate and cover with plastic wrap. Cook in the microwave on high power until the slices shrink and release about ½ cup fat but are neither browned nor crisp, 1 to 3 minutes. Transfer the bacon to paper towels until cool, 2 to 3 minutes. Wrap each piece of pork with 1 slice bacon and secure with 2 toothpicks where the ends of the bacon strip overlap, inserting the toothpicks on an angle and gently pushing them through to the other side (see photo below). Season the pork with pepper (do not salt) and proceed with step 2 of the recipe for Thick-Cut Pork Tenderloin Medallions (time for searing the sides may be slightly longer).

GETTING IT RIGHT:
Two Tricks to Tidier Medallions

Thick medallions allow for more browning, but they can flop over in the pan. To prevent this, tie each piece with twine or a strip of precooked bacon secured with two toothpicks.

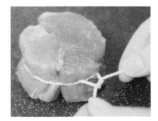
Butcher's Twine

Bacon "Twine"

---

2. Pour off any fat from the skillet in which the pork was cooked. Add 1 tablespoon of the butter and heat over medium heat until melted and the foaming subsides. Add the shallots and apple and cook, stirring occasionally, until softened and beginning to brown, 1 to 2 minutes. Remove the skillet from the heat and add the Calvados. Return the skillet to the heat and cook about 1 minute, scraping the bottom of the skillet with a wooden spoon to loosen any

EQUIPMENT CORNER:
Bargain Sauté Pans

BACK IN 2001, ALL-CLAD WAS THE WINNER OF OUR testing of sauté pans, but now our top choice costs more than $180. While a sauté pan—basically, a lidded skillet with straight rather than flared sides—is essential when you pan-fry cutlets and braise chicken parts or vegetables, it seems like an awful lot of money for a pan that might see action just once or twice a week, even in a busy home kitchen. Given the dizzying number of choices in the cookware aisle these days, we wondered if we could get similar performance for less money.

To find out, we assembled a lineup of eight "bargain" brands (under $100) to compete against the All-Clad: Cuisinart, Emerilware, Farberware, Gourmet Standard, Henckels, Oneida, Scanpan, and Sitram. Every pan had a capacity of 3 to 3½ quarts and a traditional (rather than nonstick) cooking surface, the better choice for developing the sticky browned bits—fond—that give pan sauces and braises deep flavor.

For our first test, we prepared white rice. All nine batches came out well. When we sautéed chopped onions over medium heat, a few pans browned them very quickly, while others left them pale—but slightly adjusting the temperature easily corrected either tendency. Evenly pan-fried chicken cutlets? Check. Nice pan sauce from the drippings? Check. As every pan passed every test without incident, we wondered how much we'd overspent on cookware over the years—until we had our first casualty.

During the crêpe-making session—an unconventional test for finding hot or cool spots on a pan's cooking surface—every pan produced perfect crêpes except one: The Sitram's crêpes turned dark brown around the edges. The problem was obvious. The thick aluminum disk stamped to the pan's bottom did not quite extend to the pan's outer edge, leaving an unprotected ¾-inch ring.

If dark-edged crêpes were the Sitram's only problem, all would be forgiven. But in a subsequent test—browning chicken thighs—that unprotected ring wreaked havoc again, burning the fond.

Clearly, an expensive sauté pan isn't crucial for basic tasks. But what if we pushed these pans to their limits? After combing through the test kitchen's recipe archive, we had just the challenge: pan-seared steaks—five minutes per side over very high heat (450 to 500 degrees). To see how well the pans negotiated the fiery heat below versus the cold steaks above, we fastened a temperature probe to the cooking surface.

Our test taught us several lessons, the first of which revealed itself before the steaks even hit the pan. With the probes in place, we let the pans preheat until the surface reached 500 degrees. The variance in preheating times was shocking. From fastest to slowest: Scanpan (2:55), Gourmet Standard (3:07), All Clad (3:11), Henckels (4:22), Cuisinart (4:45), Oneida (4:50), Sitram (5:00), Farberware (5:01). Emerilware? A whopping 7:36. No wonder the Emerilware had been on the slow side in some of the other tasks—it was probably still preheating!

The four fastest pans (Scanpan through Henckels) had one thing in common: clad-style construction, meaning that the entire pan is made of layers of stainless steel sandwiched around an aluminum core. The slowest five (Cuisinart through Emerilware) all had thick aluminum-core disks attached to the bottom. Because the clad pans were much thinner on the bottom than the disk pans, they heated up more efficiently: At 0.05 inches thick, the Scanpan was the responsiveness champ, while the 0.30-inch-thick Emerilware—six times thicker—was the least responsive of all.

Of course, responsiveness is only part of the equation. A pan also needs to retain heat well. When the cold steaks hit the pan, the tables turned: The heat-retention champs were the Emerilware and the Farberware, two thick, disk-bottomed pans that kept the cooking surface between 450 degrees and 500 degrees for almost the full 10 minutes. The clad pans were much more volatile—dropping precipitously, then recovering, only to drop off again when we flipped the steaks. Despite the drama, the clad pans produced fine steaks, with the exception

monitoring the temperature roller coaster. The clad-style All-Clad, Gourmet Standard, and Henckels and the disk-bottomed Oneida struck that balance well.

Although performance was our key concern, design details figured in as well. First, the size of the cooking surface matters. The pans tested ranged in diameter from 8⅜ inches to 9½ inches, and that extra inch is not insignificant: We easily fit a cut-up 3½-pound chicken in the larger pans, but the smaller models were too cramped.

Most pans had long metal handles that stayed cool, but the stubby Henckels handle heated up uncomfortably. Only one pan (Oneida) had a plastic handle, which stayed cool on the stovetop but precluded use in an oven hotter than 375 degrees. Five pans came with a "helper" handle, a small, loop-shaped second handle that made it easier to keep the pan level during transport. A dealbreaker? No. The occasional tiebreaker? Yes. In the end, it turns out you can get a great sauté pan for less than $100. The modestly priced Gourmet Standard ($74) matched the performance of the All-Clad ($184) task for task.

PAN BOTTOMS: Thick or Thin?

As a group, the disk-bottomed pans in our lineup were more than twice as thick on the bottom as the clad-style pans. We found that the thicker the pan's bottom, the better it maintained a constant temperature—but it took a long time to get there. The thinner the bottom, the faster the pan responded to temperature changes, which can be a good or bad thing. To illustrate the difference, we had our local hardware store slice through the middle of our thinnest (left) and thickest (right) sauté pans.

Thin Bottom
Superior responsiveness

Thick Bottom
Superior heat retention

---

of the hyper-responsive Scanpan, which heated up to such extremes that it scorched the steaks and ruined the fond.

The steak test convinced us that the ideal sauté pan would balance responsiveness and heat retention—too much of one or the other meant either having to wait forever to get the pan hot enough or having to be super-vigilant in

Rating Bargain Sauté Pans

WE TESTED AND EVALUATED EIGHT "BARGAIN" ($100 OR LESS) SAUTÉ PANS ALONGSIDE OUR LONGTIME (AND EXPENSIVE) favorite from All-Clad. We selected pans with a 3-quart capacity (or as close to it as we could find in that manufacturer's line) that were available in open stock according to the following criteria: sauté speed, performance (sautéing onions, searing chicken cutlets, browning thighs, and searing steaks), and design (handle shape and heat sensitivity as well as lid seal). All stovetop cooking tests were performed over 15,000-BTU gas burners on a Thermador range in our test kitchen. The pans are listed in order of preference. See www.americastestkitchen. com for up-to-date prices and mail-order sources for top-rated products.

RECOMMENDED
All-Clad Stainless 3 Quart
$183.95
Narrowly eked out another win thanks to as tiny a detail as its helper handle, a feature many staffers deemed crucial. Not to diminish its first-class performance: gorgeous sautéed onions, nicely browned steaks and cutlets, and impressive responsiveness. The most spacious cooking surface.

RECOMMENDED
Gourmet Standard Tri-Ply 10-Inch
$73.50
If it weren't for the absence of a helper handle, the near-tie for first place might have broken in this modestly priced pan's favor. Aced every test thrown its way, and a thicker gauge helped it maintain composure in the steak test just a hair better than our winner.

RECOMMENDED WITH RESERVATIONS
Oneida Stainless Steel Cook & Pour 10-Inch Deep
$29.99
The cheapest pan surprised us by stumbling on nary a task, and testers appreciated the deep sides. Because of a plastic handle, it's ovensafe to only 375 degrees, and the construction had "a chintzy feel." But, hey—it's 30 bucks. No helper handle.

RECOMMENDED WITH RESERVATIONS
Cuisinart Chef's Classic Stainless 3½ Quart
$99.99
Aced the steak test, where it maintained a steady temperature better than most, and the crêpe cooked evenly. But keep an eye on the heat during delicate tasks: Once the thick base heated up, the sauté pace raced, yielding patches of overbrowned onions.

RECOMMENDED WITH RESERVATIONS
Henckels International Classic Clad 3 Quart
$79.99
Onions cooked evenly, and chicken cutlets browned well. But eight chicken pieces proved a tight fit, and the handle heated up quickly. The narrow surface also affected the pan's ability to maintain a consistent temperature during our steak test. No helper handle.

RECOMMENDED WITH RESERVATIONS
Emerilware Stainless Steel 3 Quart
$69.95
Slow and steady was this pan's motto, but it's not for the weak of arm—that composure comes from heaviness, almost a full pound heavier than the next-lightest pan. But the real dealbreaker was the time it took to preheat: "Who wants to wait seven minutes every time you sear steaks?"

RECOMMENDED WITH RESERVATIONS
Scanpan 10¼-Inch Fusion 5
$99.99
A veritable roller coaster, this pan plummeted in temperature when cold steaks were added, then heated up enough to burn the fond, yielding a bitter-tasting sauce. The thinnest pan bottom.

RECOMMENDED WITH RESERVATIONS
Farberware Advantage Stainless Steel 10-Inch
$69.99
Browned the chicken cutlets with gusto, but overbrowned a good portion of the sautéed onions. Snug fit for the chicken; along with the Henckels and the Sitram, we would leave out a drumstick to ensure proper browning.

NOT RECOMMENDED
Sitram Profiserie 3.3-Quart Commercial Stainless Steel
$49.99 (without lid); $14.99 for lid
This pan's stamped disk bottom isn't flush with its sides, leaving an unprotected gap between the disk and the outer edge of the pan. The result? A dark brown outside ring on our crêpes and burnt chicken fond. No helper handle, a cramped cooking surface, and slow to preheat.

Bridget uses a wooden skewer to test the doneness of the cornbread topping on our Skillet Tamale Pie.

FASTER FAMILY *favorites*

In theory, quick recipes sound terrific—but we've found most streamlined recipes end up sacrificing flavor for speed and convenience. Take chicken pot pie. Most recipes for quick chicken pot pie feature a filling that is not much more than leftover chicken stirred into canned cream of chicken soup and a paltry amount of vegetables—sometimes even canned. These versions are not even close to the dinner that's always been a family favorite. We aimed to do better. We wanted a really flavorful chicken stew topped with a biscuit crust, and, yes, we wanted it fast.

Tamale pie, an already quick dish, has fallen victim to the dump-and-bake approach: combine a can of chili and a can of creamed corn; top with cornbread mix and bake. Tossing cans (and boxes) aside, we set out to make a fresh-tasting, quick tamale pie with a juicy, spicy mixture of meat and vegetables and a quick, homemade cornbread topping.

With these quick recipes, you'll be able to get dinner on the table in a reasonable amount of time—and they'll taste good, too.

CHICKEN POT PIE

WHAT WE WANTED: A weeknight chicken pot pie with moist, tender chicken, a flavorful sauce, and an easy home-made biscuit topping.

Most recipes for quick chicken pot pie are terrible. Leftover chicken and canned soup are often the culprits. The chicken dries out and the canned soup just doesn't have the depth of flavor of the original dish's rich gravy. We wanted to create a quick and fresh-tasting pot pie that didn't rely on bad shortcuts.

For the filling, we lightly browned boneless, skinless chicken breasts in butter over medium heat to keep their exteriors tender, not tough. We then set the chicken aside and built a sauce using onion, celery, thyme, vermouth, and chicken broth. Flour thickened the liquid to the proper pot pie consistency, and heavy cream added richness and a velvety texture. Once the sauce was at a gentle simmer, we returned the browned chicken to the skillet to poach and cook through. The sauce picked up flavor from the chicken, and the chicken benefited greatly from gently simmering in the sauce, cooking up perfectly tender, moist, and juicy. All that was left to do was slice (or shred) the chicken and stir in the vegetables (we opted for frozen peas and carrots). We next moved on to the topping.

While some quick recipes suggest a biscuit topping made with refrigerated biscuit dough, we thought we could come up with a quick, homemade recipe. We opted for a simple baking powder biscuit with just a few ingredients: flour, sugar, salt, baking powder, and heavy cream. We simply whisked together the dry ingredients, then stirred in the cream until a dough formed. After a brief knead, we cut the dough into rounds or wedges. We found it was best time-wise to bake the biscuits first, while we assembled the stew. By the time the stew was cooked, we simply placed the hot biscuits on top and brought the skillet to the table. For a nicer presentation, you could also transfer the stew to a pie dish and top with the biscuits. A rich, meaty stew topped with tender homemade biscuits couldn't be easier or tastier.

WHAT WE LEARNED: Prepare the biscuits first, so that while they bake you can assemble the stew. Lightly brown chicken breasts in butter over medium heat for the best flavor. Simmer the stew gently to prevent the chicken from becoming dried out and stringy. And instead of relying on canned soup, make a real sauce with chicken broth, white wine, and cream.

TECHNIQUE: Shaping Biscuits

1. On a lightly floured work surface pat the dough into a ¾-inch-thick circle.

2A. For rounds: Use a biscuit cutter to punch out rounds. Push together the scraps, pat into a ¾-inch-thick circle, and punch out more.

2B. For wedges: With a sharp knife or bench scraper, cut the dough into 8 wedges.

SKILLET CHICKEN POT PIE WITH BISCUIT TOPPING

Serves 4

If you don't have time to make your own biscuits for the topping, then use packaged refrigerated biscuits and bake them according to the package instructions. We prefer the flavor of Pillsbury Golden Homestyle Biscuits but you can use your favorite brand (you will need anywhere from 4 to 8 biscuits depending on their size). Serve this pot pie right from the skillet, or transfer the mixture to a large pie plate and top with the biscuits.

biscuits

- 2 cups (10 ounces) unbleached all-purpose flour, plus extra for the work surface
- 2 teaspoons sugar
- 2 teaspoons baking powder
- ½ teaspoon salt
- 1½ cups heavy cream

filling

- 1½ pounds boneless, skinless chicken breasts
  Salt and ground black pepper
- 4 tablespoons unsalted butter
- 1 medium onion, minced (about 1 cup)
- 1 celery rib, sliced thin
- ¼ cup unbleached all-purpose flour
- ¼ cup dry vermouth or dry white wine
- 2 cups low-sodium chicken broth
- ½ cup heavy cream
- 1½ teaspoons minced fresh thyme leaves
- 2 cups frozen pea-carrot medley, thawed

1. FOR THE BISCUITS: Adjust an oven rack to the upper-middle position and heat the oven to 450 degrees.

2. Whisk the flour, sugar, baking powder, and salt together in a large bowl. Stir in the cream with a wooden spoon until a dough forms, about 30 seconds. Turn the dough out onto a lightly floured work surface and gather into a ball. Knead the dough briefly until smooth, about 30 seconds.

3. Pat the dough into a ¾-inch-thick circle. Cut the biscuits into rounds using a 2½-inch biscuit cutter or cut into 8 wedges using a knife (see the illustrations on page 62).

4. Place the biscuits on a parchment paper–lined baking sheet. Bake until golden brown, about 15 minutes. Set aside on a wire rack.

5. FOR THE FILLING: While the biscuits bake, pat the chicken dry with paper towels and season with salt and pepper. Melt 2 tablespoons of the butter in a 12-inch skillet over medium heat until the foam subsides. Brown the chicken lightly on both sides, about 5 minutes total. Transfer the chicken to a clean plate.

6. Add the remaining 2 tablespoons butter to the skillet and return to medium heat until melted. Add the onion, celery, and ½ teaspoon salt and cook until the onion is softened, about 5 minutes. Stir in the flour and cook, stirring constantly, until incorporated, about 1 minute.

7. Stir in the vermouth and cook until evaporated, about 30 seconds. Slowly whisk in the broth, cream, and thyme, and bring to a simmer. Nestle the chicken into the sauce, cover, and cook over medium-low heat until the thickest part of the breast registers 160 degrees on an instant-read thermometer, 8 to 10 minutes.

8. Transfer the chicken to a plate. Stir the peas and carrots into the sauce and simmer until heated through, about 2 minutes. When the chicken is cool enough to handle, cut or shred it into bite-sized pieces and return it to the skillet. Season the filling with salt and pepper to taste.

9. FOR SERVING: Place the cooked biscuits on top of the skillet or individual servings.

SKILLET TAMALE PIE

WHAT WE WANTED: A quick and easy tamale pie with a fresh-tasting, well-seasoned filling and a moist and tender cornbread topping.

Tamale pie is a casserole comprised of a tomatoey ground beef and corn filling with a corn bread topping. It's simple and relatively quick and kids typically love the dish, making it a terrific choice for a weeknight meal. Too often, though, this recipe has fallen into the convenience food trap—a can of beef and bean chili mixed with a can of creamed corn—the whole then topped with a cornbread mix instead of a fresh cornbread topping. We also found in our research that some recipes used fresh ground beef, but then relied on dusty packets of taco seasoning mix for flavor. This dish was in need of some serious rescuing.

For the filling, we found that we liked the flavor and texture of 90 percent lean ground sirloin—anything less than 90 percent was simply too greasy. We added rinsed canned black beans, for heartiness and texture. Onion and garlic were a given for seasoning, and cooking a generous 2 tablespoons of chili powder in with the onion helped bloom the spice's flavor, for a rounded, well-seasoned filling. Canned diced tomatoes were another good addition for their juicy flavor and cilantro lent a bright, fresh note. We then stirred in cheddar cheese not only for flavor and richness, but also to help to thicken the mixture.

With the filling in place, we zeroed in on the topping. We admit that nothing beats the convenience of cornbread mixes—just pour into a bowl, add milk (and sometimes egg), mix, and bake; however, we found that it was almost as quick and easy to cobble together a recipe from scratch. A simple cornbread batter comes together quickly and is spread over the hot filling in the skillet. The skillet pie is then transferred to the oven to bake the topping through, which takes just ten to fifteen minutes. As we expected, the moist, tender crumb, subtle sweetness, and corn flavor of our homemade version was superior to all of the mixes we tried, and the perfect complement to the spicy filling. That said, you can use a cornbread mix if you're really pressed for time.

WHAT WE LEARNED: Use 90 percent lean ground sirloin for a meaty filling that is not greasy. Cook the chili powder with the onion to mellow its bite a bit and to allow its complex flavors to "bloom." Drained canned dice tomatoes give the filling just enough moisture and rich, tomatoey flavor. Stir in shredded cheddar cheese to thicken the filling and add richness and flavor. For best flavor, prepare a simple cornbread topping, instead of using a mix.

SKILLET TAMALE PIE

Serves 4

tamale filling

2 tablespoons vegetable oil
1 medium onion, minced
2 tablespoons chili powder
    Salt
2 medium garlic cloves, minced or pressed
    through a garlic press (about 2 teaspoons)
1 pound 90 percent lean ground sirloin
1 (15-ounce) can black beans, drained and rinsed
1 (14.5-ounce) can diced tomatoes, drained
3 ounces cheddar cheese, shredded (1 cup)
2 tablespoons minced fresh cilantro leaves
    Ground black pepper

cornbread topping

¾ cup (3¾ ounces) unbleached all-purpose flour
¾ cup (3¾ ounces) yellow cornmeal
3 tablespoons sugar
¾ teaspoon baking powder
¼ teaspoon baking soda
¾ teaspoon salt
¾ cup buttermilk
1 large egg
3 tablespoons unsalted butter, melted and cooled

1. Adjust an oven rack to the middle position and heat the oven to 450 degrees.

2. FOR THE TAMALE FILLING: Heat the oil in a 12-inch skillet over medium heat until shimmering. Add the onion, chili powder, and ½ teaspoon salt and cook until the onion is softened, about 5 minutes. Stir in the garlic and cook until fragrant, about 30 seconds.

3. Stir in the ground sirloin, beans, and tomatoes, and bring to a simmer, breaking up the meat with a wooden spoon,

about 5 minutes. Stir the cheddar and cilantro into the filling and season with salt and pepper to taste.

4. FOR THE CORNBREAD TOPPING: Whisk the flour, cornmeal, sugar, baking powder, baking soda, and salt together in a large bowl. In a separate bowl, whisk the buttermilk and egg together. Stir the buttermilk mixture into the flour mixture until uniform. Stir in the butter until just combined.

5. Dollop the cornbread batter evenly over the filling and spread into an even layer. Bake until the cornbread is cooked through in the center, 10 to 15 minutes. Serve.

TASTING LAB: Bottled Italian Dressings

OIL AND VINEGAR MAKE THE SIMPLEST SALAD DRESSING, one that's easy enough to put together yourself. So why would anyone purchase a bottled salad dressing? We can think of a couple of reasons. Sometimes you are just too tired to do it yourself. But the better reason is that sometimes you want something with more personality and zip. Italian dressing, for example, contains not just oil and vinegar but garlic, red pepper, oregano, and other herbs and spices. Sounds good, but several of those ingredients need to be finely chopped, which can add up to a lot of work.

To find out if any bottled Italian dressings are worth buying, we rounded up seven leading brands. Of the dressings we selected, most had similar ingredient lists: oil, vinegar, water, sugar, and salt, along with garlic, onion, red bell pepper, various herbs and spices, stabilizers, and preservatives. (A key ingredient in these dressings is xanthan gum, a stabilizer that gives them their signature thickness.)

Were any of these dressings good enough to buy? We found only two. The winner, Good Seasons, requires that you add your own oil and vinegar at home, so it was closest to homemade. In second place, Kraft Seven Seas Italian was OK but on the sweet side.

Rating Bottled Italian Dressings

TWENTY MEMBERS OF THE AMERICA'S TEST KITCHEN STAFF TASTED SEVEN DIFFERENT BOTTLED ITALIAN DRESSINGS ON PIECES OF iceberg lettuce. The dressings are listed in order of preference based on their scores in the tastings. All the salad dressings are available in supermarkets nationwide.

RECOMMENDED
Good Seasons Italian All Natural Salad Dressing Mix

$2.39 (includes cruet and 2 packets with dried seasonings; each packet yields 8 ounces of dressing)

It is easy to understand why this brand came out on top. Adding our own oil and vinegar (plus a little bit of water per packet instructions) made this dressing taste "most like homemade." The packet provides the right balance of herbs and spices, especially in the garlic and black pepper departments.

RECOMMENDED
Kraft Seven Seas Viva Italian Dressing

$2.79 for 16 ounces

This zesty dressing brought many tasters back to their childhood, with comparisons to "lunchroom cafeteria Italian dressing." Several tasters thought it would be a "good dressing for kids" because it had a sweet garlic and red pepper flavor to balance out the vinegar.

RECOMMENDED WITH RESERVATIONS
Wish-Bone Italian Dressing

$2.79 for 16 ounces

"Tart," "tangy," and "garlicky" were the words most often used to describe this dressing. While tasters appreciated its sharp and assertive flavor, they complained about its texture, which was described as "too thick."

RECOMMENDED WITH RESERVATIONS
Newman's Own Family Recipe Italian

$3.19 for 16 ounces

This dressing includes Romano cheese and anchovies. It was no surprise that tasters mistook this dressing for Caesar. They liked the strong garlic and black pepper flavors but not the overabundance of oil and the weak vinegar kick.

NOT RECOMMENDED
Kraft House Italian Dressing

$2.79 for 16 ounces

Like Newman's Own, this dressing also contains cheese, both Parmesan and Romano. Combined with a "dried herb" and "strong garlic" flavor, it reminded tasters of "bad pizza."

NOT RECOMMENDED
Ken's Steakhouse Italian Dressing and Marinade

$2.69 for 16 ounces

This bare-bones dressing contains few of the herbs and spices found in the other dressings sampled. Beyond oil, vinegar, salt, garlic, and onion, it featured only a long list of stabilizers and preservatives. Tasters felt that this dressing did not have enough personality to qualify as Italian.

NOT RECOMMENDED
Cains Italian Dressing

$2.79 for 24 ounces

Tasters were hard-pressed to say anything nice about this exceedingly sweet dressing. The flavor of "freeze-dried herbs" and "stale oregano" predominated; the red pepper "floaties" tasted "artificial."

To mimic the flavorful breading of fried cutlets, pre-toast the crumbs with a little olive oil and then bake the breaded chicken on a rack set over a baking sheet so hot air can circulate all around.

LIGHTER FAMILY *favorites*

Whether we like to admit it or not, there are some dishes that while tasty, are just too high in fat and calories to be enjoyed on a regular basis. Even a modest portion of such dishes as macaroni and cheese and chicken Parmesan is prohibitive. But do they need to be? What if we could create lighter versions of these dishes so we could enjoy them more often?

In our research we tried dozens of versions of "light" macaroni and cheese, and again and again we were met with disappointing dishes. Gluey sauces full of tasteless, rubbery nonfat cheeses were the norm. Versions made with ricotta and cottage cheese also showed up. We wanted a creamy macaroni and cheese with real cheesy flavor.

Light recipes for chicken Parmesan often fall short too. Again and again we were met with soggy crusts and rubbery, nonfat cheese. We wanted a really crisp crust for our chicken and we wanted great flavor.

With these lightened recipes, your favorites will be able to appear on the table as often as you crave them.

LIGHTER MACARONI AND CHEESE

WHAT WE WANTED: A lighter version of the family favorite—macaroni in a creamy (not rubbery or grainy), cheesy sauce—with a fraction of the calories.

Weighing in at about 650 calories and 40 grams of fat per serving, a bowl of homemade mac and cheese should really be a treat every once in awhile, like a slice of cheesecake. The truth, however, is that it winds up on the dinner table much more often because it's easy to prepare and kids will eat it without complaint.

We wanted to develop a macaroni and cheese recipe that could be used as a weekly workhorse meal with reasonable amounts of calories and fat, but without losing too much of the cheesy flavor and creamy texture that make it such a perennial favorite. Starting off in our cookbook library, we found dozens of recipes for low-fat mac and cheese. Making a few of these lightened recipes to get the lay of the land, we wondered if we had bitten off more than we could chew. Some of the recipes were downright awful, producing flavorless, rubbery mixtures due to large amounts of nonfat cheese, while other recipes turned out versions with a grainy texture because they included ricotta or cottage cheese. Obviously, we were on our own here.

Heading into the kitchen with the motto "Make the fat count," our philosophy was that every calorie and gram of fat needed to work for us and that none would slip by unaccounted for. With lots of ideas to test, we decided to focus on the cooking method first, then tweak the ingredients and flavors. The most common cooking method for mac and cheese is to make a béchamel (a milk sauce thickened with butter and flour) and then stir in the cheese and cooked macaroni. Another popular test kitchen method involves slowly cooking a mixture of milk, eggs, cheese, butter, and cooked macaroni over low heat until it thickens and becomes creamy. Yet a third, and somewhat unusual, method calls for boiling the pasta in a small amount of milk (the pasta starch thickens the milk to a sauce-like consistency), then stirring in cheese to finish. Giving these three methods a whirl, we were able to eliminate two right off the bat. The popular method of cooking a mixture of milk, eggs, cheese, butter, and cooked macaroni over low heat simply doesn't work without the eggs and lots of cheese. Also, cooking the pasta right in the milk turned the pasta gummy. Making a béchamel was the winning approach so far, but we still had a lot of calories and fat to trim. Using 2 percent, 1 percent, or skim milk instead of whole milk in the béchamel was an obvious way to reduce more fat and calories. Testing them side by side in batches of mac and cheese, tasters didn't like the sauces made with 1 percent and skim milk because they tasted too thin and didn't coat the pasta well. The sauce made with 2 percent milk, however, was acceptable and helped to trim about 2 grams of fat per serving.

Wanting to reduce the fat in the sauce further, we took a closer look at the roux (butter and flour mixture) used to thicken the milk into a béchamel. Cutting back on the butter as far as we could from the original 3 tablespoons, we found we needed at least 1 tablespoon of butter to make a roux with the flour. But even 1 tablespoon of butter adds a fair amount of fat and we wondered if we could lose it altogether. Making two sauces without any butter, we tried thickening the milk with either a flour slurry (flour dissolved in a liquid) or a cornstarch slurry (cornstarch dissolved in a liquid). Both slurries were able to thicken the milk to an appropriate sauce consistency, but tasters described the sauce thickened with flour as tasting grainy and pasty, while the sauce thickened with cornstarch had a smooth, silky texture. Using cornstarch instead of a traditional roux had saved us another 10 or so grams of fat per serving.

The cheese is obviously one of the heavier ingredients in the dish, and using low-fat cheese was an easy way to trim even more off the calorie and fat counts. Most mac and cheese recipes use about 12 ounces of cheddar per

½ pound pasta (serving 4 to 5 people), and we made batches of mac and cheese using incrementally less cheese until the tasters cried uncle. Eight ounces of cheese turned out to be the breaking point, beyond which tasters thought the mac and cheese tasted too bland. We then tested several batches of mac and cheese substituting other types of cheese (including Parmesan, Monterey Jack, and Gouda) for some of the cheddar, but tasters preferred the flavor of the cheddar alone. Finally, we made two more batches pitting nonfat cheddar against low-fat cheddar, and the tasters unanimously hated the rubbery texture and sweet flavor of the nonfat cheddar. Using 8 ounces of low-fat cheddar in place of the 12 ounces of regular cheddar, however, had already saved us a whopping 72 grams of fat in the overall recipe.

By now our recipe had been substantially reduced to just 422 calories and 13 grams of fat per serving, but we realized that somewhere along the line, we had lost the creamy, velvety texture of the original. Had we gone too far? Looking into how we could add back some of that silky texture, we landed on the idea of evaporated milk

(an ingredient used in the test kitchen method which we had dismissed earlier). Substituting a can of evaporated milk for some of the milk in the sauce, we hit the jackpot. The evaporated milk rounded out the texture of the sauce and even fooled some of the tasters into thinking that they were eating the real deal—full-fat mac and cheese. Testing the difference between whole evaporated milk, 2 percent evaporated milk, and skim evaporated milk in the béchamel, we found that tasters preferred the texture, flavor, and fat content of the 2 percent evaporated milk. Using low-fat (2 percent) evaporated milk not only helped the mac and cheese's texture, but it actually reduced its fat and calorie count even further, to just 360 calories and 10 grams of fat per serving.

WHAT WE LEARNED: Replace full-fat cheddar with low-fat—its flavor and texture are vastly superior to nonfat cheddar. Swap in 2 percent milk for the whole milk and add some 2 percent evaporated milk to ensure a creamy consistency. You can eliminate butter entirely by thickening the sauce with cornstarch instead of a classic roux.

EVERYDAY MACARONI AND CHEESE

Serves 5

Don't be tempted to use either preshredded or nonfat cheddar cheese in this dish—the texture and flavor of the macaroni and cheese will suffer substantially. For best results, choose a low-fat cheddar cheese that is sold in block form and has roughly 50 percent of the fat and calories of regular cheese (we like Cabot brand).

　 Salt
½　pound elbow macaroni (about 2 cups)
1　(12-ounce) can 2 percent reduced-fat evaporated milk
¾　cup 2 percent milk
¼　teaspoon dry mustard
⅛　teaspoon garlic powder or celery salt (optional) Pinch cayenne
2　teaspoons cornstarch
8　ounces 50 percent light cheddar cheese, grated (about 2 cups)

1. Bring 2½ quarts water to a boil in a large saucepan. Stir in 2 teaspoons salt and the macaroni; cook until the pasta is completely cooked and tender, about 5 minutes. Drain the pasta and leave it in the colander; set aside.

2. Add the evaporated milk, ½ cup of the 2 percent milk, mustard, garlic powder (if using), cayenne, and ½ teaspoon salt to the now-empty saucepan. Bring the mixture to a boil, then reduce to a simmer. Whisk the cornstarch and remaining ¼ cup milk together, then whisk it into the simmering mixture. Continue to simmer, whisking constantly, until the sauce has thickened and is smooth, about 2 minutes.

3. Off the heat, gradually whisk in the cheddar until melted and smooth. Stir in the macaroni, and let the macaroni and cheese sit off the heat until the sauce has thickened slightly, 2 to 5 minutes, before serving.

EVERYDAY MACARONI AND CHEESE WITH HAM AND PEAS

It is not necessary to thaw the peas before adding them to the macaroni.

Follow the recipe for Everyday Macaroni and Cheese, adding 2 ounces deli-style baked ham, cut into ⅓-inch pieces, and ¾ cup frozen peas with the macaroni in step 3.

TECHNIQUE:
Two Tips for Easier Cheese Grating

A. Semisoft cheeses such as cheddar or commercial mozzarella can stick to a box grater and cause a real mess. Here's how to keep the holes on the grater from becoming clogged.

Use nonstick cooking spray to lightly coat the coarse side of the box grater, then shred the cheese as usual. The cooking spray will keep cheese from sticking to the surface of the grater.

B. Grating hard cheeses is an easy, but often messy, affair. Here's a neater way to go about it.

Use a clean plastic bag (such as a large zipper-lock bag or a grocery store shopping bag) to hold both grater and cheese. By placing the bag around the grater and the cheese, you can grate cheese with clean hands and eliminate flyaway bits. Leftover grated cheese is ready for storage in a handy bag.

LIGHTER CHICKEN PARMESAN

WHAT WE WANTED: Crisp cutlets of breaded chicken topped with tomato sauce and gooey melted cheese, but with less fat and calories than the traditional fried version.

The best part of chicken Parmesan—breaded, fried chicken cutlets topped with tomato sauce, Parmesan cheese, and mozzarella—is the crisp, golden coating on the cutlets. Unfortunately, this terrific breaded coating is the result of frying the cutlets in a generous amount of oil. Sure there are lots of recipes for low-fat or "unfried" chicken Parmesan that bake the breaded cutlets, but none come close to the flavor or crispness of a traditional fried recipe. We wondered if we couldn't develop a better low-fat version, one actually worth eating.

Setting the issue of the sauce and cheese aside, we started with how to cook the breaded cutlets. Deep-frying and pan-frying the cutlets were both out—these methods simply use too much oil to be low fat. That left us with just the oven, but simply breading the cutlets (using the classic breading of flour, then egg—in this case egg whites, then bread crumbs) and baking them on a cookie sheet didn't work. The breading never turned brown or crisp, the bottoms became soggy, and the chicken was dry. We had our work cut out for us.

Homing in on the issue of oven temperature first, we found that baking the cutlets for 15 minutes at 475 degrees produced the most tender and juicy chicken. We tried coating the baking sheet with a thin film of oil to encourage browning, but the bread crumbs merely soaked up the oil and turned greasy. Baking the chicken on a wire rack set over a baking sheet quickly solved the soggy bottom issue, and spraying the tops with vegetable oil spray helped the breading on top of the cutlets crisp up nicely. We still, however, had issues with their bland flavor and pale color.

Then it hit us—why don't we toast the bread crumbs before breading the cutlets? We toasted the bread crumbs in a skillet over medium heat until golden, then breaded the cutlets, sprayed the tops with vegetable oil, and baked them on the rack. These cutlets were a big improvement, with an even browned color and crisp fried texture. The flavor of the breading, however, still needed help. Adding a tablespoon of olive oil to the crumbs as they toasted gave them a nice "fried" flavor without turning them greasy, and tossing them with some grated Parmesan cheese helped boost their flavor dramatically. The cutlets now actually tasted like a traditional chicken Parmesan—we were getting somewhere. Testing the difference among store-bought dried bread crumbs, fresh bread crumbs, and panko (Japanese-style bread crumbs), the test kitchen universally disliked store-bought dried bread crumbs. Both the fresh bread crumbs and the panko were well liked. However, tasters preferred the neutral flavor and ultra-crisp texture of panko (though fresh bread crumbs can be used if panko is unavailable).

With our cutlets down, we tried layering them into a casserole dish with tomato sauce and low-fat shredded mozzarella. Returning the casserole dish to the oven so that the mozzarella could melt, we were disappointed at how quickly the crisp breading turned soggy. Looking for a better method, we decided to leave the cutlets right on the rack and spoon just a small portion of the sauce and mozzarella onto the center of each piece of chicken, leaving the edges clean. Returning the rack to the oven, the edges and bottoms of the breaded cutlets remained crisp while the mozzarella cheese melted. Bingo! Served with extra sauce and grated Parmesan on the side, these oven-baked chicken Parmesan cutlets really do taste just as good as the traditional version.

WHAT WE LEARNED: Toast the bread crumbs (preferably Japanese-style panko) with a bit of oil before breading to mimic the crisp golden brown breading of the fried version. Bake the breaded cutlets on a wire rack set over a baking sheet, so air can circulate, which gives the chicken a crisp crust all around. A modest amount of Parmesan and low-fat mozzarella makes for a flavorful cheesy topping.

LIGHTER CHICKEN PARMESAN

Serves 6

If you are tight on time, you can substitute 2 cups of your favorite plain tomato sauce for the Simple Tomato Sauce. Two cups of fresh bread crumbs can be substituted for the panko. Because these cutlets are breaded, we found that one cutlet per person was plenty—but try to buy the largest chicken breasts you can to ensure good-sized portions.

1½ cups panko (Japanese-style bread crumbs)
1 tablespoon olive oil
1 ounce Parmesan, grated (about ½ cup), plus extra for serving
½ cup unbleached all-purpose flour
1½ teaspoons garlic powder
  Salt and ground black pepper
3 large egg whites
1 tablespoon water
  Vegetable oil spray

3 large boneless, skinless chicken breasts (about 8 ounces each), trimmed of excess fat and sliced into cutlets (see the illustration on page 92)
1 recipe Simple Tomato Sauce (recipe follows), warmed
3 ounces low-fat mozzarella, shredded (about ¾ cup)
1 tablespoon minced fresh basil leaves

1. Adjust an oven rack to the middle position and heat the oven to 475 degrees. Combine the bread crumbs and oil in a 12-inch skillet and toast over medium heat, stirring often, until golden, about 10 minutes. Spread the bread crumbs in a shallow dish and cool slightly; when cool, stir in the Parmesan.

2. In a second shallow dish, combine the flour, garlic powder, 1 tablespoon salt, and ½ teaspoon pepper together. In a third shallow dish, whisk together the egg whites and water.

3. Line a rimmed baking sheet with foil, place a wire rack on top, and spray the rack with vegetable oil spray. Pat the chicken dry with paper towels, then season with salt and pepper. Lightly dredge the cutlets in the flour, shaking off the excess, then dip into the egg whites, and finally coat with the bread crumbs, following the illustrations on page 75. Press on the bread crumbs to make sure they adhere. Lay the chicken on the wire rack.

4. Spray the tops of the chicken with vegetable oil spray. Bake until the meat is no longer pink in the center and feels firm when pressed with a finger, about 15 minutes.

5. Remove the chicken from the oven. Spoon 2 tablespoons of the sauce onto the center of each cutlet and top the sauce with 2 tablespoons of the mozzarella. Return the chicken to the oven and continue to bake until the cheese has melted, about 5 minutes. Sprinkle with the basil and serve, passing the remaining sauce and Parmesan separately.

SIMPLE TOMATO SAUCE

Makes about 2 cups

This easy sauce also works well with pasta.

1   (28-ounce) can diced tomatoes
4   medium garlic cloves, minced or pressed
    through a garlic press (about 4 teaspoons)
1   tablespoon tomato paste
1   teaspoon olive oil
⅛   teaspoon red pepper flakes
1   tablespoon minced fresh basil leaves
    Salt and ground black pepper

Pulse the tomatoes in a food processor until mostly smooth, about ten 1-second pulses; set aside. Cook the garlic, tomato paste, oil, and pepper flakes in a medium saucepan over medium heat until the tomato paste begins to brown, about 2 minutes. Stir in the pureed tomatoes and cook until the sauce is thickened and measures 2 cups, about 20 minutes. Off the heat, stir in the basil and season with salt and pepper to taste. Cover and set aside until needed.

TECHNIQUE: Breading Cutlets

1. Lightly dredge the cutlets thoroughly in flour, shaking off the excess.

2. Using tongs, dip both sides of the cutlets in the egg mixture and allow the excess to drip back into the dish to ensure a very thin coating. Tongs keep the egg from coating your fingers.

3. Dip both sides of the cutlets in the bread crumbs, pressing the crumbs with your fingers to form an even, cohesive coat.

4. Place the breaded cutlets in a single layer on a wire rack set over a baking sheet—this prevents the bottom of the cutlets from becoming soggy.

EQUIPMENT CORNER: Indoor Grills

THANKS LARGELY TO GEORGE FOREMAN'S LEAN MEAN FAT
Reducing Grilling Machine (55 million Foreman grills have
been sold since 1995), indoor electric grills have become
common kitchen appliances. But the champ now has plenty
of competition, so we brought seven models, all priced
under $80, into the test kitchen for some culinary sparring.
We grilled hamburgers, salmon, zucchini, grilled cheese
sandwiches, and thick Cubano panini (roast pork, ham, and
cheese on sub rolls).

Fat drainage is one of the popular selling points for
many indoor grills, but in our tests the removable reser-
voirs on four models never filled with much, if any, fat.
And, the moats surrounding the other three grills never
overflowed.

Removable grill plates are easy to clean, but we noticed
a tradeoff in performance. The grills with removable plates
(the George Foreman Next Generation, both Hamilton
Beach models, and the Black & Decker) had noticeable hot
spots or a top plate that ran hotter than the bottom. The
grills with fixed plates (Krups, George Foreman Hot Metals,
and Villaware) produced even heat across.

With both a top and bottom heat source, an indoor
grill will take roughly half the time of conventional stovetop
cooking. However, aside from the speed, hamburgers and
salmon didn't gain anything other than some attractive grill
marks. With a few extra minutes, a skillet could have done
just as well and offers more possibilities (like deglazing the
pan to make a sauce). On the other hand, indoor grills made
shatteringly crisp sandwiches and panini.

The size of the cooking surfaces ranged from 62 square
inches on both Hamilton Beach grills to 110 square inches
on the Krups. While the Krups grill could accommodate
five burgers or two large panini, the smaller grills could
handle just two burgers or one panini at a time.

We used an infrared thermometer to measure the
temperature of the cooking surfaces when fully preheated
and found slight variations that didn't correlate with performance. A better gauge of performance was the width of
the ridges (the portion of the cooking surface that actually
touches the food) and the distance between those ridges.
The Krups (with wide, closely spaced ridges) has nearly half
its cooking surface in contact with the food. The narrow,
widely spaced ridges on both Hamilton Beach grills meant
that just a fraction of the cooking space was in contact
with the food. This means less heat applied to the food, less
browning, and sandwiches that are less crisp.

In the end, our testing revealed one clear winner. The
Krups is a must-have if you like grilled sandwiches, but for
burgers and fish a heavy pan is just as good.

Rating Indoor Grills

WE TESTED SEVEN INDOOR GRILLS, ALL UNDER $80. TESTING INCLUDED GRILLING HAMBURGERS, SALMON, ZUCCHINI, and sandwiches. The grills are listed in order of preference. See www.americastestkitchen.com for up-to-date prices and mail-order sources for top-rated products.

HIGHLY RECOMMENDED
Krups Universal Grill and Panini Maker FDE312
$79.95

The largest grill and the only one to pass all our tests with flying colors. Burgers and salmon were deeply browned, zucchini was absolutely even, and sandwiches were golden and crisp. Spaciousness and performance make the extra cleanup associated with the fixed grill plates worth the bother.

RECOMMENDED
George Foreman Hot Metals Family Size Grill GR26SBTMR
$58.88

Second only to the Krups in size. Tops of burgers and salmon browned a little more than the bottoms. Top plate floated above thin pieces of zucchini, which colored only on the bottom. Cool-touch exterior is a plus.

RECOMMENDED WITH RESERVATIONS
Villaware Uno Two-Way Grill 2030
$68.99

Reservoir cup takes away from the grilling surface area, so even two burgers were crowded. Salmon and sandwiches turned out fine. Good for a one- or two-person household.

RECOMMENDED WITH RESERVATIONS
Black & Decker Grill and Wafflebaker G48TD
$49.88

Reversible plates transform this grill into an able waffle iron. The other side is a flat griddle (not grill), so forget about grill marks. Large items, if not relatively flat, kept the lightweight "lid" off kilter, resulting in lopsided sandwiches.

NOT RECOMMENDED
George Foreman Next Generation with Removable Plates GRP4
$59.99

Removable plates make cleanup easy, but performance pales, literally, in comparison to the top-rated grills. Browning was faint in all of our tests, especially at the front half of the narrow, elongated grill. The grill's front-heavy "lid" made for asymmetric sandwiches.

NOT RECOMMENDED
Hamilton Beach Grill/Griddle with Removable Grids 25295
$49.99

We had better luck with the griddle, or flat, grates, but that isn't saying much. Sandwiches ended up soggy and burgers and salmon looked more steamed than grilled. The second set of grill grids showed even more lackluster performance.

NOT RECOMMENDED
Hamilton Beach Grill with Removable Grids 25285
$39.99

The tall, sharp ridges on the cooking surface cut into both grilled cheese sandwiches and sturdy hamburgers. Browning was pale, and the sandwiches weren't as crisp as they should have been.

Rating Whole Wheat Pasta

THIRTEEN MEMBERS OF THE AMERICA'S TEST KITCHEN STAFF TASTED NINE DIFFERENT WHOLE WHEAT PASTAS, WHICH WERE cooked per the package directions. The pastas are listed in order of preference based on their scores in this tasting. The pastas are available nationwide in supermarkets and natural foods stores.

RECOMMENDED

Ronzoni Healthy Harvest Whole Wheat Blend Spaghetti

$1.79 for 13.25 ounces

The only pasta that tasted "undeniably wheaty" without a gummy or grainy texture.

NOT RECOMMENDED

Annie's Homegrown Organic Whole Wheat Spaghetti

$1.99 for 16 ounces

Full-flavored to some, "intense" to others. Several tasters swore they detected cinnamon.

NOT RECOMMENDED

Deboles Organic Whole Wheat Spaghetti

$1.99 for 8 ounces

Thin noodles were "sticky" and "gluey." Texture overshadowed their "moderately wheaty" flavor.

RECOMMENDED

Bionaturae 100% Stone Ground Whole Durum Wheat Spaghetti

$2.29 for 16 ounces

The texture of this mild-mannered, "not very wheaty" pasta rivals that of conventional pasta. "A good introduction" to whole wheat pasta.

NOT RECOMMENDED

De Cecco Whole Wheat Spaghetti

$2.29 for 17.5 ounces

The most dietary fiber, but the "gritty, grainy" texture "feels healthy." The flavor was mild.

NOT RECOMMENDED

Natural Value 100% Organic Whole Wheat Spaghetti

$2.54 for 16 ounces

"Toothless" pasta reminded tasters of rice. Lack of flavor didn't help, either.

RECOMMENDED

Westbrae Natural Organic Whole Wheat Spaghetti

$2.49 for 16 ounces

The flavor merely "hints at wheat." Several tasters noticed traces of "gumminess."

NOT RECOMMENDED

Eden Biodynamic 100% Whole Grain Wheat Spaghetti

$2.06 for 14 ounces

Tasters decried the "sandy" texture.

NOT RECOMMENDED

Hodgson Mill Whole Wheat Whole Grain Spaghetti

$2.39 for 16 ounces

"Doughy," "mealy," "sour," and "dusty" sum it up.

TASTING LAB: Whole Wheat Pasta

A COARSE, GUMMY TEXTURE AND OUT-OF-PLACE "OATMEAL" flavor plagued too many of the whole wheat pastas we've tried in years past. Recently, however, the options available have multiplied, so we decided to take another look.

Eight of the nine contenders were made from whole durum wheat, the notably hard, dense wheat from which semolina, the primary ingredient in traditional pasta, is processed. Though texture has improved overall since our previous tastings, several of the pastas were almost as gritty and gluey as we remembered. However, our top finisher, Ronzoni Healthy Harvest Whole Wheat Blend Pasta, blends regular semolina with wheat bran and wheat fiber—so it's not 100 percent "whole" wheat. But the combination of a pleasantly chewy texture and deep, wheaty flavor was worth the minor nutritional trade-off.

TASTING LAB: Alternative Pasta

TODAY, EVEN THE LEAST AMBITIOUS SUPERMARKETS ARE stocking alternative-grain pastas alongside standard pastas. Fad diets and food allergies aside, how do they taste? We bought five packages of spaghetti to find out.

Texture turned out to be the downfall of three of these pastas, which were gritty, mushy, or overly delicate. Tinkyáda Organic Brown Rice Pasta passed the texture test, but some tasters found it "completely flavorless." Only VitaSpelt—made from spelt, a grain that's similar to wheat—got decent marks across the board. (Unlike the other four pastas, however, VitaSpelt is not gluten-free.)

So where did we come out? On its own, the VitaSpelt outperformed all others in the taste category. Matched with a substantial enough sauce, however, the VitaSpelt and the Tinkyáda pastas were nearly indistinguishable from semolina wheat pasta. If your diet can't admit gluten, then Tinkyáda is your best option.

Rating Alternative Pasta

SIXTEEN MEMBERS OF THE AMERICA'S TEST KITCHEN STAFF tasted five different alternative pastas, which were cooked per the package directions. The pastas are listed in order of preference based on their scores in this tasting. The pastas are available nationwide in supermarkets and natural foods stores.

RECOMMENDED WITH RESERVATIONS
VitaSpelt Spelt Spaghetti
$2.29 for 8 ounces
Odd gray color aside, this pasta has a "healthy, earthy" flavor and a texture reminiscent of traditional pasta.

RECOMMENDED WITH RESERVATIONS
Tinkyáda Organic Brown Rice Pasta Spaghetti Style
$2.99 for 12 ounces
"Awesome texture" was a highlight, but "mild," "nondescript" flavor needs a potent sauce.

NOT RECOMMENDED
Deboles Rice Pasta Spaghetti Style
$1.99 for 8 ounces
"Is this Uncle Ben's?" asked one taster. The coarse, gritty appearance and texture of this pasta were its downfall.

NOT RECOMMENDED
Deboles Corn Pasta Spaghetti Style
$1.99 for 8 ounces
Cornmeal lent an "intensely grainy" texture. "Extreme starchiness" made this pasta the gummiest of the lot.

NOT RECOMMENDED
Ancient Harvest Wheat-Free Supergrain Pasta Spaghetti Style
$1.99 for 8 ounces
Quinoa and corn flour blend yielded extremely fragile pasta that disintegrated quickly into a "gummy, grainy mess."

Bridget lifts a perfectly battered fish fillet out of hot oil. The secret? Augment some of the flour in the coating with cornstarch and baking powder for a crisp, airy texture.

FISH AND CHIPS
at home

The problem with English-style fish and chips is that you've got to hop a plane across the Atlantic to really enjoy the dish. Most American restaurants that tackle England's most popular fast food do so poorly—turning out a greasy mess of fish and potatoes. We aimed to create a home-cook-friendly recipe for the real thing: large pieces of moist cod coated in a delicate, crisp batter and chips cut thick and served up crispy, with soft interiors.

To start, we'd first need to tackle frying for the home cook. While most restaurants have dedicated frying workstations, deep-frying in a home kitchen is a different matter. Cramped space, spattering oil, and inappropriate equipment all conspire to take the fun out of the job. But it needn't be an onerous task: With a bit of organization and some basic working knowledge, you'll be turning out fish and chips that will rival those found in the best English shops.

Along the way, we'd also need to figure out how to organize the process so that everything made it to the table at once—meaning that both fish and chips are served piping hot. Anything less just wouldn't be acceptable.

FISH AND CHIPS

WHAT WE WANTED: English-style fish and chips—large pieces of moist and delicate cod in a crisp and tender coating with thick-cut fries—crispy on the outside and soft on the inside. And we wanted both elements of the dish on the table at the same time.

English-style fish and chips—fried pieces of moist cod and thick-cut fries (or chips) typically doused in malt vinegar—is truly a guilty pleasure. While you can find this dish in pubs and restaurants across the U.S., it's a rare occasion to find a version that measures up to what you'd find in England. We wanted to create a recipe for the home cook—a foolproof recipe that would conquer anyone's fear of frying. In addition we wanted to ensure that the fish and chips were prepared in sync, so they could be enjoyed together, just like the real thing.

Unsure how we would resolve this logistical challenge, we decided to focus first on developing a recipe for a batter that would perform two important functions. First, protection. A piece of plain fish dropped into hot oil overcooks almost instantly. While a coating of flour or bread crumbs provides a modicum of defense, a wet batter is the best defense because it completely coats the fish, allowing it to steam gently as it cooks. Second, the batter must form a coating that provides crisp contrast with the moist fish.

In the bulk of the recipes we surveyed, the batter (usually a 50/50 mix of flour and beer) excelled at the first task and flunked the second. The fish came out moist, but the coating was bready and thick. Worse, as the fish drained on paper towels, it continued to produce steam; minutes later, the crust was falling off the fish. We tried thinning the batter with more beer so that less steam would be trapped, but that brought new problems. The liquid in the batter began to boil almost immediately upon hitting the oil, and the coating failed to survive.

If we couldn't thin the batter, perhaps we could adjust its structure. The obvious culprit behind the bready texture was gluten, the protein that gives bread its structure. What if we replaced some of the all-purpose flour with a starch that doesn't develop gluten? Various tests led us to a 3 to 1 ratio of flour to cornstarch. This thinner (but not wetter) mixture survived the hot oil and fried up crisp. Finally, a teaspoon of baking powder created tiny bubbles in the batter, giving the coating an airier texture.

One problem lingered: While the texture of the coating was great, it tended to puff away from the fish as it fried, ultimately flaking off in large pieces with the first bite. We had been drying the fish well and dredging it in flour before battering—techniques meant to stop this from happening—but it was still a problem. We tried spreading extra flour on a baking sheet, and, after dredging and battering each piece, we coated the fish with flour again. Success! The resulting coating had a slightly crumbly, irregular texture that clung tightly to the fish. A bit of cayenne for spice and a sprinkle of paprika for color finished the deal.

A recipe developed years ago in the test kitchen confirmed what any restaurant line cook knows well: The best fries are cooked twice. They're "blanched" in low-temperature oil to cook the centers, then finished in hotter oil to crisp the outsides to a golden brown. Our plan was to blanch the fries, turn up the heat on the oil and fry the fish, then keep the fish warm while the fries finished.

There were two problems with this plan. First, the fish was not as crisp as it had been before. We suspected the "used" oil was the problem: The 3 pounds of potatoes we had already dumped into the oil released a lot of moisture, much of which bubbled away as steam but some of which remained in the oil, diluting it and thus diminishing its ability to make things crisp. The oil was in even worse condition after the fish had fried, which exacerbated the second problem: The blanched, oversized fries took about 10 minutes to turn golden brown and crisp, by which time the cooling fish was several minutes past its prime.

A colleague had developed a recipe for skillet potatoes that involved first parcooking sliced potatoes in a microwave. Could we parcook the fries to get rid of some of the excess water before the potatoes hit the oil? Yes, but if microwaved too long (until completely tender), the thick fries began to crumble and fall apart. They would still have to blanch in the oil, but the microwave head start let us blanch at a higher temperature, partially browning the fries in advance to shave crucial minutes off of the final frying time. To further improve the quality of the oil, we tried adding some fresh oil to the pot just before frying the fish and found the crispness of the final products to be greatly improved.

This patchwork method—alternating the fish and the fries (see "Technique" page 84)—was quick and easy, and it resulted in fish and chips that were done in sync. Finally, we had a recipe to keep us satisfied until our next trip across the Atlantic.

WHAT WE LEARNED: For the chips, parcook the sliced potatoes in the microwave before frying, then alternate frying the potatoes and the fish. For the fish, replace some of the flour in the batter with lower-gluten cornstarch, for a crisp, not bready, coating. In addition, dredging the fish in flour both before and after battering helps the coating adhere to the fish once it has been fried. A bit of baking powder gives the batter an airy delicate texture. And, for optimal crispness, refresh the oil in the pot before frying the fish.

FISH AND CHIPS
Serves 4

For safety, use a Dutch oven with at least a 7-quart capacity. Serve with traditional malt vinegar or with Tartar Sauce (recipe follows).

3	pounds russet potatoes (about 4 large potatoes), peeled, ends and sides squared off, and cut lengthwise into ½-inch by ½-inch fries
3	quarts plus ¼ cup peanut oil or canola oil
1½	cups unbleached all-purpose flour
½	cup cornstarch
½	teaspoon cayenne
½	teaspoon paprika
⅛	teaspoon ground black pepper
	Salt
1	teaspoon baking powder
1½	pounds cod or other thick white fish fillet, such as hake or haddock, cut into eight 3-ounce pieces about 1 inch thick
1½	cups (12 ounces) cold beer

1. Place the cut fries in a large microwaveable bowl, toss with ¼ cup of the oil, and cover with plastic wrap. Microwave on high power until the potatoes are partially translucent and pliable but still offer some resistance when pierced with the tip of a paring knife, 6 to 8 minutes, tossing them with a rubber spatula halfway through the cooking time. Carefully pull back the plastic wrap from the side farthest from you and drain the potatoes into a large mesh strainer set over a sink. Rinse well under cold running water. Spread the potatoes onto a few clean kitchen towels and pat dry. Let rest until the fries have reached room temperature, at least 10 minutes and up to 1 hour.

2. While the fries cool, whisk the flour, cornstarch, cayenne, paprika, pepper, and 2 teaspoons salt in a large mixing bowl; transfer ¾ cup of the mixture to a rimmed baking sheet. Add the baking powder to the bowl and whisk to combine.

3. In heavy-bottomed Dutch oven, heat 2 quarts of the oil over medium heat to 350 degrees. (Use an instant-read thermometer that registers high temperatures or clip a candy/deep-fat thermometer onto the side of the pan before turning on the heat.) Add the fries to the hot oil and increase the heat to high. Fry, stirring with a mesh spider or slotted metal spoon, until the potatoes turn light golden and just begin to brown at the corners, 6 to 8 minutes. Transfer the fries to a thick paper bag or paper towels to drain.

4. Reduce the heat to medium-high, add the remaining quart of oil, and heat the oil to 375 degrees. Meanwhile, thoroughly dry the fish with paper towels and dredge each piece in the flour mixture on the baking sheet; transfer the pieces to a wire rack, shaking off any excess flour. Add 1¼ cups beer to the flour mixture in the mixing bowl and stir until the mixture is just combined (the batter will be lumpy). Add the remaining beer as needed, 1 tablespoon at a time, whisking after each addition, until the batter falls from the whisk in a thin, steady stream and leaves a faint trail across the surface of the batter. Using tongs, dip 1 piece of fish in the batter and let the excess run off, shaking gently. Place the battered fish back onto the baking sheet with the flour mixture and turn to coat both sides. Repeat with the remaining fish, keeping the pieces in a single layer on the baking sheet.

5. When the oil reaches 375 degrees, increase the heat to high and add the battered fish to the oil with the tongs, gently shaking off any excess flour. Fry, stirring occasionally, until golden brown, 7 to 8 minutes. Transfer the fish to a thick paper bag or paper towels to drain. Allow the oil to return to 375 degrees.

6. Add all of the fries back to the oil and fry until golden brown and crisp, 3 to 5 minutes. Transfer to a fresh paper bag or paper towels to drain. Season the fries with salt to taste and serve immediately with the fish.

TECHNIQUE:

Getting the Fish and Chips in Sync

To ensure that the fish and chips are done at the same time, we crafted this sequence of steps that also minimizes mess.

1. Microwave potatoes
Microwave oil-tossed potatoes until softened and pliable.

2. Rinse potatoes
Rinse potatoes under cold running water and pat dry.

3. Fry potatoes
Fry potatoes in 350-degree oil until just beginning to brown.

4. Fry fish
Add more oil to the pot, heat oil to 375 degrees, turn the heat to high, and fry fish until golden brown.

5. Fry potatoes again
Return fries to oil and cook until crisp and golden.

TARTAR SAUCE

Makes about 1 cup

This classic sauce for fried seafood can be stored and refrigerated in a covered container for several days. If you like, prepare this sauce with one of our recommended light mayonnaises from our tasting on this page.

¾   cup mayonnaise
1½ tablespoons minced cornichons (about 3 large),
     plus 1 teaspoon cornichon juice
  1 tablespoon minced scallions
  1 tablespoon minced red onion
  1 tablespoon capers, minced

Stir all the ingredients together in a medium bowl until combined. Cover and refrigerate until the flavors blend, at least 30 minutes.

TASTING LAB: Light Mayonnaise

BECAUSE MAYONNAISE IS FATTY BY DEFINITION (IT'S mostly oil and egg yolks), reduced-fat mayonnaise is a popular product. But is it possible for a light mayo to be as flavorful as the full-fat original?

In the past, Hellmann's Light Mayonnaise has won taste tests here in the test kitchen, beating out four other leading brands of light mayonnaise. (And among leading brands of full-fat mayonnaise, Hellmann's full-fat has also come in first.) That's why we were interested when we discovered that Hellmann's now makes another, even lighter, mayonnaise

called Hellmann's Reduced-Fat Mayonnaise, which has only 2 fat grams per tablespoon compared to Hellmann's Light, which has 4.5 grams of fat per tablespoon. (Regular mayonnaise has about 11 grams of fat per tablespoon.) We thought a little testing was in order to see if there would be a significant difference between these two light mayos.

Because mayonnaise is a key ingredient in Tartar Sauce (this page), we prepared batches using each low-fat mayonnaise. Tasters found little difference between the batches made with Hellmann's Light and Hellmann's Reduced Fat. As we already knew, there is a significant difference in fat grams between the two: ¾ cup of Hellmann's Reduced Fat Mayonnaise has 24 grams of fat compared to Hellmann's Light, which has more than twice as much—54 grams.

We also tasted each mayonnaise on its own and spread on bread. This time the Hellmann's Light won out. Tasters complained that on its own Hellmann's Reduced Fat has an off sweet flavor.

Our conclusion: Hellmann's Light is great for spreading on a sandwich, especially when you're using a modest amount, but in recipes where significant amounts of mayo are called for (and fat grams are a concern), Hellmann's Reduced Fat Mayonnaise is perfectly fine.

BEST LOW-FAT MAYONNAISE

Hellmann's Light
Bright, balanced flavors make this mayo the best choice for sandwiches.

Hellmann's Reduced Fat
Fine in dips and dressings, but this mayo is too sweet on its own.

EQUIPMENT CORNER:
Candy Thermometers

CANDY THERMOMETERS ARE DESIGNED FOR STOVETOP recipes where close monitoring of temperature is key—especially candy-making and deep-frying. The thermometer stays in the liquid during cooking. But which brand is best? To find out, we brought 13 models into the test kitchen and made multiple batches of caramel.

Thermometers with the simplest style—a plain glass tube—worked fine, but they are also fragile and the gradations were hard to read. What's more, a few models had a tendency to slide down and touch the bottom of the pan, giving a false reading. Similar thermometers with a metal "foot" to keep the thermometer off the pan bottom didn't work in a small (shallow) batch of caramel and were also hard to read. Dial-face thermometers required as much as 2½ inches of liquid—a rarity when making candies.

The best of the bunch were the digital models, which have easy-to-read consoles and alarm features that warn the cook when the caramel is done. But they tend to be top-heavy, with a precarious grip on the saucepan. Maverick's Redi-Chek Digital Oil & Candy Thermometer ($34.95) had the most reliable grip, and it's a decent choice. An alternative is an instant-read thermometer capable of registering temperatures up to 400 degrees, such as ThermoWorks' Thermapen ($79), which is just as reliable and can also be used to check the temperatures of roasts, breads, sauces, and more.

BEST CANDY THERMOMETER

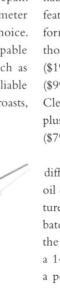

Easy to read and with an alarm feature that alerts the cook when the target temperature has been reached, the Maverick's Redi-Chek ($34.95) was the best we found.

EQUIPMENT CORNER:
High-End Deep Fryers

FROM PAST TESTS, WE KNOW A DECENT DEEP FRYER CAN BE had for less than $80. Spend more and you'll get fancy features like oil filtration systems. But what about basic performance? To find out, we embarked on a french-fry marathon with six high-end models—Masterbuilt Turk'N'Surf ($199.95), Deni Multi-Fryer ($99.99), DeLonghi Dual Zone ($99.95), Waring Professional ($129.95), T-Fal Ultimate EZ Clean ($119.95), and DeLonghi Cool-Touch ($129.95)—plus our favorite inexpensive model, the Oster Immersion ($79.95).

All the models turned out tasty fries—eventually. The difference between good performance and great hinged on oil capacity. The more capacity, the less severe the temperature drop once the food hit the oil, which allowed for fewer batches and quicker recovery between batches. For instance, the Masterbuilt, which holds 2 gallons of oil (enough to fry a 14-pound turkey!), dropped 34 degrees when we added a pound of fries. In contrast, the DeLonghi Cool-Touch,

which uses a mere 1.3 quarts (it rotates food into and out of the oil), lost a whopping 114 degrees. What that means in practical terms is that the Masterbuilt can effectively cook an entire batch of fries; by the time the smallest model finished its fourth partial batch, the rest of the fries were soggy and limp.

Every model was equipped with a built-in thermostat—an essential feature, to our minds. But other "deluxe" features seemed extraneous. Transparent lids are nice in theory but quickly rendered useless by emanating steam. T-Fal's so-called EZ Clean—the oil is filtered and drained into a container—is anything but easy.

Ideally, we'd fry our fries in one batch, but pouring 2 gallons of oil into the Masterbuilt seems excessive. If you don't often fry fish and chips, the Oster—the cheap model—is all you really need.

The hallmark of great chicken Kiev is the rich butter filling that melts into a sauce inside the chicken bundles and contrasts perfectly with the crisp bread crumb crust.

CHICKEN kiev

Popularized during the heyday of Manhattan's now-shuttered Russian Tea Room, chicken Kiev became one of the restaurant's premier offerings in the 1960s. The well-heeled were quite familiar with this elegant dish of pounded, breaded, and fried chicken breast stuffed with an herb butter that melted into a sauce. Although chicken Kiev's Ukrainian roots remain unclear, its current fate is hardly in dispute: It has become a greasy bundle of poultry with a sandy, disconcertingly peelable exterior and a greasy, leaky center. Commonly found in banquet halls and at catered events, this once highbrow dish has become a self-parody. But after preparing several cookbook versions, we realized that pairing a crisp-fried coating with a delicately flavored butter sauce was a great idea that deserved a revival.

A dish as special as chicken Kiev deserves a side dish with equal dazzle. We settled on broccoli and turned to pan-roasting, because it works well with many vegetables, imparting a toasty, caramelized flavor. Broccoli, however, can be fussy because the hardy stalks and delicate florets require different handling. We'd need to find a way to get around those issues.

IN THIS CHAPTER

THE RECIPES
Chicken Kiev

Pan-Roasted Broccoli
Pan-Roasted Broccoli with
  Lemon Browned Butter
Pan-Roasted Broccoli with Spicy
  Southeast Asian Flavors
Pan-Roasted Broccoli with
  Creamy Gruyère Sauce

EQUIPMENT CORNER
Cookbook Holders

TASTING LAB
Sandwich Breads

CHICKEN KIEV

WHAT WE WANTED: Crisp breaded chicken breasts stuffed with a delicately flavored herb butter.

Chicken Kiev is a recipe that elevates the humdrum boneless, skinless chicken breast to star status. Traditionally, the dish is a crisp fried chicken breast encasing a buttery herb sauce that dramatically oozes out when knife meets fork. But today, the dish has sunk to the level of bad banquet food—a greasy, bread crumb–coated chicken breast whose meat is dry and chalky despite the butter filling. This was a dish that truly needed its greatness restored.

Chicken Kiev has three distinct parts: the chicken, the butter, and the coating. The chilled butter is stuffed inside the boneless chicken breast, and the whole thing is rolled in a coating, then fried up crisp. As was clear from the flawed recipes we tried in our research, getting the butter to survive cooking without leaking was key. So we started there.

Some recipes call for cutting a slit in the thickest part of the breast and inserting a disk of butter. That was easy, but it became apparent that providing any path of egress was a bad idea. One false move and the butter came streaming out—a dangerous proposition when frying in hot oil.

We had to encase the butter completely. Some recipes pounded the chicken, put a chilled disk of butter on top, then rolled the cutlet around it. This method worked much better, but it was hard to pound the chicken thin and wide enough to encase the butter without tearing the flesh. We next tried butterflying the breasts lengthwise (yielding cutlets twice as wide but half as thick as the original) before pounding. Much better: Less pounding meant less damage. Experimenting with various thicknesses, we settled on ¼ inch.

Flattened, our cutlets resembled large teardrops. Using a rolling-and-folding technique, we placed the butter disk just above the tapered end of the "teardrop" and proceeded as if wrapping a burrito: rolling the tapered end completely over the butter, folding in the sides, then continuing to roll until we had a tight bundle. We were on the right track, but occasionally the folded-in sides refused to stay put. We quickly diagnosed the problem. The ¼-inch-thick sides, once folded over, were double the thickness of the rest of the bundle. Easy enough: We simply pounded the outer edges of the cutlets a little thinner (⅛ inch) than the rest. Obsessive precision? Okay, we admit it. But the foolproof result—no leaks—was worth it. (That said, pounding the cutlets down to a uniform ¼-inch thickness is almost as reliable.)

With four compact chicken bundles at the ready, we could focus on the exterior. We began with a standard breading procedure: dusting each stuffed cutlet with seasoned flour, dipping it in beaten egg, then rolling it in bread crumbs. But breading the chicken just after stuffing was a hazardous affair: The seam sometimes opened up, and the entire bundle became less compact (thus undoing all our anti-leak-protection work). Once, after leaving the unbreaded stuffed chicken in the refrigerator (uncovered) for an hour while we tended to other tasks, we noticed that the edges had begun to stick together, nearly gluing shut. From then on, we purposely placed the Kievs in the refrigerator to set up before attempting to bread them.

No matter what type of crumbs we used—fresh or dried, coarse or fine—deep-frying gave the Kievs a homogeneous, corndog-like quality. By the time the chicken was fully cooked, the exterior was a hard, tan-colored shell that desperately needed to be drained of grease. Not very appetizing. If only we could do away with deep-frying altogether. We tried pan-frying the bundles in a small amount of oil just until the crumbs became crisp. Once they were browned, we finished cooking them up to temperature in the oven. So far, so good—well, mostly. While the tops and bottoms of the chicken were nicely browned, it was hard to get the sides evenly colored without manhandling the Kievs, which often caused unraveling.

That's when we made the decision that would effectively transform our chicken Kiev from greasy banquet food to elegant dinner showpiece: toasting the bread crumbs in the oven first. Starting with already-browned bread crumbs meant we could skip the pan-frying step and cook the Kievs completely in the oven. We simply dredged the Kievs in seasoned flour, dipped them in egg, coated them with the browned bread crumbs, and threw them in the oven. No more frying, no more skillet, no more spotty browning.

All we had left to do was to perk up the plain filling. Traditional recipes stuff the Kievs with butter spiked with nothing more than parsley and chives. Tasters preferred the more aromatic minced shallots over chives and a small amount of chopped tarragon for a hint of sweetness. A squeeze of lemon juice tamed the rich butter with a bit of acidity, and Dijon mustard, whisked into the egg wash (for coating the chicken), provided another layer of flavor.

WHAT WE LEARNED: For chicken bundles that won't leak the butter filling, butterfly the chicken breasts, then pound the cutlets ¼ inch thick, with the edges pounded slightly thinner to ⅛ inch thick. Instead of deep-frying, oven-fry the chicken for crisp, not greasy, Kiev. And, toasting the bread crumbs prior to breading mimics the golden browned crust of the deep-fried version.

CHICKEN KIEV

Serves 4

Unbaked, breaded chicken Kievs can be refrigerated overnight and baked the next day or frozen for up to one month. To cook frozen chicken Kievs, increase the baking time to 50 to 55 minutes (do not thaw the chicken).

herb butter

8	tablespoons unsalted butter (1 stick), softened
1	tablespoon minced shallot
1	tablespoon minced fresh parsley leaves
½	teaspoon minced fresh tarragon leaves
1	tablespoon juice from 1 lemon
⅜	teaspoon salt
⅛	teaspoon ground black pepper

chicken

4–5	slices white sandwich bread, cut into ¾-inch cubes
	Salt and ground black pepper
2	tablespoons vegetable oil
4	boneless, skinless chicken breasts (7 to 8 ounces each), tenderloins removed
1	cup unbleached all-purpose flour
3	large eggs, beaten
1	teaspoon Dijon mustard

1. FOR THE HERB BUTTER: Mix the ingredients in a medium bowl with a rubber spatula until thoroughly combined. Form into a 3-inch square on a sheet of plastic wrap; wrap tightly and refrigerate until firm, about 1 hour.

2. FOR THE CHICKEN: Adjust an oven rack to the lower-middle position and heat the oven to 300 degrees. Add half of the bread cubes to a food processor and pulse until the cubes are coarsely ground, about sixteen 1-second pulses. Transfer the crumbs to a large bowl and repeat with the remaining bread cubes (you should have about 3½ cups crumbs). Add ⅛ teaspoon salt and ⅛ teaspoon pepper to

1. Starting on the thinnest side, butterfly the breast by slicing lengthwise almost in half. Open the breast up to create a single, flat cutlet.

2. With the cutlet between sheets of plastic wrap, pound (starting at the center) to ¼-inch thickness. Pound the outer perimeter to ⅛ inch.

3. Place the butter piece near the tapered end of the cutlet and roll up the end to cover completely. Fold in the sides and continue rolling to form a cylinder, pressing on the seam to seal.

the bread crumbs. Add the oil and toss until the crumbs are evenly coated. Spread the crumbs on a rimmed baking sheet and bake until golden brown and dry, about 25 minutes, stirring twice during the baking time. Let cool to room temperature (you should have about 2½ cups bread crumbs).

3. Prepare the cutlets, following illustrations 1 and 2 above. Unwrap the herb butter and cut it into 4 rectangular pieces. Place a chicken breast cut side up on a work surface; season both sides with salt and pepper. Following illustration 3, place 1 piece of butter in the center of the bottom half of the breast. Roll the bottom edge of the chicken over the butter, then fold in the sides and continue rolling to form a neat, tight package, pressing on the seam to seal. Repeat with the remaining butter and chicken. Refrigerate the chicken, uncovered, to allow the edges to seal, about 1 hour.

4. Adjust an oven rack to the middle position and heat the oven to 350 degrees. Place the flour, eggs, and bread crumbs in separate pie plates or shallow dishes. Season the flour with ¼ teaspoon salt and ⅛ teaspoon pepper; season the bread crumbs with ½ teaspoon salt and ¼ teaspoon pepper. Add the mustard to the eggs and whisk to combine. Dredge 1 chicken breast in the flour, shaking off the excess, then coat with the egg mixture, allowing the excess to drip off. Coat all sides of the chicken breast with the bread crumbs, pressing gently so that the crumbs adhere. Place on a wire rack

set over a rimmed baking sheet. Repeat the flouring and breading of the remaining chicken breasts.

5. Bake until an instant-read thermometer inserted into the center of the chicken (from the top) registers 160 degrees, 40 to 45 minutes. Let rest 5 minutes on the wire rack before serving.

GETTING IT RIGHT:
Ensuring a Leakproof, Crisp Crust

Problem: Compound butter leaks.
Solution: Pounding the chicken thin (and thinner at the edges) and refrigerating to let the seams set produced butter-tight Kievs.

Problem: Pan-fried coating browns unevenly, and sides remain pale.
Solution: Browning the bread crumbs before coating and baking the chicken yielded a uniform crust.

EQUIPMENT CORNER:
Cookbook Holders

COOKING FROM AN OPEN COOKBOOK CAN PRESENT REAL challenges: The book may not lie flat, pages flip over, splatters soil the pages, and pages can be difficult to turn with slippery hands. Short of photocopying the recipe or rewriting it on a separate sheet of paper, the obvious solution is to use a cookbook holder.

Arguably, any book holder can act as a cookbook holder, but we felt that at the very least a cookbook holder should have a shield that protects pages from splatters. Making this our baseline requirement for purchase, we ordered seven candidates and evaluated them according to several criteria.

First we looked at the size of each holder. A quality cookbook holder should accommodate a book of any size, regardless of whether the recipe is in the front, middle, or back of the book. Ease of use is important, too. It should be easy to insert cookbooks into and remove them from the holder. (This is especially important if the recipes run to a second page.)

Stability is also a factor we examined among the cookbook holders. We wanted a holder that would stay put and not slide around on a wet surface.

As for the shields on the cookbook holders we wanted a shield large enough to protect the entire page from splatters. The cook should have no trouble reading through the shield. The shield should also be durable: stain and scratch resistant and easy to clean.

Last, because counter space is at a premium in most home kitchens, we also wanted a cookbook holder that folded flat for easy and efficient storage.

What did we find? One holder, the $30 Clear Solutions Deluxe, trumped the field, earning a highly recommended rating. It remained stable while holding books of all sizes and weights. Inserting and removing a book was a snap—the front cover is hinged, allowing the user to fold it down to insert a book. The holder also stores easily, as the back support detaches to lie flat on the base, and the shield folds flat as well. Finally, with a cherry-wood base, it was the most attractive holder we tested. Clear Solutions offers a smaller version of the Deluxe model with many similar features, but it could not firmly hold the largest cookbooks we tested and did not provide exceptional shield coverage. Still, it is a good alternative when space is a concern.

We also recommend one unusual option if storage space is tight. Not technically a holder, the $10 Norpro Cookbook Shield is a heavy sheet of clear, flexible acrylic, with marbles inserted in folds along the two outside edges for weight. The shield lies on top of an open book, keeping the pages open and protected. At 21 inches across, it actually did the best job of all the samples at protecting big pages. And it was certainly the easiest to store, rolling into an 11-inch tube just 2 inches in diameter. This roll-up feature also makes it easy to tote along on vacations to use at a cottage or cabin. All of these good points notwithstanding, we still preferred reading books that were propped up rather than lying flat on the counter.

BEST COOKBOOK HOLDER

The Clear Solutions Deluxe Cookbook Holder ($30) was the only holder that held cookbooks of all sizes (even the coffee-table-sized hardbacks). It was also the easiest to use; insertion required only that we fold the front flap forward. All of its components fold flat for easy storage.

TASTING LAB: Sandwich Breads

WITH ALL THE HYPE ABOUT ARTISANAL BREAD, THE SLICED stuff in the plastic bags doesn't get much attention these days, but it should. In the test kitchen, we still go through several loaves of sandwich bread every week. So why not buy the best? We gathered eight leading brands of white sandwich bread, in country styles with larger slices whenever possible, and held a blind tasting.

For our first test, tasters sampled the bread plain. Because some of the breads are not available in large slices, we cut the samples into pieces so tasters would focus on taste and texture, not size. Tasters weren't fooled. They gave top marks to the hearty texture of Arnold Country Classics and Pepperidge Farm Farmhouse. These brands also have larger-than-usual slices—1½ ounces each versus 1 ounce for the competition.

Tasters detected big flavor differences, too. Top-rated Arnold and Pepperidge Farm were deemed the "sweetest" breads in the lineup. There were many complaints about

"sour" and "off" notes in the lower-rated brands. It turns out that some of these brands contain vinegar (often added to increase shelf life). Lower-rated breads also contain almost twice as many ingredients as our top-rated breads, with many more additives and preservatives, which may also explain the unpleasant aftertaste.

We then asked tasters to try the breads in grilled cheese sandwiches. Though volunteers for this tasting were plentiful, clear winners were not—all the breads were pretty good. In short, once you slather your bread with butter and load it up with cheese, it gets very hard to tell one brand from another.

For our final test, we prepared simple croutons seasoned only with olive oil and salt. Again, Arnold and Pepperidge Farm swept the tasting. They were consistently ranked as crunchier than the other brands.

Based on our tests, we recommend Arnold Country Classics and Pepperidge Farm Farmhouse. Their hearty texture and slightly sweet (not sour) flavor put them a cut above the competition.

Rating Sandwich Breads

TWENTY-THREE MEMBERS OF THE AMERICA'S TEST KITCHEN STAFF TASTED EIGHT DIFFERENT SANDWICH BREADS THREE WAYS: plain, in grilled cheese sandwiches, and in croutons seasoned with olive oil and salt. The breads are listed in order of preference based on their combined scores from these three tastings. The breads are available in supermarkets nationwide.

RECOMMENDED

Arnold Country Classics White

$3.19 for 24 ounces

"This is what I expect from sandwich bread," wrote one taster of our top-rated brand. Others agreed, praising its "perfect structure" and "subtle sweetness."

RECOMMENDED

Pepperidge Farm Farmhouse Hearty White

$2.50 for 24 ounces

Tasters deemed this top-rated bread "well balanced," "likeable," and "flavorful (for white bread!)," with a "familiar" taste that was "not overly sweet—just enough."

NOT RECOMMENDED

Wonder Country White

$2.69 for 24 ounces

This upscale version of the bread many of us grew up with was panned as "rather dry and cardboard-like," with a "blah" flavor and "slightly sour aftertaste."

NOT RECOMMENDED

Sunbeam Giant White

$2.39 for 22 ounces

Described as "classic packaged American white bread," this "squishy" bread had a "strong sour flavor" and a "texture like cotton candy" that turned off tasters.

NOT RECOMMENDED

Freihofer's Country White

$2.69 for 24 ounces

There were few fans of this bread, which was described as "tasteless," "too soft," and "borderline gummy."

NOT RECOMMENDED

J.J. Nissen ButterTop White

$2.39 for 20 ounces

"Who calls this fluff 'bread'?" asked one taster of this "really soft and spongy" bread with "nonexistent" flavor. More "like eating air" than bread, said another.

NOT RECOMMENDED

Home Pride Butter Top White

$2.39 for 20 ounces

Tasters found this "plasterboard sample" to be so "coarse and dry" that it would be "great for exfoliating your feet"; otherwise, a "waste of flour."

NOT RECOMMENDED

Country Kitchen Giant White

$2.49 for 22 ounces

This "gutless" bread was deemed "ridiculously soft and bland," with a "plasticky" flavor that "tastes like additives."

PAN-ROASTED BROCCOLI

WHAT WE WANTED: Tender, not dry, bright green broccoli with a toasted, slightly sweet flavor.

Pan-roasting broccoli is an intriguing idea, but that method (dry pan, high heat) often yields dried-out, shriveled florets and chewy stalks—leaving plenty of room for improvement.

The first step was to transform a head of broccoli into pieces that would cook evenly—trimming the florets into small pieces and the stalks into oblong coins. Next we assembled the pieces in an even layer in a hot, lightly oiled skillet. We had hoped the heat would promote caramelization and that the bit of oil would keep things from drying out, but it became clear that some moist heat (in other words, steam) was needed if the broccoli was to cook through without burning or drying out.

Once the pieces began to brown, we added water seasoned with salt and pepper, covered the skillet, and let the pieces steam. When the broccoli turned bright green, we removed the lid and let the excess moisture evaporate. Because the hardier stalks take longer to cook than the delicate florets, we found that adding the pieces in a two-step process (browning the stalks first, then tossing in the florets) prevented the florets from becoming limp.

After spending just 10 minutes at the stove, we had a flavorful broccoli dish with bright green florets and toasty-brown stalks that were tasty enough to be eaten simply as is—but hearty enough to stand up to assertive flavorings, such as a garlicky lemon browned butter in one; Southeast Asian flavors—garlic, peanut, chili sauce, and basil—in another; and in a third, creamy Gruyère sauce.

WHAT WE LEARNED: Brown then steam the broccoli in a covered skillet with salt-and-pepper-seasoned water. Once the broccoli turns bright green, remove the lid to evaporate excess moisture. Also, start cooking the hardier stalks first, then follow with the more delicate florets.

PAN-ROASTED BROCCOLI
Serves 4

- 3 tablespoons water
- ¼ teaspoon salt
- ⅛ teaspoon ground black pepper
- 2 tablespoons vegetable oil
- 1¾ pounds broccoli, florets cut into 1½-inch pieces, stalks trimmed, peeled, and cut on the bias into ¼-inch-thick slices about 1½ inches long (about 5 cups florets and ¾ cup stalks)

1. Stir the water, salt, and pepper together in a small bowl until the salt dissolves; set aside. In a 12-inch nonstick skillet with a tight-fitting lid, heat the oil over medium-high heat until just beginning to smoke. Add the broccoli stalks in an even layer and cook, without stirring, until browned on the bottoms, about 2 minutes. Add the florets to the skillet and toss to combine; cook, without stirring, until the bottoms of the florets just begin to brown, 1 to 2 minutes longer.

2. Add the water mixture and cover the skillet; cook until the broccoli is bright green but still crisp, about 2 minutes. Uncover and continue to cook until the water has evaporated, the broccoli stalks are tender, and the florets are tender-crisp, about 2 minutes more, and serve immediately.

VARIATIONS
PAN-ROASTED BROCCOLI WITH LEMON BROWNED BUTTER
This buttery variation goes especially well with fish or chicken.

- 1 recipe Pan-Roasted Broccoli
- 4 tablespoons unsalted butter
- 1 small shallot, minced (about 1½ tablespoons)

2 medium garlic cloves, minced or pressed through a garlic press (about 2 teaspoons)
¼ teaspoon salt
⅛ teaspoon ground black pepper
1½ teaspoons juice from 1 lemon
½ teaspoon minced fresh thyme leaves

1. Follow the recipe for Pan-Roasted Broccoli; transfer the broccoli to a medium bowl and set aside.

2. Melt the butter in the now-empty skillet over medium-high heat and continue to cook, swirling occasionally, until the butter is browned and releases a nutty aroma, about 1½ minutes. Off the heat, add the shallot, garlic, salt, and pepper and stir until the garlic and shallot are fragrant, about 1 minute. Stir in the lemon juice and thyme. Add the broccoli to the skillet, toss to coat with the browned butter, and serve immediately.

PAN-ROASTED BROCCOLI WITH SPICY SOUTHEAST ASIAN FLAVORS
Serve this Asian-inspired variation with steamed white rice.

1 tablespoon creamy peanut butter
1 tablespoon hoisin sauce
2 teaspoons juice from 1 lime
2 medium garlic cloves, minced or pressed through a garlic press (about 2 teaspoons)
1 teaspoon light or dark brown sugar
¾ teaspoon Asian chili sauce
1 recipe Pan-Roasted Broccoli
¼ cup coarsely chopped fresh basil leaves
2 tablespoons chopped roasted unsalted peanuts

1. Stir together the peanut butter, hoisin sauce, lime juice, garlic, brown sugar, and chili sauce in a medium bowl until combined; set aside.

2. Follow the recipe for Pan-Roasted Broccoli; during the last minute of cooking, add the basil and cook, stirring, until the leaves wilt, about 30 seconds. Add the peanut butter mixture and toss until the broccoli is evenly coated and heated through, about 30 seconds. Transfer to a serving dish, top with chopped peanuts, and serve immediately.

PAN-ROASTED BROCCOLI WITH CREAMY GRUYÈRE SAUCE
This ultra-rich variation is especially good with a pan-seared steak.

1 recipe Pan-Roasted Broccoli
1 tablespoon unsalted butter
1 medium shallot, peeled and sliced into thin rings (about 2 tablespoons)
½ cup heavy cream
½ teaspoon Dijon mustard
½ teaspoon dry sherry
Pinch cayenne
⅛ teaspoon salt
3 tablespoons grated Gruyère (about ¾ ounce), plus additional 1 to 2 tablespoons
1 teaspoon juice from 1 lemon

1. Follow the recipe for Pan-Roasted Broccoli; transfer the broccoli to a medium bowl and set aside.

2. Melt the butter in the now-empty skillet over medium heat. When the foaming subsides, add the shallot and cook, stirring frequently, until golden and softened, about 2 minutes. Stir in the cream, mustard, sherry, cayenne, and salt. Increase the heat to medium-high and cook until the mixture bubbles and thickens, about 1 minute. Off the heat, add the cheese and lemon juice and stir until the cheese is melted. Add the broccoli and stir to reheat and coat. Transfer to a serving dish, sprinkle with the additional cheese, and serve immediately.

To tame the bite on her pepper-crusted filet mignon, Bridget first simmered the peppercorns in oil before blending them into a thick paste.

MEAT AND POTATOES
CHAPTER 10
for company

Few main courses are as impressive as filet mignon, but such cachet comes with a hefty price tag. The hallmark of this luxury cut is its buttery, tender texture, but some argue that the beefy flavor is too mild, lacking the oomph of fattier (albeit chewier) cuts like the rib eye. So we aimed to boost the meat's flavor with a lively peppercorn crust and a rich pan sauce. Peppercorn crusts, however, have their issues. They can be overwhelmingly spicy, masking, rather than enhancing, the flavor of the meat. We'd need to strike just the right balance. Getting the crust to evenly adhere to the meat would be a challenge too.

In looking for a potato dish to serve alongside our steak, we quickly settled on the simple, but elegant, potatoes Lyonnaise—sautéed slices of buttery potato sweetened with caramelized strands of onion. But getting this dish just right can be a challenge. Buttery potatoes can easily turn greasy. And caramelizing the onion alongside the potatoes is difficult to do without steaming them. We'd need to find a way to get these two ingredients in sync.

When you're aiming to impress and willing to splurge a bit, you can be confident that these dishes will deliver.

PEPPER-CRUSTED FILET MIGNON

WHAT WE WANTED: To boost the flavor of tender but mild filet mignon with a crunchy peppercorn crust—without the stinging heat that usually accompanies it.

Filet mignon may be revered as the elite superstar of steaks, but it needs serious help in the kitchen to live up to that reputation on the palate. Chefs compensate for the relatively mild flavor of beef tenderloin—the lean, ultra-tender muscle from which filet mignon steaks are cut—by wrapping it in bacon or puff pastry, searing it to develop a dark, flavorful crust, and serving it with rich wine sauces or flavored butters.

Another popular way to dress up a filet is with a crust of cracked black peppercorns. Surveying a stack of published recipes, we envisioned the pleasing contrast of a thick center of pink, soft-as-butter beef and a crunchy, spicy coating—a peppery hit with every bite. But peppercorn crusts fall off in the pan, interfere with the meat's browning, and—used in sufficient quantity to create a real crust—deliver punishing pungency.

An earlier recipe developed in the test kitchen for steak au poivre solved these problems by coating only one side of each steak with the cracked peppercorns. The overall heat level was reduced by half, and the uncoated side got nicely browned, contributing flavor to the steaks and providing the necessary fond (browned bits in the pan) to create the brandy-cream sauce that accompanies the classic French dish. A neat solution, but not one that could help us this time. That recipe used strip steaks cut from the loin that were, at most, an inch thick. Because the eye of the tenderloin muscle is small, filet steaks are usually cut almost twice as thick. We suspected a one-sided crust would not be sufficient, and a quick test proved it: Too many bites came with little or no crust. Flavor was also an issue. When we did get a bite with peppercorns, peppercorns were all we tasted.

Thick, lean, tender, mild—how best to use peppercorns to complement these traits without overwhelming them? We started with the test kitchen's standard technique

for cooking a filet mignon: searing it first in a hot pan with a small amount of oil, then finishing it in the oven. Immediately, we encountered a problem. The cracked pepper kept the meat from making direct contact with the hot pan, so beneath the crust the steaks were unappealingly pale. We tried adding extra oil to the skillet, hoping it would bridge the gap between the pan and the meat, and this was a partial success. On the downside, peppercorns were still falling off. Next, we made a thick paste of cracked peppercorns and oil, which we rubbed over the raw steaks. Before cooking, we pressed down on each peppercorn-adorned steak through a sheet of plastic wrap. Problem solved.

Now we had steaks that were well browned and coated in an attractive pepper crust, but some tasters preferred to admire them from afar, as the overall heat level was still intense. Inspired by an article on blooming spices in infused oils, we wondered how heating the peppercorn-oil paste might affect its flavor, especially the spiciness. We brought the mixture to a gentle simmer in a saucepan, as aromas of flowers, chocolate, and toasted nuts wafted up. When we cooked up steaks coated with this mixture, we were amazed at the change. In place of the stinging heat was a pleasant warmth. (For an explanation, see "Taming Peppercorn Heat," page 102.) Now we could have a substantial peppercorn crust without the usual punishing heat.

To augment the flavor of the steaks' thick interior, we took a cue from the prior testing with beef tenderloin, in which the meat is rubbed with salt an hour before grilling; the salt penetrated into the interior, seasoning it and drawing out a beefier flavor. We hoped this same technique would work here, but rather than include a separate salting step we simply added a tablespoon of salt to the peppercorn paste and let the steaks sit, covered, for an hour before cooking. Sure enough, the meat became noticeably beefier—and flavorful enough to stand up to the assertive pepper crust.

As for accompaniments, the salting step buys plenty of time to simmer a rich reduction sauce. And because it is so lean, filet mignon is also excellent with flavored butters.

WHAT WE LEARNED: Gently simmering the peppercorns with oil helps tame their raw bite and harsh heat, while adding salt to the peppercorn mixture after it has cooled helps draw out the beefy flavor of the steaks. And to ensure that the crust adheres to the steak, rub the paste all over the meat, then press down gently with plastic wrap.

PEPPER-CRUSTED FILET MIGNON
Serves 4

If you prefer a very mild pepper flavor, drain the cooled peppercorns in a fine-mesh strainer in step 1, toss them with 5 tablespoons of fresh oil, add the salt, and proceed. Serve with Port-Cherry Reduction or Blue Cheese–Chive Butter (page 102).

5 tablespoons black peppercorns, cracked (see illustration on page 103)
5 tablespoons plus 2 teaspoons olive oil
1 tablespoon kosher salt
4 center-cut filets mignons, 1½ to 2 inches thick, 7 to 8 ounces each, trimmed of fat and silver skin

1. Heat the peppercorns and 5 tablespoons of the oil in a small saucepan over low heat until faint bubbles appear. Continue to cook at a bare simmer, swirling the pan occasionally, until the pepper is fragrant, 7 to 10 minutes. Remove from the heat and set aside to cool. When the mixture is at room temperature, add the salt and stir to combine. Rub the steaks with the pepper mixture, thoroughly coating the top and bottom of each steak with the peppercorns. Cover the steaks with plastic wrap and press gently to make sure the peppercorns adhere; let stand at room temperature for 1 hour.

2. Meanwhile, adjust an oven rack to the middle position, place a rimmed baking sheet on the oven rack, and heat the oven to 450 degrees. Heat the remaining 2 teaspoons oil in a 12-inch heavy-bottomed skillet over medium-high heat until faint smoke appears. Place the steaks in the skillet and cook, without moving the steaks, until a dark brown crust has formed, 3 to 4 minutes. Using tongs, turn the steaks and cook until well browned on the second side, about 3 minutes. Remove the pan from the heat and transfer the steaks to the hot baking sheet. Roast 3 to 5 minutes for rare, 5 to 7 minutes for medium-rare to medium. Transfer the steaks to a wire cooling rack and let rest, loosely tented with foil, for 5 minutes before serving.

TECHNIQUE: Key Steps for Pepper-Crusted Filet Mignon

Simmer
Gently simmer the peppercorns in olive oil to mellow the heat.

Coat
Coat the tops and bottoms of the steaks with the pepper mixture, pressing the excess onto the sides.

Rest
Cover with plastic, pressing to make sure the peppercorns adhere. Let rest one hour.

Brown
Sear the steaks in a well-oiled skillet until browned beneath the peppercorn layer.

Roast
Finish cooking in a hot oven to ensure browning on the sides of the steaks.

PORT-CHERRY REDUCTION

Makes about 1 cup, enough for 4 steaks

1½ cups port
½ cup balsamic vinegar
½ cup dried tart cherries
1 large shallot, minced (about 3 tablespoons)
2 sprigs fresh thyme
1 tablespoon unsalted butter
   Salt

1. Combine the first five ingredients in a medium saucepan; simmer over medium-low heat until the liquid is reduced to ⅓ cup, about 30 minutes. Set aside, covered.

2. While the steaks are resting, reheat the sauce. Off the heat, remove the thyme, then whisk in the butter until melted. Season with salt to taste. Serve, passing the sauce at the table with the steak.

BLUE CHEESE–CHIVE BUTTER

Makes about ½ cup, enough for 4 steaks

3 tablespoons unsalted butter, softened
⅓ cup crumbled mild blue cheese, room temperature
⅛ teaspoon salt
2 tablespoons minced chives

Combine the butter, cheese, and salt in a medium bowl and mix with a stiff rubber spatula until smooth. Fold in the chives. While the steaks are resting, spoon 1 to 2 tablespoons butter on each one.

SCIENCE DESK: Taming Peppercorn Heat

TEST-KITCHEN STAFFERS WITH MORE SENSITIVE PALATES were relieved to learn that the pungent heat of black peppercorns can be mellowed by a brief simmer in oil. We were pleased with the effect but curious as to the cause.

Research revealed that the natural irritant in peppercorns is called piperine. As peppercorns age, the piperine is converted into closely related molecules (called isomers) that have different flavor characteristics and that are less irritating to the nose and throat. Left sitting at room temperature in your cupboard, the peppercorns may take years to undergo this reaction, but the hot oil serves as a catalyst, driving the conversion at hundreds of times its natural speed, quickly tempering the pepper's pungency. As a bonus, piperine and its isomers are oil-soluble, so that during the simmer some of the remaining pepper heat and flavor leaches out of the peppercorns into the surrounding oil. This oil can then be discarded to further reduce the heat of the dish.

TASTING LAB:
Mail-Order Filet Mignon

LIKE IT OR HATE IT, THERE'S NO DISPUTING BEEF TENDER-loin's cachet, thanks in large part to the distinctively high prices it commands. Supermarket meat counters are bad enough ($15 a pound at the low end), but mail-order filets mignons can run as high as $80 for two 8-ounce steaks. We ordered 34 steaks from four mail-order retailers to see if these cash cows tasted any better.

Outrageous price aside, we identified two problems. First, most of these steaks are USDA Prime—the highest grade, based on a high percentage of intramuscular fat, or marbling. Pronounced marbling is highly desirable when it comes to a rib eye or a strip steak (when the fat melts, it leaves behind great flavor and texture). But tenderloin is so tender to begin with that extra marbling didn't help much—at least according to our panel of tasters. It certainly didn't seem worth the premium price tag. Also, most of our mail-order steaks were packed with dry ice and frozen solid. Freezing creates ice crystals in the meat, turning these already-tender steaks mushy once thawed.

Our favorite filets were USDA Choice (the next grade down), purchased at $19.99 per pound—$40 for a dinner for four. The only mail-order steaks that weren't frozen solid on arrival, Lobel's ($207.93 for six steaks, including shipping) landed in second place. For those prices, it's cheaper to hit a swanky steakhouse—and you won't have to do the dishes.

TECHNIQUE: Cracking Peppercorns

Use the back of a heavy pan and a rocking motion to grind the peppercorns on a cutting board.

Rating Filet Mignon

SEVENTEEN MEMBERS OF THE AMERICA'S TEST KITCHEN staff tasted seven different steaks, which were pan-seared to medium doneness and seasoned with salt. The filets are listed in order of preference based on their scores in this tasting.

HIGHLY RECOMMENDED
Supermarket Filet Mignon
$19.99 per pound
Tasters found this USDA Choice steak to have a clean, "beefy-chew" that was "more meaty than mushy"—tasters' biggest complaint with lesser steaks. "Buttery" flavor won tasters over.

RECOMMENDED
Lobel's Filet Mignon
$65.67 per pound, including shipping
While a few tasters thought this "good-n-beefy" steak "melts in your mouth," most thought it was a little "too tender."

NOT RECOMMENDED
Omaha Steaks Private Reserve Filets Mignons
$44.00 per pound, including shipping
These frozen steaks cross the point where "tender" meets "mushy." Flavor is mild, but soft texture trumps any positives. Fork-tender steak? No, thanks.

NOT RECOMMENDED
Allen Brothers Choice Filets
$53.57 per pound, including shipping
An OK steak texture-wise; downgraded for tasting "like nothing."

NOT RECOMMENDED
Allen Brothers Prime Filets
$65.48 per pound, including shipping
One taster deemed this steak "cafeteria beef." Most didn't go that far, merely calling it "livery," "mineral-y," and "mealy."

NOT RECOMMENDED
Dean & Deluca Prime Filet
$68.29 per pound, including shipping
Tasters called these steaks "wet" (as in watery) rather than "juicy" (as in moist and beefy). Sponge-like texture didn't win over any tasters.

NOT RECOMMENDED
Omaha Steaks Filets Mignons
$30.85 per pound, including shipping
Dry ice is no friend of filet mignon. These steaks were so mushy one taster compared them to "mashed potatoes."

POTATOES LYONNAISE

WHAT WE WANTED: A foolproof version of France's elegant, buttery potato and onion dish—and one that didn't require leftover potatoes to make.

One of the hallmark dishes of France's premier gastronomic city, pommes de terre Lyonnaise (aka potatoes Lyonnaise) is a study in simple elegance. Although originally conceived as a dish of economy (an easy way to use up leftover boiled potatoes), it came to represent the best of classic French bistro cuisine: buttery, browned potato slices interwoven with strands of sweet, caramelized onion and fresh, grassy parsley—a simple yet complex four-ingredient skillet potato dish.

The reality, however, is too often far removed from that buttery, earthy ideal. Most versions we tested were greasy and heavy rather than rich and complex. A few were so bad—with sodden spuds and waterlogged onions—that we were reminded how often the simplest dishes are the most difficult to execute properly. Each component would have to be handled with the utmost care.

Having no leftover cooked potatoes on hand (the case with most home cooks), we wondered if we could proceed with raw spuds without precooking. Starting with a large skillet, we sautéed the raw slices on fairly high heat and got dismal results: The exteriors had cooked to a near-blackened crisp before the interiors got even remotely tender. On moderate heat, however, the potatoes took forever to develop a nice, browned crust. Cooking the potatoes covered got us closer to what we wanted. Still, the potatoes were too dry. Some sort of parcooking would have to be a first step.

Borrowing a technique used in the test kitchen for an American short-order classic (home fries), we began by microwaving the ¼-inch-thick slices of potato in a tablespoon of melted butter until barely tender. This gave them the head start they needed. The time it took the potatoes to brown was now also sufficient to cook them through. Using just one more tablespoon of butter (most classic recipes call for 4 to 6 tablespoons), a simple brown-and-flip approach, and medium-high heat, we cooked the potatoes in less than 15 minutes.

This technique was fast and gave the potatoes great color, but the russets we'd been using often came out mealy. In a spud-to-spud taste test, creamy, golden-fleshed, medium-starch Yukon Gold potatoes beat out the high-starch russets and the "rubbery," low-starch Red Bliss by a comfortable margin.

Potatoes Lyonnaise would just be sautéed potatoes if not for the addition of onions, the definitive ingredient of dishes prepared à la Lyonnaise. For sweet, concentrated flavor, the onions would have to be cooked separately from the potatoes. Cooking them all the way through over medium-high heat dried them out. Covering the skillet and cooking them on medium once they had released some moisture created an environment of gentle, moist heat. Deglazing the pan with a small amount of water gave them the chance to cook in their own flavorful juices.

To put the steps together in an efficient manner was easy. While the onions cooked, the potatoes began their warm-up in the microwave. Once the onions finished cooking and were removed to a nearby bowl, the potatoes had a turn in the pan. To meld the flavors and heat everything through, we added the onions back into the pan and briefly sautéed the two together. A sprinkling of minced fresh parsley gives the dish a bit of color and a fresh finish. Now we had an updated version of a French classic that was good enough (and quick enough) to make even without leftover potatoes.

WHAT WE LEARNED: Use Yukon Gold potatoes for their creamy texture. Caramelize the onions in a skillet while the potatoes parcook in the microwave. Remove the onions from the skillet and brown the parcooked potatoes until they become tender. Return the onions to the pan to allow the flavors to meld.

POTATOES LYONNAISE

Serves 3 to 4

Toss the potatoes halfway through the microwave session to prevent uneven cooking. If using a lightweight skillet, you will need to stir the potatoes more frequently to prevent burning.

3	tablespoons unsalted butter
1	large onion (about 14 ounces), halved pole to pole and sliced ¼ inch thick (about 3 cups)
¾	teaspoon kosher salt (or ½ teaspoon table salt)
2	tablespoons water
1½	pounds medium Yukon Gold potatoes, peeled and sliced crosswise into ¼-inch rounds
¼	teaspoon ground black pepper
1	tablespoon minced fresh parsley leaves

1. Heat 1 tablespoon of the butter in a 12-inch heavy nonstick skillet over medium-high heat. When the foaming subsides, add the onion and ¼ teaspoon salt and stir to coat; cook, stirring occasionally, until the onions begin to soften, about 3 minutes. Reduce the heat to medium and cook, covered, stirring occasionally, until the onions are light brown and soft, about 12 minutes longer, deglazing with water when the pan gets dry, about halfway through the cooking time. Transfer to a bowl and cover. Do not wash the skillet.

2. While the onions cook, microwave 1 tablespoon more butter on high power in a large microwave-safe bowl until melted, about 15 seconds. Add the potatoes to the bowl and toss to coat with the melted butter. Microwave on high power until the potatoes just start to turn tender (see the photos at right), about 6 minutes, tossing halfway through the cooking time. Toss the potatoes again and set aside.

3. Melt the remaining tablespoon of butter in the now-empty skillet over medium-high heat. When the foaming subsides, add the potatoes and shake the skillet to distribute evenly. Cook, without stirring, until browned on the bottom, about 3 minutes. Using a spatula, stir the potatoes carefully and continue to cook, stirring every 2 to 3 minutes, until the potatoes are well browned and tender when pierced with the tip of a paring knife, 8 to 10 minutes more. Sprinkle with the remaining salt and the pepper.

4. Add the onions back to the skillet and stir to combine. Cook until the onions are heated through and the flavors have melded, 1 to 2 minutes. Transfer to a large plate, sprinkle with the parsley, and serve.

GETTING IT RIGHT:
Parcooking Potatoes in the Microwave
A few crucial seconds in the microwave separate perfectly parcooked potatoes from overdone and underdone misfires. Because microwave ovens vary in terms of power, it's important to check the look and texture during cooking.

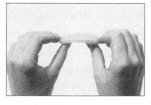 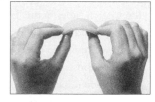

Undercooked
Potatoes look translucent and feel rubbery when bent.

Just Right
Mostly opaque potatoes resist slightly when bent.

EQUIPMENT CORNER: Cocktail Shakers

COCKTAIL SHAKERS BRING A SENSE OF STYLE TO A PARTY: Think of James Bond having his vodka martini shaken, not stirred, or William Powell in an old Thin Man movie shaking Manhattans while revealing the murderer. But for our tests, we focused on more pragmatic concerns: We wanted a comfortable-to-use, leakproof shaker that would combine liquors and flavorings effectively, efficiently chill the liquid, and pour the mixture easily into a V-shaped martini glass. We encountered a lot more problems than we anticipated.

Before we could start testing, we had to narrow the field. At the time of publication, eBay alone listed 641 shakers for sale, very few of which were identical. Most shakers manufactured today, however, are one of two types: cobbler (glass, stainless steel, or acrylic) or Boston (a combination of glass and stainless steel).

The cobbler shaker is the type usually found in home bars. It's normally made of three pieces: a metal, glass, or acrylic base, a lid (usually stainless steel) with a built-in strainer, and a small cap that fits over the lid. Ice and liquid are added to the base, the top sections are attached, the mixture is shaken, the cap is removed, and the liquid is poured through the strainer into the glass. The problems? The lid wasn't snug enough, so liquid sprayed everywhere during shaking; the lid fit too snugly, so that once the metal contracted from the chill, we had to wait for the metal to warm up and expand before we could unscrew the lid; and the strainer holes in the lid were so small that surface tension caused liquid to pool on top of the holes, causing overflow when we removed the cap.

The Boston shaker is the shaker of choice for professionals; when handled properly, it affords the bartender better control and security against leakage. It's a two-tumbler operation, in which a large metal tumbler is inverted over a smaller glass tumbler and the two are then shaken. If arranged properly, a seal forms between the two tumblers that prohibits leaking; a light tap just below the joint will break the seal.

The problems? The making and breaking of the seal, both of which take practice. Some of our testers complained that the Boston shaker demands a two-handed, two-step operation: After shaking, the tumbler is topped with a separate strainer that holds back the ice when the cocktail is poured. That said, two of our testers who had been professional bartenders in previous careers recommend the Boston style for anyone who mixes a lot of drinks. Our favorite Boston shaker was the WMF Manhattan Collection Boston Shaker.

For most home-entertaining purposes, though, we recommend the safer, easier-to-use cobbler style. We developed three general preferences in this category. First, we preferred stainless steel to glass and acrylic. Stainless steel shakers chill more quickly, the material doesn't break, and the lids on these shakers formed the most secure seal. (In fact, despite a rubber ring, one of the glass shakers was the worst leaker.) Second, we found that the shakers made with stronger stainless steel (18/10 or 18/8) rather than lighter stainless steel were better at managing the contracting/expanding problem that creates tight, hard-to-remove lids, though there were exceptions. Finally, we found that the strainer holes had to be large enough to prevent the surface tension that causes liquid to pool on top of the strainer after shaking (that liquid then tends to spill when the cap is removed). Only the Bullet Cocktail Shaker met all of our requirements: no stray sprays, no problem removing the lid, no pooling of liquid atop the strainer, and easy pouring.

Rating Cocktail Shakers

WE TESTED NINE COCKTAIL SHAKERS IN TWO STYLES: THE COBBLER-STYLE AND THE BOSTON-STYLE (WHICH IS THE CHOICE OF most professional bartenders). The cocktail shakers were rated on ease of use, leak resistance, chill effectiveness, and pourability. The shakers are listed in order of preference. See www.americastestkitchen.com for up-to-date prices and mail-order sources for top-rated products.

RECOMMENDED

The Bullet Cocktail Shaker by Metrokane

Stainless steel, 28 ounces, Cobbler-style

$28.99

Besides meeting our primary qualifications—no leaking, no problem unscrewing lid, no pooling on strainer, and easy pouring—even testers with small hands found that they could use it to shake a cocktail with just one hand.

RECOMMENDED

WMF Boston Cocktail Shaker, Manhattan Collection

Glass and stainless steel, 16 ounces, Boston-style

$29.99

For experienced bartenders, this shaker had no drawbacks: When fitted together properly, it didn't leak, and when tapped just right, the two tumblers came apart easily. But inexperienced users had problems creating a leakproof seal.

RECOMMENDED WITH RESERVATIONS

Oggi Dial-a-Drink Stainless Steel Cocktail Shaker

Stainless steel, 34 ounces, Cobbler-style

$34.95

While this shaker passed our primary tests, two vigorous testers caused its outside base to fly off, creating a risk for those standing nearby. Testers with smaller hands also felt that it was too big for one-handed shaking.

NOT RECOMMENDED

Acryl Cocktail Shaker

Acrylic, 20 ounces, Cobbler-style

$7.95

Initially, we thought this would be a great shaker to bring on picnics: It's light and unbreakable, it didn't leak, and the lid comes off easily. But when we took the cap off, our hands were drenched with liquid.

NOT RECOMMENDED

Norpro Recipe Cocktail Shaker

Stainless steel, 34 ounces, Cobbler-style

$34.99

The lid on this shaker fits too tightly and the revolving base makes it hard to get a good grip. The strainer holes are also small, which made for messy pooling and an awkward pour.

NOT RECOMMENDED

Norpro Cocktail Shaker Set

Stainless steel, 15 ounces, Boston-style

$19.95

Norpro's version of the Boston shaker has a rubber rim on the glass tumbler to help amateurs create a tight seal. Unfortunately, the rubber seal leaked like a sieve. Once wet, the rubber gripped the metal tumbler, making it difficult to get the lid off.

NOT RECOMMENDED

WMF Stainless Steel Cocktail Shaker with Built-In Strainer

Stainless steel, 22 ounces, Cobbler-style

$29.99

The sleek design looks great, but its ill-fitting cap not only leaked but also came off during shaking. Some testers found it hard to hold all three pieces of the shaker together because of its elongated design.

NOT RECOMMENDED

Precidio Olives Cocktail Shaker

Glass tumbler, metal lid and cap, 20 ounces, Cobbler-style

$17.95

This shaker was a poor performer. Even with the rubber seal on the cap, the shaker leaked. It's also heavy, and the large top made one-handed shaking a challenge.

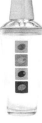

NOT RECOMMENDED

Liss Mesh Cobbler Shaker

Glass surrounded by aluminum mesh, metal lid and cap, 16 ounces, Cobbler-style

$39.99

Some users found the aluminum mesh uncomfortable, like "grabbing onto a chain-link fence." The real problem was the diminutive size of the lid, strainer holes, and cap. The tiny strainer holes prevented easy drainage, and the opening was too small to wash without the help of a bottle brush.

Try serving a saucy stir-fry over an Asian-style noodle cake instead of the usual rice. The test kitchen found that a crisp noodle cake with a tender interior starts by boiling fresh Chinese egg noodles for just 2 or 3 minutes before draining them.

STAYING IN FOR
CHAPTER II chinese takeout

We love a good stir-fry served with rice, but sometimes a change of pace is welcome. A noodle cake, a savory round of tender noodles sautéed in a skillet until the exterior is crisp, is the perfect base for a saucy stir-fry. We've enjoyed noodle cakes in restaurants, but never at home. We set out to find the best way to make one. While we were at it, we also aimed to develop a chicken stir-fry with really juicy chicken in a fresh-flavored sauce. Too often, chicken can turn dry and stringy in a stir-fry and no amount of sauce can rescue dry meat.

Another Asian classic, also more familiar at the restaurant table than in the average American home kitchen, is hot and sour soup—a spicy, bracing broth filled with pork, tofu, and wisps of egg. But is visiting your local Chinese restaurant the only way to enjoy it? We wanted to make this complex-flavored soup at home. But with a host of hard-to-find ingredients and a long simmering time, we had our work cut out for us. We'd need to strategically choose our ingredients and find reasonable substitutions for those that are just too difficult to find at the supermarket. At the same time, we'd need to take a hard look at streamlining the soup's lengthy preparation. And, we wouldn't settle for a pale imitation of this heady soup—it would need to stand up to authentic versions.

CHICKEN STIR-FRY WITH CRISPY NOODLE CAKE

WHAT WE WANTED: A stir-fry with juicy, tender chicken and crisp vegetables. And, instead of serving rice with our stir-fry, we wanted a thick noodle cake with contrasting textures: crisp on the outside with a moist, slightly chewy interior.

Quick to cook yet complex in flavor, stir-fries are the quintessential weeknight dinner. The problem is that they are usually served on a lackluster mound of steamed rice. On several excursions to Chinatown, we've learned that there is an alternative: stir-fry served on top of a pan-fried noodle cake, a superior marriage of protein and starch. The cake, crispy and crunchy on the outside and tender and chewy in the middle, appeared to be the antidote to the tedium of rice.

Finding a noodle that would achieve this textural balance, however, was difficult. A stroll down the international aisle of the local supermarket turned up an overwhelming number of dried Asian noodles of all sizes and flavors, ranging from thin somen to wide lo mein. Back in the test kitchen, we boiled up batches of noodles and pan-fried numerous cakes, and the results were, for the most part, disastrous. Thin noodles lacked enough body to achieve the balance of crispy outside and tender inside, and they produced a cake that was overly dry, almost similar in texture to raw pasta. Wide noodles were not much better. They wouldn't hold together to form a cake and so did not develop the contrasting textures we were looking for.

We finally hit upon a solution when we tried fresh Chinese egg noodles. These noodles tend to be starchy. As a result, they yielded a cohesive cake, one with a crunchy exterior and a chewy interior. Given our success with fresh Chinese noodles, we wondered if fresh Italian pasta would work. Although not as starchy as the fresh Chinese noodles, fresh Italian spaghetti from the supermarket refrigerator case performed well in kitchen tests, better than any dried Asian noodle.

Now that we had determined the type of noodle to use, we had to come up with a technique that would consistently yield good cakes. A nonstick skillet turned out to be crucial (to avoid sticking and the need for excess oil), and 2 tablespoons of oil per side was just the right amount to achieve a crispy exterior that was neither greasy nor burnt. Trying to flip this unwieldy disk was also a challenge. In the end, the best (and safest) method turned out to be sliding the cake onto a plate, inverting it onto another plate, and then sliding the cake back into the skillet, browned side up.

With the noodle cake down, it was on to our stir-fry. Chicken becomes dry and stringy when cooked over high heat, so we sought to find a method to prevent this. We considered brining, which imparts seasoning and moisture to meat, but brining takes more time than we'd like to spend on a quick-cooking dish like a stir-fry. Instead, we turned to a quick marinade for seasoning along with a traditional Chinese technique called "velveting," which involves coating chicken pieces in a thin cornstarch and egg white or oil mixture, then parcooking in moderately heated oil.

Cornstarch mixed with egg white yielded a cakey coating; tasters preferred the more subtle coating provided by cornstarch mixed with peanut oil. This velveted chicken was supple, but it was also pale, and again, this method seemed far too involved for a quick weeknight dinner.

We wondered if the same method—coating in a cornstarch mixture—would work if we eliminated the parcooking step. It did. This chicken was not only juicy and tender, but it also developed an attractive golden brown coating. Best of all, the entire process was quick. The only problem was that the coating, which was more of an invisible barrier than a crust, became bloated and slimy when cooking in the sauce. After researching the issue, we learned that the cornstarch was absorbing liquid from the sauce, causing the slippery finish. Cutting the cornstarch with flour turned out to be the solution. It created a negligible coating—not too thick, not too thin—that still managed to keep the juices inside the chicken. Substituting sesame oil for the peanut oil added a rich depth of flavor.

For the vegetables, we liked bok choy and red bell pepper with the chicken. And as for the sauce, the test kitchen has found that chicken broth, rather than soy sauce, makes the best base because it's not overpowering. Soy sauce, sherry, and oyster sauce work nicely as flavoring ingredients. We have also tested the addition of cornstarch to help the sauce coat the meat and vegetables and have found that a small amount is necessary. Otherwise the sauce is too thin and does not adhere properly. Juicy, stir-fried chicken, crisp bok choy, and red pepper is hard to beat, and the combination, coupled with the noodle cake, gives a welcome twist to the usual stir-fry dinner.

WHAT WE LEARNED: Fresh Chinese noodles yield a cohesive cake that won't fall apart once cooked. For a crisp noodle cake that's not greasy, use a nonstick skillet, which requires less oil. A quick marinade gives our chicken welcome flavor, and a modified version of the Chinese technique called velveting prevents the chicken from drying out over high heat.

STIR-FRIED CHICKEN WITH BOK CHOY AND CRISPY NOODLE CAKE

Serves 4

Fresh Chinese noodles are often kept in the produce section of the grocery store. If you can't find them, substitute an equal amount of fresh Italian spaghetti.

noodle cake

1   (9-ounce) package fresh Chinese egg noodles
1   teaspoon salt
2   scallions, sliced thin
4   tablespoons vegetable oil

stir-fry sauce

¼   cup low-sodium chicken broth
2   tablespoons soy sauce
1   tablespoon dry sherry
1   tablespoon oyster-flavored sauce
1   teaspoon sugar
1   teaspoon cornstarch
¼   teaspoon red pepper flakes

chicken and vegetables

1   pound boneless, skinless chicken breasts, patted dry with paper towels, trimmed, and cut into 1-inch squares (see the illustrations on page 112)
1   tablespoon soy sauce
1   tablespoon dry sherry
2   tablespoons toasted sesame oil
1   tablespoon cornstarch
1   tablespoon unbleached all-purpose flour
1   tablespoon minced fresh ginger
1   medium garlic clove, minced or pressed through a garlic press (about 1 teaspoon)
8   teaspoons peanut oil or vegetable oil
1   small head bok choy, stalks sliced on the bias into ¼-inch slices, and greens cut into ½-inch strips
1   small red bell pepper, cut into ¼-inch strips

1. Separate the tenderloin from the breast. Starting at the thick end, cut the breast into ¼-inch slices. Stop slicing when you reach the tapered triangle end.

2. With the flat side of the knife, press the tapered triangle end to an even ¼-inch thickness and then cut all slices into 1-inch squares.

3. Use the same technique for the tenderloin, flattening it with the side of the knife and then cutting it into 1-inch pieces.

1. FOR THE NOODLE CAKE: Bring 3 quarts water to a boil over high heat in a large pot. Add the noodles and salt to the boiling water; cook the noodles until tender, 2 to 3 minutes (do not overcook). Drain thoroughly through a colander. Add the scallions to the noodles in the colander and toss to combine; set aside.

2. FOR THE SAUCE: Meanwhile, whisk together the sauce ingredients; set aside.

3. FOR THE CHICKEN AND VEGETABLES: Toss the chicken with the soy sauce and sherry; set aside. In a large bowl, whisk together the sesame oil, cornstarch, and flour; set aside. In a small bowl, mix together the ginger, garlic, and 1 teaspoon peanut oil; set aside.

4. While the chicken marinates, cook the noodle cake. Heat 2 tablespoons of the vegetable oil in a 12-inch nonstick skillet over medium heat until shimmering. Spread the noodles evenly across the bottom of the skillet and press with a spatula to flatten into a cake. Cook until crisp and golden brown, 5 to 8 minutes.

5. Slide the noodle cake onto a large plate. Add the remaining 2 tablespoons vegetable oil to the skillet; swirl to coat. Invert the noodle cake onto a second plate and slide it, browned side up, back into the skillet. Cook until golden brown on the second side, about 5 to 8 minutes.

6. Slide the noodle cake onto a cutting board and let sit for at least 5 minutes before slicing into wedges and serving. (The noodle cake can be transferred to a wire rack set over a baking sheet and kept warm in a 200-degree oven for up to 20 minutes.)

7. Stir the marinated chicken into the sesame oil–cornstarch mixture until uniformly combined. Heat 2 teaspoons peanut oil in a 12-inch nonstick skillet over high heat until smoking; add half of the chicken to the skillet in a flat, even layer. Cook, without stirring, but gently separating the pieces, until golden brown on the first side, about 1 minute; turn the chicken pieces and cook until lightly browned on the second side, about 30 seconds. Transfer the chicken to a clean bowl. Repeat with an additional 2 teaspoons peanut oil and the remaining chicken; cover to keep warm.

and continue to cook until the stalks are tender-crisp, about 30 seconds longer. Stir in the bok choy greens and cook until beginning to wilt, about 30 seconds.

10. Return the chicken to the skillet. Whisk the sauce to recombine, then add to the skillet and cook, tossing constantly, until the sauce is thickened and the chicken is heated through, about 30 seconds. Transfer to a serving platter and serve immediately with the noodle cake.

8. Add the remaining 1 tablespoon peanut oil to the now-empty skillet and return to high heat just until smoking. Add the bok choy stalks and red bell pepper and cook until lightly browned, 2 to 3 minutes.

9. Push the vegetables to the sides of the skillet to clear the center; add the garlic-ginger mixture to the clearing and cook, mashing the mixture with a spoon, until fragrant, 15 to 20 seconds, then stir the mixture into the vegetables

TECHNIQUE: Preparing Bok Choy

1. Trim the bottom inch from the head of bok choy. Wash and pat dry the leaves and stalks. With a chef's knife, cut the leafy green portion away from either side of the white stalk.

2. Cut each white stalk in half lengthwise and then crosswise into ¼-inch slices.

3. Stack the leafy greens and then slice them crosswise into ½-inch strips.

HOT AND SOUR SOUP

WHAT WE WANTED: A spicy, rich version of the classic Chinese soup without shopping for hard-to-find ingredients or spending all day in the kitchen.

The hot and sour soup we eat in Chinese-American restaurants today isn't much different from the Sichuanese original. Named for its potent peppery and vinegary flavors, the lightly thickened soup contains strips of pork, cubes of tofu, and wisps of egg. According to the cookbooks and Chinese-cooking experts we consulted, hot and sour soup encapsulates the Taoist principle central to Chinese culture: yin and yang, the notion of balancing the universe's opposing yet complementary forces. In the kitchen, that means creating balanced dishes by strategically combining flavors, textures, colors, and temperatures—some yin, some yang.

Balancing universal forces we'd have to leave to the philosophers. (All we were after was a good soup.) But balancing flavors, textures, and temperatures? That was familiar territory. At the very least, we figured, the yin/yang principle left us some leeway to explore stand-ins for hard-to-find ingredients that show up in some authentic versions—for instance, mustard pickle, pig's-foot tendon, and dried sea cucumber—without sacrificing the spirit of authenticity. So armed with thoughts of yin, yang, and the inventory of the local supermarket, we headed to the test kitchen to work on a balanced and (philosophically) authentic take on hot and sour soup.

The heat in hot and sour soup traditionally comes not from fresh chiles but from ground white (or sometimes black) peppercorns. Unlike chiles, pepper delivers direct spiciness but doesn't leave a lingering burn in its wake. An all-black-pepper soup was sharp but one-dimensional; a half-black, half-white combination was an improvement. Better still was a version made with a full teaspoon of distinctive, penetrating white pepper. Nice, but we suspected that a second heat source might deliver yet another layer of

complexity. Sure enough, chili oil—a bit unconventional for this recipe—supported the white-hot heat of the pepper, laying the groundwork for the opposing flavor of vinegar. This yin/yang balancing act was turning out easier than we'd anticipated.

Until the very next experiment, that is. Made from toasted rice, Chinese black vinegar (the traditional sour component) has an elusive flavor that almost defies description. Because it can be difficult to find, we needed to identify a substitute. Emboldened by the success of our first improvisation, we raided the test kitchen pantry and assembled 14 bottles of vinegar. Drop by drop, we confidently sniffed and tasted our way through the lineup, ultimately deciding that balsamic, cider, malt, rice, and red wine vinegar most closely resembled black vinegar. Next, we supplemented the vinegars, alone and in combination, with everything from angostura bitters to molasses to vermouth to Worcestershire sauce. A smidgen of this, a drizzle of that, and so it went. Sadly, every concoction was exceedingly harsh. To adhere to the yin/yang principle, we needed a substitute that would support, not outshine, the pepper.

We then reexamined the black vinegar label and noticed an acidity level of 1.18 percent. Most American vinegars measure in the 5 to 7 percent range, so we would have to use a lot less of the substitute vinegars. After several more rounds, we finally settled on a tablespoon each of dark, fruity balsamic and robust red wine vinegar as a workable substitute for 5 tablespoons of black vinegar. (That said, black vinegar is so unique that we recommend seeking it out.)

Now that we had carefully balanced the flavors of the soup, we turned our focus to texture. Cornstarch is the standard thickener, but a heavy hand resulted in a goopy gravy instead of a silky broth. We found that just 3 tablespoons yielded an agreeable, not-too-thick consistency that would gently support the other textures in the soup. To activate its thickening power, cornstarch is best added to the soup in the form of a cool slurry (cornstarch mixed

with water); the soup is then brought to a boil while being stirred constantly.

In addition to its role as thickener, cornstarch is believed by many Chinese cooks to play the part of meat (or protein) tenderizer. To test what seemed a dubious theory, we prepared two batches of soup, adding cornstarch to a simple soy sauce marinade for one julienned pork chop and omitting it in the marinade for another. The cornstarch-marinated pork was noticeably more tender. The cornstarch created a protective sheath that bought us the few extra minutes we needed to finish the soup without overcooking the pork.

After the pork is cooked and the soup thickened, beaten egg is drizzled in to create yet another complementary texture: fine, feathery shreds. The problem is that if the egg doesn't set immediately, it can blend into the soup and muddy the appearance of the broth. Wanting to make this step foolproof, we tried mixing the egg with vinegar and cornstarch. The vinegar instantly coagulated the egg, whereas the cornstarch, once again, was the miracle worker: The cornstarch molecules stabilized the liquid proteins, preventing them from contracting excessively when they hit the hot liquid. The result? Lighter, softer eggs. (See

"Cornstarch as Tenderizer" on page 117.)

Spicy, bracing, pungent, tender, fluffy—our soup was already replete with pleasing balances of flavor and texture. But we weren't quite done yet. Almost all authentic hot and sour soup recipes start with reconstituted dried wood ear mushrooms and lily buds. Wood ear mushrooms, also known as tree ear or cloud ear, offer snappy texture but little else. We swapped in commonly available dried porcini and shiitake mushrooms, but their woodsy notes had a negative influence on the flavor equilibrium we'd worked so hard to achieve. Fresh, mild shiitake mushrooms were a better choice. Lily buds, or golden needles, are the dried buds of the tiger lily flower. Tangy, mildly crunchy canned bamboo shoots closely approximated the musky, sour flavor of lily buds and added textural variety (a crisp foil for the fluffy wisps of egg).

As for the tofu, we had one basic question: Must it be pressed? The answer was a simple yes. Spongelike tofu is full of water, and weighting it beneath a heavy plate yielded firmer, cleaner-tasting cubes. Marinating was a mistake; an occasional bite of plain, mild (yin) tofu was a necessary respite in the mostly yang soup.

Many recipes call for passing potent toasted sesame oil at the table, but a generous pour overwhelmed the other flavors. We took a low-risk approach and added a measured amount to the marinade for the pork. A sprinkle of raw, crisp, green scallions (raw versus cooked) symbolized a final embrace of the yin/yang philosophy.

WHAT WE LEARNED: White pepper and chili oil provide a complex layer of heat that balances the sour component of Chinese black vinegar (though a combination of balsamic and red wine vinegar can be substituted). Cornstarch is a key ingredient: it not only thickens the soup but helps keep the pork tender and creates lighter, softer wisps of egg. Fresh shiitake mushrooms and canned bamboo shoots make good substitutes for hard-to-find wood ear mushrooms and lily buds.

HOT AND SOUR SOUP

Serves 6 to 8

To make slicing the pork chop easier, freeze it for 15 minutes. We prefer the distinctive flavor of Chinese black vinegar; look for it in Asian supermarkets. If you can't find it, a combination of red wine vinegar and balsamic vinegar approximates its flavor. This soup is very spicy. For a less spicy soup, omit the chili oil altogether or add only 1 teaspoon.

7   ounces extra-firm tofu, drained
4   tablespoons soy sauce
1   teaspoon toasted sesame oil
3   tablespoons plus 1½ teaspoons cornstarch
1   boneless center-cut pork chop (½ inch thick, about 6 ounces), trimmed of fat and cut into 1-inch by ⅛-inch matchsticks
3   tablespoons plus 1 teaspoon cool water
1   large egg
6   cups low-sodium chicken broth
1   cup bamboo shoots (from one 5-ounce can), sliced lengthwise into ⅛-inch-thick strips
4   ounces fresh shiitake mushrooms, stems removed, caps sliced ¼ inch thick (about 1 cup)
5   tablespoons Chinese black vinegar or
    1 tablespoon red wine vinegar plus
    1 tablespoon balsamic vinegar (see note)
2   teaspoons chili oil (see note)
1   teaspoon ground white pepper
3   medium scallions, sliced thin

1. Place the tofu in a pie plate and set a heavy plate on top. Weight with 2 heavy cans and let stand at least 15 minutes (the tofu should release about ½ cup liquid). Whisk 1 tablespoon soy sauce, sesame oil, and 1 teaspoon cornstarch in medium bowl; toss the pork with the marinade and set aside for at least 10 minutes (but no more than 30 minutes).

2. Combine 3 tablespoons of the cornstarch with 3 tablespoons of the water in a small bowl and mix thoroughly;

set aside, leaving the spoon in the bowl. Mix the remaining ½ teaspoon cornstarch with the remaining 1 teaspoon water in a small bowl; add the egg and beat with a fork until combined. Set aside.

3. Bring the broth to a boil in a large saucepan over medium-high heat. Reduce the heat to medium-low and add the bamboo shoots and mushrooms and simmer until the mushrooms are just tender, about 5 minutes. While the broth simmers, dice the tofu into ½-inch cubes. Add the tofu and pork, including the marinade, to the soup, stirring to separate any pieces of pork that stick together. Continue to simmer until the pork is no longer pink, about 2 minutes.

4. Stir the cornstarch mixture to recombine. Add it to the soup, increase the heat to medium-high, and cook, stirring occasionally, until the soup thickens and turns translucent, about 1 minute. Stir in the vinegar, chili oil, pepper, and remaining 3 tablespoons soy sauce and turn off the heat.

5. Without stirring the soup, use a soupspoon to slowly drizzle very thin streams of the egg mixture into the pot in a circular motion. Let the soup sit 1 minute, then return the saucepan to medium-high heat. Bring the soup to a gentle boil, then immediately remove from the heat. Gently stir the soup once to evenly distribute the egg; ladle into bowls and top with the scallions.

Beating an egg with cornstarch before drizzling it into the thickened soup helps the egg to set up on the soup's surface—keeping it light, wispy, and cohesive rather than tough or curdled.

1. Turn off the heat so the surface of the soup is calm, then use a spoon to drizzle the egg onto the surface in thin streams.

2. Let sit for 1 minute. Turn the heat back on and stir gently to finish cooking the egg and break it into ribbons.

SCIENCE DESK:
Cornstarch as Tenderizer

MOST COOKS KEEP A BOX OF CORNSTARCH ON HAND FOR a single purpose: thickening. So did we—until we noticed that cornstarch was working its magic in other ways as well. Predictably, adding cornstarch (3 tablespoons) to our soup thickened it. What was surprising, however, were the two other uses we found for cornstarch. Adding just 1 teaspoon of cornstarch to the pork marinade of soy sauce and sesame oil caused the marinade to coat the meat during cooking, creating a protective sheath that slowed the inevitable rise in temperature that separates moist, tender pork from dry, chalky pork jerky. And adding just ½ teaspoon of cornstarch to the egg that's drizzled into the soup at the end of cooking seemed to have a tenderizing effect. Cornstarch stabilizes liquid proteins when they're heated, staving off excessive shrinkage and contraction. So this last bit of cornstarch helped the eggs cook up lighter and softer.

EQUIPMENT CORNER:
Small Nonstick Saucepans

A SMALL SAUCEPAN SEES PLENTY OF ACTION—MAKING rice, heating milk, melting butter, or warming up a little soup. Because most of these tasks don't involve browning (and many involve sticky foods), in the test kitchen we use nonstick 2-quart saucepans almost exclusively. Do pans that cost close to $100 offer significant performance, stick-resistance, or design advantages over models costing a quarter as much? We decamped to the test kitchen with nine 2-quart nonstick saucepans to find out.

We designed our initial tests around the smaller, less complicated jobs for which these small saucepans are suited best, including steaming rice, scalding cream, and making pastry cream (using a nonstick-friendly nylon or silicone whisk). The pastry cream test illustrated several design differences that separated those pans we'd reach for every day from those that would remain parked eternally in the cabinet. Pouring hot cream from a saucepan is much neater if the pan from which you're pouring has either a spout, like the pans from Look, Bialetti, and Revere, or a rolled lip, like the Cuisinart and, again, the Bialetti. An ample diameter and sloped sidewalls make it easier to carry out the constant whisking necessary to prevent pastry cream from scorching. Diameters (measured across the top) ranged from just shy of 7 inches for the Anolon to nearly 9½ inches for the Calphalon.

In the process of making pastry cream or rice, a pan can spend 30 minutes (or more) on the burner, so there's a clear advantage to handles that remain cool to the touch. All but three of the pans had hard thermal plastic or Santoprene (soft plastic) handles, which passed this test with no problem. Even the metal handles, which heated up alarmingly at the point of attachment, maintained a sufficiently comfortable temperature at the far end. While steaming rice, we also developed a preference for transparent lids, which make it easier to monitor cooking progress.

There are two common ways to attach a handle to a saucepan—with rivets or screws—but, in our opinion, only one works effectively. Simply put: Rivets are sturdier than screws.

The Calphalon, Cuisinart, Anolon, and Circulon handles were riveted securely in place, while the Revere handle appeared to be soldered. To our displeasure, the handles on all of the other pans in our group, including the pricey $95 Swiss Diamond, $85 Look, and $70 Berndes, were screwed into place, a fact that we find hard to tolerate on an expensive piece of cookware. Worse yet, the Look's handle was loose from the get-go.

To get at performance issues such as the evenness and speed of heat distribution, we sautéed chopped onions and cooked eggs in each pan. Weight, rather than materials (which were similar in all pans tested), was the deciding factor. The onions were lightly and evenly colored in the two heaviest pans, the Calphalon and the Look, each of which weighs close to 2½ pounds. In contrast, onions darkened faster in some of the lighter pans, including the Bialetti, Circulon, and Cuisinart, which all weigh 1¾ pounds or less. In the past, we have often downgraded heavy skillets for being too slow and unwieldy, but a heavy saucepan is actually a good thing. Even the heftiest pan in our lineup was easy to maneuver, and many saucepan tasks involve prolonged cooking over low heat, where gentleness, not speed, is paramount.

Fresh from the box, all of the pans exhibited excellent stick resistance. In fact, it wasn't until we subjected the pans to a purposeful abuse test, designed to bring about the sort of cooking mistake we all hope never to make, that we noticed any difference in the stick-resistance of our pans. What evil did we visit upon our victims? Caramel. In each pan, we cooked sugar and water until it reached a deep amber hue. Caramel is no sin in and of itself, but what we did next was. We just walked away, leaving the sticky, sugary messes to harden overnight. We returned in the morning to face solid disks of caramel set hard into the pans, clinging with the force of epoxy. To remove the caramel, we tried

bashing it with a wooden spoon and then whacked the pan upside down against the rim of a trash can with the hope that pieces of caramel would tumble out. If the caramel held fast after five tries, then we filled the pan with water, brought it to a boil, and melted it out.

Strictly speaking, we felt it would be unfair to count the results of this extreme trial in the chart at right, but it certainly separated the men from the boys; so we used this information to help break ties. In only two pans, the Revere and the Anolon, did we have to resort to boiling. On the other hand, the Calphalon and the Swiss Diamond pans discharged the caramel with ease.

In the end, the performance differences were subtle—most of the pans will do a fine job of heating up soup or making rice. Design differences were more significant, and the sturdy Calphalon pan—with its riveted handle, wide diameter, sloped sides, and superior nonstick coating—came out on top. The final factor, price, was the most decisive. The Calphalon pan costs just $30, a far cry from the second-place Swiss Diamond at $95.

Rating Small Nonstick Saucepans

WE TESTED NINE SMALL NONSTICK SAUCEPANS (2-QUART CAPACITY, OR AS CLOSE AS WE COULD COME IN A GIVEN LINE) AND evaluated them according to design, performance, and sauté speed. When manufacturers offered more than one saucepan that satisfied our rubric, we chose a competitively priced or best-selling model. The pans are listed in order of preference. See www.americastestkitchen.com for up-to-date prices and mail-order sources for top-rated products.

RECOMMENDED
Calphalon Contemporary Nonstick Short & Saucy 2.5-Quart Shallow Saucepan with Cover
$29.99

Heavy, solid, and priced right, this pan is a hybrid—part plain saucepan and part classic saucier—just as the name, shallow shape, and generous diameter suggest. Sauté pace was a little slow, though easy to control, and hardened caramel nearly jumped out of the pan.

RECOMMENDED WITH RESERVATIONS
Bialetti Casa Italia Italian Collection 2-Quart Covered Saucepan
$24.99

This lightweight pan wasn't perfect (the onions overbrowned a bit), but given its low price, design features (rolled lip, pouring spout, glass lid, wide diameter, and stay-cool handle), and excellent performance in the caramel abuse test, we're willing to turn down the heat a little.

RECOMMENDED WITH RESERVATIONS
Cuisinart Chef's Classic Non-Stick Hard Anodized 2-Quart Saucepan
$29.99

Well designed, with riveted handle, rounded corners, rolled lip, and clear lid, but hot-headed in the sauté department—the onions came close to burning.

RECOMMENDED
Swiss Diamond 2.2-Quart Covered Saucepan
$94.99

Onions and eggs browned evenly and slipped out effortlessly, and this pan practically ejected the sticky caramel. But c'mon . . . for almost a hundred bucks, don't we deserve a riveted handle?

RECOMMENDED WITH RESERVATIONS
Circulon Total 2-Quart Covered Saucepan
$40.00

The stainless steel lid lacked the see-through convenience of glass, a few pieces of onion overbrowned, and the caramel required a soak to come clean. Dealbreakers? Maybe not, but with stronger contenders in the lineup, we'd look elsewhere.

RECOMMENDED WITH RESERVATIONS
Revere Convenience 2-Quart Saucepan
$23.99

Nicely rendered with wide, almost 8-inch diameter, rounded corners, and pouring spouts, but performance didn't match design. Rice did not cook evenly, and onions and eggs were slightly darker than ideal. The caramel clung for dear life and had to be boiled away.

RECOMMENDED
Berndes SignoCast Classic 2-Quart Saucepan
$69.99

Flared sides and rounded corners meant easy whisking, and the nonstick finish performed well in the abuse test. Not cheap, though, and the handle is not riveted.

RECOMMENDED WITH RESERVATIONS
Anolon Advanced 2-Quart Covered Saucepan
$60.00

Curiously, eggs cooked up a little dark, yet the onions, while impressively even, were on the light side. Run-of-the-mill nonstick performance was fine overall, but lacking in the caramel abuse test.

RECOMMENDED WITH RESERVATIONS
Look 7-Inch 2.5-Quart Covered Saucepan
$85.00

Handle was loose on delivery, and the lid was so ill-fitting that it flipped upside down on the pan with even the slightest provocation. Very slow sauté pace.

Becky shows Chris that blade steak is the best cut for Thai chile beef because it remains tender even when fully cooked and its meaty flavor stands up to the spicy, bold flavors in this dish.

NOT YOUR AVERAGE
stir-fry

CHAPTER 12

Thai-style stir-fries are a refreshing alternative to Chinese stir-fries. Spicy, sweet, sour, and salty, the flavors are well-balanced and complex. But who has the ingredients often required, such as shrimp paste, tamarind pulp, galangal, and palm sugar? And while the more familiar Chinese stir-fry is fairly quick to prepare, a Thai stir-fry can take hours. For our starting point, we looked to a restaurant favorite—Thai chile beef—and set out to streamline this dish without compromising its interesting combination of flavors.

Potstickers are another Asian favorite we wanted to enjoy at home. At their best, potstickers are light dumplings filled with a well-seasoned mix of pork and cabbage. Dunked into a soy dipping sauce, they make a terrific start to a meal. Unfortunately, we've eaten more than our share of truly awful potstickers—leaden balls of pasty meat in a doughy wrapper. All it took was one bite for us to put our chopsticks down. We wanted to find out the secret to making great potstickers—the right filling, the right wrapper, and a method of assembly that wasn't overly complicated and didn't take all day. Most of all we wanted these potstickers to be so good, we'd rather make them ourselves than call for our favorite takeout.

THAI CHILE BEEF

WHAT WE WANTED: Thai chile beef translated for the American home kitchen. We wanted a complex dish with carefully balanced flavors—without an extensive list of hard-to-find ingredients and hours in the kitchen.

Based on a sophisticated combination of four flavors—spicy, sweet, sour, and salty—Thai chile beef promises to be vastly more interesting than most everyday stir-fries. According to our recipe research, this simple transformation would be built on a foundation of just four ingredients: chiles, sugar, lime juice, and fish sauce.

We set out with high hopes, rounding up and testing cookbook recipes and even ordering Thai chile beef from three neighborhood restaurants. The net result of all this tasting and testing, however, was disappointment—with one notable exception. One "authentic" Thai recipe produced a wonderful dish. It contained no vegetables (restaurants frequently add vegetables to reduce the cost per serving), and the meat was sauced in a thick, complex, well-balanced chile jam. The problem? For starters, the ingredient list, which contained dried prawns, shrimp paste, tamarind pulp, galangal, and palm sugar. And then there was the three-hour prep time, which involved deep-frying many of the ingredients separately. While we had tasted the ultimate Thai chile beef, we had to wonder how we could possibly re-create it for an American home kitchen.

We started with the key ingredient: the beef. We stir-fried four easy-to-find cuts (filet, sirloin steak, strip steak, and blade steak) and compared them with our usual choice, flank steak.

The flank steak fared well, as expected. Mild filet, the choice in several recipes, could not stand up to the assertive Thai flavors. Sirloin and strip steaks both fared poorly because stir-fried meats tend to end up thoroughly cooked, making these cuts chewy and dry. The cheapest cut of all, the blade steak, was the surprise winner of the tasting. Generally, beef with the biggest flavor is tough, but blade steak is an exception. Cut from the chuck—the forequarter of the animal—this inexpensive, well-marbled cut delivered more than enough flavor to stand up to its spicy competition yet was more tender than flank steak when thoroughly cooked.

Here in the test kitchen, we marinate beef for Chinese stir-fries in soy sauce, a practice that seasons and tenderizes the meat. For this recipe, salty soy sauce would be replaced with the salty, fermented fish sauce that is traditional in Thai chile beef. The fish sauce simulated the briny flavors of the dried shrimp and shrimp paste listed in the original recipe, but something was missing. We dug deeper into a few Thai cookbooks and discovered that white pepper is a key ingredient—and for good reason. It is deeply spicy and penetrating. We added a smidgen (a little goes a long way) to the marinade, along with citrusy coriander. This was a huge hit with tasters and substantially boosted the complexity and sophistication of the dish, even though the meat was marinated for a mere 15 minutes.

We also added some of the sweet element in this dish to the marinade as a strategy for developing extra caramelization on the beef. Palm sugar is the traditional sweetener used in Thai cooking, but we found light brown sugar to be a perfect substitute. A mere teaspoon was just the right amount; any more caused scorching.

Tiny, narrow Thai bird chiles are the classic choice for this recipe, but we weren't about to hunt down exotic peppers for a Wednesday-night stir-fry. A taste test suggested that moderately hot serranos or milder jalapeños are the best stand-ins. (Insanely hot habanero chiles, tasting of tropical fruit, were admired by some but panned by most, who found the heat level punishing.)

After settling on the chiles, a new problem emerged: wild inconsistency in heat levels. Using a constant number of jalapeños, some stir-fries were flaming hot, while others didn't even send up sparks. We came up with a straightforward solution that can be used in any recipe calling for chiles. The trick is to use not one but two sources of heat, one of which is easily controlled (unlike fresh chiles). We tested cayenne and hot red pepper flakes, and both produced likeable results, but the winner was Asian chili-garlic paste, which provided a complex mix of flavors—spicy, toasty, and garlicky.

The last step in a stir-fry is to deglaze the hot pan with sauce ingredients. After many trials, we realized the importance of reintroducing every member of the Thai quartet at this stage. Adding fish sauce and brown sugar to the marinade boosted flavor, but the inclusion of both in the sauce really punched up the finished dish. For the sour component, both rice vinegar and tamarind paste fared better than lime juice—less acidity and more sweetness brought us closer to our goal of balanced flavors. We settled on rice vinegar because we usually keep it in our pantry.

The only remaining considerations were the fresh, raw ingredients added just before serving. Thai basil is traditional, contributing freshness and adding a cooling counterpoint to the chiles. Unfortunately, this herb can be hard to find (it was often out of stock at a large Asian supermarket here in Boston), so we made a substitution that we've used successfully in other recipes: fresh mint and cilantro. Used in tandem, they carry a complexity similar to that of Thai basil. The sweet basil that's readily available in most supermarkets is not a good substitute; Thai basil is tangier and spicier. We also added chopped peanuts for crunch. A fresh squirt of lime juice at the table was the final touch.

WHAT WE LEARNED: Blade steak is our cut of choice for the meat—its beefy flavor is bold enough to stand up to the other strong ingredients and it remains tender even when thoroughly cooked. Fish sauce, white pepper, and coriander add complexity to the marinade, while a bit of brown sugar not only adds sweetness but also helps to caramelize the beef. Serrano or jalapeño chiles make a good replacement for Thai bird chiles, and the addition of Asian chili-garlic paste allows you to control the heat. Rice vinegar adds the sour component and a combination of mint and cilantro makes a good substitute for hard-to-find Thai basil.

STIR-FRIED THAI-STYLE BEEF WITH CHILES AND SHALLOTS

Serves 4

If you cannot find blade steak, use flank steak; because flank steak requires less trimming, you will need only about 1¾ pounds. To cut a flank steak into the proper-sized slices for stir-frying, first cut the steak with the grain into 1½-inch strips, then cut the strips against the grain into ¼-inch-thick slices. White pepper lends this stir-fry a unique flavor; black pepper is not a good substitute. Serve the stir-fry with steamed jasmine rice.

beef and marinade

- ¾ teaspoon ground coriander
- ⅛ teaspoon ground white pepper
- 1 teaspoon light brown sugar
- 1 tablespoon fish sauce
- 2 pounds blade steaks, trimmed (see the illustrations on page 26)

stir-fry

- 2 tablespoons fish sauce
- 2 tablespoons rice vinegar
- 2 tablespoons water
- 1 tablespoon light brown sugar
- 1 tablespoon Asian chili-garlic paste
- 3 medium garlic cloves, minced or pressed through a garlic press (about 1 tablespoon)
- 3 tablespoons vegetable oil
- 3 serrano or jalapeño chiles, halved, seeds and ribs removed, chiles cut crosswise ⅛ inch thick
- 3 medium shallots, trimmed of ends, peeled, quartered lengthwise, and layers separated
- ½ cup fresh mint leaves, large leaves torn into bite-sized pieces
- ½ cup fresh cilantro leaves
- ⅓ cup roughly chopped roasted unsalted peanuts Lime wedges, for serving

1. FOR THE BEEF AND MARINADE: Combine the coriander, white pepper, brown sugar, and fish sauce in a large bowl. Add the beef, toss well to combine, and marinate 15 minutes.

2. FOR THE STIR-FRY: In a small bowl, stir together the fish sauce, vinegar, water, brown sugar, and chili-garlic paste until the sugar dissolves; set aside. In a small bowl, mix the garlic with 1 teaspoon of the oil; set aside. Heat 2 more teaspoons oil in a 12-inch nonstick skillet over high heat until smoking and add one-third of the beef to the skillet in an even layer. Cook, without stirring, until well browned, about 2 minutes, then stir and continue cooking until the beef is browned around the edges and no longer pink in the center, about 30 seconds. Transfer the beef to a medium bowl. Repeat with additional oil and the remaining meat in 2 more batches.

3. After transferring the last batch of beef to the bowl, reduce the heat to medium and add the remaining 2 teaspoons oil to the now-empty skillet and swirl to coat. Add the chiles and shallots and cook, stirring frequently, until beginning to soften, 3 to 4 minutes. Push the chile-shallot mixture to the sides of the skillet to clear the center; add the garlic-oil mixture to the clearing and cook, mashing the mixture with a spoon, until fragrant, about 15 seconds. Stir to combine the garlic with the chile-shallot mixture. Add the fish-sauce mixture to the skillet; increase the heat to high and cook until slightly reduced and thickened, about 30 seconds.

4. Return the beef and any accumulated juices to the skillet, toss well to combine and coat with the sauce. Stir in half of the mint and cilantro and serve immediately, sprinkling individual servings with portion of the peanuts and remaining herbs and passing the lime wedges separately.

GETTING IT RIGHT:
The Best Cut for Thai Chile Beef

We tested five cuts of beef—blade steak, filet, strip steak, sirloin steak, and flank steak—for this stir-fry. Blade steak was the clear winner, flank steak the runner-up. Tasters liked blade steak for its generous fat marbling, which gives this cut its tenderness and its "very beefy flavor." At just $3.69 per pound, blade steak was also the cheapest option tested. One minor inconvenience: The line of gristle running down the center should be removed (see page 26).

Blade Steak

PERFECT POTSTICKERS

WHAT WE WANTED: A foolproof recipe for great potstickers at home, with a light filling, the right wrapper, and the perfect mix of flavors.

We can count on one hand the times we've had truly great potstickers. At their best, these staples of Chinese dim sum are soft, savory pillows filled with tender ground meat and crunchy cabbage spiked with a pleasing hit of garlic, ginger, and soy. But the usual fare is nowhere near so glorious: dense, flavorless meatballs wrapped in a doughy blanket.

After sampling so many grim prospects, we assumed potstickers must require special talents or somehow be complicated. However, when we surveyed dozens of authentic potsticker recipes, we were surprised to find out how straightforward most were: Mix ground pork, cabbage, and seasonings; spoon it all into dumpling wrappers; then steam and fry in a wok. But time logged in the test kitchen revealed that tough fillings, bland flavors, and bad wraps are not just the bane of busy restaurants. Could we make this simple recipe more foolproof?

First, we needed to lighten up the filling. Ground pork has a tendency to form a dense, solid mass when it's shaped and cooked, a phenomenon test kitchen staffers began calling "the meatball effect." One bite into the dumpling and the small, dense "meatball" hidden inside would fall out onto the plate. Not very appetizing. The scallions and cabbage, folded into the pork, are meant to mitigate this problem by providing moisture and textural variety, but they just weren't doing the trick.

We tried increasing the amount of cabbage. Tasters loved the looser consistency of the filling but complained that the cabbage flavor and texture were too dominant. Forgoing the raw cabbage we'd been using, we tried sautéing it briefly to mellow the sharp flavor, but tasters missed the crunch. We tried salting and draining the cabbage to get rid of excess moisture, a trick we often use in the test kitchen.

This approach was a winner. After a 20-minute rest in the colander, the salted cabbage no longer dominated the filling, yet it still contributed a slightly bitter, crunchy edge.

Tasters continued to complain that the filling still seemed a bit hard and dense. This time we borrowed a trick from meat loaf cookery and added lightly beaten egg whites to the pork-cabbage mixture. The theory is that the egg whites will puff up as they cook, almost like a soufflé, incorporating tiny air bubbles into the otherwise compact ground meat. Sure enough, the outcome was perfect: we now had a light and tender filling.

A thick, doughy wrapper, often encountered in restaurant versions, was out, but the wrapper had to survive the cooking process, so it couldn't be paper-thin. Two ready-made versions are widely available (we were unwilling to make wrappers from scratch). Wonton wrappers—made

with flour, egg, and salt—are a bit thin for this application. We found the better choice to be gyoza wrappers. Made without egg, they are sturdier and hold up better when pan-fried. Also, the more substantial texture seemed a better match for the flavorful filling.

So far, we had been spooning the filling into the center of a round gyoza wrapper, folding it in half, then pressing the edges to seal. We placed the dumplings in a hot nonstick skillet seam side up to get a crisp, browned bottom, poured in some water, covered the pan, and let them steam until soft. Finally, we removed the cover to re-crisp the bottoms.

While mostly successful, this procedure did present a problem: The seam was drying out in the final stages of cooking. We increased the steaming time, but tasters still complained of toughness. The solution was easy. Instead of sautéing the dumplings standing straight up, we knocked them on their sides so that the seam would lie against the bottom of the pan. One side became crisp, while the rest of the dumpling remained pleasantly tender and chewy.

Placing 12 dumplings in a preheated skillet takes time and burns fingertips. By the time the last dumpling was in the pan, the first one was already browned, giving us an unevenly colored batch. The answer was to place the dumplings in a cold, lightly oiled skillet before turning on the burner. Success. To cook the second batch, we took the pan off the heat, wiped it out with bunched-up paper towels, and started the process again.

A few of the potstickers were not holding their filling well after steaming. While steaming one batch, we peeked under the lid and saw some of the dumplings ballooning out like blowfish. When we removed the lid, they seemed to deflate back to normal, but a few still had an air bubble trapped inside that kept the interior of the wrapper from making contact with (and clinging to) the filling. As a result, one bite would send the filling crashing down onto the plate. The solution? More diligence in removing all the air while filling the wrappers. Trying several approaches, we came up with the best sequence: Fold the meat-filled wrapper into a half-moon, pinch the middle closed, then carefully seal the remaining edges while lightly pressing the filling to ensure that no air remains.

All our potstickers needed now was the right dipping sauce—not the heavy-handed kind demanded by dumplings with ho-hum flavor but a simple, bracing blend of soy sauce, rice vinegar, mirin (a sweet Japanese cooking wine), and toasted sesame oil, with just a touch of chili oil to kick up the heat. Now our potstickers were not only light and flavorful but virtually foolproof as well.

WHAT WE LEARNED: Add more cabbage to the filling for a looser consistency, but salt and drain the cabbage first so its flavor isn't overwhelming. Adding lightly beaten egg white also helps keep the filling light and tender. Ready-made gyoza wrappers are convenient, sturdy, and hold up well to pan-frying. Sautéing the dumplings on their side rather than standing straight up creates a pleasing textural contrast, allowing one side to crisp while the rest remains tender and chewy.

POTSTICKERS WITH SCALLION DIPPING SAUCE

Makes 24 dumplings, serving 6 as first course

We prefer to use gyoza wrappers. You can substitute wonton wrappers, but the cooking time and recipe yield will vary (see the chart on page 128). Potstickers are best served hot from the skillet; we recommend that you serve the first batch immediately, then cook the second batch. To freeze potstickers, place filled, uncooked dumplings in the freezer in a single layer on a plate until frozen, then transfer to a storage bag. There's no need to thaw frozen potstickers; just proceed with the recipe. The dipping sauce can be prepared and refrigerated in a covered container up to 24 hours ahead of serving.

scallion dipping sauce

¼	cup soy sauce
2	tablespoons rice vinegar
2	tablespoons mirin
2	tablespoons water
1	teaspoon chili oil (optional)
½	teaspoon toasted sesame oil
1	medium scallion, minced

filling

3	cups minced napa cabbage leaves
¾	teaspoon salt
¾	pound ground pork
6	tablespoons minced scallions (about 4 medium)
⅛	teaspoon ground black pepper
4	teaspoons soy sauce
1½	teaspoons grated ginger
1	medium garlic clove, minced or pressed through a garlic press (about 1 teaspoon)
2	egg whites, lightly beaten
24	round gyoza wrappers (see note)
4	teaspoons vegetable oil

1. FOR THE DIPPING SAUCE: Combine all the ingredients in a bowl; set aside. (The dipping sauce can be refrigerated in a covered container overnight.)

2. FOR THE FILLING: Toss the cabbage and salt in a colander or mesh strainer set over a medium bowl. Let stand until the cabbage begins to wilt, about 20 minutes; press the cabbage gently with a rubber spatula to squeeze out excess moisture. Combine the cabbage and all the other filling ingredients in a medium bowl and mix thoroughly. Cover the bowl with plastic wrap and refrigerate until the mixture is cold, at least 30 minutes and up to 24 hours.

3. Place 4 wrappers flat on a work surface (keep the remaining wrappers covered with plastic wrap). Following photograph 1 on page 129, place one slightly rounded tablespoon of filling in the center of each wrapper. Using a pastry brush

---

GETTING IT RIGHT: Perfect Potstickers

During testing, we discovered that air left between wrapper and filling can cause "ballooning" during steaming, as the wrapper puffs up and away from the meat. The result? A messy first bite. Once we were mindful to press the air out before sealing the wrappers, our potstickers came out right every time.

Air = Messy Bite

No Air = Tidy Bite

or fingertip, moisten the edge of the wrapper with water. Fold each wrapper in half; starting in the center and working toward the outside edges, pinch the edges together firmly to seal, pressing out any air pockets (photographs 2 and 3). Position each dumpling on its side and gently flatten, pressing

down on the seam to make sure it lies flat against the work surface (photograph 4). Repeat to form 24 dumplings. (The filled dumplings can be refrigerated overnight in a single layer on a baking sheet wrapped tightly with plastic wrap.)

4. Add 2 teaspoons of the oil to a 12-inch nonstick skillet and quickly spread the oil with a paper towel to distribute evenly. Arrange 12 dumplings in the skillet, lying flat on one side, with all the seams facing the same direction, overlapping just slightly, if necessary. Place the skillet over medium-high heat and cook, without moving, until the dumplings are golden brown on the bottoms, about 5 minutes. Reduce the heat to low, add ½ cup water to the skillet, and cover immediately. Cook, covered, until most of the water is absorbed and the wrappers are slightly translucent, about 10 minutes. Uncover the skillet and increase the heat to medium-high; cook, without stirring, until the dumpling bottoms are well browned and crisp, 3 to 4 minutes more. Turn off the burner and slide the dumplings from the skillet onto a double layer of paper towels, browned side down, to blot excess oil.

5. Transfer the dumplings to a platter and serve immediately with the dipping sauce. Let the skillet cool until just warm, then wipe the skillet clean and repeat with the remaining dumplings and oil.

TECHNIQUE: Grating Ginger

Most cooks who use fresh ginger have scraped their fingers on the grater when the piece of ginger gets down to the tiny nub. Instead of cutting a small chunk of ginger off of a larger piece and then grating it, we like this method. Simply peel a small section of a large piece of ginger. Then grate the peeled portion, using the rest of the ginger as a handle, to keep fingers safely away from the grater's teeth.

TECHNIQUE: Wrapping Potstickers

The instructions below are for round wrappers, our preferred shape. If using square wrappers, fold diagonally into a triangle (step 2) and proceed with the recipe. For rectangular wrappers, fold in half lengthwise.

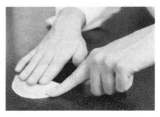

1. Fill

Place a rounded tablespoon of the filling in the center of each gyoza wrapper.

2. Fold

After moistening the edge of the wrapper, fold it in half to make a half-moon shape.

3. Pinch

With forefinger and thumb, pinch dumplings closed, pressing out any air pockets.

4. Flatten

Place dumpling on its side and press gently to flatten bottom.

EQUIPMENT CORNER:
Nonstick Skillets

YOU CAN SPEND UPWARD OF $150 ON A LARGE NONSTICK skillet. But the trouble is nonstick coatings peel and chip. We think it makes more sense to buy a reasonably priced pan (under $50) so it won't be so hard to part ways when the time comes. To find the best option, we gathered eight 12-inch nonstick skillets ranging in price from $17.99 to $49.99 and prepared omelets, cooked onions, and seared salmon, all the while judging the usability of each pan.

First, we considered the pans' design. Though all the pans sported a similar dark nonstick interior and all food released easily, other design features varied greatly. Exterior materials ranged from stainless steel and copper to enamel and anodized aluminum, though this didn't prove to be a factor in performance. Handle styles, on the other hand, could make or break the pan. We had two criteria: comfort and stability. In terms of comfort, we looked for handles that fit well in the hand and didn't get too hot during cooking. As for stability, we found welded or riveted handles to be sturdier than those that were simply screwed on.

Size also determined how well the pans fared. Sure, they're all 12-inch skillets (manufacturers measure pans across the top), but the cooking surface is considerably smaller. The diameter of the bottom of our top-rated skillet, the Cuisinart, was more than 2 inches larger than that of the low-rated Innova pan. That extra space means less crowding in the pan and more even cooking.

Some pans couldn't stand up to high heat. While all of the pans produced good omelets, several struggled with the salmon test, which was conducted over higher heat. The best pans turned out fish with beautiful brown crusts; the worst pans produced blackened or unevenly cooked salmon.

The ability to maintain even heat during prolonged cooking is a must as well. To measure this trait, we cooked diced onions in each pan for 10 minutes over medium heat. Our goal: soft, evenly cooked, golden brown onions with no signs of charring. More often than not, we got dark brown onions, indicating a faster cooking speed, or, even worse, onions that were browned on the edges yet still crunchy in the middle.

What did we find? Because testers put a premium on cooking space, the heavy-duty Cuisinart pan earned the top slot—but only by a hair.

Rating Inexpensive Nonstick Skillets

WE TESTED AND EVALUATED EIGHT 12-INCH NONSTICK SKILLETS RANGING IN PRICE FROM $17.99 TO $49.99. TESTS INCLUDED preparing omelets, cooking onions, and searing salmon. The pans are listed in order of preference. See www.americastestkitchen.com for up-to-date prices and mail-order sources for top-rated products.

RECOMMENDED
Cuisinart Chef's Classic Nonstick Hard Anodized Omelet Pan
$41.95

Bottom Diameter: 10½ inches

With the largest cooking area of all the skillets, this pan impressed us with its sturdiness and heft. Salmon was beautifully and evenly browned, though onions cooked at a moderately fast pace.

RECOMMENDED
Farberware Millennium Soft Touch Stainless Steel Omelet Pan
$39.95

Bottom Diameter: 9½ inches

Its rubber-coated handle was comfortable and stayed cool through most tests, though the bare metal closest to the pan got hot toward the end of the salmon test. Onions were beautifully cooked, though the salmon was somewhat unevenly browned.

RECOMMENDED
KitchenAid Gourmet Essentials Nonstick French Skillet
$39.95

Bottom Diameter: 9 inches

Heavy and sturdy, with solid riveted handles, this skillet impressed us with excellent crust formation on the salmon, though the onions were unevenly cooked. The rubber-coated handle is comfortable, and the grip opposite the main handle is a nice touch.

RECOMMENDED
Simply Calphalon Stainless Omelet Pan with Nonstick Interior
$49.99

Bottom Diameter: 8¾ inches

Though a bit oddly shaped, the contoured metal handle stayed cool through all of our cooking tests. Onions cooked unevenly, though salmon developed a nice brown crust. We wish this smallish pan was a little bit bigger.

RECOMMENDED WITH RESERVATIONS
Revere Copper Ellipse Nonstick Skillet
$49.49

Bottom Diameter: 9¾ inches

This pan aced every cooking test, but the hollow metal handle got very hot during cooking. Some complained about the weight of this heavy pan, too.

NOT RECOMMENDED
Circulon 2 Nonstick French Skillet
$49.99

Bottom Diameter: 9¼ inches

It wasn't the strange circular ridges inside of the pan (hence the name) that turned us off, it was the burnt onions and charred salmon. This lightweight pan simply couldn't compare with other pans that cost much less.

NOT RECOMMENDED
Innova Kitchen Basics Stainless Steel Frypan with Nonstick Interior
$39.99

Bottom Diameter: 8¼ inches

Omelets were unevenly browned and onions and salmon charred to an even black. The flimsy design, including a screwed-on plastic handle that got uncomfortably warm during cooking, inspired little confidence.

NOT RECOMMENDED
T-fal Initiatives 12.5" Nonstick Sauté Pan
$17.99

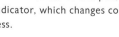

Bottom Diameter: 10¼ inches

The lightest pan in the group, the T-fal produced slightly charred onions and burned one side of the salmon. The screwed-on handle only accentuated the flimsiness of the pan, and we found the "Thermo-Spot" heat indicator, which changes color when the pan is hot, to be utterly useless.

Stir-Fried Chicken and Bok Choy with Crispy Noodle Cake **page 111**

Hot and Sour Soup **page 116**

132

Glazed All-Beef Meat Loaf **page 6**

Thick-Cut Pork Tenderloin Medallions **page 54**

134

Stir-Fried Thai-Style Beef with Chiles and Shallots **page 123**

Glazed Pork Chops **page 48**

"Stuffed" Roast Butterflied Chicken **page 38**

Carbonnade à la Flamande **page 25**

Chicken Parmesan **page 74**

Pepper-Crusted Filet Mignon **page 101**

Skillet-Roasted Potatoes **page 10**

Marinara Sauce **page 165**

Potstickers with Scallion Dipping Sauce **page 127**

143

Chicken Kiev **page 91**

Potatoes Lyonnaise **page 105**

Chicken Fajitas **page 149**

TEX-MEX
CHAPTER 13 *favorites*

We love good Tex-Mex, but depending on which part of the country you live in, chances are you'd be better off preparing it yourself at home. We wanted to take a look at two Tex-Mex favorites, chicken fajitas and huevos rancheros, and create authentic, tasty versions we could stand behind.

Chicken fajitas aren't as easy a proposition as beef fajitas. Beef, by nature, packs a lot more flavor, while chicken fajitas seem to rely on a host of condiments to mask its lack of flavor, or worse, its dry texture. We wanted tender, juicy chicken, and we wanted it well seasoned. We wanted the same for our vegetables—too many vegetables in fajitas are treated as a bland afterthought.

Huevos rancheros are the answer to a hungry man's (or woman's) breakfast. But too often we've stared at what looks like a dish of fried eggs crossed with nachos. First, we wanted to pare back this breakfast classic to its tasty essentials. We'd next need to focus on the fiery roasted salsa that typically is part of this dish. And without access to fresh corn tortillas, we needed to find a way to turn rubbery supermarket corn tortillas into a crisp, not greasy, base for our eggs. Last, we needed to figure out how to coordinate cooking the eggs with the other elements, so that everything comes together simultaneously—hot and fresh.

No matter where you live, with these recipes, you can enjoy authentically flavored Tex-Mex anytime.

CHICKEN FAJITAS

WHAT WE WANTED: Chicken fajitas that don't rely on a truckload of toppings for flavor—just smoky grilled vegetables and tender, well-seasoned pieces of chicken that taste great on their own.

With or without the sizzling cast-iron skillet, what passes for chicken fajitas in most restaurants these days is about as authentic as Belgian toaster waffles. Guacamole, sour cream, and salsa are slathered on in a weak attempt to mask the bland, soggy flavors of the underlying ingredients. We wanted to go back to the basics, a simple combination of smoky grilled vegetables and strips of chicken, wrapped up at the table in warm flour tortillas.

While the skirt steak in classic beef fajitas has no need for a marinade to add juiciness or flavor, boneless chicken breasts need all the help they can get. Starting with a mixture of lime juice, vegetable oil, garlic, salt, and pepper as our base, we tried several marinating methods. Grilling the chicken plain and tossing the cooked strips into the marinade (now really a sauce) left the chicken with only superficial flavor. Brining—soaking in a saltwater solution—seasoned the chicken and kept it juicy, but tasters found the meat too moist—waterlogged, even. "It might as well have been poached," said one. Making a "brinerade" (a cross between a brine and a marinade) by adding the marinade to a concentrated 2-cup brine only weakened the final flavors. Up to this point, soaking the chicken breasts directly in the marinade yielded the best results: tender browned chicken with bright, unadulterated tang. The high-acid mixture (⅓ cup lime juice and 4 tablespoons oil) not only added fresh citrus flavor notes but also reduced the marinating time to a mere 15 minutes—any longer and the meat started to "cook" in the acid, like a "chicken ceviche" of sorts.

Although moving in the right direction, the marinade still lacked smokiness and depth. After trying numerous (and unsuccessful) flavor additions, we finally hit upon Worcestershire sauce, an unlikely candidate for chicken but one that has some of the characteristics of *umami*, an overused and little-understood culinary term that refers to a fifth taste sensation beyond the familiar sweet, sour, bitter, and salty. (Some simply liken it to "meaty," while many think of umami as an unusual, sophisticated juxtaposition of flavors that provides a unique taste experience.) A mere tablespoon of Worcestershire was plenty to add another layer of saltiness and smoke without revealing its true identity. A bit of brown sugar helped round out the salty flavors, and minced jalapeño and cilantro added freshness.

Both green and red bell peppers gave the fajitas some needed contrast, not just in terms of color but in their bitter and sweet flavors. Quartering the peppers allowed them to lie flat on the grill and cook evenly on both sides. Onion wedges cooked unevenly, while rounds were both pretty and practical. We quickly discovered that whereas the chicken needed blazing-hot coals, the vegetables, which are more prone to burning, required more moderate heat. Placing them over medium-hot coals helped them brown nicely as well as cook through without burning.

To allow the chicken and vegetables to cook side by side at slightly different heat levels, we created a simple two-level fire. We started with a full chimney of ignited coals spread in a single layer on the bottom of the grill, then added another 20 unlit coals to just one side of the grill, and waited until that side became hot (the coals on the other half of the grill were just medium-hot). Once the cooking grate was in place, the chicken cooked for 8 to 10 minutes on the hotter side of the grill, while the vegetables cooked safely on the cooler side.

As for the flour tortillas, 8- to 10-inch rounds yielded too much excess tortilla; small (but not dainty) 6-inch tortillas were the perfect size. Heating each side of the tortillas for 20 brief seconds on the cooler end of the grill allowed them to puff up and lose their raw, gummy texture. Quickly wrapping the warmed tortillas in a clean kitchen towel or foil prevented them from becoming dry and brittle.

With the warm tortillas steaming in the wrapper and the requisite toppings ready to go, all that was left to do was separate the onion into rings and slice the bell peppers and chicken breasts into strips. But something was still missing. By tossing just a small amount of unused reserved marinade back in with the chicken strips and vegetables, we were able to give them a burst of fresh flavor. It wasn't until we'd eaten our way through half of a chicken fajita that we realized we'd forgotten to add any condiments.

WHAT WE LEARNED: Briefly marinate the chicken breasts in an acidic mixture of lime juice and oil (along with a little Worcestershire for smokiness and depth and some jalapeño and cilantro for brightness) for best flavor. A combination of green and red bell peppers creates a pleasing contrast of bitter and sweet. Use a two-level fire to allow the chicken and vegetables to cook at the same time (the vegetables cook on the cooler side of the grill so they don't burn). Toss a small amount of extra marinade with the chicken and vegetables just before serving for an added burst of flavor.

CHICKEN FAJITAS FOR A CHARCOAL GRILL
Serves 4 to 6

The chicken and vegetables in these fajitas are only mildly spicy. For more heat, include the jalapeño seeds and ribs when mincing. When you head outside to grill, bring along a clean kitchen towel or a large piece of foil in which to wrap the tortillas and keep them warm as they come off the grill. Although the chicken and vegetables have enough flavor to stand on their own, accompaniments (guacamole, salsa, sour cream, shredded cheddar or Monterey Jack cheese, and lime wedges) can be offered at the table. For our recipe for guacamole, see page 152. The chicken tenderloins can be reserved for another use or marinated and grilled along with the breasts.

⅓ cup juice from 3 or 4 limes

6 tablespoons vegetable oil

3 medium garlic cloves, minced or pressed through a garlic press (about 1 tablespoon)

1 tablespoon Worcestershire sauce

1½ teaspoons brown sugar

1 jalapeño chile, stemmed, seeded, and minced

1½ tablespoons minced fresh cilantro leaves
Salt and ground black pepper

3 boneless, skinless chicken breasts (about 1½ pounds), trimmed of fat, tenderloins removed, breasts pounded to ½-inch thickness

1 large red onion (about 14 ounces), peeled and cut into ½-inch-thick rounds (do not separate the rings)

1 large red bell pepper (about 10 ounces), quartered, stemmed, and seeded

1 large green bell pepper (about 10 ounces), quartered, stemmed, and seeded

8–12 (6-inch) flour tortillas

1. In a medium bowl, whisk together the lime juice, 4 tablespoons of the oil, garlic, Worcestershire, brown sugar, jalapeño, cilantro, 1 teaspoon salt, and ¾ teaspoon pepper.

Reserve ¼ cup of the marinade in a small bowl; set aside. Add another teaspoon salt to the remaining marinade. Place the chicken in the marinade; cover with plastic wrap and refrigerate 15 minutes. Brush both sides of the onion rounds and peppers with the remaining 2 tablespoons oil and season with salt and pepper.

2. Meanwhile, using a large chimney starter, ignite 6 quarts charcoal briquettes (about 90 briquettes) and burn until the coals are fully ignited, about 20 minutes. Empty the coals into the grill, spreading them in an even single layer; place an additional 20 unlit coals over the lit coals on one side of the grill to create a two-level fire. Position the cooking grate over the coals and heat the grate for 5 minutes; scrape clean with a grill brush.

3. Remove the chicken from the marinade and place the chicken smooth side down on the hotter side of the grill; discard the remaining marinade. Place the onion rounds and peppers (skin side down) on the cooler side of the grill. Cook the chicken until well browned, 4 to 5 minutes; using tongs, flip the chicken and continue grilling until the chicken is no longer pink when cut into with a paring knife or when an instant-read thermometer inserted into the thickest part registers 160 degrees, 4 to 5 minutes longer. Meanwhile, cook the peppers until spottily charred and crisp-tender, 8 to 10 minutes, turning once or twice as

needed; cook the onions until tender and charred on both sides, 10 to 12 minutes, turning every 3 to 4 minutes. When the chicken and vegetables are done, transfer them to a large plate and tent with foil to keep warm.

4. Working in 2 or 3 batches, place the tortillas in a single layer on the cooler side of the now-empty grill and cook until warm and lightly browned, about 20 seconds per side (do not grill too long or the tortillas will become brittle). As the tortillas are done, wrap them in a kitchen towel or large sheet of foil.

5. Separate the onions into rings and place in a medium bowl; slice the bell peppers lengthwise into ¼-inch strips and place in the bowl with the onions. Add 2 tablespoons reserved unused marinade to the vegetables and toss well to combine. Slice the chicken into ¼-inch strips and toss with the remaining 2 tablespoons reserved marinade in another bowl; arrange the chicken and vegetables on a large platter and serve with the warmed tortillas.

VARIATIONS
CHICKEN FAJITAS FOR A GAS GRILL

1. Follow the recipe for Chicken Fajitas for a Charcoal Grill through step 1.

2. Light all the burners on a gas grill and turn to high, cover, and heat the grill until hot, about 15 minutes; scrape the cooking grate clean with a grill brush. Leave one burner on high heat while turning the remaining burner(s) down to medium. Continue with the recipe from step 3, cooking the chicken and vegetables covered.

3. When the grill is empty, set all the burners to medium. Working in batches, if necessary, place the tortillas in a single layer on the grate and grill until warm and lightly browned, about 20 seconds per side. As they are done, wrap the tortillas in a kitchen towel or large sheet of foil. Proceed as directed in step 5 of Chicken Fajitas for a Charcoal Grill.

INDOOR CHICKEN FAJITAS

Our indoor version is just as delicious as our grilled recipe.

1. Follow the recipe for Chicken Fajitas for a Charcoal Grill through step 1.

2. Adjust one oven rack to the upper-middle position (about 8 inches from the heating element) and the second rack to the lower-middle position; heat the broiler.

3. Meanwhile, arrange the onion rounds and peppers (skin sides up) in a single layer on a rimmed baking sheet. Wrap the tortillas securely in foil in two packets, each containing half of the tortillas.

4. Remove the chicken from the marinade and pat dry with paper towels; discard the marinade. Heat 2 teaspoons oil in a 12-inch nonstick or cast-iron skillet over medium-high heat until just beginning to smoke. Swirl the oil to coat the skillet, then arrange the chicken smooth side down in the skillet in a single layer; cook without moving the chicken, until well browned, about 3 minutes. Using tongs, flip the chicken; continue to cook until the second sides

are well browned, about 2 minutes. Reduce the heat to medium and continue to cook, turning the chicken once or twice, until the chicken is no longer pink when cut into with a paring knife or when an instant-read thermometer inserted into the thickest part registers 160 degrees, 3 to 5 minutes longer. Transfer the chicken to a large plate and let rest 5 minutes.

5. While the chicken is cooking, place the baking sheet with the vegetables in the oven on the upper rack; place the tortilla packets on the lower rack. Broil the vegetables until spottily charred and the peppers are crisp-tender, 6 to 8 minutes. Using tongs, transfer the peppers to a cutting board. Flip the onion rounds and continue to broil until charred and tender, 2 to 4 minutes longer. Turn off the broiler and remove the onions, leaving the tortillas in the oven until needed. Proceed as directed in step 5 of Chicken Fajitas for a Charcoal Grill.

1. Start by slicing around the pit and through both ends with a chef's knife. With your hands, twist the avocado to separate the two halves.

2. Stick the blade of the chef's knife sharply into the pit. Lift the knife, twisting the blade to loosen and remove the pit.

3. Don't pull the pit off the knife with your hands. Instead, use a large wooden spoon to pry the pit off the knife safely.

TECHNIQUE: Dicing an Avocado

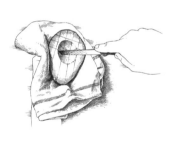

1. Use a dish towel to hold the avocado steady. Make ½-inch crosshatch incisions in the flesh of each avocado half with a dinner knife, cutting down to but not through the skin.

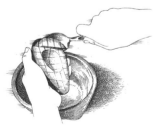

2. Separate the diced flesh from the skin using a spoon inserted between the skin and the flesh and gently scoop out the avocado cubes.

CHUNKY GUACAMOLE

Makes 2½ to 3 cups

Ripe avocados are essential here. We prefer Hass avocados (the variety with dark, pebbly skin), which are creamier and more flavorful than large, smooth-skinned varieties. If you like, garnish the guacamole with diced tomatoes and chopped cilantro just before serving. See the illustrations at left to pit and dice the avocados.

3   medium ripe avocados, preferably pebbly skinned Hass
2   tablespoons minced onion
1   medium garlic clove, minced or pressed through a garlic press (about 1 teaspoon)
1   small jalapeño chile, stemmed, seeded, and minced
¼   cup minced fresh cilantro leaves
     Salt
½   teaspoon ground cumin (optional)
2   tablespoons juice from 1 or 2 limes

1. Halve one of the avocados, remove the pit, and scoop the flesh into a medium bowl. Mash the flesh lightly with the onion, garlic, chile, cilantro, ¼ teaspoon salt, and cumin (if using) with the tines of a fork until just combined.

2. Halve, pit, and cube the remaining 2 avocados. Add the cubes to the bowl with the mashed avocado mixture.

3. Sprinkle the lime juice over the diced avocado and mix the entire contents of the bowl lightly with a fork until combined but still chunky. Adjust the seasonings with salt, if necessary, and serve. (The guacamole can be covered with plastic wrap, pressed directly onto the surface of the mixture, and refrigerated for up to 1 day. Return the guacamole to room temperature, removing the plastic wrap at the last moment, before serving.)

EQUIPMENT CORNER:
Nonstick Grill Pans

BASICALLY A SKILLET (OR SAUTÉ PAN) WITH RAISED RIDGES splayed across the cooking surface, a grill pan is designed to deliver grill marks similar to those made on an outdoor grill. But can a grill pan really replicate some of the flavor produced on a real grill?

First, we had to narrow the field: Grill pans come in a dizzying array of materials, shapes, and sizes. We purchased representatives of each and embarked on a pretesting marathon that included pounds and pounds of beef, vegetables, and fish. Shape and size turned out to matter much less than material, and it soon became apparent that aluminum was the only way to go. Why? The aluminum pans were lighter and so much easier to handle, and they produced more distinct grill marks than their cast-iron counterparts. The full testing, then, would focus on aluminum, nonstick-coated grill pans. An afternoon of shopping yielded eight models, with prices ranging from $40 to over three times as much.

To gauge how well the pans produced attractive grill marks, we needed to cook something with a fairly uniform surface. Boneless chicken breasts? Eggplant planks? Not quite the uniformity we were looking for. But a trip to the home-improvement store produced exactly what we needed: standard two-by-four pine boards cut into 8-inch lengths. Back in the test kitchen, we spent two days burning grill marks into wood, as colleagues looked on in disbelief. It was an odd notion, but it worked. We ended up with an equitable and permanent memento of each pan's performance. In general, the pans with wider ridges produced wider, deeper grill marks than pans with narrow ridges. Illustrative as the charred lumber was, we figured we'd better cook some real food, too. Full testing of the eight pans with hamburgers, flank steak, salmon fillets, swordfish steaks, chicken breast cutlets, panini (Italian-style grilled sandwiches), and sliced zucchini taught us a few things about cooking with grill pans.

First, to develop appetizing grill marks, the pan must be preheated. Second, it's best to use a modicum of fat. In our tests, a light coating of oil resulted in nicer stripes than dry food in a dry pan. (Besides, for safety's sake you should not overheat an empty nonstick pan.) Third, cooking foods with wide, flat surfaces will help any grill pan do its best. For instance, broad, flat swordfish steaks developed deeper, more consistent grill marks than salmon fillets, which have naturally uneven surfaces.

All of our winners shared one trait: the design of the ridges. Our favorite pans had wide ridges ($5/16$ inch or more), which begat wide, substantial grill marks on the food—resulting in larger areas of caramelization and, thus, flavor. In contrast, pans with the narrowest ridges ($3/16$ inch or less) produced thinner, less-developed marks.

Finally, we noticed a fairly consistent correlation between performance and the method used to construct the ridges. There are two basic approaches: Either the ridges are punched into the metal from the bottom, leaving indentations open to the heat source, or the pan is cast from molten metal, meaning that the ridges are formed by the mold. Cast pans have a solid bottom surface, without exposed indentations. In general, the pans with open indentations delivered better grill marks. Why? The interior of each ridge was directly exposed to the heat source, which facilitated heat transfer. (The exception to this rule is the Swiss Diamond, which has a solid bottom surface but was also the heaviest pan in the group.)

The recommended grill pans had proved their ability to dress a variety of foods for success in dark, even, nicely charred stripes. But did they deliver any advantage in terms of flavor? Happily, yes—though the grill pans could not caramelize food as efficiently as an outdoor grill and, hence, provided a subtler grill flavor. Are grill pans, then, worth buying? Certainly, they can't replace a real grill, but for wintertime in the Snow Belt, our tests proved that a grill pan can make a practical substitute. And with its modest $40 price tag, wide ridges, and easily cleaned nonstick surface, the Calphalon grill pan is our top choice.

Rating Nonstick Grill Pans

WE TESTED EIGHT NONSTICK ALUMINUM GRILL PANS (SQUARE SHAPED, WHENEVER POSSIBLE) AND EVALUATED THEM according to ridge width, performance (color, evenness, and quality of grill marks), and ease of cleanup. Tests were performed over gas burners on the professional-grade ranges in our test kitchen. The pans are listed in order of preference. See www.americastestkitchen.com for up-to-date prices and mail-order sources for top-rated products.

RECOMMENDED

Simply Calphalon Nonstick 13" Round Grill Pan
$39.95

The wide-body of the lineup turned out an impressive flank steak, with wide, nicely developed grill marks. Best-in-class pricing and generous cooking area pushed it to the top slot.

RECOMMENDED

All-Clad LTD. 11" Square Grille Pan
$69.99

Matched the other recommended pans in most ways, but stood out in none. Unevenly marked zucchini cost it a crucial performance point.

RECOMMENDED

Pampered Chef Professional Cookware 11" Square Grill Pan
$95.00

Gorgeous swordfish emerged from this pan, drawing a crowd of admirers, forks in hand and poised to pounce. Nary a misstep in any test. Available only from Pampered Chef sales reps.

RECOMMENDED WITH RESERVATIONS

Berndes 12" Square Grill Pan
$99.95

Closely spaced ridges are to thank for faint, uninspiring grill marks—and utter lack of charred flavor—in nearly every test.

RECOMMENDED

Anolon Advanced 12" Covered Deep Round Grill Pan
$49.95

An even-tempered performer that won't break the bank. Impressive showing on the burgers, swordfish, chicken cutlets, and zucchini.

RECOMMENDED WITH RESERVATIONS

Look 10½" Nonstick Square Grill Pan
$90.00

Grill marks? Pass the magnifying glass, please. Choked on both heavy and light searing tasks, with grill marks as disappointing on the fish as they were on the zucchini.

RECOMMENDED

Swiss Diamond 11" Square Grill Pan
$129.99

A heavy-searing star that produced beautiful grill marks. Its weight helped it overcome the cast design (we generally preferred hollow ridges).

RECOMMENDED WITH RESERVATIONS

Scanpan Classic 10½" Nonstick Square Grill Pan
$104.95

Tall, tight ridges made it harder to clean than some, and for what? Faint grill marks and a significantly lightened wallet.

HUEVOS RANCHEROS

WHAT WE WANTED: Authentic-tasting huevos rancheros translated for the American table using only supermarket staples.

Huevos rancheros, or "rancher-style eggs," is a dish born of ease and convenience: a quick, satisfying meal that makes use of leftover salsa and corn tortillas to serve as a simple Mexican breakfast alongside hearty refried beans. While there are many variations on this theme, most often the eggs are quickly fried, slipped onto a corn tortilla base, then napped with a fiery, roasted tomato-chile salsa.

North of the border, it's a different story: The huevos rancheros found on American brunch menus more closely resemble heaping plates of nachos. The eggs are lost under any number of untraditional ingredients—meat, gobs of melted cheese, shredded lettuce, and slices of avocado—the tortillas become soggy, and the flavors are muddied.

But even with an authentic recipe, making this dish at home is no less problematic when the cook is faced with mediocre supermarket ingredients such as pale, mealy tomatoes and rubbery packaged tortillas. We wanted to do right by this dish and produce a version as close to authentic as we could with the materials at hand.

Salsa is the star in most authentic versions, so that's where we began. We tried oblong plum tomatoes as well as the usual round orbs. The plum tomatoes had slightly more complexity than the round tomatoes and a more compact, less watery texture. In an effort to increase their flavor, we turned to roasting the tomatoes, which did the trick.

While we were at it, we wondered if the chiles and onions would also benefit from roasting. Indeed, roasting improved their flavor, adding a deeper, sweeter intensity. Heady garlic was a welcome addition to this mix, as were cumin for its nutty flavor and cayenne pepper for extra zing. For more color and depth of flavor, we first coated all the ingredients with a tablespoon of tomato paste. Once we had

given the roasted vegetables a quick turn in the food processor, we added lime juice and fresh cilantro for brightness. As a final touch, we reserved one jalapeño and added it, finely chopped, at the end for a zesty, clean chile flavor.

After the rigmarole of roasting the salsa ingredients (though it was certainly worth the effort), we were chagrined to find that the simple fried-egg preparation we were expecting turned out to be a sloppy mess on the plate. Four gently fried eggs looked beautiful in the skillet but, once separated, appeared haphazard and irregular on top of a round tortilla—if we didn't break the yolks getting them there. While poaching the eggs is not traditional, we had seen this technique in a few recipes; indeed, these eggs were easily (and neatly) scooped out of their poaching liquid.

As we monitored our two adjacent cooking vessels full of bubbling liquid—poaching eggs and simmering salsa—we realized we might be able to make things even easier. Adding all the hot salsa to a skillet, we scooped out four small wells and cracked an egg into each, then fit a lid over the top for even cooking. We finally achieved the look we were after, and even better, the eggs benefited from the flavor boost—not to mention one less pot to wash.

Most authentic recipes call for fresh, handmade corn tortillas. We were stuck with all-but-stale supermarket versions. Some recipes attempt to "soften" the tortillas with a five-second shallow fry, but this produced sodden, greasy results. Instead, we brushed the tortillas lightly with oil, sprinkled with a little salt, and toasted them until golden brown at 450 degrees. These tortillas were crisp and dry—a perfect foil for the soft, creamy poached eggs and the deep, roasted flavors of the fiery salsa.

WHAT WE LEARNED: Get great flavor out of average supermarket tomatoes by roasting them. For ease and an attractive presentation, cook the eggs by nestling them into the salsa while it simmers. Get the best results from supermarket tortillas by toasting them briefly in the oven.

HUEVOS RANCHEROS

Serves 2 to 4

To save time, make the salsa the day before and store it in the refrigerator. If you like, serve with Refried Beans (below right).

- 3 jalapeño chiles, halved, seeds and ribs removed
- 1½ pounds ripe plum tomatoes (about 8 medium), cored and halved
- ½ medium yellow onion, cut into ½-inch wedges
- 2 medium garlic cloves, peeled
- 1 tablespoon tomato paste
  Salt
- 3 tablespoons vegetable oil
- ½ teaspoon ground cumin
- ⅛ teaspoon cayenne
- 3 tablespoons minced fresh cilantro leaves
  Ground black pepper
- 1–2 tablespoons juice from 1 or 2 limes, plus an additional lime cut into wedges, for serving
- 4 corn tortillas
- 4 large eggs

1. FOR THE SALSA: Adjust an oven rack to the middle position and heat the oven to 375 degrees. Mince one jalapeño and set aside. In a medium bowl, combine the tomatoes, remaining jalapeños, onion, garlic, tomato paste, 1 teaspoon salt, 2 tablespoons of the oil, cumin, and cayenne; toss to mix thoroughly. Place the vegetables cut side down on a rimmed baking sheet. Roast until the tomatoes are tender and the skins begin to shrivel and brown, 35 to 45 minutes; cool on the baking sheet for 10 minutes. Increase the oven heat to 450 degrees. Using tongs, transfer the roasted onion, garlic, and jalapeños to the workbowl of a food processor. Process until almost completely broken down, about 10 seconds, pausing halfway through to scrape down the sides of the bowl with a rubber spatula. Add the tomatoes and process until the salsa is slightly chunky, about 10 seconds more. Add 2 tablespoons of the cilantro, reserved minced jalapeño, salt, pepper, and lime juice to taste.

2. FOR THE TORTILLAS: Brush both sides of each tortilla lightly with the remaining tablespoon oil, sprinkle both sides with salt, and place on a clean baking sheet. Bake until the tops just begin to color, 5 to 7 minutes; flip the tortillas and continue to bake until golden brown, 2 to 3 minutes more.

3. FOR THE EGGS: Meanwhile, bring the salsa to a gentle simmer in a 12-inch nonstick skillet over medium heat. Remove from the heat and make four shallow wells in the salsa with the back of a large spoon. Break 1 egg into a cup, then carefully pour the egg into the well in the salsa; repeat with the remaining eggs. Season each egg with salt and pepper to taste, then cover the skillet and place over medium-low heat. Cook until desired doneness: 4 to 5 minutes for runny yolks, 6 to 7 minutes for set yolks.

4. TO SERVE: Place the tortillas on serving plates; gently scoop one egg onto each tortilla. Spoon the salsa around each egg, covering the tortillas, but leaving a portion of the eggs exposed. Sprinkle with the remaining cilantro and serve with the lime wedges.

REFRIED BEANS

Makes about 3 cups

- ¾ cup low-sodium chicken broth
- 2 (15-ounce) cans pinto beans, drained and rinsed
- ½ teaspoon salt
- 3 slices (about 3 ounces) bacon, minced
- 1 small onion, chopped fine (about ¾ cup)
- 1 large jalapeño, stemmed, seeded, and minced (about 2 tablespoons)
- ½ teaspoon ground cumin
- 2 medium garlic cloves, minced or pressed through a garlic press (about 2 teaspoons)
- 2 tablespoons minced fresh cilantro leaves
- 2 teaspoons juice from 1 lime

1. Process the broth, all but 1 cup of the beans, and the salt in a food processor until smooth, about 15 seconds, scraping down the sides of the bowl with a rubber spatula if necessary. Add the remaining beans and process until slightly chunky, about ten 1-second pulses.

2. Cook the bacon in a 12-inch nonstick skillet over medium heat until the bacon just begins to brown and most of the fat has rendered, about 4 minutes; transfer to a small bowl lined with a strainer; discard the bacon and add 1 tablespoon bacon fat back to the skillet. Increase the heat to medium-high, add the onion, jalapeño, and cumin and cook until softened and just starting to brown, 3 to 5 minutes. Stir in the garlic and cook until fragrant, about 30 seconds. Reduce the heat to medium, stir in the pureed beans and cook until thick and creamy, about 4 to 6 minutes. Off the heat stir in the cilantro and lime juice and serve.

TECHNIQUE: Better Huevos Rancheros

Roast

Slow-roasting improved the flavor of supermarket tomatoes while intensifying the other salsa ingredients.

Toast

Crisping store-bought tortillas in the oven yielded the best texture—light and crispy, not tough or greasy.

Poach

Poaching the eggs in small wells made in the salsa improved their flavor and left us with just one pot to wash.

TASTING LAB: Refried Beans

TRADITIONAL FRIJOLES REFRITOS START WITH DRIED PINTO beans that are cooked, "fried well" in lard, then mashed. They make a terrific accompaniment to Huevos Rancheros (opposite) and most other Tex-Mex fare. Making your own refried beans is not rocket science, but it is certainly time-consuming, so many cooks opt for a store-bought version instead.

We sampled six brands of refried beans to determine if any were worth a spot beside our huevos rancheros. Only two brands, Old El Paso Traditional and Ortega, use lard (the rest use vegetable oil), but to our tasters, lard offered no advantage in flavor or texture.

As for flavor, Taco Bell was described as "well-seasoned," and tasters found that Goya had an "earthy," straightforward flavor. Otherwise, flavor fell short among the other brands.

Texture, however, turned out to be key—Spackle is still Spackle, even if it contains garlic and onions. But even the best brands mustered only enough points to earn our "Recommended with Reservations" rating. And whatever you do, steer clear of dehydrated, instant refried beans. These were consistently stale and unappealing.

BEST SUPERMARKET REFRIED BEANS

Although none of the supermarket refried beans could compare to homemade, and no brand tested earned higher than a "Recommended with Reservations" rating, Taco Bell Home Originals Refried Beans were described by tasters as "well seasoned" and "super smooth."

Jack explains that there is indeed a difference among brands of canned whole tomatoes—some are bland and mushy, while others are juicy, firm-textured, and flavorful.

ITALIAN classics

CHAPTER 14

Just when we think we've become familiar with every Italian recipe under the sun, we're pleasantly surprised to come across a dish we'd somehow overlooked. Take chicken francese. It's true that this Italian-style chicken cutlet dish isn't as well known as chicken parmigiana or chicken Marsala, but it's no less delicious. Coated with a thin eggy crust, the cutlets are served in a light, lemony white wine sauce. With just a few simple elements, it's hard to believe that such dish can go wrong, but versions we tried proved otherwise. In some recipes, the egg crust was unappetizingly thick and tough, or turned soggy once coated with the sauce. The sauces we tried weren't much better. While we couldn't detect any lemon flavor in some, others made us pucker, or the wine was too overpowering, giving the sauce an unpleasant boozy flavor. We aimed to conquer these issues and turn out a lemony cutlet dish that we'd want to incorporate into our Italian classics repertoire to make again and again.

Another Italian classic, the rich tomato sauce marinara, is not a new discovery, but it's one worth a second look in terms of simplifying. The hallmark of this sauce is a depth of flavor achieved by hours of cooking, but what if we didn't have all day? After all, for the modern cook, an all-day marinara just isn't a reasonable option. We set out to create an authentic marinara with complex flavors without the hours of work involved.

Join us as we resurrect one Italian classic and streamline another.

CHICKEN FRANCESE

WHAT WE WANTED: Tender chicken cutlets with a soft, eggy coating and a generous amount of silky, well-balanced sauce full of bright lemon flavor.

You've probably never heard of chicken francese. This simple but refined dish consists of pan-fried chicken cutlets with a light but substantial eggy coating and a bright lemony sauce. Although its name hints at a rich pedigree—one account claims that Italians once made this dish for Napoléon Bonaparte—there is no classic French or Italian version. Instead, chicken francese is most strongly identified with Italian-American cooking in and around New York City. It's a humble dish with a fancy name.

Hazy background aside, we found that chicken francese was related to the familiar but loosely defined group of thin-cut chicken (and sometimes veal) dishes that includes scaloppine, parmigiana, Milanese, piccata, and Marsala. But francese also has much in common with a well-known egg-coated breakfast dish: French toast. While many of the other thin-cut chicken dishes are dusted with flour or shrouded in crisp bread crumbs, chicken francese has a soft, rich, eggy coating. The silky lemon sauce nestles into nooks in this soft coating so that each bite reveals just the right balance of chicken, coating, and sauce. Although this dish has fallen out of favor, it's simple, it's quick, and it's chicken—three things almost every home cook appreciates.

For the chicken, we started with untrimmed and unpounded chicken breast halves. These proved too thick; the egg coating burned before the meat cooked through. Store-bought cutlets (roughly half the thickness of breast halves) were ragged and uneven, causing the edges of the cutlets and the coating to dry out by the time the chicken cooked through. We decided to trim and pound the breast halves into cutlets ourselves to get the evenness and thickness we wanted. By trimming off the tenderloins and slicing the breasts in half horizontally, we were able to get the

thickness close to our desired ¼ inch. A few whacks with a meat pounder got us all the way there. Yes, this step did take five extra minutes, but the results were far superior to any we got with supermarket cutlets.

In all the recipes we could find, some combination of eggs and flour was used to create the soft coating. Although the ingredients were set, the method was not. Some recipes dredged the chicken in flour first, some in egg first, and still others combined the eggs and flour to create a batter. The batter approach seemed promising because it was simpler, but the resulting coating was tough and rubbery. Adding baking soda and/or baking powder to the mixture for lightness also added uncharacteristic crispness and an off-flavor. Some batter recipes called for water or milk. Milk made the coating more tender, but the batter became too thin and dripped off the chicken.

We abandoned the batter approach and methodically tested the other options. In the end, dredging the cutlets in flour, dipping them in beaten egg, and then adding a second coating of flour worked best. This technique guaranteed that the coating would stay put and, because the last coating consisted of flour (as opposed to bread crumbs, for instance), the finished cutlets were delicate and soft. We wondered if the eggs would benefit from a little milk (something that had worked in the tests with a batter coating). Sure enough, just a couple of tablespoons all but guaranteed a tender—not rubbery—coating.

Sauces made with whole lemon slices were unbearably bitter because of the zest and pith. We quickly skipped over them in favor of fresh lemon juice, augmented with wine and chicken broth. Although not traditional in chicken francese, we also tested garlic, onion, and shallot. Only onion made the cut, providing a mellow, sweet background flavor that balanced the lemon while still letting the citrus lead the way.

Thin, watery sauces saturated the coating, making it peel right off; a thicker sauce, we reasoned, would cling to (but not penetrate) the coating we had worked so hard to attain. Reducing the wine, broth, and lemon juice was not sufficient. Finishing the sauce with butter or cornstarch helped to thicken it, but neither was perfect. The best solution was to make a classic roux of flour and butter cooked together. The roux was a more reliable thickener than either butter or cornstarch alone.

Cutlets sautéed in butter tasted better than cutlets sautéed in oil, but the butter burned. Adding some oil to the butter raised its smoke point without diluting its flavor impact. By using a nonstick skillet, we could get away with just a tablespoon each of oil and butter for each batch of cutlets. To make sure that the second batch looked as nice as the first, we found it helpful to wipe out the pan between batches. Once the second batch was done and in the oven, we wiped out the pan again and finished the lemon sauce.

At this point, we thought we were done. Tasters loved the sauce and the chicken. Maybe they loved the sauce too much—they wanted more. At first we thought, no problem, just make more sauce. But additional lemon juice, wine, and broth needed additional time to simmer and reduce. By the time the sauce was done, the cutlets in the oven had dried out. The solution was switching the recipe around and starting with the sauce, then cooking the chicken. Is it unconventional to make the sauce before cooking the chicken? You bet. But now we could deliver on the promise of this "lost" recipe.

WHAT WE LEARNED: For cutlets of even thickness, avoid packaged cutlets and instead pound your own cutlets from chicken breasts. Dredging the chicken in flour, then into a mixture of egg and milk, and then coating in flour again gives the cutlets a soft, tender coating. Sautéing the cutlets in butter augmented by oil prevents the butter from burning without diluting its flavor. A combination of fresh lemon juice, white wine, and chicken broth yields a sauce with bright flavors, and thickening the sauce with flour and butter gives it a silky consistency that clings to, but doesn't turn, the chicken's coating soggy.

CHICKEN FRANCESE
Serves 4

The chicken breasts will be easier to slice into cutlets if you freeze them for about 15 minutes until they are firm but not fully frozen. To slice in half, place one hand on top of a chicken breast to secure it, hold a chef's knife parallel to the cutting board, and slice through the middle of the breast horizontally. Note that just 1 tablespoon of the butter for the sauce is used in step 2; the remaining 2 tablespoons are used in step 5. The sauce is very lemony—for less tartness, reduce the amount of lemon juice by about 1 tablespoon.

sauce

- 3 tablespoons unsalted butter
- 1 very small onion, minced (about ⅓ cup)
- 1 tablespoon unbleached all-purpose flour
- ½ cup dry white wine or vermouth
- ⅓ cup juice from 2 lemons
- 2¼ cups low-sodium chicken broth
  Salt and ground black pepper

chicken

- 1 cup unbleached all-purpose flour
  Salt and ground black pepper
- 2 large eggs
- 2 tablespoons milk
- 4 boneless, skinless chicken breast halves (6 to 8 ounces each), tenderloins removed, breasts trimmed of excess fat, halved horizontally (see note), and pounded to an even ¼-inch thickness
- 2 tablespoons unsalted butter
- 2 tablespoons olive oil
- 2 tablespoons minced fresh parsley leaves

1. Adjust an oven rack to the middle position and heat the oven to 200 degrees. Set a wire rack on a rimmed baking sheet and place the sheet in the oven.

2. FOR THE SAUCE: Heat 1 tablespoon of the butter in a medium nonreactive saucepan over medium heat. When the foaming subsides, add the onion and cook, stirring occasionally, until translucent, 2 to 3 minutes. Add the flour and stir until light golden brown, about 1 minute. Whisk in the wine, lemon juice, and broth; increase the heat to high and bring to a boil, whisking constantly. Lower the heat to medium-high and cook, whisking occasionally, until the mixture is reduced to 1½ cups, 10 to 15 minutes. Strain the sauce through a mesh strainer, return to the saucepan, and set aside.

3. FOR THE CHICKEN: Set a second wire rack on a second rimmed baking sheet on the counter. Whisk together the flour, 1 teaspoon salt, and ¼ teaspoon pepper in a pie plate. In a second pie plate, whisk the eggs and milk until combined. Season both sides of each cutlet with salt and pepper. Using tongs and working with 2 cutlets at a time, coat the cutlets in seasoned flour; shake off the excess flour. Transfer the cutlets to the egg mixture; coat evenly and let the excess run off. Return the cutlets to the seasoned flour; coat evenly and shake off the excess flour. Place the coated cutlets on the wire rack on the counter.

4. Heat 1 tablespoon each butter and oil in a 12-inch nonstick skillet over medium-high heat; when the foaming subsides, place 4 cutlets in the skillet. Cook until well browned, 1½ to 2 minutes. Carefully flip the cutlets and continue to cook until lightly browned on the second side, 30 to 60 seconds. Transfer the chicken to the wire rack in the oven. Wipe out the skillet with paper towels. Repeat, using the remaining 1 tablespoon each butter and oil to cook the remaining cutlets in the now-empty skillet. After transferring the chicken to the oven, wipe out the skillet with paper towels.

5. TO FINISH THE SAUCE AND SERVE: Transfer the sauce to the now-empty skillet and set over low heat; cook until the sauce is heated through, about 1 minute. Whisk in the remaining 2 tablespoons butter and season with salt and pepper to taste. Remove the baking sheet with the chicken from the oven and transfer 4 cutlets to the skillet; turn to coat with the sauce, then transfer each serving (2 cutlets) to individual plates. Repeat with the remaining cutlets. Spoon 2 tablespoons additional sauce over each serving and sprinkle with the parsley. Serve immediately, passing the extra sauce separately.

VARIATION

CHICKEN FRANCESE WITH TOMATO AND TARRAGON
Fresh tomato and tarragon lend a lively complexity to the lemon sauce in this variation.

Follow the recipe for Chicken Francese, adding 1 sprig fresh parsley and 1 sprig fresh tarragon to the sauce along with the wine, lemon juice, and broth in step 2. Discard the herbs after the sauce is reduced. Add 1 medium tomato, seeded and cut into ¼-inch dice (about ¾ cup), to the sauce before spooning additional sauce over each serving in step 5. Substitute 1 tablespoon minced fresh tarragon for 1 tablespoon of the minced fresh parsley.

GETTING IT RIGHT: Cast of Coatings

Thick and Eggy   **Thin and Insubstantial**   **Just Right**

A batter coating (made by mixing flour and eggs) was too thick and rubbery (left). A dusting of flour and a dip in beaten egg made a coating that was too thin (center). We obtained the best results by dusting cutlets with flour, dipping them in eggs beaten with milk, and coating them again with flour (right). This coating remained soft and tender but was sturdy enough to stand up to the lemon sauce.

MARINARA SAUCE

WHAT WE WANTED: A homemade tomato sauce with complex, fresh flavors made in less than an hour.

There's something great about a quick tomato sauce: fast, furious, and fresh. But what a quick sauce offers in convenience it lacks in the complexity of a slowly simmered tomato sauce, the best known of which may be marinara.

Unfortunately, complexity of flavor means lots of time in the kitchen, which is in short supply on a Tuesday night. Our goal was to produce a multidimensional sauce in less than an hour, starting the clock the moment we entered the kitchen and stopping it when dinner was on the table. Weeding through hundreds of marinara recipes, we settled on testing not only a variety of "quick" versions but also some that were cooked for longer than an hour. The differences were readily apparent. The quick sauces were generally thin and lacked depth of flavor. The long-cooked sauces got the complexity right, but most relied on an ambitious laundry list of ingredients to achieve it—not to mention a lot of time. The sauce we were after had to capture some of these robust flavors within the confines of fairly quick cooking.

Because prime fresh tomatoes are available for such a limited time during the year, we opted for canned. But canned tomatoes take up nearly half an aisle at the supermarket. Which variety should we choose?

Crushed, pureed, and diced tomatoes offered the ultimate ease in sauce making: Open can, dump contents into pan. But all three options have downsides. Pureed tomatoes go into the can already cooked, which imparts a stale, flat flavor to the final sauce. Crushed tomatoes are generally packed in tomato puree: same problem. With these, the sauces came out tasting like unremarkable homemade versions of the jarred spaghetti sauces sold at the supermarket. With canned diced tomatoes, the problem was texture, not flavor. In the past, we've learned that manufacturers treat diced tomatoes with calcium chloride to keep them from turning to mush and losing their shape. That's fine for many dishes, but for recipes in which a smooth consistency is desired, calcium chloride does its job too well, making the tomatoes harder to break down—and the resulting sauces oddly granular.

The only choice left, then, was canned whole tomatoes. (While whole tomatoes are also treated with calcium chloride, the chemical has direct contact with a much smaller percentage of the tomato.) The big drawback of using whole tomatoes in a sauce is that they have to be cut up. Chopping them on a cutting board was a mess. The solution was to dump the tomatoes into a strainer over a bowl and then hand-crush them, removing the hard core and any stray bits of skin.

That's when we made the first of several decisions that would enable us to get long-simmered complexity in a short time. Most marinara recipes call for simply adding a can (or two) of tomatoes to the pot, juice and all—and some even call for throwing in a can of water. Now that we were separating the solids from the juice anyway, why not experiment with adding less of the reserved liquid? The trick worked: By adding only 2½ cups of the drained juice from two cans of whole tomatoes (rather than the full 3½ cups we had collected) and omitting the extra water, we managed to cut the simmering time by almost 20 minutes.

Up until now we had been following the standard marinara procedure of sautéing aromatics (onions and garlic) in olive oil in a saucepan before adding the tomatoes, liquid, and flavorings, then simmering. That's fine if you have all day, but we had only an hour. So we switched from a saucepan to a skillet, hoping the greater surface area would encourage faster evaporation and, thus, faster concentration of flavors.

It was faster, all right—down to just under an hour— but we felt that the sauce could use gutsier tomato flavor. Not only was the solution simple, but it was the key step in

giving our quick sauce the complexity of a long-simmered one. Before adding the liquids and simmering, we sautéed the tomato meats until they glazed the bottom of the pan. Only then did we add the liquids, a normally routine step that, by essentially deglazing the pan, added crucial flavor to our sauce.

With the tomato flavor under control, it was time to develop more depth of flavor. Onions added a pleasant sweetness, but carrots, although sweet, added an earthy flavor that diminished that of the tomatoes. Sugar, added at the end of cooking, proved to be the working solution to balance the flavors: too much and our sauce began to taste like it came out of a jar; too little and the acidity overwhelmed the other flavors. Tasters loved the robust, complex flavor of red wine, and a mere ⅓ cup was just the right amount. But not just any bottle: Wines with a heavy oak flavor rated lower than those with little to no oak presence. (Chianti and Merlot scored particularly high marks.)

We now had a good marinara ready to ladle and serve in less than an hour—about half the time of many recipes. Could we further bolster the complexity without adding minutes? On a hunch, we tried reserving a few of the uncooked canned tomatoes and adding them near the end

of cooking. When we served this sauce alongside the earlier version, tasters were unanimous in their preference for the new sauce; just six tomatoes pureed into the sauce at the end added enough brightness to complement the deeper profile of the cooked sauce.

So far the sauce had little flavor from herbs beyond oregano. Fresh basil, also added at the end, contributed a floral aroma that complemented the sauce's careful balance of sweet and acid. Adjusting the salt and pepper and adding extra-virgin olive oil rounded things out.

WHAT WE LEARNED: For a year-round marinara with consistent flavor, use canned whole tomatoes. Drain the tomatoes, reserving the juice, and use just a portion of the juice, so as not to dilute the tomato flavor. Sauté the tomatoes (reserving a small portion) to concentrate their flavor further in a short amount of time, then add the juices to deglaze. Add the reserved tomatoes toward the end of cooking to give the sauce a contrasting brightness. Cook the sauce in a skillet, which has greater surface area than a saucepan, allowing for faster evaporation. A red wine with little or no oak presence adds a robust complexity to the sauce, and fresh basil, added toward the end of cooking, brings fresh floral notes that complement the rich tomato flavors.

MARINARA SAUCE

Makes 4 cups

This recipe makes enough to sauce more than a pound of pasta; leftovers can be refrigerated or frozen. Because canned tomatoes vary in acidity and saltiness, it's best to add salt, pepper, and sugar to taste just before serving. If you prefer a chunkier sauce, give it just three or four pulses in the food processor in step 4.

2	(28-ounce) cans whole tomatoes packed in juice
2	tablespoons olive oil
1	medium onion, chopped fine (about 1 cup)
2	medium garlic cloves, minced or pressed through a garlic press (about 2 teaspoons)
½	teaspoon dried oregano
⅓	cup dry red wine, such as Chianti or Merlot
3	tablespoons chopped fresh basil leaves
1	tablespoon extra-virgin olive oil
	Salt and ground black pepper
1–2	teaspoons sugar, as needed (see note)

1. Pour the tomatoes into a strainer set over a large bowl. Open the tomatoes with your hands and remove and discard the fibrous cores; let the tomatoes drain excess liquid, about 5 minutes. Remove ¾ cup tomatoes from the strainer and set aside. Reserve 2½ cups tomato juice and discard the remainder.

2. Heat the olive oil in a large skillet over medium heat until shimmering. Add the onion and cook, stirring occasionally, until softened and golden around the edges, 6 to 8 minutes. Add the garlic and oregano and cook, stirring constantly, until the garlic is fragrant, about 30 seconds.

3. Add the tomatoes from the strainer and increase the heat to medium-high. Cook, stirring every minute, until the liquid has evaporated and the tomatoes begin to stick to the bottom of the pan and a brown fond forms around the pan edges, 10 to 12 minutes. Add the wine and cook until thick and syrupy, about 1 minute. Add the reserved tomato juice and bring to a simmer; reduce the heat to medium and cook, stirring occasionally and loosening any browned bits, until the sauce is thick, 8 to 10 minutes.

4. Transfer the sauce to a food processor (or transfer to a saucepan and insert a hand blender; see Equipment Corner on page 169) and add the reserved tomatoes; process until slightly chunky, about eight 2-second pulses. Return the sauce to the skillet, add the basil and extra-virgin olive oil, and salt, pepper, and sugar to taste.

GETTING IT RIGHT:
Slow-Simmered Flavor Fast

Drain Juice

A can of tomatoes has more juice than solids. We jump-start flavor concentration by draining off almost a cup of juice beforehand.

Caramelize Solids

Caramelizing the tomato solids briskly in a large skillet before deglazing with liquid ingredients further deepens the flavor profile.

Add Raw Tomatoes

Reserving a few uncooked tomatoes to add near the end of cooking contributes an extra note of freshness to the cooked sauce.

TASTING LAB: Canned Whole Tomatoes

WHEN IT COMES TO COOKING, WE PREFER TO GO WITH good canned tomatoes. Juice-drenched seasonal tomatoes, available only a few weeks a year, are reserved for eating raw on mayonnaise-slathered bread or straight off the cutting board.

Are some brands better than others? To find out, we brought 10 brands into the test kitchen for a series of blind tastings. Tasters sampled the tomatoes straight from the can, drained and cooked simply in a quick tomato sauce, and long-simmered in a more complex sauce (undrained) with herbs and wine.

The first surprising discovery was the utter defeat of the four Italian brands in our lineup—all of which landed at the bottom of our chart. In every tasting, panelists found these samples bitter and stale tasting, and the textures were consistently on the mushy side. The American brands, by contrast, were generally deemed bright, fresh, and well-balanced.

For decades, Italy has been synonymous with superior tomato quality, so these results were puzzling. First, we checked the tomato variety used for each brand, in case the difference was as simple as plum versus round. All of the Italian samples were plums, while the American samples (our top five brands) were split down the middle between plum and round. But tomato variety proved to have little to do with taster preference.

The stale taste of the Italian brands in our lineup, it turns out, has more to do with trade laws than crop differences. In 1989, the United States imposed debilitating punitive tariffs on imported European fruits and vegetables—from 13.6 percent to an exorbitant 100 percent. Unsurprisingly, Italian tomato prices went through the roof, and sales of imported tomatoes dropped off dramatically. To avoid paying the steep duty, Italian tomato canners eventually began packing their tomatoes in tomato puree rather than juice. The loophole? When packed in juice,

Rating Canned Whole Tomatoes

TWENTY MEMBERS OF THE AMERICA'S TEST KITCHEN STAFF TASTED TEN CANNED WHOLE TOMATOES STRAIGHT OUT OF THE CAN (raw); cooked into a quick, simple sauce with olive oil (drained); and slowly simmered in a more complex sauce with herbs and wine (undrained). For each brand, we list origin (domestic or Italian), tomato type (plum or round), and packing medium (juice or puree). The labels for two brands, Rienzi and Pastene, indicate that they were packed in juice, but the thick, grainy consistency and cooked taste said otherwise; here, we have designated that possible discrepancy as "puree-style 'juice.'" The tomatoes are listed in order of preference.

RECOMMENDED
Progresso Italian-Style Whole Peeled Tomatoes with Basil
$1.89 for 28 ounces; drained weight: 11.6 ounces
pH: 3.93 (domestic, plum, juice)
The winner in all three tastings. "Mmmm—bright, lively flavor and silky texture," said one taster. "The perfect balance of acidic and fruity notes," said another.

RECOMMENDED
Redpack Whole Peeled Tomatoes in Thick Puree
$1.29 for 28 ounces; drained weight: 12.6 ounces
pH: 3.95 (domestic, round, puree)
This "bright, sweet, and balanced" brand might have come out on top if the tomatoes hadn't been packed in a puree with a slightly "processed-tasting ketchup" quality.

RECOMMENDED
Hunt's Whole Tomatoes
$1.39 for 28 ounces; drained weight: 10.3 ounces
pH: 3.97 (domestic, round, juice)
Tasters praised the bright, "straightforward" flavor. On tasting the quick sauce, one panelist said, "This one tastes the most like ripe, fresh tomatoes."

RECOMMENDED WITH RESERVATIONS
Tuttorosso Italian-Style Peeled Plum Tomatoes with Natural Basil Flavor
$1.19 for 28 ounces; drained weight: 12.8 ounces
pH: 3.97 (domestic, plum, juice)
"Basil—with just a hint of tomato," joked one taster, referring to the prominent herbal notes. But even those distracted by the "vegetal, perfumey" overtones had to admit that the tomatoes underneath were bright and nicely balanced.

RECOMMENDED WITH RESERVATIONS
Muir Glen Organic Whole Peeled Tomatoes
$2.59 for 28 ounces; drained weight: 12.3 ounces
pH: 4.15 (domestic, round, juice)
The sweet flavor was pleasant, but most tasters craved fuller flavor. The real downfall, though, was a water-logged texture.

RECOMMENDED WITH RESERVATIONS
Rienzi Peeled Tomatoes
$1.29 for 28 ounces; drained weight: 10.8 ounces
pH: 4.36 (Italian, plum, puree-style "juice")
The best-scoring Italian brand had fine tomato flavor, but the dull, "stale" taste of the puree was distracting. Several tasters detected "metallic, tinny" off-tastes.

RECOMMENDED WITH RESERVATIONS
Cento Italian Peeled Tomatoes with Basil Leaf
$2.39 for 35 ounces; drained weight: 11.0 ounces
pH: 4.37 (Italian, plum, puree)
Tasters complained about overcooked, "canned" flavors and a broken-down texture. Strong tomato flavor, but one tinged with "tinny" flavors.

NOT RECOMMENDED
Pastene Italian Peeled Tomatoes with Basil Leaf
$1.79 for 28 ounces; drained weight: 8.5 ounces
pH: 4.44 (Italian, plum, puree-style "juice")
"All I taste is the can—it's like sucking on aluminum," said one participant. "Tastes like overripe tomato paste," said another.

NOT RECOMMENDED
Muir Glen Organic Fire Roasted Whole Tomatoes
$2.19 for 28 ounces; drained weight: 12.1 ounces
pH: 4.10 (domestic, round, juice)
"Not good for spaghetti—but maybe for enchiladas?" ventured one polite taster, but that's as genteel as the comments got. The texture of the tomatoes was fine, but no one thought the charred, smoky variation was a good idea.

NOT RECOMMENDED
Sclafani Italian Peeled Tomatoes
$2.39 for 35 ounces; drained weight: 8.8 ounces
pH: 4.48 (Italian, plum, puree)
The least acidic tomato in the lineup elicited grimaces across the board. "Bitter, plastic tasting—I would never voluntarily eat this!" complained one taster (who apparently felt coerced).

tomatoes are considered a "vegetable"; when packed in puree, they're a "sauce," which carries a much lower customs duty. Sure enough, the Italian brands were all packed in a thick puree (even though two brands inaccurately call it "juice" on the label).

Unfortunately, tomato puree, which is made by pulverizing and then cooking tomatoes, imparts a "cooked" flavor to the fresh, uncooked tomatoes packed in it; tomato juice, by contrast, is uncooked. Taster comments fell in line with that hypothesis. The Italian brands were indicted repeatedly for metallic off-notes and "overcooked, stale" qualities, among other faults. By contrast, most of the domestic brands were packed in a thin juice.

But there's more to the story than just puree versus juice. The best-performing American brands were praised for "refreshing, clean acidity," while the Italian brands were consistently faulted for lack of brightness. To see what was really going on, we decided to measure the pH (an indicator of relative acidity) of every sample. Sure enough, the levels ranged from a moderately acidic pH 4.48 to a more acidic pH 3.93, and all of the American brands were more acidic than the Italian. (The difference between pH 4.48 and pH 3.93 is more dramatic than it looks: It means that the most acidic tomatoes in our lineup were more than three times as tart as the least acidic brand.) Even more fascinating was how perfectly the pH values aligned with taster preference: Like clockwork, the top eight brands were ranked in precise descending order from lowest pH (most acidic) to highest. The more acidic the canned tomato, the better.

The only missing piece of the puzzle was why textures differed so substantially, and (once again) we found the answers listed on the label. The top five brands—the five American brands—contain calcium chloride, an additive manufacturers use to maintain tomato firmness. None of the Italian brands contained calcium chloride, and all were criticized for their mushy, mealy texture. In the raw tasting, some panelists objected to the pronounced sturdiness of the American brands. But as soon as the tomatoes were cooked, those with this additive were preferred unanimously over the ones without, which quickly lost even the meager structure they had to begin with.

Finally, because some recipes call for drained whole tomatoes, we drained one 28-ounce can of each of the brands, then weighed the solids. The results were shocking. The drained weights of our top seven brands ranged between 10.3 ounces (Hunt's) and 12.8 ounces (Tuttorosso). But the two Italian brands in our "Not Recommended" category yielded a measly 8.8 ounces—or less! What wasn't shocking is that the drained-weight values correlated directly with the scores tasters gave each sample for "Fullness of Tomato Flavor." Less tomato meat means less tomato flavor.

So where did we come out? For canned whole tomatoes, some extra processing goes a long way toward making a better product. Let the label be your guide: Check for evidence of domestic origin, citric acid, calcium chloride, and tomato juice rather than puree (the one exception was the puree-packed Redpack). Progresso was the tasters' clear favorite, while the few who disliked the addition of basil preferred Redpack.

TECHNIQUE:
No-Mess Canned Tomato Chopping

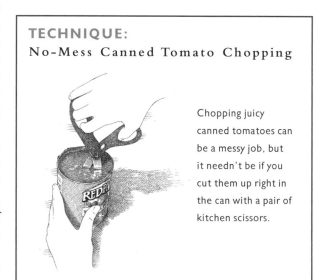

Chopping juicy canned tomatoes can be a messy job, but it needn't be if you cut them up right in the can with a pair of kitchen scissors.

Rating Hand Blenders

WE TESTED NINE HAND BLENDERS BY PUREEING BROCCOLI SOUP AND PREPARING PESTO. THE BLENDERS ARE LISTED in order of preference. See www.americastestkitchen.com for up-to-date prices and mail-order sources for top-rated products.

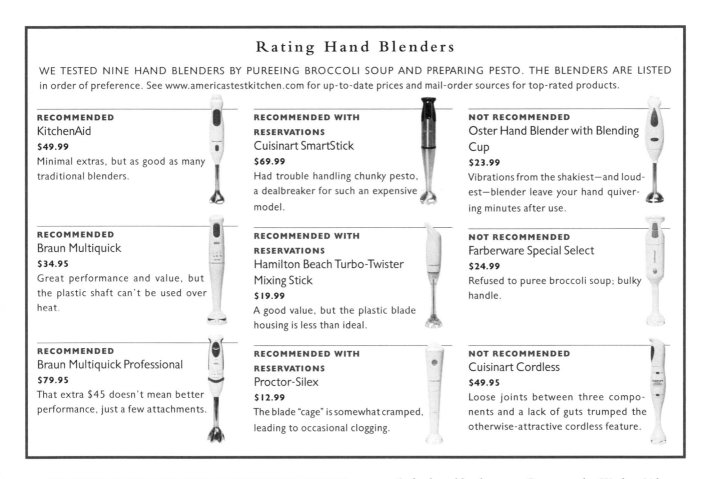

RECOMMENDED
KitchenAid
$49.99
Minimal extras, but as good as many traditional blenders.

RECOMMENDED
Braun Multiquick
$34.95
Great performance and value, but the plastic shaft can't be used over heat.

RECOMMENDED
Braun Multiquick Professional
$79.95
That extra $45 doesn't mean better performance, just a few attachments.

RECOMMENDED WITH RESERVATIONS
Cuisinart SmartStick
$69.99
Had trouble handling chunky pesto, a dealbreaker for such an expensive model.

RECOMMENDED WITH RESERVATIONS
Hamilton Beach Turbo-Twister Mixing Stick
$19.99
A good value, but the plastic blade housing is less than ideal.

RECOMMENDED WITH RESERVATIONS
Proctor-Silex
$12.99
The blade "cage" is somewhat cramped, leading to occasional clogging.

NOT RECOMMENDED
Oster Hand Blender with Blending Cup
$23.99
Vibrations from the shakiest—and loudest—blender leave your hand quivering minutes after use.

NOT RECOMMENDED
Farberware Special Select
$24.99
Refused to puree broccoli soup; bulky handle.

NOT RECOMMENDED
Cuisinart Cordless
$49.95
Loose joints between three components and a lack of guts trumped the otherwise-attractive cordless feature.

EQUIPMENT CORNER: Hand Blenders

A HAND, OR IMMERSION, BLENDER CAN SAVE TIME AND effort: no need to blend in batches, no need to wash a food processor—just rinse it off and toss it back in the drawer. But which brand is best? To find out, we gathered nine models, priced between $13 and $80, and put them to the test.

To start, all nine blenders whirred the chunks out of our marinara sauce easily, so we upped the ante. Pureeing broccoli soup was a more telling task: A few models finished the job in just 30 seconds, while the weaker blenders were still batting around small chunks after a minute. (Several manufacturers advise against continuous running for more than a minute.) What separated the movers from the shakers was pesto. Only three blenders, two Brauns and a KitchenAid, dispatched the herbs and nuts in quick order.

So what makes a better hand blender? The differences aren't obvious. As we've found in past tests, wattage means nothing when it comes to most appliances: The 200- and 400-watt Braun models performed equally well. We did, however, end up with a few design preferences: Stainless steel shafts (rather than plastic) were not better performers, but they do resist staining and can be used in pots sitting over a flame. And come cleanup time, a removable blade end is best. In the end, KitchenAid's immersion blender ($49.99) was our favorite. Aside from a blending beaker, it offers no extras (some models come with fancy attachments), but it did as good a job at blending as most traditional blenders.

Bridget shows Chris that the best steak Diane begins by cooking the steak in batches to ensure maximum development of fond—the browned meaty bits that stick to the pan and boost the flavor of pan sauces.

FLAMBÉ
CHAPTER 15
at home

Fifty years ago, steak Diane, pan-seared steak in a rich,

peppery pan sauce, was a hot menu item at fancy restaurants. Prepared tableside, it included a burst of pyrotechnics supplied by a match and some cognac. Sure, such theatrics might seem a bit dated and silly, but who can resist having a little fun—especially when entertaining? To give this old-school dish a modern twist, we wanted to find a more reasonable substitute for the laborious veal stock that is the traditional basis for the pan sauce. While we were at it, we wanted to slim down the sauce a bit—yes, we love butter and cream, but many of the recipes we tried were just too rich tasting. And, as for the flambé method, we'd need to come up with a foolproof process that wouldn't intimidate the home cook.

While we were on the flambé bandwagon, it occurred to us we could continue the theme in the form of crêpes suzette, a stunning dessert consisting of warm tender crêpes served in a bright orange-flavored sauce. But most restaurants that prepare this dish do so for just two. Could we adapt this classic to serve a tableful of hungry guests for our next dinner party? We were ready to find out.

STEAK DIANE

WHAT WE WANTED: A modern version of this French old-school classic. We aimed to determine the right cut of steak, create a lighter, less labor-intensive sauce, and find a foolproof method for cooking the meat.

We never tire of steak. And for entertaining, steak easily fits the bill. In looking for something different from the usual pan-seared steak, we came across the French classic—steak Diane. But then we noticed that the demanding rich sauce is based on an all-day veal stock reduction. And, on closer inspection, after reviewing 27 recipes and testing 5, our enthusiasm waned further. Recipes were consistent in requiring a sauce based on a labor-intensive veal stock reduction, an abundance of butter and cream, and varying amounts of shallot, mustard, and Worcestershire sauce. They varied widely when it came to what cut of steak to use (sirloin shell, rib eye, strip, or tenderloin), how to prepare it (paper-thin or as thick as it comes), and how to cook it (some were lightly browned, some deeply caramelized, others practically stewed in butter). Our goal, we then decided, would be to develop a straightforward recipe that fit modern tastes and modern time constraints. In the end, we hoped to sit down to a dinner of tender, perfectly cooked steak napped in a deeply satisfying pan sauce—having done it all in less than an hour.

The cornerstone of the sauce for this dish is veal stock, which imparts a silky texture and deep flavor. Because homemade veal stock—a staple in any half-decent restaurant—was out of the question, we had to come up with a good stunt double that could be made in less than an hour. (See page 176 for tips on buying veal stock.) We started our test by browning onions, carrots, and garlic to develop flavor and then deglazing the pan with red wine. For depth of flavor, we tried equal parts beef and chicken broths (both low sodium) and reduced the mixture by half. The result? The color of this concoction was murky, its consistency watery, and its flavor lacking. Progress, it seemed, would be slow.

We revisited some tried-and-true French cookbooks and were reminded that veal stocks typically contain tomato in some form. We wondered what would happen if we sautéed tomato paste in oil before adding the vegetables to the pan. The tomato paste lost its neon color and turned a deep reddish-brown, and when the vegetables were added it coated them with rich flavor. The only problem was that the paste began to burn before the vegetables were fully browned. The solution that came to mind was water.

We added 2 tablespoons to the pan just as the paste was about to burn and then scraped the browned bits from the pan bottom. We let the deep red liquid reduce almost to the point of no return and then added another 2 tablespoons of water. The flavors intensified each time, giving the richest "roasted" flavor possible. To enhance the meaty flavor, we cut back on the chicken broth, doubled the beef broth, and added red wine, fresh thyme, bay leaf, and a hefty amount of black peppercorns. Then we let that mixture reduce for 35 minutes. We had now distilled 54 ounces of watery liquid to 10 ounces of concentrated stock, and the results were worth the wait: The flavor was right on. But we weren't done yet, as our faux veal stock was still thin.

To thicken our stock, we experimented with cornstarch, arrowroot, gelatin, and flour. Cornstarch and arrowroot gave the sauce the gluey substance of bad takeout Chinese food. Gelatin turned it into something resembling beef Jell-O. It turned out that a small amount of flour, sprinkled over the browned vegetables, added the perfect viscosity without masking flavors. We now had an intensely flavored foundation with a consistency similar to serious veal stock reductions. Not as good as the real thing, to be sure, but outstanding considering the modest investment in time.

Of the four cuts of meat we had cooked for our first tests, we ruled out sirloin shell for its toughness and rib eye for the mass of trimmings that ended up in the garbage. Both tenderloin and strip steaks were well liked, but tasters preferred the flavorful strip to the less beefy and more

pricey tenderloin. We wanted to be able to cook four steaks quickly, so we trimmed them of excess fat and tested a range of thicknesses, from ⅛ inch to 1 inch. The deciding factor turned out to be the diameter of the bottom of our 12-inch skillet (we were using a traditional skillet with flared sides, meaning that the measure across the top was greater than across the bottom), which let us cook two 4½-inch-wide steaks at a time. This meant that we could pound each of the steaks to a ½-inch thickness. Unfortunately, the steaks were not browning as evenly as we had hoped. We discovered that weighting them with a heavy-bottomed skillet or Dutch oven as they cooked on the second side gave us the color we were looking for and added more fond, or flavorful browned bits, to the pan bottom.

With the steaks cooked, it was time to take our faux veal stock and create a sauce. Because the sauce base included red wine, we tested Madeira, sherry, white wine, and brandy. Madeira and sherry were too sweet, and white wine made the sauce too acidic. Brandy was the winner, so we went on to taste cognac and Armagnac, both straight up and in the sauce. Armagnac had a bitter aftertaste, so we settled on cognac.

We had now reached the denouement of recipe development for steak Diane: It was time to introduce the flambé. Once we finished cooking the steaks and removed them from the pan, we added minced shallot and 6 tablespoons of cognac and tipped the pan toward the gas burner. The flames shot up into the ventilation system. We cut back to 4 tablespoons of cognac, allowed the alcohol vapors to evaporate slightly, and then tipped the pan toward the flame. This time we got what we wanted: a nice flambé, with no need for the fire extinguisher. But we wondered, was the flambé crucial to the flavor of the dish, or was it just for show? To answer this question, we conducted a head-to-head blind taste test of two sauces, one flamed, one unflamed. The clear winner was the flambéed sauce, which was more balanced and slightly sweeter. The question now was, why? A bit of scientific examination was in order. (To see what we found out, read "Is Flambé Just for Show?" on page 176.)

Once the cognac had been flamed and the browned bits scraped from the skillet, we added the faux veal stock we had prepared earlier and focused on the final seasonings. Dijon mustard was well received, but tasters took issue with the quantity of Worcestershire sauce used in most recipes, so we reduced it to a mere teaspoon. After sampling sauces finished with cream, butter, and a combination of the two, we realized that while cream may add body to a pan sauce with a thin base, it was diluting the flavors of our base. A simple finish with butter added luster and sheen.

Finally, we plated the steaks individually and spooned just enough of the sauce over the center of each to moisten them, not to drown them. A colorful sprinkling of fresh chives, and our skillet steak was ready to serve.

WHAT WE LEARNED: For a rich sauce base that mimics the complexity of labor-intensive veal stock in a fraction of the time, use a flavorful combination of sautéed tomato paste, aromatics such as garlic, onion, and carrots, a combination of beef broth and chicken broth, red wine, peppercorns, and herbs. Skip the cream, which we found dilutes the intensity of the sauce, and use cognac for its slightly sweet, complex flavor. Choose strip steaks for great beefy flavor and ease of preparation. To brown the steaks evenly and develop enough fond (the flavorful browned meaty bits that cling to the pan and give pan sauces their rich, meaty flavor), weight the steaks with a heavy-bottomed skillet or Dutch oven when cooking the second side.

SAUCE BASE FOR STEAK DIANE

Makes 1¼ cups

This recipe yields a sauce base that is an excellent facsimile of a demi-glace, a very labor-intensive and time-consuming classic French sauce base. Because the sauce base is very concentrated, make sure to use low-sodium chicken and beef broths; otherwise, the base may be unpalatably salty. The sauce base can be made ahead and refrigerated for up to three days.

- 2 tablespoons vegetable oil
- 4 teaspoons tomato paste
- 2 small onions, chopped medium (about 1⅓ cups)
- 1 medium carrot, chopped medium (about ½ cup)
- 4 medium garlic cloves, peeled
- ¼ cup water
- 4 teaspoons unbleached all-purpose flour
- 1½ cups dry red wine
- 3½ cups low-sodium beef broth
- 1¾ cups low-sodium chicken broth
- 2 teaspoons black peppercorns
- 8 sprigs fresh thyme
- 2 bay leaves

1. Heat the oil and tomato paste in a Dutch oven over medium-high heat and cook, stirring constantly, until the paste begins to brown, about 3 minutes. Add the onions, carrot, and garlic and cook, stirring frequently, until the mixture is reddish brown, about 2 minutes. Add 2 tablespoons water and continue to cook, stirring constantly, until the mixture is well browned, about 3 minutes, adding the remaining water when needed to prevent scorching. Add the flour and cook, stirring constantly, 1 minute. Add the wine and, using a heatproof rubber spatula, scrape up the browned bits on the bottom and sides of the pot; bring to a boil, stirring occasionally (the mixture will thicken slightly). Add the beef and chicken broths, peppercorns, thyme, and bay leaves; bring to a boil and cook, uncovered, occasionally scraping the bottom and sides of the pot with a spatula, until reduced to 2½ cups, 35 to 40 minutes.

2. Strain the mixture through a fine-mesh strainer, pressing on the solids to extract as much liquid as possible; you should have about 1¼ cups.

STEAK DIANE

Serves 4

If you prefer not to make the sauce base, mix ½ cup glace de viande (see the veal stock tasting on page 176) with ¾ cup water and ¼ cup red wine and use this mixture in place of the base in step 2. For this recipe, use a traditional skillet. The steaks leave behind more fond (browned bits) than they do in a nonstick skillet, and more fond means a richer, more flavorful sauce. A superb embellishment for steak Diane is a drizzle of white truffle oil just before serving. Before preparing the sauce, read "Tips for Fearless Flambé" (opposite) or if you do not wish to flambé, simmer the cognac in step 2 for 10 to 15 seconds for a slightly less sweet flavor profile.

steaks

- 2 tablespoons vegetable oil
- 4 strip steaks (about 12 ounces each), trimmed of all excess fat and pounded to even ½-inch thickness (see photos opposite)
  Salt and ground black pepper

sauce

- 1 tablespoon vegetable oil
- 1 small shallot, minced (about 2 tablespoons)
- ¼ cup cognac
- 1 recipe Sauce Base for Steak Diane (see note)
- 2 teaspoons Dijon mustard
- 2 tablespoons cold unsalted butter
- 1 teaspoon Worcestershire sauce
- 2 tablespoons minced fresh chives

1. FOR THE STEAKS: Heat 1 tablespoon of the oil in a 12-inch heavy-bottomed skillet over medium-high heat until smoking. Meanwhile, season the steaks with salt and pepper. Place 2 steaks in the skillet and cook until well browned, about 1½ minutes. Using tongs, flip the steaks and weight with a heavy-bottomed pan; continue to cook until well browned on the second side, about 1½ minutes longer. Transfer the steaks to a large platter and tent with foil. Add the remaining tablespoon oil to the now-empty skillet and repeat with the remaining steaks; transfer the second batch of steaks to the platter.

2. FOR THE SAUCE: Off the heat, add the oil and shallot to the now-empty skillet. Using the skillet's residual heat, cook, stirring frequently, until the shallot is slightly softened and browned, about 45 seconds. Add the cognac and let stand until the cognac warms slightly, about 10 seconds, then set the skillet over high heat. Using a chimney match, ignite the cognac and shake the skillet until the flames subside, then simmer the cognac until reduced to about 1 tablespoon, about 10 seconds. Add the sauce base and mustard and simmer until slightly thickened and reduced to 1 cup, 2 to 3 minutes. Whisk in the butter; off the heat, add the Worcestershire, any accumulated juices from the steaks, and 1 tablespoon of the chives. Season to taste with salt and pepper.

3. Set the steaks on individual dinner plates, spoon 2 table-spoons sauce over each steak, sprinkle with the remaining chives, and serve immediately, passing the remaining sauce separately.

GETTING IT RIGHT:
Preparing the Steaks

Untrimmed   **Trimmed and Pounded**

The steak at left has not been trimmed. To keep the sauce from becoming too fatty, trim the fat from the perimeter of the steak, and to ensure even cooking, use a meat pounder or mallet to pound the steak to an even ½-inch thickness, as in the steak at right.

GETTING IT RIGHT:
Tips for Fearless Flambé

Flambéing is more than just tableside theatrics: As dramatic as it looks, igniting alcohol actually helps develop a deeper, more complex flavor in sauces—thanks to flavor-boosting chemical reactions that occur only at the high temperatures reached in flambéing. But accomplishing this feat at home can be daunting. Here are some tips for successful—and safe—flambéing at home.

Be prepared: Turn off the exhaust fan, tie back long hair, and have a lid at the ready to smother flare-ups.

Use the proper equipment: A pan with flared sides (such as a skillet) rather than straight sides will allow more oxygen to mingle with the alcohol vapors, increasing the chance that you'll spark the desired flame. If possible, use long, chimney matches, and light the alcohol with your arm extended to full length.

Ignite warm alcohol: If the alcohol becomes too hot, the vapors can rise to dangerous heights, causing large flare-ups once lit. Inversely, if the alcohol is too cold, there won't be enough vapors to light at all. We found that heating alcohol to 100 degrees Fahrenheit (best achieved by adding alcohol to a hot pan off heat and letting it sit for five to 10 seconds) produced the most moderate, yet long-burning, flames.

If a flare-up should occur: Simply slide the lid over the top of the skillet (coming in from the side of, rather than over, the flames) to put out the fire quickly. Let the alcohol cool down and start again.

If the alcohol won't light: If the pan is full of other ingredients (as is the case in Crêpes Suzette, page 181), the potency of the alcohol can be diminished as it becomes incorporated. For a more foolproof flame, ignite the alcohol in a separate small skillet or saucepan; once the flame has burned off, add the reduced alcohol to the remaining ingredients.

SCIENCE DESK: Is Flambé Just for Show?

A FLAMBÉ LOOKS IMPRESSIVE AND IS EASY ENOUGH TO execute, but we wondered if it really improves the flavor of a sauce and, if so, why. Blind taste tests quickly revealed that flambéing the sauce for steak Diane did indeed improve its flavor; a flamed sauce was richer and sweeter than a sauce that had not been ignited.

A flambé is the ignition of the alcohol vapor that lies above the pan, a reaction that generates significant amounts of heat. To measure this heat, we used an infrared thermometer and discovered that the temperature at the surface of the cognac quickly climbed past 500 degrees; this heat would indeed affect the cognac below. Curious to know whether the high heat served to remove all of the alcohol from the pan, we sent samples of the flambéed cognac as well as the completed sauce to a food lab for alcohol analysis. Tests revealed that the flambé removed 79 percent of the alcohol from the cognac. (The simmering of the sauce that followed the flambé removed almost all of the remaining alcohol.) So the flambé was removing most of the alcohol, but what effect was the high heat having on flavor?

Many of the great, flavor-boosting chemical reactions of cooking require high heat. Reactions involving sugar, such as caramelization and browning, occur at temperatures higher than 300 degrees. Because the surface had reached above 500 degrees, we noticed some of this type of flavor development. A simmered cognac, in contrast, maintains a steady temperature of about 180 degrees at its surface.

Another benefit of the flambé is that at very high heat, molecules can absorb enough energy to isomerize, or change shape. The consequences of this reconfiguration might include improved solubility and changed flavor perception. The mystery was solved. A flambéed sauce burns off most of its alcohol and gains flavor from several high-heat cooking reactions. The final result is a sauce with a hint of alcohol and great depth of flavor.

TASTING LAB: Veal Stock

REAL RESTAURANT-QUALITY VEAL STOCK TAKES HOURS OF roasting and simmering, all of which results in a highly reduced stock referred to as either a demi-glace or glace de viande. (Strictly speaking, a demi-glace is a reduced brown sauce, whereas a glace de viande is simply a meat stock that has been reduced to a thick syrup.) Sure, homemade veal stock is immensely flavorful, but does the average home cook have time to make it? Not most of us, which is why we set out to see what was available on the market and if any of it was worth using.

We tested four demi-glace products and three that were labeled "glace de viande." The demi-glace offerings were universally disliked by tasters. Typical comments were "no meat flavor" and "vegetal and sour." The demi-glaces also had ingredient lists that were as long (and confusing) as a four-star chef recipe. The glace de viande products (also called glace de veau) were far superior, no doubt because they contained recognizable ingredients. Our favorites were Provimi and CulinArte' Bonewerks. Both companies offer frozen 1-pound envelopes for about $14 each.

BEST VEAL STOCK

Provimi Glace de Veau   **CulinArte' Bonewerks Glace de Veau**

The two veal stocks that rated the highest in our tasting were Provimi Glace de Veau (left), which was described as "sweet and meaty" and "balanced," and CulinArte' Bonewerks Glace de Veau (right), which earned similar praise. Both products are available through mail order. See www.americastestkitchen.com for up-to-date prices and mail-order sources for top-rated products.

TASTING LAB: Beef Broth

IN OUR 1998 TASTING OF BEEF BROTH, THE TEST KITCHEN found most products to be downright dreadful. The problem boiled down to an appalling lack of beef flavor. Lots of salt, plenty of vegetal flavors, a few metallic off-notes—but hardly anything that said beef beyond the brownish hue. When we learned that the U.S. Department of Agriculture (USDA) requires only 1 part beef to every 135 parts water, we weren't surprised that most products came up short. While commercial chicken broth, similarly, gets by on a paltry amount of poultry, chicken's less saturated fat goes much further when it comes to flavor than the same amount of beef. In fact, when we make homemade broth in the test kitchen, we use twice as much beef as chicken to flavor the same amount of liquid.

Since our original tasting of beef broths, an impressive collection of new products has hit the supermarket shelves, so we decided to take another taste. We were especially intrigued by the increased availability of beef "bases," stock concentrates (just add water) that were once used almost exclusively by restaurants.

To narrow the field, tasters sipped 13 beef broths—

7 liquid broths and 6 made from concentrated bases—simply heated and served straight up. The top eight brands moved on to a full battery of tests: plain (again), regular strength in a simple beef soup, and reduced in an all-purpose gravy.

Some of these broths didn't taste half bad! While they were still a far cry from a homemade broth, it was clear that commercial brews had come a far piece from our earlier tasting. Even better, a few broths actually tasted like beef. Hints of mushroom, onion, other vegetables, and even chicken were still more common, but two brands—Redi-Base and Pacific—elicited consistent praise for assertive beefiness. In the end, those two broths came in first and second place (see the chart on page 179).

So what makes a better beef broth? Our hopes of finding a clear pattern based on product type (that is, liquid broths versus concentrated bases) were quickly dashed after the final results were tallied. Although Redi-Base, our top finisher overall, was indeed a beef base, three bases ended up in the lower ranks, and two others failed even to make it past the elimination round. Likewise, the liquid broth contenders evidenced no discernible pattern.

What about the presence of beef itself? Foiled again. Virtually every product in the lineup included some form of beef near the top of the ingredients list, and every manufacturer we contacted was unwilling to provide additional details. To get around this roadblock, we sent samples to an independent lab to be analyzed for protein content—but to no avail. (The highest-protein brand came in last place overall, while the next-highest came in second.)

Frustrated, we canvassed industry experts to shed light on the beefy/not-so-beefy divide. The consensus was that it would be cost-prohibitive for broth makers to stray beyond the USDA's minimum beef to water ratio. Given that meager amount, manufacturers must rely on the magic of flavor chemistry to avoid a completely tasteless brew. Well, that explained the blandness of the one beef broth that opted for the all-natural route: It was eliminated by tasters in the preliminary round. The rest of the broths were chock-full of additives.

In our lineup, every broth contained a generous amount of the most common additive—salt. Most contained some form of sugar (including plain sugar, corn syrup solids, and maltodextrin). So far, so familiar. It was when we looked more closely at the less familiar ingredients that we stumbled upon our most important clues—namely, hydrolyzed vegetable protein and autolyzed yeast extract. Many sources we consulted lumped these additives together simply as "flavor enhancers," but more diligent digging revealed that they work quite differently.

Hydrolyzed vegetable protein (made by altering soybean, corn, or other vegetable molecules through a chemical reaction, hydrolysis) merely adds flavor complexity, sort of like adding spices or salt. By contrast, autolyzed yeast extract (made by allowing yeast enzymes to feed on carefully chosen sugars and proteins until they release flavor-enhancing compounds) works like MSG (monosodium glutamate). Rather than contribute additional flavors, yeast extract amplifies flavors already present, especially savory and meaty ones. Our food science consultant explained, "Autolyzed yeast extracts literally boost the flavor of beef by as much as 20-fold. There is so little real beef protein and fat in commercial broth that [the product] wouldn't have much flavor without them." Put another way: By

including yeast extract in the mix, that USDA recipe of just 1 part beef to 135 parts water could taste like 20 parts beef instead.

With this new piece of information, things started to make sense. As we scanned the ingredients lists of our beef broths, we spotted a definite pattern. While many of the products contained yeast extract, they differed markedly in where it fell in the mix. (By law, ingredients must be listed in descending order by weight.) In our top four brands, yeast extract was placed second or third (just after beef or salt). Moving down the ranks, the placement of yeast extract began to fall dramatically—fifth, then fifteenth, then tenth, then fourteenth—and some of the brands eliminated in the first round lacked yeast extract altogether. What's more, our top five brands included no hydrolyzed vegetable protein (which the experts said can produce "metallic" off-tastes, a flaw we've often encountered in commercial beef broth). The rest of the brands included multiple forms of hydrolyzed vegetable protein—and a few of them were faulted for (you guessed it) metallic off-notes.

If yeast extract offers such a clear advantage in terms of flavor, why wouldn't all beef-broth manufacturers opt to include it in the mix? Quite simply: cost. Yeast extracts are far more expensive than hydrolyzed vegetable proteins, in large part because the technology is so much newer. According to industry literature, only in the last decade have food chemists begun to perfect yeast-extract science, and now yeast extract shows up on the ingredients lists of foods as varied as potato chips, salad dressing, processed sandwich meat, and chicken broth. Although it's only speculation, this may be the reason that beef-broth products taste better than they did in 1998.

So which broth to stock? Based on our tests, just note the first few ingredients listed on the label. We found the winning combination to be beef plus a flavor amplifier—in the form of yeast extract—near the top of the list. In our lineup, Redi-Base Beef Base and Pacific Beef Broth conformed to these rules and, more important, tasted best to our panel.

Rating Beef Broth

TWENTY-FOUR MEMBERS OF THE AMERICA'S TEST KITCHEN STAFF TASTED EIGHT BRANDS OF BEEF BROTH AND RECONSTITUTED beef broth concentrates and bases plain, in a simple beef soup (in both cases with the sodium levels adjusted to parity), and cooked in a simple gravy reduction (with sodium levels left as is). Brands are listed below in order of preference based on their combined scores in the three tastings.

RECOMMENDED

Redi-Base Beef Base

$5.95/8 ounces (makes 2½ gallons)

Tasters agreed on a "deep, dark, and hearty" character in the soup. Though many viewed the gravy as salty, they also picked up a distinct beefiness, roasted flavor, and notes of onion and mushroom.

RECOMMENDED

Pacific Beef Broth

$2.69/32 fluid ounces

In both the soup and the gravy, tasters found "toasty" or roasted notes, though the gravy was considered mild and in need of extra salt. But this was one of the few products that tasted truly beefy.

RECOMMENDED WITH RESERVATIONS

Knorr Beef Flavored Broth

$4.99/30.4 fluid ounces

Scored higher marks as a soup—which tasters found sweet, "like caramelized onions," balanced with a slight acidity and a strong "vegetal" presence—than as a gravy, which one taster pronounced to be "wicked vegetal."

RECOMMENDED WITH RESERVATIONS

Swanson Lower Sodium Beef Broth

$1.19/14 fluid ounces

When faced with this gravy, one taster declared "cardboard comes to mind," then joined the nearly unanimous cry to "please pass the salt." Even the salt-corrected soup struck numerous tasters as "nondescript" and "dull, dull, dull." At least there were no off-flavors.

NOT RECOMMENDED

Savory Basics Beef Flavor Stock Concentrate

$5.95/6 ounces (makes 1 gallon)

From "pallid" to "plain Jane," both the gravy and the soup were overwhelmingly decried as too light in color and too mild in flavor. While one detractor groaned "not worthy of the name 'gravy,'" many likened the flavor to that of chicken broth.

NOT RECOMMENDED

Orrington Farms Gourmet Beef Soup Base and Food Seasoning

$4.17/8 ounces (makes 2.8 gallons)

Detecting dried herbs and mushrooms, several tasters remarked that the bland gravy belonged on a TV dinner or a grade school hot lunch tray. Others complained of metallic and "musty, stale" aftertastes.

NOT RECOMMENDED

Superior Touch Better Than Bouillon Beef Base

$4.99/8 ounces (makes 2.4 gallons)

Our 1998 "winner" suffered in the rankings this time around, thanks to stiff competition from the beefier newbies. In the gravy, tasters picked up on mushrooms, soy, and salt. In the soup, most tasters couldn't get past vegetal, artificial, and other off-flavors.

NOT RECOMMENDED

College Inn Fat Free & Lower Sodium Beef Broth

$0.99/14.5 fluid ounces

This gravy was characterized as "bland and thin" by most tasters, several of whom also picked up distinct artificial flavor notes. Referring to plasticky and metallic aftertastes, one panelist griped that it "tastes like the can it came in."

CRÊPES SUZETTE

WHAT WE WANTED: A home cook–friendly rendition of the restaurant classic—tender, not soggy, crêpes in a buttery orange-flavored sauce. And instead of serving just two, as it's prepared in restaurants, this recipe would make enough to serve six, ideal for a dinner party.

Whﬆ's not to like about the sophisticated combination of crêpes, oranges, liqueur, and a showy flambé? Having enjoyed this dish in restaurants, we thought that it would make an impressive finale to a sophisticated dinner party. But on closer inspection, we realized that this dish prepared tableside in restaurants serves just two—not so practical for dinner parties. Our goals therefore would be twofold: develop a foolproof, home cook–friendly method for this showstopper dessert and make enough to serve six.

Our first stop was the library, where we instinctively pulled a Julia Child cookbook from the shelves. (After all, this dish is usually credited to the world's most famous French chef, Escoffier, though some suggest that a young chef accidentally flambéed a skillet full of pancakes and named the dish after Suzette, mistress to the Prince of Wales.) We copied her recipe along with five others and started comparing ingredient lists. Crêpes consist mainly of flour, milk, and egg; the accompanying orange sauce typically relies on butter, sugar, orange juice, cognac, and orange liqueur. (We ignored specifications for suzette pans and used a skillet; we wouldn't be spending $200 on a single-purpose piece of cookware.) After a morning of flipping crêpes and making sauces, we rounded up a few colleagues to witness the flambé step, which, as Julia warned, requires practice.

Tasters critiqued the sauces, calling them butter-heavy and overcooked, with a few tasting strongly of alcohol—courtesy of an inferior flambé. Working with the test kitchen's favorite crêpe recipe, we scaled back the butter in a basic sauce and continued experimenting. When frozen orange juice concentrate, lemon juice, orange marmalade, and even grenadine syrup failed to improve things, we returned to square one. Adding uncooked orange juice and zest to the usual reduction of butter, sugar, and orange juice was the answer, yielding lively, multilayered flavors.

Flambé science is simple enough. When alcohol is ignited, it reaches a temperature of about 500 degrees. This high heat causes a reaction in the sugars in the liquor, producing complex flavors that can't be achieved at the lower heat (180 degrees) of simmering. After a few shaky attempts at igniting our simmering dessert, we reached two important conclusions. First, the more crêpes in the pan, the more likely the alcohol will be quickly absorbed and then impossible to ignite. Second, the intensity of the flames is directly related to the heat in the pan.

Because we were preparing six servings and therefore had a very full skillet, we figured we'd have more success if we lit the sauce first and added the crêpes second. Yet even with this approach, the results were spotty at best. Minor variations in temperature had a dramatic effect on the results, which ranged from mere flickers (low heat) to a full-out blaze (high heat). Then it hit us: What if we simply removed the extraneous variables and started by flambéing the alcohol alone in the skillet? Voilà! This reversal (flambé first, build the sauce second) delivered great flavor, along with predictable flames.

As for the alcohol, cognac was a given. Grand Marnier is usually called for, but it's not the only orange liqueur, so we tried other options. Surprisingly, inexpensive and less alcoholic triple sec stole the show (see the tasting on page 183).

Although we had made good progress, we were having problems with crêpes that were bloated and soggy, having spent too much time swimming in sauce. This isn't much of a problem when the dessert is made rapidly for two people, but when six servings (12 crêpes) are called for, there is too much absorption time. The solution came from well-known French chef Jacques Pépin, who sprinkles unsauced crêpes with sugar and then broils them. Following his lead, we first transferred the sauce in the skillet to a serving bowl, then arranged folded, sugared crêpes in the skillet. When they emerged from the oven, we drizzled on a bit of sauce and passed the remainder at the table. Though untraditional, this brûlée technique was a real hit, forming a crunchy, sugary barrier that provided textural contrast and partially protected the crêpes from the sauce.

We reviewed our recipe for a final time. Like most, it aimed for ultra-tender crêpes and so called for resting the batter to relax the gluten, a protein that can make batters and doughs tough. Would skipping this step prove beneficial, yielding sturdier crêpes more capable of standing up to the sauce (not to mention saving two hours of prep time)? We put together one last test, and, sure enough, tasters preferred the unrested crêpes, finding that once sauced, they retained a more substantial texture than the rested batch.

WHAT WE LEARNED: For a foolproof flambé that won't create a frightening fireball or conversely not burn at all, ignite the alcohol (cognac) alone in the skillet before building the sauce. For a delicate sauce with complex flavor, enrich a reduction of butter, sugar, and fresh orange juice with additional orange juice, fresh orange zest, and triple sec (not the pricier Grand Marnier or Cointreau). For tender but sturdy crêpes that will stand up to the sauce without turning soggy, skip resting the batter before cooking. Then, once the crêpes are cooked, sprinkle them with sugar, and run them under the broiler for a sweet and crunchy coating.

CRÊPES SUZETTE

Serves 6

Note that it takes a few crêpes to get the heat of the pan right; your first two or three will almost inevitably be unusable. (To allow for practice, the recipe yields about 16 crêpes; only 12 are needed for the dish.) A dry measuring cup with a ¼-cup capacity is useful for portioning the batter. Tasters had a slight preference for crêpes made with whole milk, but low-fat or skim milk can also be used. Before you reach step 4, read "Tips for Fearless Flambé" on page 175.

crêpes

3	large eggs
1½	cups whole milk (see note)
½	cup water
1½	cups (7½ ounces) unbleached all-purpose flour
2	tablespoons cognac
3	tablespoons sugar
½	teaspoon salt
5	tablespoons unsalted butter, melted, plus extra for brushing the pan

orange sauce

4	tablespoons cognac
6	tablespoons unsalted butter, cut into 6 pieces
4	tablespoons sugar
1¼	cups juice plus 1 tablespoon finely grated zest from 3 to 4 large oranges
2	tablespoons orange-flavored liqueur, preferably triple sec

1. FOR THE CRÊPES: Combine the eggs, milk, water, flour, cognac, sugar, salt, and melted butter in a blender until a smooth batter forms, about 10 seconds. Transfer the batter to a medium bowl.

2. Using a pastry brush, brush the bottom and sides of a 10-inch nonstick skillet very lightly with melted butter and heat the skillet over medium heat. When the butter stops sizzling, tilt the pan slightly to the right and begin pouring in a scant ¼ cup batter. Continue to pour the batter in a slow, steady stream, rotating your wrist and twirling the pan slowly counterclockwise until the pan bottom is covered with an even layer of batter. Cook until the crêpe starts to lose its opaqueness and turns spotty light golden brown on the bottom, loosening the crêpe from the side of the pan with a heatproof rubber spatula, 30 seconds to 1 minute. To flip the crêpe, loosen the edge with the spatula and, with your fingertips on the top side, slide the spatula under the crêpe and flip. Cook until dry on the second side, about 20 seconds.

3. Place the cooked crêpe on a plate and repeat the cooking process with the remaining batter, brushing the pan very lightly with the butter before making each crêpe. As they are done, stack the crêpes on a plate (you will need 12 crêpes). (The crêpes can be double-wrapped in plastic wrap and refrigerated up to 3 days. If the crêpes have been refrigerated, bring them to room temperature before making the sauce.)

4. FOR THE ORANGE SAUCE: Adjust an oven rack to the lower-middle position and heat the broiler. Add 3 tablespoons of the cognac to a broiler-safe 12-inch skillet; set over medium heat just until the vapors begin to rise from the cognac, about 5 seconds. Remove the pan from the heat and wave a lit chimney match over the cognac until it ignites; shake the pan until the flames subside. (The cognac should burn for about 15 seconds; reignite if the flame dies too soon.)

5. Add the butter, 3 tablespoons of the sugar, and 1 cup of the orange juice and simmer briskly over high heat, whisking occasionally, until many large bubbles appear and the mixture reduces to a thick syrup, 6 to 8 minutes. (You should have just over ½ cup sauce.) Transfer the sauce to a small bowl; do not wash the skillet. Stir the remaining ¼ cup orange juice, zest, liqueur, and the remaining tablespoon cognac into the sauce. Cover to keep warm.

6. TO ASSEMBLE: Fold each crêpe in half, then in half again to form a wedge shape. Arrange 9 folded crêpes

---

TECHNIQUE: Making Crêpes

For the tenderest crêpes, most recipes call for resting the batter for two full hours to let the gluten relax. Given that our crêpes get crisped under a broiler and are then drenched in a sticky sauce, we wanted just the opposite. Our sturdier crêpes require no resting—just mix the batter and go.

1. Tilt the buttered and heated nonstick skillet slightly to the right and begin pouring in a scant ¼ cup batter.

2. Continue tilting the pan slowly, in a counterclockwise motion, until a thin, even crêpe is formed.

3. Loosen the edge with a heatproof rubber spatula and, with your fingertips on the top side, grab the edge and flip.

around the edge of the now-empty skillet, with the rounded edges facing inward, overlapping as necessary to fit. Arrange the remaining 3 crêpes in the center of the pan. Sprinkle the crêpes evenly with the remaining tablespoon of sugar. Place the skillet in the oven and broil until the sugar caramelizes and the crêpes turn spotty brown, about 5 minutes. (Watch the crêpes constantly to prevent scorching; turn the pan as necessary.) Remove the pan from the oven and pour half of the sauce over the crêpes, leaving some areas unsauced. Transfer the crêpes to individual serving dishes and serve immediately, passing the extra sauce separately.

TASTING LAB: Orange Liqueurs

WHEN MAKING CRÊPES SUZETTE, SHOULD YOU SHELL OUT big bucks for a name brand, such as Grand Marnier or Cointreau, or will a cheaper orange liqueur do? We started by tasting triple sec, a sweet, clear spirit flavored with the peels of sweet and bitter oranges (and sometimes lemons). Out of eight brands, 30-proof Leroux ($7.99 for 750 ml) was the favorite. Another option, curaçao, is flavored with the peel of bitter oranges, specifically those native to the Caribbean island of the same name. Manufacturers may tint their curaçaos blue, but color doesn't affect flavor. We tasted two brands and preferred 30-proof Hiram Walker ($11.99 for 750 ml). Infused cognac is well known to most home cooks as Grand Marnier, but there are other, less expensive, brands. Out of seven orange-infused cognacs, we liked La Belle Orange from France ($18 for 750 ml).

After much drinking, we were ready to cook. We sampled the three winners of our first tasting—Leroux Triple Sec, Hiram Walker Curaçao, and La Belle Orange—alongside the two premium 80-proof choices—Grand Marnier ($29.95 for 750 ml) and Cointreau ($34.95 for 750 ml)—in crêpes suzette. While the high-priced liqueurs may be better for sipping, for cooking we found that the cheaper choices worked just fine. The unexpected winner was Leroux Triple Sec. La Belle Orange captured second place, with tasters noting a more intense but appealing bitterness. High-priced Grand Marnier finished third, just ahead of Hiram Walker Curaçao and pricey Cointreau.

BEST ORANGE LIQUEUR
Leroux Triple Sec is our top choice for crêpes suzette.

Julia shows Chris that you need some patience—and a gentle folding motion—to produce truly great scrambled eggs.

HEARTY EGGS
for breakfast

Most of us might not have time to prepare (and enjoy) egg dishes during the week, but come the weekend, eggs are a terrific way to begin a leisurely day. In this chapter, we wanted to take a look at a couple of our favorite egg dishes—scrambled eggs and omelets—and see how we could make the most of them.

Sometimes you want something heartier than simple scrambled eggs. But adding meats, cheeses, and vegetables weighs down the eggs' fluffy texture and, worse, turns the eggs watery. We wanted to solve these problems and turn out scrambled eggs that could stand up to the addition of hearty ingredients. And we also wanted an interesting mix of additions, so we'd be inclined to make these eggs for dinner, too.

Omelets made for one or two aren't difficult to prepare. But what if you're making omelets for the whole family? You don't want to be standing at the stove playing the part of short-order cook, right? We wanted to create one big omelet, big enough to serve 4. Working with such a large omelet wouldn't be easy—we'd need to figure out how to cook through such a large omelet without it drying out, how to add the fillings (and heat them through), and how to turn the omelet out of the pan without it breaking apart.

With these foolproof recipes, you just might find yourself making time to enjoy eggs a bit more often.

HEARTY SCRAMBLED EGGS

WHAT WE WANTED: Fluffy (not watery) scrambled eggs, packed with flavorful meats, cheeses, and vegetables.

What's not to love about fluffy, creamy yellow, feather-light scrambled eggs? From prior testing, we'd discovered that adding milk to the eggs makes the curds soft, while cooking them over high heat in a constant folding motion coagulates the eggs quickly and efficiently. It was, therefore, a great disappointment when we discovered that our simple recipe ran into trouble as soon as we attempted to add any other ingredients. Just a sprinkle of sautéed vegetables or browned sausage caused the eggs to become watery and discolored. As it turned out, the difference between scrambled eggs and "hearty" scrambled eggs was much bigger than we expected.

The biggest problem was "weeping." Additional ingredients seemed to promote water loss in the eggs during cooking. Our first thought was that the temperature of the added ingredients might be a key factor. But from tests in which we tried adding both room temperature and refrigerated ingredients, we learned that their temperature made little difference to the eggs. We thought perhaps adding a binder would inhibit water loss, so we tried cornstarch, cream cheese, mayonnaise, and bread crumbs—all to no avail. Then we suspected that milk, one of the ingredients in the original recipe, might be the source of the problem, considering that it is mostly water. We eliminated the milk but found that the recipe could not live without it; dairy-free scrambled eggs were tough.

Another thought was that the high heat of the recipe was causing the eggs to cook too quickly and seize, squeezing out their moisture (evident in the gray, unappetizing puddle of liquid on our plate). Although even the slightest bit of overcooking will cause eggs to lose their moisture and high heat makes split-second timing essential, the heat itself was not the problem. To the contrary, the steam created by cooking over high heat was crucial to the light, fluffy

texture that was the hallmark of our recipe. Nonetheless, to reduce the margin of error, we reduced the heat to medium. The texture of these eggs was slightly more substantial but certainly not inappropriate for a hearty egg dish. So far, so good—but the added ingredients were still causing our scrambled eggs to turn watery.

We wondered if the method we were using to combine the ingredients in the pan was a factor. Our current approach was to sauté onions, add the beaten eggs, and then fold the ingredients together until the eggs cooked through. For the next test, we removed the sautéed onions from the pan and wiped it clean before cooking the eggs, folded in the sautéed onions when the eggs were nearly done, then let the eggs finish cooking off the heat. Finally, some good news. The weeping was reduced, and the eggs had managed to hold on to their pristine yellow hue.

Because the onions were adding moisture to the eggs, we wondered if we should reduce the liquid elsewhere. We knew that some dairy was important for a soft texture, but perhaps instead of milk we should be using half-and-half or cream, both of which contain less moisture and more fat. We tested them and decided that heavy cream made the eggs too rich and heavy; half-and-half, however, was perfect. These eggs were substantial, soft, and able to accept most of the ingredients we threw at them. Among the ingredients that were consistently successful were drier leafy greens, crunchy vegetables, and breakfast meats; there was nary a puddle on our breakfast plate. But we found it best to avoid very watery ingredients, such as mushrooms or ham steaks.

WHAT WE LEARNED: For tender eggs, half-and-half is preferred over milk and heavy cream. To guard against weepy eggs, don't crowd all the ingredients into the skillet at once. Instead, cook in stages. First, cook the aromatics like onion, then remove from the pan, and wipe the skillet dry. Next, proceed with scrambling the eggs over medium, not high, heat. Finally, off the heat, gently fold in the remaining ingredients.

SCRAMBLED EGGS WITH BACON, ONION, AND PEPPER JACK CHEESE

Serves 4 to 6

Note that you'll need to reserve 2 teaspoons of bacon fat to sauté the onion. After removing the cooked bacon from the skillet, be sure to drain it well on paper towels so that it won't turn the eggs greasy.

12	large eggs
¾	teaspoon salt
¼	teaspoon ground black pepper
6	tablespoons half-and-half
4	slices bacon (about 4 ounces), halved lengthwise, then cut crosswise into ½-inch pieces
1	medium onion, chopped (about 1 cup)
1	tablespoon unsalted butter
1½	ounces pepper Jack or Monterey Jack cheese, shredded (about ½ cup)
1	teaspoon minced fresh parsley leaves (optional)

1. Crack the eggs into a medium bowl; add the salt, pepper, and half-and-half. Beat with a dinner fork until thoroughly combined.

2. Cook the bacon in a 12-inch nonstick skillet over medium heat, stirring occasionally, until browned, 4 to 5 minutes. Using a slotted spoon, transfer the bacon to a paper towel–lined plate; discard all but 2 teaspoons bacon fat. Add the onion to the skillet and cook, stirring occasionally, until lightly browned, 2 to 4 minutes; transfer the onion to a second plate.

3. Thoroughly wipe out the skillet with paper towels, add the butter, and set over medium heat. When the butter foams, swirl to coat the bottom and sides of the skillet, then pour in the eggs. With a heatproof rubber spatula, stir the eggs constantly, slowly pushing them from side to side, scraping along the bottom of the skillet and then around the sides, and lifting and folding the eggs as they form curds. Do not overscramble, as the curds formed will be too small. Cook the eggs until large curds form but the eggs are still very moist, 2 to 3 minutes. Off the heat, gently fold in the onion, cheese, and half of the bacon until evenly distributed; if the eggs are still underdone, return the skillet to medium heat for no longer than 30 seconds. Divide the eggs among individual plates, sprinkle with the remaining bacon and parsley, and serve immediately.

SCRAMBLED EGGS WITH SAUSAGE, SWEET PEPPERS, AND CHEDDAR CHEESE

Serves 4 to 6

While we prefer sweet Italian sausage here, especially for breakfast, you can certainly use spicy sausage, if desired.

12 large eggs
¾ teaspoon salt
¼ teaspoon ground black pepper
6 tablespoons half-and-half
1 teaspoon vegetable oil
8 ounces sweet (or hot) Italian sausage, casing removed, sausage crumbled into ½-inch pieces
1 medium red bell pepper, stemmed, seeded, and cut into ½-inch cubes (about 1 cup)
3 medium scallions, white and green parts separated, both sliced thinly on the bias
1 tablespoon unsalted butter
1½ ounces sharp cheddar cheese, shredded (about ½ cup)

1. Crack the eggs into a medium bowl; add the salt, pepper, and half-and-half. Beat with a dinner fork until thoroughly combined.

2. Heat the oil in a 12-inch nonstick skillet over medium heat until shimmering. Add the sausage and cook until beginning to brown but still pink in the center, about 2 minutes. Add the red bell pepper and scallion whites; continue to cook, stirring occasionally, until the sausage is cooked through and the peppers are beginning to brown, about 3 minutes. Spread the mixture in a single layer on a medium plate; set aside.

3. Thoroughly wipe out the skillet with paper towels, add the butter, and set over medium heat. When the butter foams, swirl to coat the bottom and sides of the skillet, then pour in the eggs. With a heatproof rubber spatula, stir the eggs constantly, slowly pushing them from side to side, scraping along the bottom of the skillet and then around the sides, and lifting and folding the eggs as they form curds. Do not overscramble, as the curds formed will be too small. Cook the eggs until large curds form but the eggs are still very moist, 2 to 3 minutes. Off the heat, gently fold in the sausage mixture and cheese until evenly distributed; if the eggs are still underdone, return the skillet to medium heat for no longer than 30 seconds. Divide the eggs among individual plates, sprinkle with the scallion greens, and serve immediately.

SCRAMBLED EGGS WITH ASPARAGUS, PROSCIUTTO, AND PARMESAN

Serves 4 to 6

If your asparagus spears are very fat, cut them on the bias into ⅜-inch lengths after halving them lengthwise.

12 large eggs
¾ teaspoon salt
¼ teaspoon ground black pepper
6 tablespoons half-and-half
1 teaspoon vegetable oil
8 ounces asparagus, bottoms trimmed, each spear halved lengthwise, then cut on the bias into ½-inch lengths (about 1½ cups)
1 tablespoon unsalted butter
½ cup grated Parmesan cheese (1 ounce)
3 ounces thinly sliced prosciutto, cut into ½-inch squares

1. Crack the eggs into a medium bowl; add the salt, pepper, and half-and-half. Beat with a dinner fork until thoroughly combined.

2. Heat the oil in a 12-inch nonstick skillet over medium heat until shimmering. Add the asparagus and cook, stirring occasionally, until lightly browned and tender but still crisp, 3 to 4 minutes. Spread the asparagus in a single layer on a small plate; set aside.

3. Thoroughly wipe out the skillet with paper towels, add the butter, and set over medium heat. When the butter foams, swirl to coat the bottom and sides of the skillet, then pour in the eggs. With a heatproof rubber spatula, stir the eggs constantly, slowly pushing them from side to side, scraping along the bottom of the skillet and then around the sides, and lifting and folding the eggs as they form curds. Do not overscramble, as the curds formed will be too small. Cook the eggs until large curds form but the eggs are still very moist, 2 to 3 minutes. Off the heat, gently fold in the cheese and prosciutto until evenly distributed; if the eggs are still underdone, return the skillet to medium heat for no longer than 30 seconds. Divide the eggs among individual plates and serve immediately.

EGGS IN A HOLE

Serves 2 to 4

Want another way to enjoy eggs? This quick, double-duty dish combines the best of the breakfast world—crisp buttered toast and creamy fried eggs—the eggs cook through while the bread toasts. Use a substantial sliced sandwich bread, such as Pepperidge Farm, which has a fine crumb, for this recipe. Soft breads, such as Wonder, or slices from a thick-crusted rustic loaf, for that matter, are not options here.

> 4 slices high-quality white sandwich bread
> 2 tablespoons unsalted butter
> 4 large eggs
> Salt and ground black pepper

Adjust an oven rack to the middle position and heat the oven to 200 degrees. Using a 2½-inch biscuit cutter, cut and remove a hole from the center of each slice of bread. Melt 1 tablespoon of the butter in a 12-inch nonstick skillet over medium-high heat until it just begins to brown, swirling to coat the pan. Crack an egg each into 2 small bowls. Place 2 slices of the bread in the skillet and slide 1 egg into each hole. Sprinkle with salt and pepper and cook until the egg whites begin to set and the bread is well

browned, about 1½ minutes. Carefully flip the bread and eggs over and continue to cook until the eggs have reached your desired doneness, up to 70 seconds longer. Slide the bread slices onto a plate and keep warm in the oven. Wipe out the skillet and return to medium heat. Repeat with the remaining tablespoon of butter, bread, and eggs.

SCIENCE DESK:
How Scrambled Eggs Work

COOKING CAUSES PROFOUND CHANGES IN THE STRUC-ture of egg proteins. Heat encourages these proteins to unfold, stick together, and form a latticed gel (compare illustrations 1 and 2 on the following page). As a result, eggs transition from a liquid to a semisolid that you can pick up with a fork.

Most scrambled egg recipes call for some sort of dairy. Both the water and the fat in dairy ingredients keep the eggs from becoming tough by getting in between the protein strands, preventing them from joining too tightly (illustration 3). The water also helps to incorporate pockets of air and steam into the eggs as they are gently folded. This translates into fluffy scrambled eggs.

When we added hearty ingredients (each containing some water) to our scrambled egg recipe, however, the eggs became watery and weepy. That's because eggs can hold only a limited amount of water—too much and they weep as they coagulate (illustration 4). Our solution to the problem of weepy eggs was to reduce the amount of liquid we had been using by 50 percent and to make our liquid of choice half-and-half rather than milk. While these scrambled eggs were not quite as fluffy as those made with milk, the extra fat in the half-and-half made for a pleasing texture, and the added heaviness of the eggs was imperceptible once sausage, bacon, and vegetables were folded in just before serving.

GETTING IT RIGHT:
Watery Versus Fluffy Eggs

The illustrations below demonstrate how the protein strands in eggs behave from (1) their raw state to (2) scrambled, then to (3) scrambled with just enough liquid, and (4) scrambled with too much liquid. See the Science Desk (page 189) for more information.

1. Raw Eggs
Protein strands fold over on themselves.

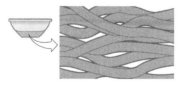

2. Scrambled Eggs
Protein strands unfold and stick to each other.

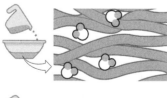

3. Fluffy Eggs: Just enough liquid
Water and fat separate protein strands.

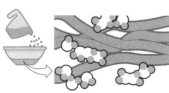

4. Wet Eggs: Too much liquid
Protein strands are saturated and shed excess water.

TASTING LAB: Breakfast Sausage

AMERICANS KNOW BREAKFAST SAUSAGE TO BE A MIXTURE of ground meat (both lean and fat, and usually pork), salt, pepper, and spices that you fry up crisp and brown to accompany eggs or pancakes. A simple list of ingredients, maybe, but selecting a sausage can be a complicated affair. Shape (link, patty, roll, or bulk) and flavor (mild through "zesty") are just two of the obvious choices. But for our tasting we explored another option that many home cooks might not even consider: the choice between fully cooked sausage, which requires only a bit of heating (often referred to as "brown and serve"), and fresh sausage, which requires full cooking. Brown-and-serve sausage has two things going for it: It's less perishable than fresh, capable of withstanding months in the freezer, and it takes precious little time to prepare. But how much flavor do you have to sacrifice for such convenience?

In an informal poll, almost everyone in the test kitchen agreed that they would buy fresh over fully cooked, frozen breakfast sausage. That sounded like a challenge to us, so we conducted a tasting to find out if fresher really is better. These were the rules: pork only (nothing identified as beef, poultry, or meatless), in link form, and in the simplest possible flavor profile. Fresh and fully cooked sausages were prepared by pan-frying according to package instructions. First, we evaluated the fresh sausages alone, then we sampled the fully cooked sausages along with the winning fresh sausage for reference.

Fresh and brown-and-serve sausages are fabricated in much the same way, at least up to a point. Pork trimmings from several primal cuts are ground, blended with ice (to help maintain temperature) and water (for workability), and seasoned. Several experts stressed that the trimmings are not scraps but pieces of lean meat and fat removed from large primal cuts during the fabrication of retail cuts. Inquiries to manufacturers about specific types and grades of trimmings, lean to fat ratios, particle sizes, quantities of water, seasonings, and casings were unerringly met with the word "proprietary."

If sausages are to be sold as a brown-and-serve product, they are sent through gigantic cookers that often use steam and convection to cook them to 170 degrees. The sausages then may or may not be sent to a browning chamber, where gas-fired flame jets enhance both color and flavor. Some sources suggest that a less expensive way to color the steam-cooked sausages is to dip them in caramel coloring. The sausages are then quickly cooled and blast-frozen.

With all this in mind, it came as a huge surprise that the fully cooked, brown-and-serve sausages did extremely well in the tasting, so well that the best sausage overall was the brown-and-serve product from Farmland, which scored a full two points higher (out of 10) than the highest-ranked fresh sausage—also from Farmland. After conversations with meat-processing experts, we concluded that the explanation for our findings is control.

Roger Mandigo of the University of Nebraska pointed out that fully cooked sausage introduces many variables, among them the evaporation of moisture, rendering of fat, and denaturing (reconfiguration) of proteins. But these variables are also opportunities for manufacturers to engineer the product. With specific appearance, flavor, and texture attributes in mind, manufacturers can manipulate the recipe and cooking temperature(s) and time with great exactitude.

For instance, a Farmland representative mentioned one method that the company uses to help control the texture of its brown-and-serve sausage. Immediately after steam cooking, excess fat on the surface of the sausage is blown off at high pressure to reduce the perception of greasiness by the consumer. This kind of manipulation ensures a more consistent product when the sausages are reheated at home.

Robert Delmore Jr. at California Polytechnic State University mentioned another possible advantage of manufacturing brown-and-serve sausage. Oxidation of fat, he said, degrades flavor. Many companies combat this effect by adding preservatives such as propyl gallate, citric acid, butylated hydroxyanisole (BHA), and butylated hydroxytoluene

(BHT), but the quick deep freeze that brown-and-serve sausages undergo during processing adds an extra level of protection against oxidation. Sure enough, our tasting bore out this theory, as tasters were more likely to use terms such as "off," "musty," "stale," and "not fresh" to describe the fresh sausage than to describe the brown and serve.

We next turned to the issue of fat, which provides both flavor and juiciness in sausage. We enlisted an independent food lab to measure fat content and uncovered large disparities. Some brands had as little as 22 percent fat, while others were nearly 50 percent fat (the maximum allowable amount, according to the U.S. Department of Agriculture). Comparing these figures with our tasting results, the success of Farmland makes a lot of sense.

With its relatively high fat content (44 percent), Farmland's fresh sausage was described by tasters as being juicy and tasting strongly of pork. (The two fresh sausages with higher fat contents, Hormel and Swift, failed for unrelated reasons.) In contrast, tasters considered Owens, near the bottom of the fat content scale at 23 percent, too bland. Likewise, many tasters found Jimmy Dean fresh sausage, with its relatively low fat content of 27 percent, to be dry. Among the brown-and-serve sausages, Farmland topped the fat ratings at nearly 41 percent, which helps explain why tasters found it to possess "big pork flavor" and juiciness.

Another point raised by the experts was seasoning. Tasters scrutinized every sample for saltiness, sweetness, and spiciness and marked down samples they perceived as too salty, sweet, or spicy. The lab could not analyze for specific spices, and none of the manufacturers we contacted would reveal their seasoning blend (there was that word "proprietary" again), but balance was important to our tasters, who regarded Farmland favorably in this regard.

What, then, to buy? If what you desire most in your pork breakfast sausage is convenience, you may now approach fully cooked, frozen products without fear of sacrificing flavor and reliable texture. This is one of those rare cases in which a "processed" food may in fact be superior to the "real thing."

Rating Breakfast Sausages

TWENTY-THREE MEMBERS OF THE AMERICA'S TEST KITCHEN staff tasted 14 different supermarket pork sausages, including both fresh and frozen, fully cooked brown-and-serve samples. The sausages were pan-fried to the same degree of doneness (165 degrees on an instant-read thermometer) per the manufacturers' cooking instructions, and tasted warm. Fresh and fully cooked sausages were tasted separately. The top-rated fresh sausage was included in the tasting of fully cooked sausages as a point of reference. The sausages are listed, separated by type, in order of preference based on their scores in these tastings. The sausages are available nationwide.

BEST OVERALL SAUSAGE
Farmland Pork Sausage Links, Fully Cooked
$2.69 for 12 ounces, Fat: 40.82%
Tasters lauded this link for "big pork flavor," good balance of salt and sweet, and "nice, lingering spiciness." Accolades didn't end there; compliments also garnered for tender, "super-juicy" meat. And, this fully cooked frozen sausage was even preferred to its fresh counterpart, making it our best overall sausage.

FULLY COOKED, FROZEN SAUSAGES

RECOMMENDED WITH RESERVATIONS
Armour Brown 'N Serve Original Fully Cooked Sausage Links
$1.99 for 7 ounces, Fat: 33.79%
Armour's hallmark was tenderness, so much so that one taster thought the texture was "suspicious." A few complaints about saltiness, but most found the sweetness and saltiness well balanced and the pork flavor "decent."

RECOMMENDED WITH RESERVATIONS
Owens Express Fully Cooked Regular Microwavable Pork Sausage Links
$2.89 for 8 ounces, Fat: 31.05%
The middle-of-the-road fat content made for a middle-of-the-road link, with discernible flavors of pork and spice that some perceived as mild, even "boring." Texture viewed as fine and firm.

RECOMMENDED WITH RESERVATIONS
Jones Golden Brown Fully Cooked & Browned Sausage, Mild Links
$2.59 for 8 ounces, Fat: 38.86%
Pork flavor was lost on tasters, who cried "stale," "funky," and "bizarre." Comments on texture were split almost evenly between "greasy" and "juicy."

RECOMMENDED WITH RESERVATIONS
Bob Evans Express Fully Cooked Original Microwavable Pork Sausage Links
$2.59 for 8 ounces, Fat: 28.70%
Nearly every taster thought the casing was tough, giving the link "too much snap . . . like a hot dog." Most deemed the flavor fresh and subtle, though some complained of "massive sage overload."

NOT RECOMMENDED
Swift Premium Sizzle 'N Serve Fully Cooked Sausage
$3.59 for 8 ounces, Fat: 35.66%
Nearly every taster was overwhelmed by salt, so much so that several likened this link to a "salt lick." Tasters who could get beyond the salt were bothered by a "cafeteria flavor."

NOT RECOMMENDED
Jimmy Dean Fresh Taste. Fast! Original Fully Cooked Pork Sausage Links
$4.19 for 9.6 ounces, Fat: 36.15%
Instead of pork flavor, more tasters noted hints of bacon, beef, and hot dogs, as well as a strong smokiness that "totally dominated."

FRESH SAUSAGES

RECOMMENDED
Farmland Original Pork Sausage Links
$1.89 for 12 ounces, Fat: 43.99%

Though saltiness was a common complaint, tasters still found a lot to like in this highly rated link, which earned kudos for its "straight-up pork flavor" and "spiciness that mellows with every bite." Pleasantly sweet and juicy.

RECOMMENDED WITH RESERVATIONS
Bob Evans Original Links
$3.68 for 12 ounces, Fat: 27.21%

Some tasters likened the flavor of this "not-too-sweet" link to a hot dog, but most focused on obvious ("overwhelming") dried spice flavors, including coriander, white pepper, and sage.

RECOMMENDED WITH RESERVATIONS
Owens Original Premium Pork Sausage Links
$3.75 for 12 ounces, Fat: 22.46%

Nicely balanced pork flavor, though some considered it too mild, even bland. Tasters collectively hated the texture: The words "gristly," "rubbery," and "spongy" were used repeatedly.

RECOMMENDED WITH RESERVATIONS
Jimmy Dean Original Fresh Pork Sausage Links
$3.69 for 10 ounces, Fat: 26.74%

Several tasters picked up on a "cured," "hammy" flavor that even reminded one of "Chinese wontons," but many more declared this link to be bland and dry.

RECOMMENDED WITH RESERVATIONS
Jones All Natural Pork Little Sausages
$4.49 for 12 ounces, Fat: 42.96%

The smooth texture struck tasters alternately as greasy or juicy. Notes on the flavor were positive, with praise for "big" pork flavor. A vocal minority was stunned by salt: "Get me some O.J., stat!"

NOT RECOMMENDED
Hormel Little Sizzlers Pork Sausage, Original
$2.69 for 12 ounces, Fat: 47.17%

Most tasters said "no thanks" to these "super-salty," overly spiced links, which were widely thought to resemble "Tater Tots" or "fish sticks."

NOT RECOMMENDED
Swift Premium Fresh Pork Sausage
$3.59 for 12 ounces, Fat: 47.66%

Tasted "gamey" and "processed" to many panelists, one of whom even likened the sample to Slim Jim beef jerky. Saltiness was also a common complaint.

FAMILY-SIZED OMELETS

WHAT WE WANTED: An omelet big enough to serve four, with all the merits of our best individual omelet: tender not tough eggs and a hearty filling that wouldn't weigh down the eggs.

Omelets are a terrific way to make a meal out of eggs, but omelets just aren't practical when you're making more than one or two. We set out to see if we could make one big omelet that would serve a family of four and we wanted an interesting mix of fillings to make this an attractive dinner option, not just for breakfast or brunch. Typically our favorite omelet is soft, supple, and slightly creamy. But for a large omelet, we aimed for something a bit sturdier—almost, but not quite as firm as a frittata.

With these goals in mind, we began testing. Our initial tests were disastrous, with runny eggs on top and burnt eggs underneath. Obviously, flipping a behemoth, eight-egg omelet was out of the question. We began by cooking the eggs over low heat to prevent them from scorching, but found that they took so long to cook that the eggs' texture was suffering. We increased the heat to medium and things were better, but we still had to figure out a way to cook the top of the omelet. And we wanted cheese in our omelet and needed to figure out how to melt that, too.

Sliding the omelet under the broiler worked OK, but our omelet was a little dry. Next, we wondered about simply covering the skillet with a tight-fitting lid. We found that the lid trapped the steam, cooking the eggs with its moist heat. This method also aided in partially melting the cheese. A note about the cheese: be sure to shred the cheese before you begin cooking. Eggs cook quickly and once they're in the skillet there will be no time to step away to prep the cheese.

Shaping this super-sized omelet was as simple as sliding it halfway out of the pan and then folding it over onto itself—and the residual heat was also enough to perfectly finish melting the cheese.

For our omelet with a filling, we found that the process wasn't as simple as sprinkling the filling over the eggs and folding the omelet over. When sliding our big, filled omelet out of the pan, some filling slipped out. And once cut, some portions held more filling than others. After further testing, we found that mixing the filling ingredients in with the egg mixture made our omelet much easier to handle. We also found that chopping the ingredients finely made it much easier to distribute the filling among the egg mixture, yielding an omelet with a cohesive mixture of filling and egg in every bite—and no one got shortchanged.

WHAT WE LEARNED: Cook the egg mixture in a non-stick skillet over medium heat until the bottom is set, but the top is still runny. Cover the skillet with a tight-fitting lid and reduce the heat. The lid traps the moisture, gently steaming the top of the omelet so it won't dry out. Mix the filling ingredients in with the eggs and make sure to chop the ingredients finely to ensure even distribution.

TECHNIQUE: How to Make an Oversized Omelet

Our eight-egg omelet calls for a cooking method that requires a 12-inch nonstick skillet with a tight-fitting lid.

1. To cook the omelet evenly, pull the cooked edges of egg toward the center of the pan and allow the raw egg to run to the edges.

2. When the omelet is set on the bottom but still very runny on the top, cover the skillet and reduce the heat to low.

3. After the top of the omelet begins to set, sprinkle with the cheese and let the omelet rest off the heat, covered, until the cheese has partially melted.

4. After using a heatproof rubber spatula to slide half of the omelet out onto a platter, tilt the skillet so that the omelet folds over onto itself to make the traditional half-moon shape.

FAMILY-SIZED CHEESE OMELET
Serves 4

Monterey Jack, colby, or any good melting cheese can be substituted for the cheddar.

- 8 large eggs
- ½ teaspoon salt
- ⅛ teaspoon ground black pepper
- 2 tablespoons unsalted butter
- 3 ounces cheddar cheese, shredded (about ¾ cup)

1. Whisk the eggs, salt, and pepper together. Melt the butter in a 12-inch nonstick skillet over medium heat, swirling to coat the skillet, until the foaming subsides.

2. Add the eggs and cook, stirring gently in a circular motion, until the mixture is slightly thickened, about 1 minute. Following the illustration above, use a heatproof rubber spatula to pull the cooked edges of the egg toward the center of the pan, tilting the pan so the uncooked egg runs to the cleared edge of the pan. Repeat until the bottom of the omelet is just set but the top is still runny, about 1 minute. Cover the skillet, reduce the heat to low, and cook until the top of the omelet begins to set but is still moist, about 5 minutes.

3. Remove the pan from the heat. Sprinkle the cheese evenly over the eggs, cover, and let sit until the cheese partially melts, about 1 minute. Following the illustration above, slide half of the omelet onto a serving platter using the spatula, then tilt the skillet so the remaining omelet flips over onto itself, forming a half-moon shape. Cut into wedges and serve immediately.

VARIATION
FAMILY-SIZED TOMATO, BACON, AND GARLIC OMELET

Assemble the filling ingredients before making the omelet.

- 8 slices bacon (about 8 ounces), minced
- 1 large tomato, cored, seeded, and chopped fine
- ½ green bell pepper, stemmed, seeded, and chopped fine
- 4 medium garlic cloves, minced or pressed through a garlic press (about 4 teaspoons)
- 3 ounces pepper Jack cheese, shredded (about ¾ cup)

Fry the bacon in a 12-inch nonstick skillet over medium-high heat until crisp, about 8 minutes. Stir in the tomato and bell pepper and cook until the vegetables are softened, about

6 minutes. Stir in the garlic and cook until fragrant, about 30 seconds. Transfer the mixture to a paper towel–lined plate. Wipe the skillet clean with paper towels and follow the recipe for Family-Sized Cheese Omelet, adding the bacon mixture to the pan with the eggs in step 2. Substitute pepper Jack cheese for the cheddar.

EQUIPMENT CORNER:
Plastic Nonstick Spatulas

UNLESS YOU LIKE TO EAT FLAKED-OFF NONSTICK COATING, you need to use a plastic spatula with your nonstick cookware. But with most stores stocking at least five models, how do you know which one is best?

To narrow the field, we decided to focus on one plastic spatula that would fulfill all our cooking needs. A slotted spatula that allows grease and liquid to drain but that still provides the support of a solid spatula, covers all the bases. We gathered 11 brands of plastic nonstick slotted spatulas ranging in price from $4.95 to $14.99 and went to the kitchen to flip pancakes and pan-fry fish fillets and hamburgers to see what mattered most in a spatula and how our brands stacked up.

After flipping our way through dozens of pancakes, one thing was clear: the larger the blade of the spatula, the better. Small blades caused the pancakes to droop on the sides when we flipped them, dripping batter and sometimes breaking in the process. The size of the slots, on the other hand, did not play a factor in any test; though the slots came in all shapes (circles, rectangles, ovals) and sizes, all the spatulas drained grease from burgers and fish adequately.

All of the spatulas featured blades that tapered to a thinner edge, some just at the top and others on all three sides. The best spatulas featured thin blades and even thinner edges. Blades that were too thick were difficult to slide under the pancakes and fish fillets without causing them to bunch up and, in the case of delicate fish fillets, to break apart. The blade of the top-rated Calphalon spatula was

just 2.73 mm, that of the lowest-rated iSi was a whopping 6.5 mm.

Given the range in price among our spatulas, we thought perhaps the more expensive models might be sturdier than the cheaper ones and better able to support the weight of heavy foods. To test this, we cooked up some hefty 8-ounce hamburgers and flipped them with each spatula. To our surprise, only two spatulas failed this test, bending under the burger's weight, and they were two of the most expensive: the Henckels and the iSi.

While most of the spatulas featured thick plastic handles that were comfortable in the hand, a few had sharp metal edges that made gripping difficult. The Henckels spatula was particularly uncomfortable, with not just one but two sharp edges thanks to the handle's loop design.

In the end, the cheapest spatulas were the top performers: The Calphalon and Cuisinart impressed us with their large blades and thin edges.

Rating Plastic Nonstick Spatulas

WE TESTED 11 BRANDS OF SPATULAS, RANGING IN PRICE FROM $4.95 TO $14.99. TESTS INCLUDED FLIPPING PANCAKES AND pan-frying fish fillets and hamburgers. The spatulas are listed in order of preference. See www.americastestkitchen.com for up-to-date prices and mail-order sources for top-rated products.

RECOMMENDED

Calphalon N04 Tools Large Nylon Slotted Spatula

$4.99; Blade area: 16.48 square inches; Blade thickness: 2.73 mm

The least expensive spatula impressed us with its large blade and very thin edge, which slid under pancakes and fish with ease.

RECOMMENDED

Cuisinart Nylon Turner with Soft Grip Handle

$5.95; Blade area: 15.94 square inches; Blade thickness: 2.73 mm

The large rubber handle was extremely comfortable to hold, and the large blade was tapered on all sides so we could flip from any angle.

RECOMMENDED

Oxo Good Grips Nylon Square Turner

$5.99; Blade area: 15.94 square inches; Blade thickness: 3.74 mm

The long handle was very comfortable, and the thin edge compensated for the fairly thick blade.

RECOMMENDED WITH RESERVATIONS

Messermeister Pro-Touch Teflon Spatula

$5.95; Blade area: 17 square inches; Blade thickness: 2.6 mm

This model lost points for the short, thin rubber grip at the end of the handle.

RECOMMENDED WITH RESERVATIONS

Zyliss Slotted Turner

$7.49; Blade area: 12.78 square inches; Blade thickness: 3.05 mm

This spatula shone in all but the pancake test, where the narrow blade resulted in awkward flipping.

RECOMMENDED WITH RESERVATIONS

Amco Nonstick Slotted Spatula

$7; Blade area: 12 square inches; Blade thickness: 2.69 mm

The small blade made flipping large pancakes and fish fillets a messy affair.

RECOMMENDED WITH RESERVATIONS

Emerilware Nonstick Slotted Turner

$5.99; Blade area: 14.63 square inches; Blade thickness: 4.93 mm

We liked the large molded handle and tapered edge, but the blade was too thick to slide under foods with ease.

RECOMMENDED WITH RESERVATIONS

KitchenAid Silicone Slotted Turner

$9.99; Blade area: 17.81 square inches; Blade thickness: 5.08 mm

Though it had the largest blade of the lot, it also had one of the thickest, which made flipping greasy foods a slippery task.

NOT RECOMMENDED

WMF Profi Plus Nonstick Slotted Spatula

$13.99; Blade area: 9.36 square inches; Blade thickness: 3.7 mm

The extremely small blade area and very short handle caused this model to flop in all but the hamburger test.

NOT RECOMMENDED

Henckels Twin Select Nylon Turner

$14.99; Blade area: 12 square inches; Blade thickness: 3.28 mm

The most expensive spatula in the group suffered from a small blade and a sharp and extremely uncomfortable metal handle.

NOT RECOMMENDED

iSi K8677 Silicone Meat Turner with Stainless Steel Handle

$12.07; Blade area: 15.13 square inches; Blade thickness: 6.5 mm

This spatula featured a long, narrow blade that was thick, floppy, and almost jelly-like in texture; sliding it under foods was a daunting task. The thin metal handle was uncomfortable.

For tender grilled shrimp with great smoky flavor, slide the shrimp onto skewers and grill them just until pink, then transfer them to a pan of simmering sauce to gently finish cooking.

SUMMER cooking

Grilling imparts a smoky dimension to foods that is just about impossible to replicate indoors. So it's no wonder that once the weather turns warm, we're eager to get our favorite foods like steaks and burgers onto the grill. But delicate foods, such as shrimp, are trickier to cook over the grill's intense, dry heat. We wanted to find the best way to grill shrimp so that they are tender, moist, and flavorful, not dry and rubbery. And we wanted to do so without grilling shrimp in their shells. It's true that the shells act as a protective barrier, but peeling shells at the table is cumbersome and messy, not to mention that with the discarded shells, the flavorful spice rub is also lost.

Warm weather isn't always about cooking outdoors—it's about eating outdoors, too. Cold barbecued chicken is a classic whether you're planning a picnic or packing for a road trip. But once chilled, the meat can become very dry and the skin, once thin and crisp, can turn tough and flabby. We wanted to solve these problems and turn out moist chicken with spicy flavor and we also wanted to make it easier to eat, so we didn't have to use a knife and fork or rely on a wad of napkins to wipe our hands of sticky barbecue sauce.

IN THIS CHAPTER

THE RECIPES

Charcoal-Grilled Shrimp Skewers
Gas-Grilled Shrimp Skewers
Spicy Lemon-Garlic Sauce
Fresh Tomato Sauce with Feta
  and Olives
Charmoula Sauce

Spice-Rubbed Picnic Chicken

EQUIPMENT CORNER

Skewers

SCIENCE DESK

Salting Instead of Brining?

TASTING LAB

Veggie Burgers
Lemonade

GRILLED SHRIMP

WHAT WE WANTED: Great grilled shrimp—tender, moist, and flavorful. And we wanted shrimp that could go directly from the grill to the dinner plate, so that we wouldn't have to deal with the messy task of peeling shells at the table.

I t's no secret that shrimp can turn from moist and juicy to rubbery and dry in the blink of an eye, a consequence of their small size and lack of fat. Add the unpredictability of cooking over a live fire, and the challenge is magnified. Grilling shrimp in their shells to shield them from the coals' scorching heat works well, but we're always disappointed when garlic, herbs, and other seasonings get stripped off at the table along with the shells, only to land in a discard pile. We wanted to experience tender, juicy, boldly seasoned grilled shrimp without the pesky shells.

We started by preparing the test kitchen's existing recipe for grilled shrimp, substituting peeled shrimp for shell-on. (We'd investigate flavorings later.) We followed every mandate, plumping the shrimp in a saltwater brine (which helps keep them moist), threading them onto skewers, brushing with oil, then quickly grilling over moderate heat. After a few minutes over the fire, the shrimp were tough and dehydrated—no surprise given their shell-free state. Also problematic was the absence of attractive (and flavorful) char marks.

Suspecting that brining was causing the shrimp to become waterlogged and, thus, hindering caramelization, we lit a new fire and grilled a batch of plain, unbrined samples. Sure enough, these shrimp began to pick up the flavor of the grill with a few faint, yet promising, marks.

Having discarded brining, we next built an especially hot fire by banking all the coals on one side of the grill. We seasoned a batch of shrimp with salt and pepper (plus a pinch of sugar to encourage caramelization), set them on the grate, and waited. And waited. Even with a screaming-hot fire, the only way to get sufficient charring was to leave the

shrimp on the grill for four or five minutes, yet each passing minute brought us closer to shrimp jerky and farther from a decent dinner.

Shrimp cook so quickly because of their small size. Would jumbo shrimp afford us a few extra minutes? Thirty-seven dollars later, we had the answer. Producing a charred exterior and a tender interior on these hefty specimens was a snap, but with a cost of more than $25 per pound and spotty availability, there had to be a better way.

Then, we thought of an idea: cramming several normal-sized shrimp very tightly together on a skewer, creating a faux "jumbo" shrimp. Sure enough, this homemade giant

shrimp cooked at a slightly slower pace, giving us the extra minutes of grilling time the shrimp needed for charring.

With a decent grilling method at hand, we could finally start investigating flavorings. Thus far, we'd been coating the shrimp in oil, but we wondered if yogurt, mayonnaise, coconut milk, or butter offered any advantages. Coconut milk was promising but too distinctive, so we stuck with relatively neutral olive oil. We tried to add personality to the oil with ground spices, but this was a mistake. During a moment of inattention, a flare-up torched the spice paste, turning it bitter. Minced garlic? Scorched. Fresh herbs? Scorched again.

Scanning our library shelves, we reviewed every grilled seafood recipe we could find. Eventually, we found a few recipes in which shellfish was given an initial sear over a hot fire, then transferred to a sauce waiting on the cooler side of the grill. Intrigued, we grilled a few shrimp and slid them into a sauce that simmered in a disposable foil pan. These shrimp were a tad overdone but, having soaked up the flavorful sauce, were good enough for two of us, who polished off an entire batch grill-side.

A few tries later, we started transferring the shrimp to the sauce before they were fully cooked. This way, we could concentrate on getting char marks, then switch to a more forgiving cooking method (gentle simmering in the sauce) until the shrimp were done. We finally had an infallible recipe that delivered everything we wanted in grilled shrimp: tender flesh, attractive charring, tons of flavor—and no shells.

WHAT WE LEARNED: Pack the shrimp together tightly on the skewers. This technique creates a mass of shrimp that will cook more slowly than individual shrimp and slower cooking means that the shrimp will have more time to absorb smoky flavor and develop grill marks. To promote caramelization, sprinkle one side of the shrimp with a bit of sugar. Grill the skewered shrimp just until grill marks form, but shrimp are still translucent. Then slide the shrimp off the skewers into a simmering pan of flavorful sauce to gently finish cooking through.

CHARCOAL-GRILLED SHRIMP SKEWERS
Serves 4 as a main course, 6 as an appetizer

The shrimp and sauce (recipes follow) finish cooking together on the grill, so prepare the sauce ingredients while the coals are heating. To fit all of the shrimp on the cooking grate at once, you'll need three 14-inch metal skewers. Serve with grilled bread.

1½	pounds extra-large (21/25) shrimp, peeled and deveined, tails left on
2–3	tablespoons olive oil for brushing the shrimp
	Salt and ground black pepper
¼	teaspoon sugar
1	recipe Spicy Lemon-Garlic Sauce, Fresh Tomato Sauce with Feta and Olives, or Charmoula Sauce (recipes follow)
	Lemon wedges, for serving

1. Pat the shrimp dry with paper towels. Thread the shrimp onto 3 skewers, alternating direction of heads and tails (see illustration, page 203). Brush both sides of the shrimp with the oil and season lightly with salt and pepper. Sprinkle one side of each skewer evenly with sugar.

2. Light a large chimney starter filled with charcoal (6 quarts, or about 100 briquettes) and allow to burn until the coals are fully ignited and partially covered with a thin layer of ash, about 20 minutes. Empty the coals into the grill and build a modified two-level fire by arranging the coals to cover one-half of the grill, leaving the other half empty. Position the cooking grate over the coals, cover the grill, and heat until hot, about 5 minutes; scrape the cooking grate clean with a grill brush.

3. Set the disposable pan with the sauce ingredients on the hot side of the grill and cook as directed; transfer the pan to the cooler side of the grill. Place the shrimp skewers, sugared sides down, on the hot side of the grate and use tongs to push the shrimp together on the skewers if they have

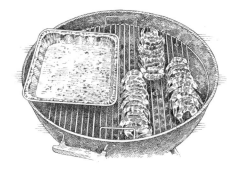

TECHNIQUE: The Right Setup

With grilled shrimp, timing can be tricky. We solved the problem by setting up two cooking zones. On the hot side, we sear the shrimp over dry heat until almost done. On the cooler side, we keep a disposable pan of simmering sauce, where the shrimp finish cooking at a gentler pace. Crowding the shrimp on the skewers bought us a few extra minutes on the hot side, giving the shrimp better charring.

separated. Grill the shrimp, uncovered, until lightly charred, 4 to 5 minutes. Using tongs, flip and grill until the second side is pink and slightly translucent, 1 to 2 minutes longer.

4. Using a potholder or oven mitt, carefully lift each skewer from the grill and use tongs to slide the shrimp off the skewers into the pan with the sauce. Toss the shrimp and sauce to combine and transfer the pan to the hot side of the grill; cook, stirring, until the shrimp are opaque and fully cooked, about 30 seconds. Remove from the grill, add the remaining sauce ingredients, and toss to combine. Transfer to a serving platter and serve immediately with lemon wedges.

VARIATION

GAS-GRILLED SHRIMP SKEWERS

Follow step 1 of the recipe for Charcoal-Grilled Shrimp Skewers. Light all the burners on a gas grill and turn to high, cover, and heat the grill until hot, about 15 minutes. Scrape the cooking grate clean with a grill brush and proceed with step 3 of the recipe, setting the sauce aside off the heat once hot and grilling the shrimp with the lid down, checking occasionally to make sure they're not burning (the timing may be a few minutes longer than in the charcoal grill recipe).

SPICY LEMON-GARLIC SAUCE

Makes enough to sauce 1½ pounds shrimp

4	tablespoons (½ stick) unsalted butter, cut into 4 pieces
4	tablespoons juice from 2 lemons
½–¾	teaspoon red pepper flakes
3	medium garlic cloves, minced or pressed through a garlic press (about 1 tablespoon)
⅛	teaspoon salt
	10-inch disposable foil pan or pie plate
⅓	cup minced fresh parsley leaves

Combine the butter, lemon juice, pepper flakes, garlic, and salt in the pan. Cook over the hot side of the grill, stirring occasionally, until the butter melts, about 1½ minutes; transfer to the cooler side of the grill (if using a charcoal grill) or set aside off heat (if using a gas grill). Proceed to grill the shrimp, adding the parsley just before serving.

TECHNIQUE:

Brushless Grate Cleaning

You should always start with a clean cooking grate. If you don't have a grill brush, this method works just as well.

Once your cooking grate is hot, fashion your own grill brush with a crumpled wad of aluminum foil and long-handled tongs.

TECHNIQUE:

Crowding Shrimp onto a Skewer

Pass the skewer through the center of each shrimp. As you add shrimp to the skewer, alternate the directions of the heads and tails for a compact arrangement of about 12 shrimp. The shrimp should be crowded and touching each other.

FRESH TOMATO SAUCE WITH FETA AND OLIVES

Makes enough to sauce 1½ pounds shrimp

Shrimp, combined with tomatoes, feta, and olives, is a classic Greek combination.

4	tablespoons extra-virgin olive oil
1	large ripe tomato, cored, seeded, and diced very small
⅛	teaspoon salt
1	tablespoon minced fresh oregano leaves 10-inch disposable foil pan or pie plate
2	tablespoons juice from 1 lemon
4	ounces feta cheese (about 1 cup), crumbled into ¼-inch pieces
⅓	cup kalamata olives, pitted and chopped fine
3	scallions, sliced very thin

Combine the oil, tomato, salt, and oregano in the pan. Cook over the hot side of grill, stirring occasionally, until hot, about 1½ minutes; transfer to the cooler side of the grill (if using a charcoal grill) or set aside off heat (if using a gas grill). Proceed to grill the shrimp, adding the lemon juice, feta, olives, and scallions just before serving.

CHARMOULA SAUCE

Makes enough to sauce 1½ pounds shrimp

Charmoula is a traditional Moroccan spice blend.

4	tablespoons extra-virgin olive oil
1	small red bell pepper, stemmed, seeded, and diced very small (about ½ cup)
½	small red onion, minced (about ⅓ cup)
1	teaspoon paprika
½	teaspoon ground cumin
¼	teaspoon cayenne
3	medium garlic cloves, minced or pressed through a garlic press (about 1 tablespoon)
⅛	teaspoon salt 10-inch disposable foil pan or pie plate
⅓	cup minced fresh cilantro leaves
2	tablespoons juice from 1 lemon

Combine the oil, bell pepper, onion, paprika, cumin, cayenne, garlic, and salt in the pan. Cook over the hot side of the grill, stirring occasionally, until the vegetables soften, about 5 minutes (2 or 3 minutes longer if using a gas grill); transfer to the cooler side of the grill (if using a charcoal grill) or set aside off heat (if using a gas grill). Proceed to grill the shrimp, adding the cilantro and lemon juice just before serving.

EQUIPMENT CORNER: Skewers

AT FIRST IT SEEMED A LITTLE SILLY TO TEST SKEWERS. AFTER all, how much "performance" difference could there really be between one pointed stick and another? But once we'd surveyed the field—and tried out the designs with our recipe for grilled shrimp and a test on grilling onions—our attitude changed. It really is possible to buy bad skewers.

First of all, forget what most grilling books say: If you're cooking over very high heat, bamboo skewers will burn and break apart—no matter how long you soak them in water beforehand. We had better luck with metal skewers. They may cost more, but they're reusable and they can handle the heartiest kebabs without bending or breaking.

Not all metal skewers are created equal, however. We had a tough time flipping food on round skewers—the skewer itself turned just fine, but the food stayed in place. Flat skewers proved much more effective. Double-pronged skewers turned the food, but some were flimsy and most had a tendency to twist out of their parallel configuration. Other models took the sturdy concept too far, with bulky skewers that severed shrimp in half. Our choice: Any flat, thin metal skewer will do. We particularly like Norpro's 12-inch Stainless Steel Skewers (six skewers for $10), which are just 3/16 inch thick.

BEST SKEWERS

Metal skewers stand up to the high heat of grilling and won't bend or break—bamboo skewers will burn, no matter how long they're soaked and most aren't sturdy enough for hearty foods. Among metal skewers, we prefer flat skewers, because the food turns along with the skewer for fuss-free maneuvering. Norpro's 12-inch Stainless Steel Skewers (six skewers for $10) came out ahead among the brands we tested.

TASTING LAB: Veggie Burgers

CHOPPING, SIMMERING, DRAINING, SHAPING, CHILLING— are homemade veggie burgers really worth the effort? Not if there was something decent to be had at the supermarket, we reasoned. So we tasted seven products, all fully cooked frozen patties that required just two kitchen skills: heating and plopping onto a bun.

All brands won high marks for convenience, but that's about it. Veggie burger veterans and first-timers alike agreed that the flavors and textures were dreadful across the board. Even more perplexing, hardly any of these burgers tasted of vegetables. The problem is that most seemed to be trying to replicate an all-beef burger in texture and taste, but no combination of soy protein, wheat gluten, or smoke flavor pulled that off convincingly.

BEST STORE-BOUGHT VEGGIE BURGERS
Gardenburger Original Burgers ($3.69 for four burgers) boasted strong mushroom and grain flavors, but the dehydrated vegetable texture was reminiscent of "stuffing mix." The best of the lot tested, but that's not saying much.

PICNIC CHICKEN

WHAT WE WANTED: Cold barbecue-seasoned chicken perfect for enjoying on a picnic. The chicken should have all the merits of barbecued chicken (moist meat with lots of spicy flavor) without the sticky mess involved in eating it—and without turning on the grill.

Cold barbecued chicken is a picnic classic. Maybe because picnics offer so much more than food (fresh air, a nice view), most people don't care that this recipe often doesn't make culinary sense. Covered with sticky sauce, the chicken is hard to eat with a fork and impossibly messy to eat with hands. And because the chicken has been cooked and then chilled, the skin is flabby and the meat is so dry it squeaks. We wanted "picnic" chicken good enough to serve whether we were picnicking or not.

For starters, great picnic chicken ought to have moist, tender meat. We decided we also wanted the robust spicy and slightly sweet flavor of barbecue. On the other hand, we didn't want to have to light the grill for a dish that would be going straight to the fridge. The oven is a much easier option for a make-ahead recipe. After sampling several mediocre recipes from various cookbooks, we knew that turning this dish into something a lot better than worse-for-the-wear leftovers was going to be a tall order.

The first advance we made was as quick as it was dramatic. About 90 percent of the recipes we found called for slathering roasted, skin-on chicken with barbecue sauce and letting it sit overnight. Given that the main problem was soggy skin, this approach seemed counterintuitive. The few remaining recipes went the dry-rub route, relying on dried spices to provide traditional barbecue flavor. Although most got the flavor wrong—and were plagued by the same bland-meat problem as the wet-sauced versions—the skin was noticeably less soggy the next day. So dry rubs were in, sticky sauces were out.

Trying some simple combinations of chili powder,

black pepper, paprika, cayenne, and a little brown sugar for that trademark barbecue sauce sweetness, we fiddled with the proportions until we were able to replicate the flavors of a good sauce. By rubbing the spice mixture all over the chicken, even under the skin, we achieved the robust barbecue flavor we'd thought only barbecue sauce could deliver. When tasters sampled the chicken the next day, it drew raves for flavor, and there were no sticky fingers in sight. Unfortunately, the skin was flabby.

Clearly, we needed to spend more time trimming the fat before cooking the chicken. The breast and especially the thighs possess some excess fat that never quite renders properly, no matter how long the chicken cooks. Right out of the oven, that fat is mildly annoying; the coagulated mess you bite into the next day is, well, disgusting.

The solution came in two parts. First, a simple but diligent trimming of the chicken pieces yielded improved results and took just a modicum of effort and time. Second, by slitting the skin with a sharp knife (and being careful not to cut into the flesh), we provided escape hatches for the melting fat during roasting; with a final blast of heat (we went all the way to 500 degrees) in the few last minutes, the skin was nicely rendered. The next day we found not tough, flabby skin but a thinner, flavorful coat on each piece of chicken. Although this skin was still less than crisp, we were making serious headway.

Up until now we had been following the test kitchen's standard procedure for roasting chicken, which includes brining (soaking in a solution of water and salt). Brining yields better flavor and moister meat, but the added moisture also makes for flabby skin. Omitting the brine in this recipe wasn't going to be easy, but perhaps we could get the salt into the meat without the water.

Back in our research library, we came across a technique used by Judi Rodgers, chef of San Francisco's Zuni Café. She salts all of her meat, vegetables, and even fish for up to three days depending on the size of the foods. The salt is thought to draw moisture out of the product initially; then, after a few hours, the reverse happens, and the salt and moisture flow back into the flesh (see "Salting Instead of Brining?" on page 207, for details). The test kitchen has used this technique successfully with some recipes for beef, a meat that we never brine, but we had never thought to try it with chicken.

Curious, we salted the chicken pieces, being careful not to under- or overseason, and then placed them in a covered dish in the refrigerator overnight. The next morning we added the spices and roasted the chicken. Tasters waited patiently as we allowed the chicken to cool to room temperature (after all, this dish wasn't going to be served hot). It was worth the wait. The chicken was well seasoned throughout and the meat very moist. Best of all, the skin was flavorful, delicate, and definitely not flabby. The salting had worked exactly as we'd hoped, both seasoning the meat and keeping it moist, even during high-heat roasting.

With the chicken where we wanted it to be, we worked on streamlining the recipe. We combined the spice rub with the salt and applied it at the same time, saving a step. We also placed the chicken pieces directly on the rack they'd be cooked on so they would be oven-ready the next morning. The final surprise, a completely unexpected bonus, was that after an overnight stay in the fridge some of the spice flavor had penetrated the meat along with the salt. Not only had we come up with a great recipe for picnic chicken, but we had stumbled across a fascinating alternative to brining, one that could produce moist meat that was also deeply flavored by means of a spice rub.

WHAT WE LEARNED: Prevent roast chicken parts with thick, flabby skin by trimming any excess fat and slitting the skin to allow the fat to render properly. And instead of brining the meat, which can turn the cooked skin tough once chilled, salt the meat. Condense steps by adding the salt to a spice rub (containing brown sugar, chili powder, paprika, pepper, and cayenne), which imparts a barbecue sauce–like flavor to the meat.

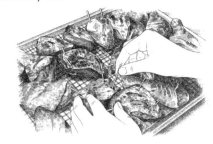

TECHNIQUE: Keeping the Skin in Place
Securing the skin with toothpicks just before roasting keeps the skin from shrinking up into an unattractive bundle and allowing the meat to dry out.

SPICE-RUBBED PICNIC CHICKEN
Serves 8

If you plan to serve the chicken later on the same day that you cook it, refrigerate it immediately after it has cooled, then let it come back to room temperature before serving. On the breast pieces, we use toothpicks to secure the skin, which otherwise shrinks considerably in the oven, leaving the meat exposed and prone to drying out. We think the extra effort is justified, but you can omit this step. This recipe halves easily.

5	pounds bone-in, skin-on chicken parts (breasts, thighs, drumsticks, or a mix with breasts cut into 3 pieces or halved if small), trimmed of excess fat and skin
2	tablespoons kosher salt
3	tablespoons brown sugar
2	tablespoons chili powder
2	tablespoons sweet paprika
2	teaspoons ground black pepper
¼–½	teaspoon cayenne

1. Use a sharp knife to make 2 or 3 short slashes in the skin of each piece of chicken, taking care not to cut into the meat. Combine the salt, sugar, and spices in a small bowl and mix thoroughly. Coat the chicken pieces with the spices, gently lifting the skin to distribute the spice rub underneath but leaving it attached to the chicken. Transfer the chicken skin side up to a wire rack set over a rimmed baking sheet, lightly tent it with foil, and refrigerate 6 to 24 hours.

2. Following the illustration on page 206, secure the skin of each breast piece with 2 or 3 toothpicks placed near the edges of the skin.

3. Adjust an oven rack to the middle position and heat the oven to 425 degrees. Roast the chicken until the thickest part of the smallest piece registers 140 degrees on an instant-read thermometer, 15 to 20 minutes. Increase the oven temperature to 500 degrees and continue roasting until the chicken is browned and crisp and the thickest parts of the breast pieces register 160 degrees, 5 to 8 minutes longer, removing the pieces from the oven and transferring them to a clean wire rack as they finish cooking. Continue to roast the thighs and/or drumsticks, if using, until the thickest part of the meat registers 170 to 175 degrees, about 5 minutes longer. Remove from the oven, transfer the chicken to a rack, and let cool completely before refrigerating or serving.

SCIENCE DESK:
Salting Instead of Brining?

IN THE TEST KITCHEN, WE'RE STRONG ADVOCATES OF brining—soaking meat in a solution of salt and water before cooking. The meat absorbs water as well as salt, with the latter helping the meat retain the moisture as it cooks. With our Spice-Rubbed Picnic Chicken, however, brining made the skin soggy. To solve this problem, we turned to salting the chicken overnight, which helped the meat retain moisture as it cooked—and didn't harm the skin.

Chicken naturally contains some salt and lots of water, which coexist in a happy balance. In coating the chicken with salt, we threw off that balance. To restore order, or equilibrium, water in the meat moved to the surface, where it dissolved the salt.

But wouldn't drawing all that water out of the chicken make the situation worse, causing the meat to dry out? It certainly did—until we figured out the timing. When we tried cooking chicken that had been salted for three hours,

the chicken cooked up drier than if we hadn't salted it. (The juices that had made it to the exterior simply evaporated in the oven.) But when we cooked the chicken after six hours, the story changed entirely. By that point, the exterior salt had pulled so much water to the surface that the balance of the salt concentration had changed. To restore equilibrium, the water simply changed directions, flowing back into the meat. But this time—and here's the key—the dissolved salt went along for the ride. Essentially, we had "brined" the chicken using its own juices instead of a bucket of water.

Once we successfully tapped into this means of delivering salt to the interior, we wondered if it was possible to deliver other flavors the same way. As it turns out, it all comes down to whether the flavoring agent is water-soluble (like salt) or fat-soluble. With the rub we used for our Spice-Rubbed Picnic Chicken, the salt and brown sugar, which dissolve easily in water, flowed right in, as did some of the distinguishing flavor compounds of the black pepper, cayenne, chili powder, and paprika. But the spiciness was waylaid at the surface. Capsaicin, the compound that gives chile peppers their spicy heat, is soluble only in fat, so it was unable to join the caravan.

TASTING LAB: Lemonade

LEMONADE IS A WOLF IN SHEEP'S CLOTHING, A SEEMINGLY natural, kid-friendly alternative to soda with about the same sugar content as Coca-Cola, which has 27 grams of sugar in every 8 ounces of cola.

Of course, that is probably why it is so popular with young and old alike. Youngsters love the sweetness, and grown-ups like to think we're drinking something somewhat healthy (it's juice!). But given the reality—lemonade is a treat—it better taste pretty good. We held a blind tasting of nine popular brands of frozen concentrate and prepared lemonades (skipping the powdered mixes) and found that despite the near-equivalent sugar content among the brands (26 to 28 grams per 8 ounces), flavor differences were vast.

At their core, all brands contain lemon juice, water, and sugar, though never in that order and not always in those forms; high-fructose corn syrup, lemon juice concentrate, and natural lemon flavors made numerous appearances. The well-rated Florida's Natural was the purest of the bunch, with a short ingredient list of just water, lemon juice, sugar, and grapefruit pulp. Compare that with the ingredients in our lowest-rated brand, Snapple: water, high-fructose corn syrup, citric acid, lemon juice from concentrate, gum acacia, natural lemon flavor with other natural flavors, salt, ascorbic acid (Vitamin C), and beta-carotene (for color). No wonder one taster described it as "not lemonade-y." Tasters clearly wanted a "natural" lemon flavor.

But great lemon flavor alone isn't enough; there's a reason we drink lemonade and not lemon juice. Winning brands were consistently described as "sweet/tart," with a "middle-of-the-road blend of sweet and sour," while low-ranked lemonades were "unbalanced," "too tart," and "sickly sweet." Brands with too much or too little lemon also failed the test.

Rating Lemonade

TWENTY MEMBERS OF THE AMERICA'S TEST KITCHEN STAFF TASTED NINE DIFFERENT LEMONADES. THE LEMONADES ARE LISTED in order of preference based on their scores in this tasting. Brands are available nationwide.

RECOMMENDED

Newman's Own Old Fashioned Roadside Virgin Lemonade

$2.29 for 64-ounce carton

Praised for its "natural-tasting lemon flavor" and "good balance of sweet and tart," this brand was deemed "just right."

NOT RECOMMENDED

Minute Maid Premium Lemonade

$2.00 for 64-ounce carton

Despite the strong showing of its frozen cousin, this refrigerated version was deemed "totally muted and boring" and "artificial."

NOT RECOMMENDED

Tropicana Lemonade

$2.00 for 64-ounce carton

The lemonade made by the company renowned for its orange juice was panned as "not lemony enough" and "candy-like." Or, as one taster put it simply: "Ick, ick."

RECOMMENDED

Florida's Natural Lemonade

$2.00 for 64-ounce carton

Many found this brand to be the "most drinkable," with "nice balance." A handful thought it was "too sweet."

NOT RECOMMENDED

Nantucket Nectars Lemonade

$1.59 for 17.5-ounce bottle

"That's not lemonade!" complained one taster of this "artificial" brand that was so tart it "makes you wince!"

NOT RECOMMENDED

Cascadian Farms Organic Lemonade Frozen Concentrate

$3.39 for 12-ounce can (yields about 60 ounces)

"Blech!" wrote one taster of the lone organic brand, and most others agreed, including one who asked, "What was that? That wasn't lemonade."

RECOMMENDED

Minute Maid Premium Lemonade Frozen Concentrate

$1.49 for 12-ounce can (yields about 60 ounces)

Fans of this frozen concentrate found it "light, clean, and tart," with "good flavor," though some found it "not lemony enough."

NOT RECOMMENDED

Odwalla Pure Squeezed Lemonade

$4.99 for 64-ounce jug

Several tasters found this "painfully sweet" lemonade to taste "like apple juice," while others complained of an "odd aftertaste."

NOT RECOMMENDED

Snapple Lemonade

$1.35 for 16-ounce bottle

Panned by all as "very bad," "sickly sweet," and "fake," with one taster going so far as to compare it to "the smell of rubber."

Erika pan-fries corn fritters in vegetable oil, which, the test kitchen discovered, is the best cooking medium due to its high smoke point and neutral flavor.

BARBECUED
CHAPTER 18
brisket and corn fritters

Summertime entertaining can often mean preparing food for groups larger than six to eight—school graduations, Fourth of July, the neighborhood block party—the list goes on. For those times, hamburgers just aren't practical—unless the cook plans on standing at the grill until everyone is fed. Instead, think brisket. This hefty piece of meat (a full cut can weigh 13 pounds) turns smoky and tender on the grill and leftovers, if there are any, are terrific. Best of all, brisket doesn't require constant attention, so the cook can enjoy the party, too. Brisket isn't without its challenges, however. On the grill, the meat can take about 12 hours to become fully tender. We wanted to find not only the best way to barbecue brisket, but a way to do so more quickly.

Summertime also calls for corn. And while we love corn on the cob, we also enjoy other preparations. Take corn fritters. These savory cakes are pan-fried and served hot. They make a terrific side dish or hors d'oeuvres, served as is, or sprinkled with hot sauce. Some recipes are short on corn flavor, but we wanted a recipe that brings the corn front and center.

When you're looking for a main course to serve a summertime crowd, or want to give a new twist to a summertime vegetable, we hope you'll turn to these recipes.

BARBECUED BRISKET

WHAT WE WANTED: A shortcut method for producing tender, smoky brisket.

Our favorite way to cook brisket is to barbecue it. When prepared correctly, the meat picks up a great smoky flavor and becomes fork-tender. Unfortunately, many a barbecued brisket ends up burnt, tough, or chewy. This is because brisket is so tough to begin with. Unless it is fully cooked, the meat is very chewy and practically inedible. Because brisket is so large (a full cut can weigh 13 pounds), getting the meat "fully cooked" can take many hours. Our goal was to make the meat as tender as possible as quickly as possible.

What does "fully cooked" mean when talking about brisket? To find out, we roasted four small pieces to various internal temperatures. The pieces cooked to 160 and 180 degrees were dry and quite tough. A piece cooked to 200 degrees was slightly less tough, although quite dry. A final piece cooked to 210 degrees had the most appealing texture and the most pleasant chew, despite the fact that it was the driest.

So what's going on here? Heat causes muscle proteins to uncoil and then rejoin in a different formation, which drives out juices in the same way that wringing removes moisture from a wet cloth. This process starts in earnest at around 140 degrees, and by the time the meat reaches 180 degrees, most of its juices have been expelled. This explains why a medium-rare steak (cooked to 130 degrees) is much juicier than a well-done steak (cooked to 160 degrees).

With tender cuts, like steak, the lower the internal temperature of the meat, the juicier and less tough the meat will be. However, with cuts that start out tough, like brisket, another process is also at work. Brisket is loaded with waxy-looking connective tissue called collagen, which makes the meat chewy and tough. Only when the collagen has been transformed into gelatin will the meat be tender. Collagen begins to convert to gelatin at 130 to 140 degrees, but the conversion process occurs most rapidly at temperatures above 180 degrees.

When cooking brisket, the gelatinization of collagen must be the priority. Thus, the meat should be cooked as fully as possible, or to an internal temperature of 210 degrees. The muscle juices will be long gone (that's why the sliced meat is served with barbecue sauce), but the meat will be extremely tender because all the collagen will have been converted to gelatin.

It is important to point out that moist-heat cooking methods (such as braising) are appropriate for cooking meats to such high internal temperatures because water is a more efficient conductor of heat than air. Meats cooked in a moist environment heat up faster and can be held at high internal temperatures without burning or drying out.

Given the fact that brisket must be fully cooked and that it can be so big, the meat needs 10 or 12 hours of barbecuing to reach the fork-tender stage. Even when butchers separate the brisket into smaller pieces, as is often the case, the cooking time is astronomical. Most cooks are not prepared to keep a fire going that long. To get around this tending-the-fire-all-day-long problem, we found it necessary to commit barbecue heresy. After much testing, we decided to start the meat on the grill but finish it in the oven, where it could be left to cook unattended.

We wondered how long the meat would have to stay on the grill to pick up enough smoke flavor. In our testing, we found that two hours allows the meat to absorb plenty of smoke flavor and creates a dark brown, crusty exterior. At this point, the meat is ready for the oven. We found it best to wrap the meat in foil to create a moist environment. (Unwrapped briskets cooked up drier, and the exterior was prone to burning.) After barbecuing, a whole brisket requires three hours or so in a 300-degree oven to become fork-tender. Barbecue purists might object to our use of the oven, but this method works, and it doesn't require a tremendous commitment of hands-on cooking time.

Some further notes about our testing. Although many experts recommend basting a brisket regularly as it cooks on the grill to ensure moistness, we disagree. Taking the lid off wreaked havoc with our charcoal fire, and the meat didn't taste any different despite frequent basting with sauce. Likewise, we don't recommend placing a pan filled with water (we also tried beer) on the grill. Some barbecue masters believe that the liquid adds moisture and flavor to the meat, but we couldn't tell any difference between brisket cooked with and without the pan of liquid.

Brisket comes with a thick layer of fat on one side. We tried turning the brisket as it cooked, thinking this might promote even cooking, but we had better results when we barbecued the brisket fat side up the entire time. This way, the fat slowly melts, lubricating the meat underneath.

WHAT WE LEARNED: Start the brisket on the grill. Barbecue fat side up (so the fat melts over the meat) for two hours. Use a dry rub for flavor. Avoid typical barbecuing methods like basting the meat or setting a pan of liquid on the cooking grate to create a moist environment—we didn't find either method effective. After two hours, wrap the meat in foil and transfer to a 300-degree oven to finish cooking. This two-track approach, although unconventional, produces fork-tender meat with real barbecue flavor in about half the time it would take if you cooked the meat entirely on the grill.

BARBECUED BEEF BRISKET FOR A CHARCOAL GRILL

Serves 18 to 24

Cooking a whole brisket, which weighs about 10 pounds, may seem like overkill. However, the process is easy, and the leftovers keep well in the refrigerator for up to 4 days. (Leave leftover brisket unsliced, and reheat the foil-wrapped meat in a 300-degree oven until warm.) Still, if you don't want to bother with a big piece of meat or if your grill has fewer than 400 square inches of cooking space, barbecuing brisket for less than a crowd is easy to do. Simply ask your butcher for either the point or flat portion of the brisket, each of which weighs about half as much as a whole brisket. Then follow this recipe, reducing the spice rub by half and barbecuing for just 1 hour and 30 minutes. Wrap the meat tightly in foil and reduce the time in the oven to 2 hours. No matter how large or small a piece you cook, it's a good idea to save the juices the meat gives off while in the oven to enrich the barbecue sauce. Hickory and mesquite are both traditional wood choices with brisket.

1 recipe Spicy Chili Rub (recipe follows)
1 whole beef brisket (9 to 11 pounds), fat trimmed to ¼-inch thickness
2 (3-inch) wood chunks
3 cups store-bought barbecue sauce

1. Apply the dry rub liberally to all sides of the meat, patting it on firmly to make sure the spices adhere and completely cover the meat. Wrap the brisket tightly in plastic wrap and refrigerate for 2 hours. (For stronger flavor, refrigerate for up to 2 days.)

2. About 1 hour prior to cooking, remove the brisket from the refrigerator, unwrap, and let it come up to room temperature. Soak the wood chunks in cold water to cover for 1 hour and drain.

3. Meanwhile, light a large chimney starter filled a bit less than halfway with charcoal briquettes (2½ quarts, or about 45 briquettes) and allow to burn until the coals are fully ignited and partially covered with a thin layer of ash. Empty the coals into one side of the grill, piling them up in a mound 2 or 3 briquettes high. Keep the bottom vents completely open. Place the wood chunks on top of the charcoal. Put the cooking grate in place, open the grill lid vents completely, and cover, turning the lid so that the vents are opposite the wood chunks to draw smoke through the grill. Let the grate heat up for 5 minutes and then scrape the cooking grate clean with a grill brush.

4. Position the brisket, fat side up, on the side of the grill opposite the fire. Barbecue, without removing the lid, for 2 hours. (The initial temperature will be about 350 degrees and will drop to 250 degrees after 2 hours.)

5. Adjust an oven rack to the middle position and heat the oven to 300 degrees. Attach 2 pieces of heavy-duty foil, 4 feet long, by folding the long edges together 2 or 3 times, crimping tightly to seal well, to form an approximately 4 by 3-foot rectangle. Position the brisket lengthwise in the center of the foil. Bring the short edges over the brisket and fold down, crimping tightly to seal. Repeat with the long sides of the foil to seal the brisket completely. (See illustrations 1 and 2 at right.) Place the brisket on a rimmed baking sheet. Bake until the meat is fork-tender, 3 to 3½ hours.

6. Remove the brisket from the oven, loosen the foil at one end to release steam, and let rest for 30 minutes. If you like, drain the juices into a bowl (see illustration 3 at right) and defat the juices in a gravy skimmer.

7. Unwrap the brisket and place it on a cutting board. Separate the meat into two sections and carve it on the bias across the grain into long, thin slices (see illustrations 4 and 5 at right). Serve with plain barbecue sauce or with barbecue sauce that has been flavored with up to 1 cup of the defatted brisket juices.

TECHNIQUE:
Key Steps to Barbecued Brisket

1. After barbecuing, place the brisket on two 4-foot sections of heavy-duty aluminum foil that have been sealed together to make a 4 by 3-foot rectangle. Bring the short ends of the foil up over the brisket and crimp tightly to seal.

2. Seal the long sides of the foil packet tightly up against the sides of the meat. Put the brisket on a rimmed baking sheet and put the sheet in the oven.

3. After the brisket comes out of the oven, use oven mitts to hold the rimmed baking sheet and carefully pour the juices into a bowl. If you like, reserve the juices and defat. They make a delicious addition to barbecue sauce.

4. Since the grain on the two sections of the brisket goes in opposite directions, separate the cuts before slicing.

5. Carve the brisket on the bias across the grain into long, thin slices.

BARBECUED BEEF BRISKET FOR A GAS GRILL

You will need a pretty large grill to cook a whole brisket. If your grill has fewer than 400 square inches of cooking space, barbecue either the point or flat end, each of which weighs about half as much as a whole brisket. Follow the directions in the note on page 213 for cooking a smaller piece of brisket.

Follow the recipe for Barbecued Beef Brisket for a Charcoal Grill through step 2, substituting 2 cups wood chips for the wood chunks and soaking them for 30 minutes in cold water to cover. Drain the chips and place them in a foil tray (see the illustrations below). Place the tray on top of the primary burner. Light all the burners and turn to high, cover, and heat until the chips are smoking heavily, about 20 minutes. Scrape the cooking grate clean with a grill brush. Turn the primary burner down to medium and turn off the other burner(s). Position the brisket, fat side up, over the cooler part of the grill. Cover and barbecue for 2 hours. (The temperature inside the grill should be a constant 275 degrees; adjust the lit burner as necessary.) Proceed as directed from step 5.

SPICY CHILI RUB

Makes about 1 cup

If you cannot abide spicy hot food, reduce or eliminate the cayenne. The rub can be stored in an airtight container at room temperature for up to a month.

4	tablespoons paprika
2	tablespoons chili powder
2	tablespoons ground cumin
2	tablespoons dark brown sugar
2	tablespoons salt
1	tablespoon ground oregano
1	tablespoon sugar
1	tablespoon ground black pepper
1	tablespoon ground white pepper
2	teaspoons cayenne

Mix all the ingredients in a small bowl.

TECHNIQUE: Making a Foil Tray for Wood Chips for a Gas Grill

1. Start with an 18 by 12-inch piece of heavy-duty foil. Make a 1-inch fold on one long side. Repeat three more times, then turn the fold up to create a sturdy side that measures about an inch high. Repeat the process on the other long side.

2. With a short side facing you, fold in both corners as if wrapping a gift.

3. Turn up the inside inch or so of each triangular fold to match the rim on the long sides of the foil tray.

4. Lift the pointed end of the triangle over the rim of foil and fold down to seal. Repeat the process on the other short side. The tray can now be filled with soaked and drained wood chips.

Many recipes call for a particular volume of charcoal, such as 4 quarts. An easy way to measure it is to use an empty half-gallon milk or juice carton. Just wash the carton thoroughly and store it with the charcoal. Each full carton equals roughly two quarts.

EQUIPMENT CORNER: Charcoal Grills

FLICKING A SWITCH TO LIGHT A GAS GRILL MAY BE CONVE-nient, but for many die-hard grillers nothing beats a live charcoal fire. The pleasure is utterly visceral: the red-hot coals, the smoke, the sizzle, the interplay of food and flame, and the aroma of searing meat. And, of course, there is the flavor. Charcoal fires infuse food with notes of wood and smoke that no gas fire can match.

Yet deciding which charcoal grill to buy is not so straightforward: Manufacturers produce grills of various sizes and shapes at various prices. We chose six grills from six manufacturers that ran the gamut from round to rectangular, bare-bones to fully loaded, small to large, and costing less than $100 to more than six times that amount. A few weeks of grilling in the alley behind the test kitchen led us to some interesting observations and, in the end, the discovery of the quintessential charcoal grill.

Grilling a mountain of food over two weeks revealed very little difference in the grills' cooking performance. Each developed a fire hot enough to sear the food, which is what charcoal grilling is all about. Each also offers vents to control airflow—and thereby the intensity of the fire—but we were not able to detect any advantages or disadvantages based on the number or position of the vents. It was possible, however, to identify two important design factors: the size of the grill and the depth of the grill cover.

After years of grilling on a small portable grill, we can speak personally about the benefits of upsizing. (The cooking areas on the smallest grills we tested were 19 inches square and 21½ inches round; the cooking area on the largest grill was 31 by 19 inches.) A large surface area is essential if you cook for large groups, and useful even when you don't, because it affords the opportunity to easily grill some extra food alongside the main course. For instance, we rarely grill a meal without covering every available inch of grill space with vegetables to have on hand for tomorrow's antipasto, pizza, or pasta salad. It is also easier to build a two-level fire (hot on one side and cooler on the other) in a large grill. Among the grills tested, the Bar-B-Chef was the size champ, with 585 square inches of grilling space.

While we generally don't use the cover when charcoal grilling over high heat, it is necessary when grill-roasting large cuts, such as a turkey or prime rib, over lower heat. To trap heat and contain any flavorful smoke generated from wood chunks or chips, the grill lid must fit comfortably over the food and form a tight seal with the grill bottom. The test kitchen recommends 12- to 14-pound turkeys for grill-roasting, and the Bar-B-Chef and Patio Classic grills were the only models on our list with lids that closed over a 14-pounder (set on a V-rack to promote even cooking). However, all of the grills in the group, except for the Arctic, were able to swallow a 12-pounder.

In some respects, charcoal grills are a little like cars. Any new car will get you from point A to point B, but extra features like traction control or antilock brakes make the car easier to drive, and goodies like a sunroof or heated

seats help you enjoy the ride more. Likewise, all charcoal grills will cook your food, but several features can make the process easier and more enjoyable.

An attached table makes a huge difference, and two are even better. After years of precariously balancing platters on deck railings and chair arms, it was a welcome relief to have a secure, accessible place to put dishes and utensils. Among our group, only the Weber One Touch Gold lacked a table of any kind (although a table/cutting board is available from Weber as an add-on).

If you plan to barbecue or grill-roast (both methods entail long cooking over a relatively low fire), some means of easily adding charcoal to the fire is crucial. The Bar-B-Chef offered the perfect solution—a door to the charcoal rack, which made it a breeze to tend the fire and add fuel. Another solution, hinged cooking grates (on the Patio Classic, Weber, and Arctic) allow you to slip in extra charcoal, but you must push food to the opposite side of the grate. To add fuel to the Cajun Grill or MECO, you must endure the aggravation of first removing the food and the scorching hot cooking grate.

Another thoughtful feature is some means of adjusting the height of either the charcoal rack or the cooking grate. If given no respite from a hot fire, many foods, such as thick steaks, pork chops, and chicken breasts, will burn on the outside before cooking through on the inside. So they must be finished over a cooler fire. This is easy to accomplish if you can adjust the charcoal rack down away from the cooking grate, as is the case with the Bar-B-Chef and the Cajun. On the MECO, the charcoal rack is fixed, but you can adjust the height of the cooking grate, so the effect is the same. Still, the ability to adjust the charcoal rack or cooking grate is not essential. On grills that do not offer such adjustability, you can build a two-level fire that is hot on one side and cool on the other to achieve the same effect. This simply takes a little extra knowledge on the part of the griller. It is easier, though, if you can change the level of the fire with the shift of a lever or the turn of a dial.

An ash catcher, a container attached to the bottom of

Rating Charcoal Grills

WE TESTED SIX CHARCOAL GRILLS AND EVALUATED THEM ACCORDING TO PERFORMANCE AND VALUE. THE GRILLS ARE LISTED in order of preference. See www.americastestkitchen.com for up-to-date prices and mail-order sources for top-rated products.

HIGHLY RECOMMENDED
Bar-B-Chef Texas Charcoal Barbecue On Cart
$499.00

If you've got $500 for a grill, this is the way to go. Too much grill for some, but there's really nothing this behemoth can't do. Charcoal rack is a cinch to screw up and down. Cavernous grill could swallow a few 14-pound turkeys.

RECOMMENDED
Patio Classic 3500 Series
$219.00

Long list of extras and two spacious tables make for a user-friendly grill at a reasonable price. One design flaw—the oversized hatch in the cooking grate (which requires moving most of the food off the grill to tend the fire)—mars an otherwise nicely outfitted grill.

RECOMMENDED
Weber One Touch Gold
$149.99

The iconic kettle grill offers only a few well-designed extras. A side table is sorely lacking but is available as an after-market add-on for about $35. Best for small patios or decks.

RECOMMENDED WITH RESERVATIONS
Arctic Steel 22½ Inch Kettle Cart Bar-B-Que Grill
$99.00

The bargain of the bunch does the job but doesn't seem built to last.

RECOMMENDED WITH RESERVATIONS
MECO Swinger II Deluxe Smoker Grill
$149.00

The design of this grill doesn't provide for a way to tend the fire and remove the ashes.

RECOMMENDED WITH RESERVATIONS
The Cajun Grill
$649.00

The charcoal lift is well designed but doesn't match the size of the cooking grate. Too much money for anything less than perfection.

the grill to trap ashes, makes life easier when it comes time to clean out the grill. The Patio Classic and Weber grills go a step further by adding a mechanism to direct ash into the catcher. Finally, when you barbecue or grill-roast, a built-in thermometer (as found on the Bar-B-Chef) is handy, though you can always put a grill thermometer through the lid vents.

In the end, our advice is to buy the largest, best-outfitted grill your budget will allow. The Bar-B-Chef isn't cheap, but it's built to last and offers everything we want in a charcoal grill and then some. That makes it a bargain in our book, especially when compared with a more expensive yet less functional grill like the Cajun. If the $499 Bar-B-Chef price tag scares you off or almost 600 square inches of grilling area is more grill than you need, the Patio Classic is just as thoughtfully featured for less than half the price. The classic Weber is bare-bones and great for folks who don't have a spacious area to grill or who need an easily transported model (as we do in the test kitchen, where we have to lug the grills to the alley in the morning and back inside at night). The Weber turns out tasty burgers and dogs just like the fully loaded big boys.

CORN FRITTERS

WHAT WE WANTED: Savory pan-fried fritters packed with fresh corn flavor.

Corn fritters are basically corn kernels (ground, grated, or chopped) enriched with egg and flour and fried until crisp. The ideal fritter is amazingly crisp and golden brown on the outside, creamy and bursting with sweet corn flavor on the inside. As our early tests demonstrated, however, most corn fritters are heavy, dense, greasy cakes with almost no corn flavor.

We first looked to see how the corn was treated. The main choices were cut, grated, pureed, and chopped. For our first batch we simply cut the kernels off the cob and then stirred them into the egg and flour batter. The result was a fritter more like a pancake, with a small amount of corn flavor showing up only if one was lucky enough to bite into a kernel. We went to the other extreme and pureed the kernels, but the amount of flour necessary to make the mixture cohesive produced a very bland, pasty fritter. We knew that we were onto something when we tried grating the corn on a box grater. This time the interior was creamy and flavorful, but the fritters lacked texture. In our next batch we included whole kernels as well as corn pulp. These fritters were packed with fresh corn flavor and texturally interesting.

Next came the binders. It was obvious that the amount of flour added would make the difference between a delicate fritter and a doorstop. We added just enough flour to keep the fritters from falling apart, but even with this small amount of flour the corn flavor was dulled significantly. Cornmeal, another binder found in several recipes, was an option, and the corn flavor that it lent was perfect. When used alone, however, the cornmeal compromised the texture of the fritters, making them unpleasantly grainy. We thought that a mixture of the flour and cornmeal would be perfect, and after trying various ratios, we agreed on equal amounts of each.

These fritters had great corn flavor and a tender texture, but they lacked the creamy richness we desired. Remembering the creamy consistency of the grated corn pulp, we added in turns a small amount of milk, buttermilk, half-and-half, and heavy cream, hoping to closely emulate the creaminess found in the corn itself. Heavy cream proved to be exactly what the batter needed—the higher amount of fat enriched the fritter yet didn't compromise its sweet corn flavor.

Next we tested frying the fritters in butter, oil, and a blend of the two. Butter scorched by the time we got around to frying the second half of our batter. Blending the butter with a bit of oil to prevent burning was not worth the trouble. Vegetable oil proved to be the best cooking medium, both for its reluctance to smoke and its neutral taste; it didn't compete with the corn. At this time we wondered how much oil was really necessary. We found pan-frying in a moderate amount of oil (¼ cup) sufficient to crisp the fritters perfectly.

Finally, we admitted to ourselves that there are times when fresh sweet corn was just not a possibility. We tried our recipe with off-season ears of corn purchased at a local supermarket but found that their moisture content and sweet flavor were greatly diminished. Frozen corn, which is much more flavorful than its canned cousin, was our only option. To obtain a texture similar to the one we got using fresh corn, we pulsed semi-defrosted kernels in the food processor. The resulting fritters had great corn flavor and texture—almost as good as those made with fresh corn.

WHAT WE LEARNED: For big corn flavor, a combination of grated corn and whole kernels works best. Equal amounts of flour and cornmeal bind the mixture together without making the fritters heavy. A bit of heavy cream adds some welcome richness. For pan-frying the cakes, vegetable oil makes the best cooking medium due to its high smoke point and its neutral flavor, which doesn't overpower the corn.

CORN FRITTERS

Makes 12 (2-inch) fritters

Serve these fritters with hot sauce, salsa, or even maple syrup.

 4 ears fresh corn, husks and silk removed
 1 large egg, lightly beaten
 3 tablespoons unbleached all-purpose flour
 3 tablespoons fine-ground cornmeal
 2 tablespoons heavy cream
 1 shallot, minced
 ½ teaspoon salt
  Pinch cayenne
 ¼ cup vegetable oil, or more as needed

1. Using a paring knife, cut the kernels from 1 or 2 ears of corn (see the illustration below right); you should have about 1 cup. Transfer the kernels to a medium bowl. Use the back of a knife to scrape any pulp remaining on the cobs and transfer it to the bowl. Following the illustrations opposite, grate the kernels from the remaining 2 or 3 ears of corn on the large holes of a box grater, then firmly scrape any pulp remaining on the cobs with the back of a knife; you should have a generous cup of kernels and pulp. Transfer the grated kernels and pulp to the bowl with the cut kernels.

2. Mix the egg, flour, cornmeal, cream, shallot, salt, and cayenne into the corn mixture to form a thick batter.

3. Heat the oil in a 12-inch heavy-bottomed skillet over medium-high heat until almost smoking, about 2 minutes. Drop heaping tablespoons of batter into the oil (half the batter, or 6 fritters, should fit into the pan at once). Fry until golden brown, about 1 minute. Using a thin metal spatula, turn the fritters and fry until the second side is golden brown, about 1 minute longer. Transfer the fritters to a plate lined with paper towels. Add more oil to the skillet if necessary and heat until almost smoking. Repeat to fry the remaining batter. Serve immediately.

VARIATIONS

CORN FRITTERS WITH CHEDDAR AND CHIVES

Tangy cheddar cheese partners well with the corn and flecks of green chives give the fritters a light, oniony flavor.

Follow the recipe for Corn Fritters, adding ⅓ cup shredded cheddar cheese, 2 tablespoons minced fresh chives, and 1 teaspoon Dijon mustard to the batter.

OUT-OF-SEASON CORN FRITTERS

When fresh corn is out of season, frozen corn makes a fine substitute. Processing the frozen kernels in a food processor approximates the texture achieved by grating fresh corn.

Follow the recipe for Corn Fritters, substituting 2 cups frozen corn kernels, thawed at room temperature for 15 minutes, for the fresh corn. Pulse the corn, egg, flour, cornmeal, cream, shallot, salt, and cayenne in the workbowl of a food processor fitted with the steel blade until the mixture forms a thick batter with some whole kernels, about ten 1-second pulses. Continue with the recipe from step 3.

TECHNIQUE:
Removing Kernels from the Cob

Hold the cob on its end inside a large, wide bowl and cut off the kernels using a paring knife.

TECHNIQUE: Milking Corn

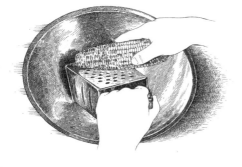

1. Start by grating an ear of corn on the large holes of a box grater.

2. Finish by firmly scraping any remaining pulp off the cob with the back of a butter knife.

TASTING LAB: Hot Sauces

As often as we use hot pepper sauce in the test kitchen, we've never given much thought to brand. Considering that most are made from a basic combination of red peppers, vinegar, and salt, does brand even matter? We rounded up eight supermarket samples to find out.

First, we sprinkled each sample on top of a portion of steamed white rice. Across the board, tasters deemed one sauce a knockout: Frank's won points for its "bright" and "tangy" notes and potent heat. Tasters also liked La Preferida Louisiana Hot Sauce, which was a tad hotter. Surprisingly, Tabasco, the brand most often found in restaurants and pantry shelves (including our own), came in dead last. Why? The searing heat masked any other flavor in the sauce, and most found the thin, watery body to be unappealing. "Bitter, like pepper skin," said one taster.

To see how our winner and loser would fare in a cooked application—with other flavors in the mix—we pitted Frank's RedHot against Tabasco in a breakfast strata made with bread, cheese, eggs, onion, and hot sauce. The results were split. Some tasters enjoyed Tabasco's spicier edge, while others preferred the fuller, more tomatoey complexity of Frank's. But for sprinkling on top of the cooked strata, however, once again nearly all tasters picked Frank's RedHot as their favorite for its fuller flavor and more "luxurious" body. As one taster put it succinctly, "Tabasco is an ingredient, while Frank's is a condiment." Save Tabasco for adding heat to recipes.

BEST HOT SAUCE
Frank's Original RedHot Cayenne Pepper Sauce ($2.39 for 12 ounces) was praised for being "bright" and "tangy," with "latent heat."

Julia found that a little mayonnaise gives pesto a creamy richness that helps it cling to pasta.

BEER CAN
chicken dinner

For many grilling and barbecue enthusiasts, there are some recipes that are never too wacky. Take beer can chicken. A whole chicken is placed over a can of beer and the chicken is set on the grill and roasted. Yes, we love the idea of grill-roasted chicken—there's nothing wrong with infusing mild-flavored chicken with the smoky flavor of the grill. But what's the point of the beer? Does the beer add moisture, flavor, or both? Does the type of beer make a difference or could we use another liquid such as white wine? We set out to answer these questions and more in developing the ultimate recipe for beer can chicken.

Tired of the same old pasta salads? We are, too. We wanted to come up with a pasta salad that showcased the bright, herbal flavors of summer—with pesto. Hot pasta tossed with pesto is a natural, but if chilled (as it would be for a salad), the pesto loses its vibrant green color. We wanted to find a way to incorporate the flavors of pesto into a pasta salad, without it turning dull and lifeless.

In this chapter, we show you how sometimes the strangest-sounding methods are the most rewarding and how a few easy tricks can give an old standby new life.

BEER CAN CHICKEN

WHAT WE WANTED: The ultimate grill-roasted chicken—smoky, spicy meat that is juicy, not dry, with crackling, crisp skin.

Beer can chicken has been a regular on the barbecue cook-off circuit for some time. The bird is rubbed with spices, and then an open, partially filled beer can is inserted into the main cavity of the chicken. The chicken is grill-roasted as it "sits" on the can, which functions as a vertical roaster. When cooking a whole chicken on the grill, we already knew that grill-roasting was the way to go. The coals are banked on each side of the grill and the chicken is placed in the center. With the heat attacking the chicken from two sides, the bird cooks evenly. (Otherwise, if cooked over direct heat, the drippings from the chicken cause unwelcome flare-ups and charred skin.) Adding a can of beer to the mix sounded downright odd, but we were willing to give it a try since barbecue masters claim it turns out smoky chicken with incredibly moist, tender meat.

First, we started with our fire. As we do with grill-roasting, we arranged the hot coals in piles on either side of the grill. About 4 quarts, or 60 briquettes, is sufficient. Any more and we run the risk of charring the chicken, and using less would make for a weaker fire that would extend our cooking time substantially. After adding some soaked wood chips to the coals, we had even heat and lots of smoke.

We next moved on to the chicken. We found 3½ pound birds to be an ideal size. Anything smaller won't accommodate a beer can. Larger birds are doable but tricky—they take longer to cook, which is a nuisance, and not everyone has a grill large enough to fit a big bird.

We decided that we wanted the beer to pull triple duty, not only as stand and steamer but as flavor container. After our first round of tests, we found that by itself the beer didn't impart a whole lot of flavor, and we found no discernible difference among various types of beer,

whether pricey or cheap. However, a few crumbled bay leaves added to the can did the trick, infusing the meat with potent herbal flavor. For another test, we emptied a soda can and filled it with water (and crumbled bay leaves). Although the differences were not dramatic, the flavor was a bit washed out and less appealing. Evidently, the beer was contributing something to the bird. We then replaced the beer with white wine in one test and lemonade in another. The white wine did nothing for flavor, but tasters

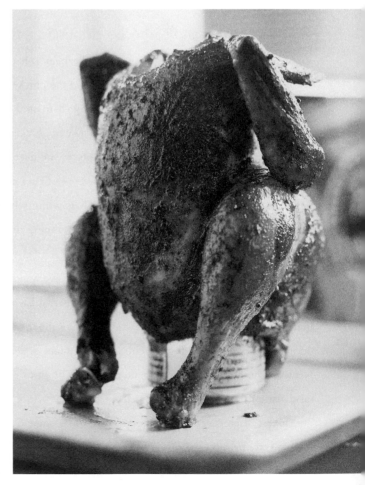

were able to detect a lightly sweet, lemon flavor in the bird cooked over lemonade, so if you prefer not to cook with beer, lemonade is a good option.

Now that we had the smoke from the grill and the flavorful steam from the can, it was time to spice things up with a spice rub. At the same time, we wanted to figure out how to achieve a crisp skin. We tried oiling the chickens before rubbing on the spices, but these birds ended up flabby and flavorless. We tried patting the chicken dry with paper towels before rubbing on the spices, and this time we rubbed them not just on the skin but under it and inside the chicken cavity. This was a big improvement, although the skin was still turning out a bit on the thick side, especially around the thighs.

Hoping to help drain the excess fat, we used a skewer to poke holes all over the skin. This worked perfectly, rendering out the fat in those hard-to-reach places and leaving an extra-crispy skin. An unexpected benefit of this technique was that the skewer captured and deposited small amounts of the rub deep into the meat. In essence, the skewer was injecting the seasonings into the chicken, making for the fullest-flavored, juiciest grill-roasted chicken we'd ever eaten.

WHAT WE LEARNED: Don't use too many coals in building your fire; too intense heat will char the chicken and too little will result in too long a cooking time. Use whatever beer you have on hand—we detected no differences between expensive and cheap brands. And, if you prefer not to use beer, lemonade makes a fine substitution. Bay leaves, crumbled into the beer, infuse the chicken with fresh herbal flavor. A 3½-pound bird is the ideal size for grill-roasting with beer—anything smaller won't accommodate a beer can (and most grills aren't big enough for large birds). For the spice rub, first pat the chicken dry then apply the spice rub all over the chicken, including inside the cavity and under the skin. Finally, poke the skin all over with a skewer to inject the seasonings into the meat and help drain away the fat for extra-crispy skin.

GRILL-ROASTED BEER CAN CHICKEN FOR A CHARCOAL GRILL

Serves 4

Using the right amount of charcoal is crucial here; using too much charcoal will burn the chicken, while using too little will extend the cooking time substantially. The temperature inside the grill should be about 375 degrees at the outset and will fall to about 300 by the time the chicken is done. For added accuracy, place a grill thermometer in the lid vents as the chicken cooks. If you prefer, use lemonade instead of beer; fill an empty 12-ounce soda or beer can with 10 ounces (1¼ cups) of lemonade and proceed as directed.

- 2 (3-inch) wood chunks or 2 cups wood chips
- 3 tablespoons Spice Rub (page 227)
- 1 whole chicken (about 3½ pounds)
- 1 (12-ounce) can beer (see note)
- 2 bay leaves
- 1 13 by 9-inch disposable foil roasting pan

1. Soak the wood chunks or chips in cold water to cover for 1 hour and drain. If using wood chips, divide them between two 18-inch squares of aluminum foil, seal to make two

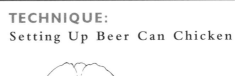

TECHNIQUE:
Setting Up Beer Can Chicken

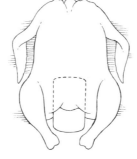

With the legs pointing down, slide the chicken over the open beer can. The two legs and the beer can form a tripod that steadies the chicken on the grill.

packets, and use a fork to create about six holes in each packet to allow smoke to escape.

2. Open the beer can and pour out (or drink) about ¼ cup. With a church key can opener, punch two more large holes in the top of the can (for a total of three holes). Crumble the bay leaves into the beer. Massage the spice rub all over the chicken, inside and out. Lift up the skin over the breast and rub the spice rub directly onto the meat (see the illustration opposite). Using a skewer, poke the skin all over. Slide the chicken over the beer can so that the drumsticks reach down to the bottom of the can and the chicken stands upright; set aside at room temperature.

3. Light a large chimney starter filled two-thirds with charcoal (4 quarts, or about 60 briquettes) and allow to burn until the coals are fully ignited and partially covered with a thin layer of ash, 15 to 20 minutes.

4. Place the disposable pan in the center of the grill. Pour half of the coals into a pile on each side of the grill, leaving the pan in the center. Nestle 1 soaked wood chunk (or 1 foil packet) on top of each coal pile. Position the cooking grate over the coals, cover the grill, and heat until hot, about 5 minutes; scrape the cooking grate clean with a grill brush.

5. Place the chicken (with the can) in the center of the cooking grate with the wings facing the coals (the ends of the drumsticks will help steady the bird, see the photo on page 224). Cover and grill-roast, until an instant-read thermometer inserted into the thickest part of the thigh registers 170 to 175 degrees, 65 to 85 minutes.

6. With a large wad of paper towels in each hand, transfer the chicken to a platter or tray, making sure to keep the can upright; let rest for 15 minutes. With paper towels, carefully lift the chicken off the can and onto a cutting board. Discard the remaining beer and can. Carve the chicken and serve.

TECHNIQUE:
Grill-Roasting Two Chickens

There are some occasions when you may want to cook more than one chicken—when you have more guests to serve or if you'd like to have leftovers on hand. Here's how.

For a Charcoal Grill: Follow the recipe for Grill-Roasted Beer Can Chicken for a Charcoal Grill, increasing the number of wood chunks to 4 (or 4 cups of wood chips), using 6 tablespoons Spice Rub, two 3½-pound chickens, 2 cans of beer, and increasing the amount of charcoal to a three-quarters full chimney (4½ quarts, or about 70 briquettes). In step 5, set the chickens (and cans) in the middle of the cooking grate, with the chickens' breasts facing one another, about 3 inches apart (keeping the chickens close together ensures that they won't hit the top of the domed grill lid). Grill-roast as directed.

For a Gas Grill: Follow the recipe for Grill-Roasted Beer Can Chicken for a Gas Grill, increasing the amount of wood chips to 4 cups, using 6 tablespoons Spice Rub, two 3½-pound chickens, and 2 cans of beer. Set the chickens (with cans) over the cool part of the grill, with a wing side facing the primary burner, allowing as much room around each chicken as possible. Grill-roast as directed.

TECHNIQUE: Beer Can Chicken with Big Flavor

Our beer can chicken is flavored through and through. Here's how we do it.

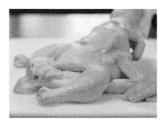

1. Use a church key can opener to punch holes in the top of the can; this will allow the maximum amount of steam to escape.

2. Loosen the skin on the breasts and thighs of the chicken by sliding your fingers between the skin and the meat.

3. Massage the spice mixture on the skin, under the skin, and inside the cavity.

4. Using a skewer, poke the skin all over to render as much fat as possible.

SPICE RUB

Makes I cup

- ½ cup sweet paprika
- 2 tablespoons kosher salt
- 2 tablespoons garlic powder
- 1 tablespoon dried thyme
- 2 teaspoons ground celery seed
- 2 teaspoons ground black pepper
- 2 teaspoons cayenne

Combine all the ingredients in a small bowl. (Extra rub can be stored [or frozen] in an airtight container for several weeks.)

VARIATION

GRILL-ROASTED BEER CAN CHICKEN FOR A GAS GRILL

Be sure not to open the lid of the gas grill too often during cooking; the temperature of the grill will drop significantly each time you open it.

Soak 2 cups wood chips in cold water to cover for 1 hour. Place the wood chips in a foil tray (see the illustrations on page 215). Place the tray on top of the primary burner of a gas grill and replace the cooking grate(s). Light all the burners and turn to high, cover, and heat until the chips are smoking heavily, about 15 minutes. Meanwhile, follow the recipe for Grill-Roasted Beer Can Chicken for a Charcoal Grill through step 2. Carefully open the grill (there may be some smoke) and scrape the cooking grate clean with a grill brush. Turn the primary burner down to medium and turn off the other burner(s). Place the chicken over the cool part of the grill with a wing side facing the primary burner. Cover and grill-roast for 35 minutes, adjusting the lit burner as needed to maintain a temperature of 325 to 350 degrees inside the grill. Rotate the chicken so that the drumstick and wing that were facing away from the lit burner are now facing toward it. Cover and continue to grill-roast until an instant-read thermometer inserted into the thickest part of the thigh registers 170 to 175 degrees, 25 to 40 minutes longer, and proceed as directed in step 6.

EQUIPMENT CORNER:
Essential Grilling Gadgets

MOST KITCHENWARE STORES WOULD HAVE YOU THINKING you couldn't grill a hamburger without investing in a staggering assortment of gadgets and gear. Not so. We've tested hundreds of pieces of grilling equipment over the years and here are our findings on what you really need.

LIGHTING THE FIRE

Chimney Starters: Chimney starters eliminate the need for lighter fluid, which some of our more sensitive tasters swear they can taste residually on the grilled food. And we prefer chimney starters to electric starters because they are faster, and you do not always have an electrical outlet nearby your grill. A chimney starter is cylindrical with an attached heatsafe handle. It resembles a huge beer mug. Inside the cylinder, just a few inches up from the bottom, a perforated metal plate separates the large upper chamber from the small lower chamber. Different models of chimney starters show very little variation. Some have wooden handles, some have plastic handles, but all do just about the same thing. One thing to keep in mind when buying a chimney is the charcoal capacity. We like a large chimney (one that holds about six quarts of charcoal briquettes and measures 12 inches high by about 7½ inches across) because it holds just the right amount for grilling most foods over medium-hot heat in a large kettle grill. Smaller chimneys necessitate extra heating time for the coals that cannot fit into the chimney. Expect to pay between $15 and $30 for a chimney starter—a very modest investment for such a useful tool.

CLEANING THE COOKING GRATE

Grill Brush: Anyone who has grilled a rack of sticky barbecued ribs has had to deal with the task of removing the sugary, burned-on mess that gets left behind. The ideal time to do this is soon after your food comes off the grill, but, if you're like most of us, you close the lid, walk away, and save the mess for the next time grill duty calls. We set out to find a grill brush that could make the tedious task of cleaning a gunked-up cooking grate more efficient. What did we find? Those brushes with stiffer bristles fared better than their softer counterparts, but none of them worked all that well. The bristles on most bent after a few strokes and trapped large quantities of gunk, thereby decreasing their efficiency. In the end, we found that the unusual but incredibly effective Grill Wizard has no brass bristles to bend, break, or clog with unwanted grease and grime. Instead, this brush comes equipped with two large woven mesh stainless steel "scrubbie" pads. The pads are able to conform to any cooking grate's spacing, size, and material, including porcelain. Best of all, the pads are detachable, washable, and replaceable.

MOVING, TURNING, AND SUPPORTING FOOD ON THE GRILL

Long-Handled Tongs: A pair of tongs is the ideal tool for turning foods as they cook. A large fork pierces foods and causes some loss of fluids. A spatula is fine for small, flat foods, especially those prone to sticking, but it is useless with flank steak or chicken parts. A pair of tongs is the most useful and versatile turner of the lot, capable of flipping something as delicate as thin asparagus spears or as heavy as a rack of ribs. Testing all manner of tongs, we groped and grabbed kebabs, asparagus, chicken drumsticks, and 3-pound slabs of ribs and found tong performance differed dramatically. Some were heavy and difficult to maneuver, and their less delicate pincers couldn't get a grip on asparagus. Other problems included sharp, serrated edges that nicked the food, flimsy arms that bent under the strain of heavy food, and pincers whose spread could not even accommodate the girth of a chicken leg. The winner? Oxo's 16-inch stainless steel kitchen tongs with soft, nonslip handles ($13), which outperformed tongs especially designed for use on the grill.

Metal Spatula: A metal spatula with a long, offset handle makes a useful supplement to a pair of tongs, especially when grilling delicate foods prone to falling apart, such as fish fillets and burgers. We prefer a spatula with a large (6 inches long by 3 inches wide), thin, stiff blade. We like the model made by Vollrath, which costs about $4.50.

Grill Grid: Grill grids, also called vegetable grids, are useful for cooking small pieces of food that might fall into the fire if placed on the cooking grate that comes with most grills. A grill grid goes on top of the grill's cooking grate, is allowed to heat up, and is then used as the cooking surface for the food. In our tests, grids made of perforated, porcelain-coated metal proved more versatile—they made it possible to cook delicate fish fillets and fish burgers which stuck easily to wire mesh grids. Nonstick and stainless steel metal grids did not brown fish burgers well. Buy a grid that covers about half your cooking grate and expect to pay about $20.

FOR MAINTAINING AND MANAGING THE FIRE

Hinged Grate: Sometimes you will need to add charcoal to a fire to maintain its temperature, as when barbecuing (cooking indirectly over a low, slow fire on a grill). A hinged cooking grate (a grate with a hinged flap that opens for easy access to the charcoal below) allows food to stay in place as you add coals. Many charcoal grills have hinged cooking grates, but some do not. Hinged grates for a 22.5-inch Weber grill cost about $18.

Plant Mister/Squirt Bottle: Keep a plant mister or squirt bottle filled with water nearby your grill. It's the best way we know to control flare-ups that can char food. Available in any hardware or discount store, usually for less than $5.

GAUGING THE TEMPERATURE OF THE GRILL AND DETERMINING DONENESS

Thermometers: We rely on a few kinds of thermometers when grilling. A grill thermometer will tell you what the temperature is inside a covered grill. Most gas grills come with this gauge. If you have a charcoal grill, you will need to buy a grill thermometer at a hardware store. This kind of thermometer has a dial face with numbers and a long stem. To use this device on a charcoal grill, simply insert it through the vents on the lid.

Instant-read thermometers are essential for determining when foods are properly cooked. The best instant-read thermometer in our tests is the Super Fast Thermapen Digital Thermometer ($85). It's fast, accurate, has a large, easy-to-read digital display, and its slender probe won't leave a gaping hole in your food.

And, for longer-cooking foods, such as a whole chicken, turkey, or roast, you can use a timer/thermometer. This thermometer includes a probe that is left in the food as it cooks and a LCD console that reads the temperature outside of the grill. Just set the desired internal temperature and activate the alarm, which will ring when that temperature is reached. Of those that we have tested, the Polder Dual Sensor Thermometer/Timer ($30) is easy and intuitive to figure out. In our tests, we have gotten different temperature readings within a very, very small area so we recommend double-checking with an instant-read thermometer.

PROTECTING DELICATE FOODS ON A CHARCOAL GRILL

Large Disposable Foil Roasting Pan: Sensitive tasters can pick up off-flavors caused by carbon residue on the inside of a charcoal grill lid used to cover foods as they cook, especially with mild-flavored foods like chicken and fish. Instead, we find that simple foil roasting pans can do the job without imparting off-flavors to food. Simply invert a foil roasting pan over delicate foods on a charcoal grill, in lieu of putting the grill lid down.

PESTO PASTA SALAD

WHAT WE WANTED: Pesto pasta salad—fresh, green, garlicky, and full of herbal flavor.

More light and refreshing than a cream-based sauce or a chunky ragù, pesto makes a top-notch accompaniment to pasta during the sultry summer months. There's nothing complicated about this uncooked Ligurian sauce, which consists of processed fresh basil, garlic, pine nuts, Parmigiano-Reggiano cheese, and olive oil. And tossing it with hot, just-cooked pasta couldn't be easier. But numerous issues arise once pesto is added to a pasta salad. The refrigerator dulls the color and flavor of the pesto, which turns greasy and clumpy as the pasta cools.

We began by trying varying ratios of the five integral ingredients: basil, garlic (blanched briefly to tame its harsh bite), Parmesan cheese, olive oil (extra-virgin), and pine nuts (toasted to enhance their nutty flavor). We found that we had to use a lot of basil (between 3 and 4 packed cups) to achieve decent herbal flavor and the bulk needed for the pesto to cling to the pasta. But when made even a few hours ahead of time, the basil turned dark and muddy. Adding another green element seemed the obvious solution. Parsley is a common trick, but we needed to use so much that it began to compete with the basil flavor. We'd seen frozen chopped spinach used in one recipe. While it turned the pesto a nice, bright shade of green, it also made the texture stringy. The easy solution was to add a small amount of fresh baby spinach (1 cup added to 3 cups of basil), which provided a lovely bright green color and smooth texture without interfering with the basil flavor. While the relatively thin consistency of traditional pesto might be fine for hot noodles, a thicker, creamier pesto was in order for room-temperature pasta. But no matter how much we fiddled with ingredient amounts, the pesto was always less than optimally creamy. Since this dish wasn't exactly an Italian classic, we decided to borrow a standard ingredient used in many American pasta salads: mayonnaise. The creamy, tangy condiment served as the perfect binder. Six tablespoons was enough to provide a creamy, luscious texture.

The best pasta shapes for this dish have a textured surface with a concave nook or two that can trap the pesto and keep it from sliding off. With its stubby form, indented center, and jagged edges, farfalle made an excellent partner. Unlike hot pasta, which should generally be cooked until al dente, the pasta used in salads should cook slightly longer, until tender. When the pesto was added straight to just-cooked pasta, it took an hour to reach room temperature. The hot pasta also "cooked" the basil, deadening its impact. Rinsing the pasta in cold water cooled it down quickly but made the surface of the pasta too slick to hold on to the pesto. The solution was to let the pasta cool in a single layer on a rimmed baking sheet, tossing in a splash of oil to prevent sticking. All our pasta salad needed was some final flavor tweaking. Lemon juice cut through the richness, and an extra ½ cup of toasted pine nuts folded into the pesto-coated pasta added a sweet, nutty note as well as textural contrast. A pint of quartered cherry tomatoes or halved grape tomatoes contributed color and small bursts of freshness.

WHAT WE LEARNED: Use a pasta shape with a textured surface, like farfalle, so that the pesto won't slide off. To ensure that the pesto coats the pasta, don't rinse the pasta after cooking. Instead, spread the pasta to cool in a single layer on a baking sheet. A splash of oil will help prevent the pasta from sticking. For the pesto, blanch the garlic to tame its harsh bite. Use lots of basil (3 cups) for vibrant herb flavor, and to keep the green color from fading, add 1 cup baby spinach. The mild flavor of the spinach won't overshadow the basil, and its fresh green color lends the salad a bright shade of green. For a creamy, not greasy, pesto, enrich it with mayonnaise. Lemon juice brightens the pesto's flavor, and an extra ½ cup of toasted pine nuts, folded into the salad, provides an extra hit of nutty flavor and a pleasant crunchy texture.

PASTA SALAD WITH PESTO

Serves 8 to 10

This salad is best served the day it is made; if it's been refrigerated, bring it to room temperature before serving. The pesto can be made a day ahead—just cook the garlic cloves in a small saucepan of boiling water for 1 minute. Garnish with additional shaved or grated Parmesan.

¾   cup pine nuts
2   medium garlic cloves, unpeeled
    Salt
1   pound farfalle (bow ties) pasta
¼   cup plus 1 tablespoon extra-virgin olive oil
3   cups packed fresh basil leaves (about 4 ounces)
1   cup packed baby spinach (about 1 ounce)
½   teaspoon ground black pepper
2   tablespoons juice from 1 lemon
1½   ounces Parmesan cheese, finely grated
    (about ¾ cup), plus extra for serving
6   tablespoons mayonnaise
1   pint cherry tomatoes, quartered, or grape
    tomatoes, halved (optional)

1. Bring 4 quarts water to a boil in a large pot. Toast the pine nuts in a small dry skillet over medium heat, shaking the pan occasionally, until just golden and fragrant, 4 to 5 minutes.

2. When the water is boiling, add the garlic and let cook 1 minute. Remove the garlic with a slotted spoon and rinse under cold water to stop the cooking; set aside to cool. Add 1 tablespoon salt and the pasta to the water, stir to separate, and cook until tender (just past al dente). Reserve ¼ cup cooking water, drain the pasta, toss with 1 tablespoon oil, spread in a single layer on a rimmed baking sheet, and cool to room temperature, about 30 minutes.

3. When the garlic is cool, peel and mince it or press through a garlic press. Place ¼ cup of the nuts, garlic, basil, spinach, pepper, lemon juice, remaining ¼ cup oil,

and 1 teaspoon salt in the workbowl of a food processor and process until smooth, scraping down the sides of the bowl as necessary. Add the cheese and the mayonnaise and process until thoroughly combined. Transfer the mixture to a large serving bowl. Cover and refrigerate until ready to assemble the salad.

4. When the pasta is cool, toss with the pesto, adding the reserved pasta water, 1 tablespoon at a time, until the pesto evenly coats the pasta. Fold in the remaining ½ cup nuts and tomatoes (if using). Serve, passing Parmesan at the table.

GETTING IT RIGHT:
Better Pesto Pasta Salad

It's not hard to make a pesto pasta salad taste good. To get the appearance and texture to live up to the vibrant flavors, we came up with two easy tricks.

Bright Color
Supplementing the basil with baby spinach helped maintain the pesto's bright green color.

Creamy Texture
Adding a touch of mayonnaise turned the too-slick pesto creamy and cohesive.

Chris explains that while you could use an umbrella to grill in inclement weather, it makes more sense to try our oven-barbecued ribs instead.

RAINY DAY

barbecue

For many of us, it doesn't seem fair that barbecue can
be enjoyed only during the short summer months—and only when
it's not raining. Take barbecued ribs. If the temperature drops or the
skies open up, we still want to satisfy our craving for this tender,
smoky meat. We aimed to develop a recipe for oven-barbecued ribs,
so no matter what kind of weather, we could have our barbecue. And
these ribs would need to stand up to their outdoor counterparts: tender, fall-off-the-bone meat infused with smoky flavor.

Rich, meaty ribs are best enjoyed with a side of tangy coleslaw—
specifically buttermilk coleslaw. But while buttermilk provides a trademark tang, it can also make a dressing so thin that it sinks to the bottom
of the bowl instead of clinging to the shreds of cabbage. Cabbage poses
its own challenges, too. We wanted even shreds that were easy to fork
and toss with the dressing. And, we wanted crisp cabbage that won't
leach moisture into our dressing, diluting its flavor and turning our
coleslaw bland.

If you're a fan of barbecue but never thought it could be replicated
indoors, our menu should change your mind.

THE RECIPES
Oven-Barbecued Spareribs
Quick Barbecue Sauce

Creamy Buttermilk Coleslaw
Creamy Buttermilk Coleslaw with
    Scallions and Cilantro
Creamy Buttermilk Coleslaw with
    Lemon and Herbs

TASTING LAB
Ketchup

RAINY DAY BARBECUE **233**

OVEN-BARBECUED RIBS

WHAT WE WANTED: Oven-barbecued ribs with the smoky flavor and tender texture of real outdoor barbecue.

The barbecue season for much of the country is cruelly short. When the temperature plunges as fall drifts into winter, it's virtually impossible to maintain the modest grill temperatures required to turn tough cuts of meat tender. When the craving strikes for crisp-crusted, smoky spareribs in midwinter, many of us have just two options: Head to the local BBQ shack or attempt them in the oven. But is it really possible to replicate outdoor ribs inside?

Barbecue is as much cooking method as flavoring agent. The low temperature and steady blanket of hardwood smoke work almost like braising, rendering the collagen—a protein in meat's tough connective tissue—to rich-tasting, silky gelatin. The low temperatures and moist environment are easy to replicate in the oven; the smoke, by contrast, is not.

The indoor barbecued rib recipes we found were a dubious lot. Most smothered racks in smoke-flavored sauce and baked them slowly. Sure, the ribs tasted OK—slather an old shoe in smoky sauce and it will taste good—but none possessed the deep, rich flavor of true barbecue. Others slicked the ribs with liquid smoke, smearing on a dry rub just before baking—not much better: There's a fundamental difference between ribs that taste of smoke and ribs that are smoked.

There was a third option: indoor smoking. Indoor smokers are essentially roasting pans fitted with a wire rack and a tight-fitting lid. Shredded wood chips are dusted across the pan bottom, the food is set on the rack, and the pan is sealed. The pan is heated on the stovetop to ignite the chips, after which it enters the oven to finish cooking. Some indoor smokers we tested worked fairly well, but the designs are so basic that we opted to rig one up from equipment we had on hand.

Before we got ahead of ourselves, we had to choose the ribs. For outdoor barbecue, we favor St. Louis–style

spareribs—pork spareribs (located near the belly) trimmed of skirt meat and excess cartilage—and saw no reason to change.

Squeezing the ribs onto a wire rack in the test kitchen's biggest roasting pan, we tossed in a handful of hickory chips and sealed it with foil. We slid the pan over a burner set on high and waited. And waited. Smoke finally began seeping out from the foil long after we were afraid the pan would melt from such heat. Once the alarm sounded, we guessed the ribs were smoky enough and transferred the pan to a 250-degree oven to finish.

The ribs tasted smoky alright, but this method certainly had flaws: It was hard finding a pan large enough to fit the ribs, it took us three trips to find wood chips (during off-season, most hardware stores switch out grilling paraphernalia for snow shovels), and the billowing smoke made the test kitchen reek of hickory for days.

Could we move the entire process to the oven, thereby containing the smoke? With no direct high heat, we could also switch to a rimmed baking sheet, which had enough room for the ribs to lie flat. We cranked the oven to 400 degrees, slid the ribs inside, and, once again, waited for smoke. An hour passed without the faintest whiff. After 1½ hours, we pulled the pan out and found gray, greasy, gristly looking ribs without a hint of smoke flavor.

Higher heat? After turning up the temperature in 25-degree increments, we finally smelled smoke at 500 degrees. Where there's smoke, there should be flavor, but no such luck. The oven still wasn't hot enough to ignite the wood.

A colleague suggested another option: tea smoking. Chinese cooks smoke a variety of foodstuffs over smoldering black tea. So we replaced the wood chips with loose tea, closed the oven door, and—while the leaves didn't burn—the distinct aroma of tea that filled the kitchen surprised us. The ribs tasted faintly of it, too. Perhaps outright combustion wasn't necessary—"roasting" was enough to unlock the tea's flavor. Smoky-tasting Lapsang Souchong tea leaves,

cured over smoldering pine or cypress boughs, seemed like the perfect candidate.

With the oven set to high heat (the leaves scattered across the bottom of the baking sheet), we could smell smoke in minutes. After 30 minutes, the ribs tasted decidedly smoky. Grinding the leaves to a fine powder (thereby maximizing the tea to baking surface ratio) imbued the ribs with an even deeper flavor. Neither as sweet as hickory nor as sharp as mesquite, the tea perfumed the ribs with a rich smokiness far deeper than that lent by barbecue sauce or liquid smoke.

The ribs were smoky, but the high heat required to "roast" the tea had also made them inedibly tough. The solution lay in the freezer. Chilling the rib racks as the oven preheated cooled them enough that they could withstand a very high heat and quickly absorb "smoke" without toughening. After just half an hour at 500 degrees, our prechilled ribs had absorbed as much of the smoky flavor as possible, and we could decrease the oven temperature dramatically.

To cook the ribs, we experimented with temperatures ranging between 200 and 300 degrees; 250 degrees proved the best compromise between texture and time. Within two hours—including the "smoking" time—the ribs were fork-tender, though moist and gummy. A pass under the high heat of the broiler quickly turned the wet exterior into a chewy, crispy crust.

Following the lead of several recipes, we tried adding liquid to the pan (and resealing the foil to contain the steam) to see if it would make the ribs moister. Water worked well but added no flavor; beer and apple juice—both common "mops" used to keep the meat moist in outdoor barbecue—

were better options. Beer brought a slightly boozy taste to the meat, but the juice added welcome sweet depth.

Smoky and tender but slightly bland, the ribs were ready for some spice. Barbecued ribs can be cooked "dry," coated with spices and served as is, or "wet," brushed with sauce shortly before serving. We've always had a weakness for the latter, but tasters argued that the big-flavored sauce masked the tea's smokiness.

We knew we wanted to keep the rub simple to make way for the ribs' smoky, pork flavor so we started with the basics: salt, pepper, paprika, and brown sugar. We added a little cayenne for heat. Still too bland. Next we tried cumin, coriander, oregano, and chili powder and only really liked the depth lent by the chili powder. Finally, a thin slathering of mustard brought just the right tangy, sharp kick to the pork and, as an added bonus, helped the spices stick fast. For an extra level of flavor, we added a few cloves of minced garlic and a spoonful of ketchup.

Smoky-tasting to the bone, tender to a fault, and judiciously spicy, these ribs were so good we might even make them in midsummer.

WHAT WE LEARNED: Pork spareribs, trimmed of skirt meat and excess cartilage (called St. Louis–style), make the best barbecued ribs. Use a baking sheet to contain the ribs—a roasting pan isn't large enough. A thin coating of mustard, ketchup, and garlic gives our ribs some welcome tang and helps our simple, but flavorful, rub adhere. Chill the ribs at least 8 hours and up to 24, then transfer to the freezer while the oven preheats so that the meat won't toughen under the oven's initial high heat. Wood chips, which are typically used in barbecue to impart smoky flavor to meat, aren't suitable for indoor cooking nor are they easy to find during the off-season. Instead, choose a Chinese trick—Lapsang Souchong tea. The tea gives the ribs an authentic smoky flavor and it's available year-round. Apple juice, added to the pan during roasting, gives the ribs flavor and welcome moisture. And, after roasting, run the ribs under the broiler to give them a browned and crispy crust.

OVEN-BARBECUED SPARERIBS

Serves 4

To make this recipe, you will need a baking stone, a sturdy baking sheet with a 1-inch rim, and a wire cooling rack that fits inside it. It's fine if the ribs overlap slightly on the rack. In step 1, removing the surface fat keeps the ribs from being too greasy. And, removing the membrane from the ribs allows the smoke to penetrate both sides of the racks and also makes the ribs easier to eat. Note that the ribs must be coated with the rub and refrigerated at least 8 hours and up to 24 hours ahead of cooking. Be careful when opening the crimped foil to add the juice, as hot steam and smoke will billow out. If desired, serve the ribs with Quick Barbecue Sauce (opposite) or your favorite store-bought brand.

ribs

2	racks St. Louis–style spareribs (2½ to 3 pounds each)
¼	cup finely ground Lapsang Souchong tea (from about 10 tea bags, or ½ cup loose tea leaves ground to a powder in a spice grinder)
½	cup apple juice

rub

6	tablespoons yellow mustard
2	tablespoons ketchup
3	medium garlic cloves, minced or pressed through a garlic press (about 1 tablespoon)
2	teaspoons ground black pepper
1	tablespoon sweet paprika
1	tablespoon chili powder
½	teaspoon cayenne
1½	tablespoons kosher salt
3	tablespoons brown sugar

1. FOR THE RIBS: Using a sharp knife, trim any surface fat from both racks. To remove the membrane (the thin white sheath that lines the concave side of the rack), insert a spoon handle between the membrane and the ribs of one rack to loosen slightly. Using a paper towel, grasp the loosened membrane and pull away gently to remove. Repeat with the second rack.

2. FOR THE RUB: Combine the mustard, ketchup, and garlic in a small bowl; combine the pepper, paprika, chili powder, cayenne, salt, and sugar in a separate small bowl. Spread the mustard mixture in a thin, even layer over both sides of the ribs and coat both sides with the spice mixture, then wrap the ribs in plastic wrap and refrigerate for at least 8 hours and up to 24 hours.

3. Transfer the ribs from the refrigerator to the freezer for 45 minutes. Adjust one oven rack to the lowest position and the second rack to the upper-middle position (at least 5 inches below the broiler). Place the baking stone on the lower rack and heat the oven to 500 degrees. Sprinkle the ground tea evenly over the bottom of the rimmed baking sheet and set the wire rack on the sheet. Place the ribs meat side up on the rack and cover with heavy-duty foil, crimping the edges tightly to seal. Set the baking sheet with the ribs directly on the stone and roast for 30 minutes, then reduce the oven temperature to 250 degrees, leaving the oven door open for 1 minute to cool. While the oven is open, carefully open one corner of the foil and pour the apple juice into the bottom of the baking sheet; reseal the foil. Continue to roast until the meat is very tender and begins to pull away from the bones, about 1½ hours. (Begin to check the ribs after 1 hour; leave loosely covered with foil for the remaining cooking time.)

4. Remove the foil and carefully flip the racks bone side up and place the baking sheet on the upper-middle oven rack. Turn on the broiler and cook the ribs until well browned and crispy in spots, 5 to 10 minutes. Flip the ribs meat side up and cook until well browned and crispy, 5 to 7 minutes more. Cool for at least 10 minutes before cutting into individual ribs. Serve with barbecue sauce, if desired.

TECHNIQUE:
Homemade Indoor Smoker

You can crowd ribs into an indoor smoker, but we prefer our roomier makeshift version. Spread tea leaves on a rimmed baking sheet, place a wire cooling rack on top, followed by the ribs and heavy-duty foil. A baking stone gets the tea smoking quickly.

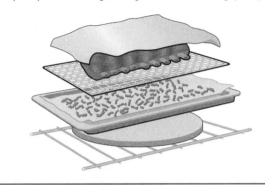

QUICK BARBECUE SAUCE

Makes about 1½ cups

Classic barbecue sauce must simmer for a long time for the whole tomatoes in it to break down. However, we found that starting with ketchup can shorten the process. Use this sauce as you would any other barbecue sauce—either brushed on foods during the last minutes of grilling or served at the table as a dipping sauce with ribs or brisket.

1	medium onion, peeled and quartered
¼	cup water
1	cup ketchup
5	tablespoons molasses
2	tablespoons cider vinegar
2	tablespoons Worcestershire sauce
2	tablespoons Dijon mustard
1½	teaspoons liquid smoke (optional)
1	teaspoon hot pepper sauce
¼	teaspoon ground black pepper
2	tablespoons vegetable oil
1	medium garlic clove, minced or pressed through a garlic press (about 1 teaspoon)
1	teaspoon chili powder
¼	teaspoon cayenne

1. Process the onion with the water in a food processor until pureed and the mixture resembles slush, about 30 seconds. Strain the mixture through a fine-mesh strainer into a liquid measuring cup, pressing on the solids with a rubber spatula to obtain ½ cup juice. Discard the solids.

2. Whisk the onion juice, ketchup, molasses, vinegar, Worcestershire, mustard, liquid smoke (if using), hot pepper sauce, and black pepper together in a medium bowl.

3. Heat the oil in a large nonreactive saucepan over medium heat until shimmering but not smoking. Add the garlic, chili powder, and cayenne and cook until fragrant, about 30 seconds. Whisk in the ketchup mixture and bring to a boil; reduce the heat to medium-low and simmer gently, uncovered, until the flavors meld and the sauce is thickened, about 25 minutes. Cool the sauce to room temperature before using. (The sauce can be refrigerated in an airtight container for up to 1 week.)

GETTING IT RIGHT:
Best Pork Ribs for Oven Barbecue

Spareribs
Ribs from near the pig's fatty belly. An acceptable choice, but needs a fair amount of home trimming.

St. Louis–Style
Spareribs that have been trimmed of skirt meat and excess cartilage. Minimal fuss—our top choice.

TASTING LAB: Ketchup

THIS CLASSIC AMERICAN CONDIMENT BEGAN IN SOUTHEAST
Asia as a salty sauce made from anchovies. When British
explorers first encountered Chinese *ke-tsiap*, Malaysian
kechap, and Indonesian *ketjap*, the sauce was more like soy
sauce or Worcestershire sauce than modern ketchup. Until
the nineteenth century, British and American ketchup was
often made from mushrooms, nuts, or fruit.

The first tomato-based ketchups were made from
unripe tomatoes and were quite thin. In the late nineteenth
century, H. J. Heinz offered an alternative made with ripe
tomatoes, and transformed ketchup into the thick condiment we know today. With sweet, ripe tomatoes as the base
for his ketchup, Heinz was able to add enough vinegar to
preserve the product naturally. Balanced out with plenty of
sweetener, ketchup as we know it was born.

Ketchup hasn't really changed for more than a century, so why run a tasting? Heinz is ketchup and ketchup is
Heinz, right? True or not, no one in our test kitchen likes
to accept things on face value. So we rounded up 8 brands
and asked 29 tasters to taste them straight from the bottle
(on spoons) and with hot french fries.

Our panel had some shocking news for ketchup
lovers. According to tasters, there's a better option than
Heinz—and it's sitting right there on the shelves of your
local supermarket. Hunt's, America's number two ketchup,
was the clear winner of our tasting. Although Heinz's new
organic ketchup was the runner-up, regular Heinz ketchup
finished in the middle of the pack. The king of ketchups
was being dethroned, and we wanted an explanation.

As we read through the tasting sheets, we noticed a lot
of comments (and complaints) about acidity. Tasters wanted
a tangy ketchup, and several brands failed on this count.
Since fat and protein (say, in a burger) temper ketchup's
acidity, ketchup needs a pronounced tang to avoid tasting
dull. Because tanginess was clearly a high priority for tasters,
we got out the kitchen's trusty pH meter to test each sample.

The three ketchups at the bottom of the ratings (see chart,
page 240) were also the least acidic (higher pH translates
to lower acidity). Our first conclusion: A tangy ketchup is
a good ketchup. Sodium, it turns out, was also important.
The brands with the lowest sodium content finished at the
bottom of the pack. Sweetness is another key ketchup trait,
and the brands with less sugar fell to the bottom of the ratings, too.

Given ketchup's use as a condiment, it makes sense that
tasters would want more of these key flavor components—
acid, salty, and sweet. But what about tomato flavor? Many
of the experts we spoke with agreed that tomato growers are
more concerned with the levels of tomato solids, the viscosity of their juice, and their color. After all, ketchup is made
from tomato paste, which has been cooked long enough to
evaporate most of the natural juices.

Where did our tasters come out on tomato flavor?
While they had much more to say about the above-
mentioned acidity, saltiness, and sweetness, there were

some complaints about "flat" tomato flavor. We sent the ketchups to a local food laboratory for an analysis of total solids (almost all of which would be tomato solids). Sure enough, the three lowest-rated brands had the lowest solids content, and our winning brand had the highest solids content. A ketchup with more tomatoes is a good ketchup.

Besides providing color and thickness, tomatoes are a source of umami, the savory quality in "meaty" foods such as soy sauce and mushrooms that is related to the presence of the amino acid glutamate. Tomatoes are also a source of bitterness. Thus ketchup triggers all five major taste sensations: sweet, sour, salty, bitter, and umami. And so we reached our final conclusion about good-tasting ketchup: It has all five elements in perfect balance.

Beyond flavor, tasters were also very picky about consistency. Ketchup has to be thick enough to keep it from turning buns and fries soggy, but it shouldn't be pasty. Pectin is typically ketchup's only thickener.

But while pectin may be the only thickener in ketchup, it's not the only thing that can affect consistency. The amount of tomato solids and the presence of calcium (often added during the processing of tomato products) also play a role. Determined to quantify the thickness of each brand, we hit upon a promising lead when a source mentioned that the thickness of ketchup is actually regulated by the federal government. In fact, there's a tool used to measure consistency in ketchup (and other products), and we were able to borrow one from a food lab. Called a Bostwick consistometer, this stainless steel trough is marked with centimeters and measures the viscosity of foods. The federal regulation calls for ketchup to flow no more than 10 centimeters in 30 seconds at room temperature while the Bostwick is level on a flat surface.

Maybe government experts have all day, but we don't. Because none of the ketchups budged when the Bostwick was placed on a level surface, we decided to differentiate the "sort of" thick ketchups from the really thick ones by setting the consistometer at 28 degrees (so

the ketchups would flow more quickly) and then timed each sample to see how long it took to travel 24 centimeters—the entire length of the trough. Most of the ketchups took between one and 2½ minutes to traverse the trough, but Muir Glen and Westbrae were noticeably slower, taking about 10 and 8 minutes, respectively. Yes, ketchup should flow slowly, but there is such a thing as too thick and too slow.

Ketchup is best when it's smooth, thick, and tangy, with balanced, bold flavors. The parameters are tight—not too thick or too thin, not too tangy or too sweet. Bright red but no chunks. Brands that deviated from this formula, such as World's Best and Westbrae, fell to the bottom of the rankings.

The remaining brands might look alike, but our tasters noted some significant flavor differences. None were unacceptable, but Hunt's possessed a balance of sweet, sour, salty, bitter, and umami flavors that stood out among the pack. We now have a new brand of ketchup in the test kitchen.

GETTING IT RIGHT:
Measuring the Consistency of Ketchup

To measure consistency of the ketchups in our tasting, we poured each sample into this troughlike device, called a Bostwick consistometer. With stopwatch in hand, we timed each sample as it crept along the trough. Most samples made it to the finish line in 1 to 2½ minutes, but two overly thick brands took more than 8 minutes to travel the length of the trough.

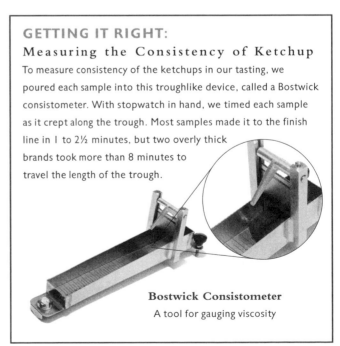

Bostwick Consistometer
A tool for gauging viscosity

Rating Ketchups

TWENTY-NINE MEMBERS OF THE AMERICA'S TEST KITCHEN STAFF TASTED THE KETCHUPS ON SPOONS AND ON FRENCH FRIES. We measured pH in the test kitchen; higher numbers indicate less acidity. A local food laboratory analyzed samples for total solids. We used a Bostwick consistometer to rate thickness, measuring the time it took each sample to slide down this device. The longer the time, the thicker the ketchup. The ketchups are listed in order of preference based on their combined scores in these two tastings.

RECOMMENDED
Hunt's Ketchup

$1.69 for 24 ounces

pH: 3.82 solids: 33.76%

Bostwick: 2 minutes, 30 seconds

This "cherry red" ketchup scored the highest for both taste and texture and was the overall winner. Tasters praised the "inviting, smooth" texture and "tangy," "fresh" flavor.

RECOMMENDED
Heinz Organic Ketchup

$1.99 for 15 ounces

pH: 3.82 solids: 31.7%

Bostwick: 1 minute, 50 seconds

Tasters liked the "vinegary tang" of this organic sample. "Color and texture are perfect," wrote one taster. The consistency was praised as "not too heavy."

RECOMMENDED
Annie's Naturals Organic Ketchup

$3.69 for 24 ounces

pH: 3.81 solids: 32.43%

Bostwick: 56 seconds

This ketchup (sweetened with sugar rather than the usual corn syrup) received solid scores for taste, texture, and color. Tasters liked the "rich, hearty, and tangy flavor," but others detected "odd smoky" notes.

RECOMMENDED WITH RESERVATIONS
Del Monte Ketchup

$1.39 for 24 ounces

pH: 3.65 solids: 32.12%

Bostwick: 1 minute, 10 seconds

Tasters were neither thrilled nor offended by this ketchup, giving it average marks in all categories. Some described it as "a little watery," and "a little cooked."

RECOMMENDED WITH RESERVATIONS
Heinz Ketchup

$1.69 for 24 ounces

pH: 3.84 solids: 32.54%

Bostwick: 50 seconds

The standard bearer fell to the middle of the pack in our taste tests, losing points for being "bland" and "too sweet." Tasters were more positive about its "fry-dipping texture" and "smooth" consistency.

RECOMMENDED WITH RESERVATIONS
Muir Glen Organic Ketchup

$3.49 for 24 ounces

pH: 4.01 solids: 29.93%

Bostwick: 10 minutes, 4 seconds

Tasters who liked "untraditional" ketchup singled out Muir Glen for its "nice texture," but others found the texture "too pasty" and "way too thick."

NOT RECOMMENDED
World's Best Ketchup

$2.99 for 10 ounces

pH: 4.29 solids: 19.46%

Bostwick: 1 minute

The most "un-ketchup-like ketchup" in our tasting. Its "chunky" texture made one taster ask, "Did I just wander into the salsa tasting?" Many said it was "too sweet."

NOT RECOMMENDED
Westbrae Natural Fruit Sweetened Ketchup

$2.39 for 14 ounces

pH: 4.15 solids: 25.92%

Bostwick: 8 minutes, 9 seconds

This brand, sweetened with fruit juice concentrate, provoked strong negative comments. One taster described it as a "molasses and tomato train wreck." Others found it "sour" and "too vinegary."

BUTTERMILK COLESLAW

WHAT WE WANTED: Coleslaw with a pickle-crisp texture in a tangy, creamy dressing.

O rder barbecue down South, and it will no doubt be accompanied by a side of buttermilk coleslaw. Unlike an all-mayonnaise coleslaw, buttermilk makes a coleslaw that is light, creamy, and refreshingly tart—a nice counterpart to a rich rack of ribs or meaty burger. The downside is that, also unlike mayonnaise, which is thick and clingy, buttermilk is thin, so it presents the unappetizing possibility of thin, watery coleslaw. Our goal was clear: crisp, evenly cut pieces of cabbage lightly dressed with an authentic, flavorful buttermilk dressing that clings to the cabbage instead of collecting in the bottom of the bowl.

The tough, squeaky leaves and compact core of a cabbage head require both a sharp knife and a good game plan. We realized it is best to quarter and core the cabbage, then disassemble each quarter into stacks containing several layers of cabbage. These stacks can then be either laid flat on a cutting board and sliced with a chef's knife or rolled and fit into the feed tube of a food processor fitted with the shredding disk.

As tempting as it is to toss freshly cut pieces of cabbage immediately with dressing, we found that such a hastily made coleslaw will weep within an hour, diluting the dressing into a puddle.

To combat the weeping problem, we tried two popular methods of dealing with the prepped cabbage: ice water and salt. Soaking the sliced cabbage in ice water turned it temporarily plump and fresh, but the dressing didn't cling to it. In the end, the soaked cabbage just made for a bigger puddle of dressing at the bottom of the bowl. Salting the cabbage, on the other hand, worked perfectly. As the salt and cabbage sat, moisture was wicked out of the cabbage cells, wilting it to a pickle-crisp texture. To eliminate excess salt and water, the wilted cabbage needed a quick rinse and towel dry. (When left unrinsed and undried, the salty moisture trapped within the thatch of the shredded cabbage ruined both the flavor and texture of the final coleslaw.) A mere teaspoon of salt was enough to draw the moisture out of half a head of cabbage.

With the cabbage cut evenly and rid of excessive moisture, we needed to find a way to bulk up the buttermilk so that it would cling to the cabbage without losing its distinctively Southern twang. First, we tried mixing the buttermilk with increasing amounts of sour cream, but the dressing tasted overly sour by the time it was thick enough to coat. Switching to mayonnaise, we were able to make a dressing with good heft and adhesiveness, but tasters disliked the way the mayonnaise muted the buttermilk's characteristic zip. But when the buttermilk was both stiffened by mayonnaise and reinforced with sour cream, the dressing adhered well to the cabbage without tasting overly potent or losing its bite. We found that ½ cup buttermilk needed help from 2 tablespoons each of sour cream and mayonnaise to dress half a head of cabbage.

For finishing touches, we added a shredded carrot for both color and sweetness, which tasters liked, and then tried celery, bell peppers, radishes, and red onions, all of which they did not like. The mild flavor of shallot was welcome, though, along with some parsley, and a pinch of sugar, mustard, and cider vinegar. The result? An authentic buttermilk coleslaw that will not weep whether it's accompanying food prepared north or south of the Mason-Dixon line.

WHAT WE LEARNED: For even shreds of cabbage, stack the leaves on a cutting board and, using a sharp chef's knife, cut into thin strips, or fit the stacked leaves into the feed tube of a food processor fitted with the shredding disk. To prevent watery coleslaw, salt, rinse, and dry the shredded cabbage. For a tangy, creamy dressing that clings to the cabbage and won't pool at the bottom of the bowl, supplement the buttermilk with mayonnaise and sour cream.

1. Start by cutting the cabbage into quarters. Cut away the hard piece of core attached to each quarter.

2. Separate the cored cabbage quarters into stacks of leaves that flatten when pressed lightly.

3. Use a chef's knife to cut each stack diagonally (this ensures long pieces) into thin shreds.

CREAMY BUTTERMILK COLESLAW

Serves 4

To serve the coleslaw immediately, rinse the salted cabbage in a large bowl of ice water, drain it in a colander, pick out any ice cubes, then pat the cabbage dry before dressing.

- 1 pound red or green cabbage (about ½ medium head), shredded fine (see illustrations above) or chopped (about 6 cups)
  Salt
- 1 medium carrot, peeled and shredded
- ½ cup buttermilk
- 2 tablespoons mayonnaise
- 2 tablespoons sour cream
- 1 small shallot, minced (about 2 tablespoons)
- 2 tablespoons minced fresh parsley leaves
- ½ teaspoon cider vinegar
- ¼ teaspoon Dijon mustard
- ½ teaspoon sugar
- ⅛ teaspoon ground black pepper

1. Toss the shredded cabbage and 1 teaspoon salt in a colander or large-mesh strainer set over a medium bowl. Let stand until the cabbage wilts, at least 1 hour and up to 4 hours. Rinse the cabbage under cold running water (or in a large bowl of ice water if serving immediately). Press, but do not squeeze, to drain; pat dry with paper towels. Combine the wilted cabbage and the carrot in a large bowl.

2. Stir the buttermilk, mayonnaise, sour cream, shallot, parsley, vinegar, mustard, sugar, ¼ teaspoon salt, and the pepper in a small bowl. Pour the buttermilk dressing over the wilted cabbage and refrigerate, covered, until ready to serve. (The coleslaw can be refrigerated for up to 3 days.)

VARIATIONS

CREAMY BUTTERMILK COLESLAW WITH SCALLIONS AND CILANTRO

Choose this coleslaw to accompany your favorite Southwestern dishes.

Follow the recipe for Creamy Buttermilk Coleslaw, substituting 1 tablespoon minced fresh cilantro leaves for the parsley and 1 teaspoon juice from 1 lime for the cider vinegar, omitting the mustard, and adding 2 scallions, sliced thin.

CREAMY BUTTERMILK COLESLAW WITH LEMON AND HERBS

This brightly flavored variation goes well with just about any main course, especially grilled chicken or fish.

Follow the recipe for Creamy Buttermilk Coleslaw, substituting 1 teaspoon juice from 1 lemon for the cider vinegar and adding 1 teaspoon fresh thyme leaves and 1 tablespoon minced fresh chives to the dressing.

Oven-Barbecued Spareribs **page 236**

Spice-Rubbed Picnic Chicken **page 206**

Barbecued Beef Brisket **page 213**

Grilled Shrimp **page 201**

Pasta Salad with Pesto **page 231**

Chicken Francese **page 161**

Sautéed Garlic-Lemon Spinach **page 43**

Pan-Roasted Broccoli with Spicy Southeast Asian Flavors **page 97**

250

Steak Diane **page 174**

Huevos Rancheros **page 156**

Crêpes Suzette **page 181**

Skillet Apple Brown Betty **page 294**

Dark Chocolate Cupcakes **page 275**

Dark Chocolate Mousse **page 272**

Key Lime Bars **page 309**

Strawberry Cream Cake **page 261**

STRAWBERRY
cream cake

Looking for a drop-dead gorgeous summer dessert?

Look no further than strawberry cream cake—a snazzier, more elegant version of strawberry shortcake. The components are almost identical—juicy strawberries, sweetened whipped cream, and layer cake (in place of biscuits). The cake, cream, and strawberries are layered, chilled, and cut into tall wedges. It's a terrific way to celebrate summer. We wanted to find the ultimate version of this dessert and solve the problems that often plague it. Because the cake, cream, and strawberries are all layered, cutting this cake can be tricky—the whipped cream can squirt out the sides or the strawberries will ooze out. The strawberries pose other problems, too—their juices can make a delicate cake soggy. Some recipes get around this pitfall by using fewer strawberries, but this results in muted fruit flavor. We wanted those strawberries front and center. In short, we wanted lots of strawberry flavor, a buttery sturdy cake that could stand up to them, and a lush whipped cream filling that would stay put, so even when sliced this cake would be a stunner.

STRAWBERRY CREAM CAKE

WHAT WE WANTED: A stunning summer dessert—buttery yellow cake layered with juicy strawberries and lush sweetened whipped cream that won't fall apart when sliced.

Nothing better showcases tangy, juicy strawberries than a strawberry cream cake. True, a simple strawberry shortcake puts the berries front and center, but its homespun, last-minute nature often doesn't suit a more dressed-up occasion.

While we found no shortage of recipes for strawberry cream cakes that looked good, we were disenchanted by their lackluster taste and texture. The problem resided with either the cake itself, which collapsed under the weight of the filling, or the whipped cream, which squirted out the sides of the cake upon slicing. But most egregious, the strawberry flavor often takes a backseat to the cake and cream. We wanted a sturdy cake, a firm filling, and strawberry flavor fit for a starring role.

With multiple layers, we needed a cake that was structurally sound. That meant butter cakes—rich but fragile—were out, so we moved on to sponge cakes. But tasters found the various sponge cakes we prepared too lean and dry. We realized that what we wanted was the structure of a sponge cake coupled with the moistness and richness of a butter cake.

There was one sponge cake we had yet to try—the chiffon cake, an American invention introduced at Hollywood's Brown Derby restaurant in the 1920s and popularized by Betty Crocker in the 1940s. Similar to an angel food cake, a chiffon cake has more fat (in the form of egg yolks and vegetable oil) than most sponge cakes, making it high and light but also moist and tender.

When we baked the test kitchen recipe for chiffon cake in a round cake pan (instead of the traditional tube pan), there was no way to hang it upside down while cooling to help the cake maintain its shape. The result was a sunken center and retracted sides. We tried increasing the flour and decreasing the liquid. The cake no longer sunk, but tasters

felt it wasn't rich enough. The answer was to switch out the oil for butter, which produced a deeper, fuller flavor.

Most recipes call for folding the sliced strawberries into whipped cream. Tasters deemed this filling one-dimensional and felt that the flavors were muddied. We decided to treat the berries as a separate layer and began focusing on enhancing their flavor. Adding sugar to the naked berries was a must. Hoping strawberry jam might act as both a sweetener and flavor enhancer, we found instead that it added a dull, cooked-berry quality.

We then drew inspiration from the test kitchen's strawberry shortcake recipe, macerating the berries in sugar for an hour, mashing a portion, and folding this mash into the remaining berries. While this helped bind the berries, it also decreased their volume, requiring us to use four pints instead of the two we'd started with. The problem was that the macerated sliced berries became soft and were not visually appealing once added to the cake layers. The solution? Dividing the berries in half: One portion was sliced and used around the edges of the filling layers for visual appeal, while the other half was macerated, pulsed in a food processor, and spread over the center.

But we found that these processed berries exuded too much juice, which made the cake soggy. We tried straining off the excess liquid, but this was vital berry flavor going down the drain. Our next step was to boil down the strained juices to evaporate the excess water, then add the syrupy remains back to the berries. This provided the perfect amount of soak for the cake, with no berry flavor lost. The final adjustment to flavor was some sweet liqueur (kirsch was the favorite), cooked along with the strained juices to eliminate any boozy overtones.

With the strawberry and cake components securely in place, all we needed to fix was the insubstantial whipped cream layer. It needed more flavor and texture to stand up to the strawberries. Pastry cream was a popular suggestion, but we didn't want to add unnecessary cooking steps. Instead,

we experimented with flavoring agents. Sour cream, yogurt, and cream cheese all offered a forward tang, but only cream cheese provided a boost in texture. When whipped with the heavy cream, cream cheese produced a stiff yet silky smooth blend that helped anchor the cake layers. Even when sliced, the cake remained cohesive.

Not only did this layered cake meet all our expectations—sturdy yet moist chiffon cake, vibrant berries, and a robust, tangy cream—it even surpassed the classic yet humble strawberry shortcake.

WHAT WE LEARNED: Chiffon cake, typically made from oil and eggs, makes a tender, yet sturdy cake, which will hold up to moisture from the strawberries and cream. But for a fuller flavor, replace the oil with butter. For a fruit filling with strong strawberry flavor, sprinkle the cut berries with sugar, which sweetens them and helps draw out their juices. Drain the berries and lightly crush them in a food processor. Simmer the reserved juice to a syrup with kirsch (cherry brandy) and add it back to the crushed berries for a thickened full-flavored fruit filling. Spread the mixture in the center of the cake and for visual appeal, arrange halved berries around the cake's edges. To thicken the whipped cream filling, use cream cheese. It gives the filling a pleasant tang and stiffens it just enough so that it will stay put, even when the cake is sliced.

STRAWBERRY CREAM CAKE

Serves 8 to 10

If using a cake pan, you will need one with straight sides that are at least 2 inches high; otherwise, use a springform pan. The cake portion can be made ahead of time, wrapped in a double layer of plastic wrap, and frozen; thaw the frozen cake, unwrapped, at room temperature for about two hours before proceeding with the recipe.

cake

- 1¼ cups (5 ounces) cake flour
- 1½ teaspoons baking powder
- ¼ teaspoon salt
- 1 cup (7 ounces) sugar
- 5 large eggs (2 whole and 3 separated), at room temperature
- 6 tablespoons unsalted butter, melted and cooled slightly
- 2 tablespoons water
- 2 teaspoons vanilla extract

strawberry filling

- 2 pounds fresh strawberries (medium or large, about 2 quarts), washed, dried, and stemmed
- 4–6 tablespoons sugar
- 2 tablespoons kirsch
- Pinch salt

whipped cream

- 8 ounces cream cheese, at room temperature
- ½ cup (3½ ounces) sugar
- 1 teaspoon vanilla extract
- ⅛ teaspoon salt
- 2 cups heavy cream

1. FOR THE CAKE: Adjust an oven rack to the lower-middle position and heat the oven to 325 degrees. Grease and flour a round 9 by 2-inch cake pan or 9-inch springform pan and line it with parchment paper. Whisk the flour, baking powder, salt, and all but 3 tablespoons sugar in a mixing bowl. Whisk in 2 whole eggs and 3 yolks (reserving the whites), butter, water, and vanilla; whisk until smooth.

2. In the clean bowl of a standing mixer fitted with the whisk attachment, beat the remaining 3 egg whites at medium-low speed until frothy, 1 to 2 minutes. With the machine running, gradually add the remaining 3 tablespoons sugar, increase the speed to medium-high, and beat until soft peaks form, 60 to 90 seconds. Stir one-third of the whites into the batter to lighten; add the remaining whites and gently fold into the batter until no white streaks remain. Pour the batter into the prepared pan and bake until a toothpick or wooden skewer inserted into the center of the cake comes out clean, 30 to 40 minutes. Cool in the pan 10 minutes, then invert the cake onto a greased wire rack; peel off and discard the parchment. Invert the cake again; cool completely, about 2 hours.

3. FOR THE STRAWBERRY FILLING: Halve 24 of the best-looking berries and reserve. Quarter the remaining berries; toss with 4 to 6 tablespoons sugar (depending on the sweetness of the berries) in a medium bowl and let sit 1 hour, stirring occasionally. Strain the juices from the berries and reserve (you should have about ½ cup). In a food processor, give the macerated berries five 1-second pulses (you should have about 1½ cups). In a small saucepan over medium-high heat, simmer the reserved juices and the kirsch until syrupy and reduced to about 3 tablespoons, 3 to 5 minutes. Pour the reduced syrup over the processed, macerated berries, add a pinch of salt, and toss to combine. Set aside until the cake is cooled.

4. FOR THE WHIPPED CREAM: When the cake has cooled, place the cream cheese, sugar, vanilla, and salt in the clean bowl of a standing mixer fitted with the whisk attachment. Whisk at medium-high speed until light and fluffy, 1 to 2 minutes, scraping down the bowl with a rubber spatula as needed. Reduce the speed to low and add the heavy

cream in a slow, steady stream; when almost fully combined, increase the speed to medium-high and beat until the mixture holds stiff peaks, 2 to 2½ minutes more, scraping down the bowl as needed (you should have about 4½ cups).

5. TO ASSEMBLE THE CAKE: Using a large serrated knife, slice the cake into three even layers. Place the bottom layer on a cardboard round or cake plate and arrange a ring of 20 strawberry halves, cut sides down and stem ends facing out, around the perimeter of the cake layer. Pour one-half of the pureed berry mixture (about ¾ cup) in the center, then spread to cover any exposed cake. Gently spread about one-third of the whipped cream (about 1½ cups) over the berry layer, leaving a ½-inch border from edge. Place the middle cake layer on top and press down gently (the whipped cream layer should become flush with the cake edge). Repeat with 20 additional strawberry halves, the remaining berry mixture, and half of the remaining whipped cream; gently press the last cake layer on top. Spread the remaining whipped cream over the top; decorate with the remaining cut strawberries. Serve, or chill for up to 4 hours.

TESTING NOTES:
Perils of Strawberry Cream Cake

1. Soggy Cake   3. Wimpy Whipped Cream
   2. Buried Berry Flavor

To rescue strawberry cream cake from the perils that often befall it, we'd need to develop a sturdy, yet tender cake that won't become soggy; intensify the berry flavor; and fortify the whipped cream so that it will sandwich neatly between the cake layers.

Building a Strawberry Cream Cake

1. With a serrated knife, use a sawing motion to cut the cake into 3 layers, rotating the cake as you go.

2. Place sliced berries evenly around the edges (they will be visible once layers are assembled).

3. Cover the center of the cake completely with half of the pureed strawberries.

4. Spread one-third of the whipped cream over the berries, leaving a ½-inch border. Repeat the layering.

5. Press the last layer into place, spread with the remaining cream, and decorate with berries.

SCIENCE DESK:
Heavy Cream versus Whipping Cream

ACCORDING TO THE U.S. GOVERNMENT'S CODE OF Federal Regulations, heavy cream must consist of at least 36 percent milk fat, whipping cream (sometimes also called light whipping cream) at least 30 percent but no more than 36 percent. This may not sound like much of a difference, but after whipping up more than a few bowls of cream and talking to some experts in the dairy industry, we learned that it can be.

We set out to purchase a pint of whipping cream and a pint of heavy cream, whip them up, and assess their performance in five categories: time to whip to stiff peaks, volume, staying power (how long the whipped cream would hold its shape), texture, and flavor. What we brought back to the test kitchen, however, were three pints of cream. We found just one kind of whipping cream in the dairy case but two kinds of heavy cream.

One type of heavy cream listed additives on its label and described their functions as follows: to help "put air into the cream as it is whipped" (mono- and diglycerides) and to help "hold the whipped cream peaks" (carrageenan). The whipping cream listed these additives, too, as well as another intended to help "create stiff peaks" (polysorbate 80). Both this heavy cream and the whipping cream were also ultrapasteurized, a process that extends shelf life (up to 60 days, unopened) while also destroying some of the proteins in the cream that promote whipping.

The other type of heavy cream that we found had no additives and listed just one ingredient—cream—and it was pasteurized, a process that is like ultrapasteurization in that it kills pathogenic microbes but does less damage to the proteins that promote whipping. (In pasteurization, which extends shelf life to only about 20 days, cream is generally heated to 145 degrees or 161 degrees, depending on the particular process used. In ultrapasteurization, cream is heated to 280 degrees or higher.) The pasteurized heavy

With our three creams in the kitchen, we took out our handheld mixer and got to work. The first category up was whipping time, and here the whipping cream was the winner by a long shot, taking just under three minutes to reach stiff peaks. The heavy creams reached stiff peaks after about five minutes. In terms of volume, all three creams doubled from 1 cup liquid to about 2 cups whipped. As for staying power, the lower-fat whipping cream lost its peaks and became watery after just a few hours in the refrigerator. The heavy creams were fine for up to a day.

Tasters found the freshly whipped whipping cream to be lighter and more airy than either of the heavy creams. It was also more fleeting, melting in your mouth almost as soon as you were able to taste it (no doubt because of the lower fat content). Of the two heavy creams, the higher fat, pasteurized cream was judged the thickest as well as the best-tasting. It was sweeter and more buttery than either the ultrapasteurized heavy cream or the whipping cream. Evidently, the additives, as well as the process of ultrapasteurization, compromise the sweet, delicate flavor of cream.

Why do manufacturers use the additives? The emulsifiers and stabilizing agents in the whipping cream and the ultrapasteurized heavy cream help compensate for the relative lack of fat. It's cheaper for a manufacturer to use a lower-fat cream with additives than a higher-fat cream without additives.

Wanting to test the creams' performance in cooking, we decided to use each one in a simple reduction sauce with chicken broth. All three creams thickened upon reduction without breaking, but the sauce with the pasteurized, highest fat cream was by far the most appealing—velvety smooth and pleasant tasting.

All told, then, pasteurized heavy cream, with a fat content of 40 percent (or 6 grams per tablespoon), is the best all-purpose cream to have on hand if you can find it. If not, the next best choice is ultrapasteurized heavy cream. We don't recommend whipping cream.

cream also contained more fat than the ultrapasteurized heavy cream, 6 grams per tablespoon versus 5 grams per tablespoon, respectively, which translates to a fat content of 40 percent versus about 36 percent.

EQUIPMENT CORNER: Standing Mixers

CHOOSING A STANDING MIXER USED TO BE A PIECE OF cake—you strolled down the KitchenAid aisle and selected a size. There just wasn't much in terms of competition. Recently, though, numerous high-end models have whirred onto the scene to give KitchenAid a run for its money. Most have raised the stakes with huge bowl sizes and seriously ramped-up wattage. While KitchenAid's largest mixer is 6 quarts (most are 5), now 7 quarts and larger aren't uncommon. KitchenAid's basic model runs on a 250-watt motor; the new models tout ratings of 700, 800, even 1,000 watts! Naturally, prices have soared. Hobart, a maker of industrial-grade mixers, has rolled out a new 5-quart consumer model priced at a cool $1,500 and change.

How much mixer does a home cook need? To test the field thoroughly, we bought 18 different mixers of every shape, size, and price, from a budget $100 model up to the $1,500 Hobart. Our lineup included Bosch (two models), DeLonghi (two), Electrolux, Farberware, Hamilton Beach (two), Hobart, Jenn-Air, KitchenAid (four), Sunbeam (two), and Viking (two).

Standing mixers should be able to beat egg whites, whip cream, incorporate butter and sugar ("creaming"), mix stiff cookie dough, and knead basic bread dough. We started with a test that would quickly thin the ranks: 15 minutes of medium-duty kneading on a rustic bread dough. (If all you need a mixer to do is beat egg whites and stir cake mix, you're better off spending $70 on a good handheld mixer instead.) Any mixer that couldn't finish the job was out of the running. Hacking, screeching, shuddering, even pausing—all fine, so long as the resulting dough was acceptable and the mixer survived.

All in all, these mixers were truly a noisy, convulsive lot. But only six failed outright, either stalling out irreversibly or leaving portions of dough unincorporated: Bosch Solitaire ($899.99; the cheaper Universal model survived), Farberware ($99.99), Hamilton Beach 5-Quart ($349.95; the

7-quart survived), Jenn-Air ($349.00), and both Sunbeams ($98.95, $129.99). Just 12 mixers, then, would advance to the remaining rounds.

For the next several weeks, the triumphant dozen tried their luck in a variety of mixer challenges: kneading pizza dough, mixing cookie dough, whipping cream, and beating egg whites. In the end, we developed clear mixer-design criteria.

First, there's mixing motion. The two most common are stationary beaters (with rotating bowl) and "planetary action," when a single beater rotates on its axis while spinning around a stationary bowl (similar to the way a planet moves around the sun). Planetary action proved far superior—the agitator simply makes it to more areas of the bowl. Three stationary models (Farberware, both Sunbeams) choked on dough in the elimination round: Either the bowl stopped moving or the beaters got too clogged to rotate. Another stationary-style mixer, albeit a more unusual design, the Electrolux DLX-2000 ($469.95) has a rotating bowl and all its inherent problems (ingredients get clogged on the agitator while the bowl spins ineffectually). One mixer opted for another approach entirely. Shaped like a food processor, the Bosch Universal ($369.99) has an agitator that rotates on a spindle. The Bosch wasn't bad at kneading, but when creaming and whipping, its tendency to fling ingredients to the sides rather than integrate them in the middle proved detrimental to the final consistency.

Second, forget cavernous bowls. Unless you regularly make multiple loaves of bread, 5 to 6 quarts is plenty. To accommodate the extra volume, DeLonghi, Hamilton Beach, and Viking built the bowls of their 7-quart models up, not out: The resulting urns are nearly impossible to scrape down without dirtying a shirt sleeve, and small amounts (think two egg whites) get lost in the depths.

We also prefer slightly squat bowls, which compensate for the lost height with a more spacious bottom surface and by flaring out to a wider mouth. By distributing ingredients lower and wider, these models had less opportunity to fling the contents up the sides beyond the beater's effective range of motion. The net result? Less need to scrape. The other

advantage of shallower distribution—coupled with a wider paddle (more leverage)—is less work by the motor.

Most mixers come with three attachments: a dough hook (for kneading), a paddle-shaped flat beater (creaming dry and wet ingredients), and a wire whisk (whipping). The minor differences from model to model aren't worth reporting, with a few exceptions. First, most flat paddles are, in fact, flat. The exceptions were the DeLonghi and Viking paddles (5-quart models only), which feature slightly bent-out edges, a three-dimensional touch that proved remarkably effective for creaming. If only the Viking could keep its slick-shaped beaters locked securely in the socket: With both Viking models we tested, the dough-caked attachments constantly plunged into the bowl during scraping sessions, thanks to a poorly designed locking mechanism and the disproportionate weight of the attachments themselves.

Finally, the DeLonghi, Hamilton Beach, and Viking mixers earned extra credit for an ingenious method of adjusting beater clearance. Each attachment can be lengthened or shortened by turning a washer near the top. With the KitchenAids, only the mixer arm can be adjusted, making it a pain for cooks who prefer closer bowl contact with one attachment than with the others.

If we hadn't included the Hobart in the lineup, we might never have discovered the sneaky truth behind wattage ratings.

Most mixers list their power in watts; Hobart is the only one to use horsepower. We were puzzled when we learned that ⅙ HP equals a mere 124 watts. How could this quiet, powerful workhorse have the lowest wattage rating in such a hacking, shuddering group (from 250 watts to 1,000 watts)? Turns out Hobart is the only mixer to list output power rather than input power. What's the difference? Output wattage is the amount of power the motor actually produces—which flows out of the motor, moves through the mixer arm, and, ultimately, smacks the ingredients around. Every other mixer lists input wattage, which is simply the power that flows from the electrical outlet into the mixer's motor.

What does input wattage tell you about the power of a mixer? Absolutely nothing—it's purely a marketing gimmick. To wit, the six models that failed the bread dough test (our initial round) had power ratings ranging from low to high, mostly high (275, 350, 400, 450, 700, 700). In addition, every other test showed absolutely no correlation between mixer performance and wattage.

Beyond output power, it was clear that design was crucial to successful mixing. For a better measure of a mixer's efficiency, then, we devised a final test. Mixing 4 cups of pizza dough in each bowl, we added 10 drops of yellow food coloring to one side of the dough and 10 drops of blue to the other. How long would each mixer take to knead the dough completely to a uniform green color—with no individual specks of yellow or blue?

Incorporation times varied significantly. The slowest mixer, the Electrolux, had gone from speckled blue and yellow to a uniform green in just over 11 minutes. The quickest? The KitchenAid Professional 600 with a speedy 3:45.

So is KitchenAid still the mixer to beat? Yes. Three mixers survived the gauntlet of tests without showing fatal flaws: the KitchenAid Professional 600 ($369.99), the 5-quart DeLonghi ($349.95), and the Hobart ($1,503.08). Given that $1,500 is far beyond most test cooks' budgets, the kitchen was split down the middle between the KitchenAid and the DeLonghi, but our test results give a slight edge to the KitchenAid.

Rating Standing Mixers

WE TESTED 18 STANDING MIXERS IN A VARIETY OF CORE TASKS; SIX MODELS FAILED THE KNEADING TEST AND WERE eliminated from consideration. Mixers are listed in order of preference, based on overall scores. See www.americastestkitchen.com for up-to-date prices and mail-order sources for top-rated products.

RECOMMENDED

KitchenAid Professional 600

6-quart capacity; "spiral" dough hook, flat beater, wire whip, pouring shield, bowl lift

$369.99

This KitchenAid model came out on top—though just barely edging out the DeLonghi.

RECOMMENDED

DeLonghi DSM5

5-quart capacity; nonstick dough hook, "crimped" nonstick flat beater, stainless steel whisk, splash guard, tilt head

$349.95

This model's flared bowl and well-sized attachments kept ingredients "low in the bowl" and minimized scraping.

RECOMMENDED

Hobart N50

5-quart capacity; dough hook, flat beater, wire whip, bowl lift

$1,503.08

This 55-pound beast calmly processed rustic dough, oatmeal cookies, and anything else we threw its way, but narrow bowl mouth made it awkward to add ingredients.

RECOMMENDED WITH RESERVATIONS

Viking VSM500

5-quart capacity; dough hook, "crimped" flat beater, wire whip, transport wheels

$440.00

The Viking's shaft-arm lock required ridiculous force to slam shut and the attachments often plummeted from the poorly designed socket during scraping breaks.

RECOMMENDED WITH RESERVATIONS

DeLonghi DSM7

7-quart capacity; nonstick dough hook, nonstick flat beater, stainless steel whisk, splash guard, tilt head

$449.95

The DSM7's tall, cavernous bowl made it difficult to whip small amounts and to scrape down its sides.

RECOMMENDED WITH RESERVATIONS

KitchenAid Artisan

5-quart capacity; dough hook, flat beater, wire whip, splash guard, tilt head

$249.99

Kneading caused audible strain on the motor. Narrow bowl mouth hindered tidy addition of dry ingredients.

RECOMMENDED WITH RESERVATIONS

KitchenAid Accolade 400

5-quart capacity; dough hook, flat beater, wire whip, splash guard, tilt head, delayed start

$299.99

More wattage (and more money) than the Artisan, but consistently performed at a lower level.

RECOMMENDED WITH RESERVATIONS

Viking VSM700

7-quart capacity; dough hook, flat beater, stainless steel whip, tilt head, transport wheels

$499.95

Same problems as the VSM500 (plummeting attachments, "slam lock" shaft design).

RECOMMENDED WITH RESERVATIONS

Hamilton Beach CPM700

7-quart capacity; dough hook, flat beater, wire whisk

$469.00

The CPM700's 5-quart sibling stalled permanently during the elimination round, and this one stalled twice before finishing the task.

RECOMMENDED WITH RESERVATIONS

Bosch Universal Kitchen Machine

6-quart capacity; dough blade, egg whip, plastic lid, 6-cup blender

$369.99

Shaped like a food processor with mixer attachments, the Bosch did a commendable job when kneading dough, but the decentralized mixing space kept less cohesive contents from meeting in the middle.

NOT RECOMMENDED

KitchenAid Classic Series

4½-quart capacity; dough hook, flat beater, wire whip, tilt head

$249.95

KitchenAid's smallest model seemed more like a toy and wasn't cut out for kneading dough.

NOT RECOMMENDED

Electrolux DLX-2000

8-quart capacity; plastic whisking bowl, dough hook, beater, roller/scraper

$469.95

Wide bowl allowed easy access and capacity for nine bread loaves, but cookies, cakes, and even single loaves got lost in the abyss.

These dark chocolate cupcakes are simply
irresistible. And the thick, fluffy frosting is
an easy-to-prepare buttercream, made with
confectioners' sugar, butter, and heavy cream.

DARK CHOCOLATE
desserts

CHAPTER 22

No matter the dessert—cookie, pudding, cake, or pie—there's nothing like the flavor of chocolate to make it truly irresistible. In this chapter, we set out to develop ultimate versions of two favorite chocolate desserts: chocolate mousse and chocolate cupcakes.

Rich, frosting-like mousse is utterly delicious—for about two spoonfuls. Yet light and silky versions often lack decent chocolate flavor. Once you start adding more chocolate, texture suffers and becomes heavy. We wanted the best of both worlds—a light and silky texture with big chocolate flavor.

Chocolate cupcakes are another treat that suffers from faint chocolate flavor. Ever try a mix? Sure they're easy, but the flavor often falls short. And most homemade chocolate cupcakes aren't much better. Some may have good chocolate flavor, but the crumb turns dense and confection-like. We aimed to develop a moist, feathery cupcake infused with chocolate flavor. And for such a homey treat, we didn't want to spend all day, so these cupcakes would need to be almost as easy as using a boxed mix.

When you're looking to satisfy a serious chocolate craving, these recipes deliver.

CHOCOLATE MOUSSE

WHAT WE WANTED: Light and silky mousse with deep chocolate flavor.

Chocolate mousse usually falls into one of two categories: rich, creamy, and dense, like a bittersweet chocolate truffle, or light and airy, but with all the flavor impact of chocolate milk. Neither is bad (we'd still eat them), but in our mind chocolate mousse is a dessert to be savored by the bowlful rather than reluctantly pushed away after a lick or two. Substantial chocolate flavor and a light, meltingly smooth texture should not be mutually exclusive.

Whisking our way through the gamut of chocolate mousse recipes, we were struck by the wide variations possible with the same basic ingredients: chocolate, eggs, sugar, and fat (butter, cream). Proportions and handling, apparently, were all that separated thick ganache from fluffy pudding.

Our perfect chocolate mousse was somewhere in between those two extremes, so our plan was to start with an average working recipe and adjust from there: Melt chocolate in a double boiler; whisk in egg yolks, butter, and heavy cream (for richness and smoothness); beat egg whites with sugar; then fold the soft peaks into the mixture (for silkiness). The resulting mousse was a fine start, but it was too dense, and the modest 4 ounces of chocolate proved little more than a tease.

Before embarking on our chocolate rampage, we decided to take a crack at lightening the texture. Where to begin? Of the recipe's six ingredients, butter, chocolate, cream, and egg yolks were all likely culprits, although it was clear we needed more chocolate, not less. Given that some tasters had complained about a residual "waxy slickness" in the first few batches, our choice seemed obvious. Sure enough, when the butter was incrementally decreased—and, ultimately, eliminated—the texture lightened considerably and the waxiness was gone.

To correct the billowy marshmallow-like quality, we reduced the egg whites from four to two, which took the texture from airy to silky. But four yolks now seemed like too many. By scaling down to two, we achieved a lighter, still-creamy mousse with good structure. Whipping the cream to soft peaks before adding it to the chocolate made up for some of the lost volume without reintroducing the "marshmallow effect."

At last, it was time for the chocolate. For days, we subjected test kitchen staffers to a whirlwind of mousses made with various styles and brands. In the end, tasters found semisweet chocolate too sweet and one-dimensional (closer to milk chocolate than dark). Bittersweet chocolate, with its higher percentage of cocoa solids, provided the more complex flavor profile we were going for. As cocoa-solid percentage varies by brand, we standardized our recipe by using our winning supermarket dark chocolate, Ghirardelli, with 60 percent cocoa solids. (Some "premium" chocolates boast even higher percentages, and we wondered if substitution would be straightforward. It wasn't, so we developed a variation using chocolate with a higher percentage of cocoa solids—see Premium Dark Chocolate Mousse on page 273.)

Armed with a shopping cart's worth of bittersweet chocolate, we set about slowly increasing the amount, in search of our mousse's breaking point. First, we tried bumping up the paltry 4 ounces we'd started with to 6 ounces. Mmm, nice—but nice wasn't enough. Seven ounces. Eight ounces. Nine ounces. At 9 ounces, we regrouped. The texture was suffering, and the mousse had become too sweet. We reduced the sugar (beaten with the egg whites) from 2 tablespoons down to 1. Better, but the dramatic increase in chocolate was still wreaking havoc on the texture.

We retreated to 8 ounces but immediately missed the more powerful flavor. What about a second form of chocolate? Adding an ounce of unsweetened chocolate made the mousse "starchy" and heavy. Two tablespoons of Dutch-processed cocoa powder, on the other hand, gave the mousse a fuller, more vibrant chocolate flavor—but it had a gritty texture.

Unwilling to sacrifice this intense, rounded flavor profile, we were determined to develop the infrastructure necessary to support so much chocolate. The texture problem was creeping up early in the process: The melted chocolate turned thick and granular as soon as we whisked in the yolks, and seizing was not uncommon. No matter how slowly, quickly, or vigorously we whisked the mixture, it remained grainy. This compromised texture subsequently affected the incorporation of the egg whites as well, leaving the mousse riddled with white particles.

Something was giving the mousse the texture of a facial scrub—but what? We knew that liquid can cause melted chocolate to seize, but we were always careful not to let any steam from the double boiler contaminate the chocolate. Could it be the moisture-laden egg yolks? Well, that didn't make sense, given that we had reduced the number of yolks from four to two, and we'd had no problems with graininess back when we were using less chocolate. Besides, some recipes call for adding several tablespoons of coffee and other liquids at this stage, with no incidence of seizing.

After researching the subject further, we discovered that we had been only half right: Liquids can cause melted chocolate to seize, but more important is the liquid to solid ratio. With small amounts of liquid, the solids absorb just enough moisture to form a gritty paste. But with more liquid (at least 1 tablespoon for every 2 ounces of chocolate), the dry cocoa solids become fluid. Suddenly, it all made sense. Early on, our recipe had just enough moisture from the 4 egg yolks and the butter to prevent 4 ounces of chocolate from becoming grainy. Once the butter was omitted, the yolks decreased, and the amount of chocolate increased, however, the story changed: The ratio of liquid to solid became too heavy on the solids.

To augment the liquid side of things, we were loath to add more cream or any other source of fat. The solution was crystal clear (literally): water. We made several more batches, increasing the water (2, 4, 6, and 8 tablespoons) each time. The more water, the looser, glossier, and more manageable the mousse became. At 8 tablespoons, we were starting to undo the deep flavor we had achieved; at 6 tablespoons, the texture was perfect: light, ethereal, and chock-full of chocolate.

All our mousse needed now was some final finessing of flavors. In other chocolate recipes, we have found that a small amount of instant espresso powder intensifies the chocolate experience. The trick worked here as well: One teaspoon added to the chocolate-cocoa-water mixture provided just the right boost. A mere ⅛ teaspoon of salt rounded out the mild sweetness.

Other common extras include vanilla and some sort of alcohol. Tasters flatly rejected vanilla for lending unwelcome floral notes to the mousse. Brandy was favored over rum and bourbon, and a meager tablespoon of the stuff (replacing an equal amount of water) added complexity without booziness. Finally, after making more than 100 batches, we had exactly the chocolate mousse we were looking for. Rich but not dense, chocolaty but not cloying, light and silky but not insubstantial, this perfectly balanced chocolate mousse could be devoured by the bowlful—or two.

WHAT WE LEARNED: Eliminate the butter that most recipes rely on—we found that omitting it made for a mousse with a lighter texture. Two eggs, rather than the 3 or 4 that most recipes call for, give the mousse richness and volume without a sticky marshmallow effect. The addition of water (to replace the lost moisture from using less eggs) prevents the mousse from seizing and turning grainy. For a deep chocolate flavor, a combination of bittersweet chocolate and cocoa powder works best. The addition of instant espresso powder underscores the chocolate flavor, and brandy provides complexity.

DARK CHOCOLATE MOUSSE

Makes 3½ cups (6 to 8 servings)

When developing this recipe, we used our winning supermarket brand of dark chocolate, Ghirardelli bittersweet, which contains about 60 percent cacao. If you want to use a chocolate with a higher percentage of cacao, see our variation, Premium Dark Chocolate Mousse, on page 273. If you choose to make the mousse a day in advance, leave it out at room temperature for 10 minutes before serving. Serve with very lightly sweetened whipped cream and chocolate shavings. A handheld mixer can do the job of a standing mixer in this recipe, though mixing times may vary slightly.

- 8 ounces bittersweet chocolate, chopped fine
- 2 tablespoons cocoa powder, preferably Dutch-processed
- 1 teaspoon instant espresso powder
- 5 tablespoons water
- 1 tablespoon brandy
- 2 large eggs, separated
- 1 tablespoon sugar
- ⅛ teaspoon salt
- 1 cup plus 2 tablespoons chilled heavy cream

1. Melt the chocolate, cocoa powder, espresso powder, water, and brandy in a medium heatproof bowl set over a saucepan filled with 1 inch of barely simmering water, stirring frequently until smooth. Remove from the heat.

2. Whisk the egg yolks, 1½ teaspoons of the sugar, and salt in a medium bowl until the mixture lightens in color and thickens slightly, about 30 seconds. Pour the melted chocolate into the egg mixture and whisk until combined. Let cool until just warmer than room temperature, 3 to 5 minutes.

3. In the clean bowl of a standing mixer fitted with a whisk attachment, beat the egg whites at medium-low speed until frothy, 1 to 2 minutes. Add the remaining 1½ teaspoons sugar, increase the mixer speed to medium-high, and beat until soft peaks form when the whisk is lifted, about 1 minute. Detach the whisk and bowl from the mixer and whisk the last few strokes by hand, making sure to scrape any unbeaten whites from the bottom of the bowl. Using the whisk, stir about one-quarter of the beaten egg whites into the chocolate mixture to lighten it; gently fold in the remaining egg whites with a rubber spatula until a few white streaks remain.

GETTING IT RIGHT: Mousse with Light and Silky Texture

Dense

Butter, unwhipped cream, and too much chocolate are often the culprits in heavy, ganache-like mousse.

Fluffy

Too many whipped egg whites produce an unappealing "marshmallow effect."

Perfect

Going easy on the egg whites, omitting the butter, and adding a small amount of water yield just the right texture.

4. In the now–empty bowl, whip the heavy cream at medium speed until it begins to thicken, about 30 seconds. Increase the speed to high and whip until soft peaks form when the whisk is lifted, about 15 seconds more. Using a rubber spatula, fold the whipped cream into the mousse until no white streaks remain. Spoon the mousse into 6 to 8 individual serving dishes or goblets. Cover with plastic wrap and refrigerate until set and firm, at least 2 hours. (The mousse may be covered and refrigerated for up to 24 hours.)

VARIATIONS

CHOCOLATE-ORANGE MOUSSE

For best flavor, the orange zest needs to steep in the heavy cream overnight, so plan accordingly. Garnish each serving of mousse with a thin strip of orange zest, if desired.

Follow the recipe for Dark Chocolate Mousse with the following changes: start by bringing the heavy cream to a simmer in a medium saucepan. Remove from the heat and transfer to a liquid measuring cup; add 3 strips of orange zest (each about 2 inches long and ½ inch wide). Cool until just warm, cover, and refrigerate overnight. Remove and discard the zest; add more heavy cream, if necessary, to replace any evaporation loss. Continue with step 1, reducing the water to 4 tablespoons and omitting the brandy. Once the chocolate is melted, stir in 2 tablespoons Grand Marnier and proceed as directed in step 2.

CHOCOLATE-RASPBERRY MOUSSE

Chambord is a raspberry-flavored liqueur and is our preferred brand in this recipe. Serve the mousse with fresh raspberries, if desired.

Follow the recipe for Dark Chocolate Mousse with the following changes: reduce the water to 4 tablespoons, omit the brandy, and once the chocolate is melted at the end of step 1, stir in 2 tablespoons of Chambord.

PREMIUM DARK CHOCOLATE MOUSSE

This recipe is designed to work with a boutique chocolate that contains a higher percentage of cacao than the Ghirardelli chocolate recommended in our Dark Chocolate Mousse.

Follow the recipe for Dark Chocolate Mousse with the following changes: replace an equal amount of bittersweet chocolate (containing about 60 percent cacao) with a bittersweet chocolate containing 62 to 70 percent cacao. Increase the water to 7 tablespoons, add one more egg (for a total of 3 eggs), and increase the sugar to 3 tablespoons (adding the extra 2 tablespoons of sugar to the chocolate mixture in step 1).

GETTING IT RIGHT:
Deep Chocolate Flavor

The toughest challenge in making chocolate mousse is ramping up the chocolate without destroying the texture. Most recipes call it quits at just 4 or 5 ounces. We accommodated 8 ounces of bittersweet chocolate plus 2 tablespoons of cocoa—and the texture is silkier than ever.

Subtle Hint

Powerful Hit

CHOCOLATE CUPCAKES

WHAT WE WANTED: A moist, buttery cupcake with a rich, deep chocolate flavor. And we wanted these cupcakes to be almost as easy to prepare as those made from a boxed mix.

No knives, no forks, no sharing: three good reasons why adults and kids alike love cupcakes. But whereas kids go gaga for confetti sprinkles and a mountain of sugary icing, adults seek quality: rich, buttery flavor; light, moist, cakey texture; and just a little sugar. This is precisely why, to the adult palate, cake mixes cannot deliver. It is also why most homemade cupcakes don't deliver. Factor chocolate into the equation and the situation is even more glum. Mixes and most recipes really choke when it comes to offering rich chocolate flavor.

Our foray into chocolate cupcakes began with a search not only for chocolate cupcake recipes but also for chocolate cake recipes; after all, cupcakes are just pint-sized cakes. What followed was a cupcake-baking marathon. We made all manner of chocolate cupcakes (well over 150): chocolate mayonnaise cupcakes, devil's food cupcakes, cocoa-only cupcakes, cupcakes with vegetable oil, cupcakes with buttermilk, and so on.

Some were OK. None were great. Solid chocolate flavor and moist, tender texture seemed not to coincide; where there was one, the other was not. Well-textured recipes seemed to use a light hand with chocolate, while those with flavor seemed to be weighed down by the chocolate.

It made sense to first determine the best mixing method, as this would probably influence the amounts of ingredients to be determined in later tests. We had three options. We could use the typical cake-making method of creaming the butter and sugar in a standing mixer until light and fluffy, adding the eggs, and then finally the wet and dry ingredients. Or we could use an easy dump-and-stir method in which the ingredients are unceremoniously combined in a mixer. The last option was the melted-butter method, a simple mixer-free method that we often use in making muffins, quick breads, and brownies.

Dump-and-stir was a failure. Unevenly textured, crumbly, under-mixed cupcakes were the result. Creaming wasn't ideal, either. The batter, fluffy with air, was so voluminous that the muffin cups were nearly filled to overflowing. And when baked, the cupcakes' caps spread too far and wide.

Cupcakes made by the melted-butter method had a light, cakey texture with a tender, fine crumb. That they were incredibly easy and quick to make was a bonus—no mixer to haul out, no butter to slowly soften. This method entailed whisking the eggs and sugar, adding the melted butter and chocolate, and then stirring in the dry ingredients in two additions, with buttermilk (deemed the best liquid in early tests) added in between. It couldn't be much easier.

Next: chocolate. Cocoa powder, unsweetened chocolate, bittersweet or semisweet chocolate, and combinations thereof were the candidates. Sorting it all out required more than a half-dozen batches. What we found was that cocoa and unsweetened chocolate alone could each provide blunt flavor (because of their high percentages of cocoa solids), but both came up short in the nuance department. Bittersweet and semisweet chocolate could supply nuance and complexity but not assertive chocolate flavor. Obviously, it was going to take two forms of chocolate to achieve the balanced flavor that we sought. Ultimately, ½ cup of cocoa powder (Dutch-processed was preferred over natural for its fuller, deeper flavor) and 2 ounces of bittersweet chocolate were the winning combination. The cupcakes were now deep, dark, and terrifically chocolaty. As a quick side note, we found that instead of treating the cocoa as a dry ingredient and combining it with the flour, it was better to mix it with the butter and chocolate as they melted, a technique that made the chocolate flavor stronger and richer.

We tried sour cream and whole milk in place of the buttermilk in our working recipe. It was nearly unanimous: Tasters found the cupcakes made with sour cream to be richer and moister (but not at all greasy).

Then came the tricky part: the leavening. Baking soda, which reacts with the acidic sour cream, was the obvious choice, but we could add only so much before it was too much. A small amount of baking soda fully neutralizes the sour cream; any excess is ineffective at leavening and can be detected as an "off-flavor" that some describe as soapy. One-half teaspoon was the baking soda ceiling, but because that amount didn't provide adequate lift, we enlisted the aid of baking powder. Three-quarters of a teaspoon of powder in addition to the baking soda encouraged the cupcakes to dome ever so slightly, the result we were looking for.

Next up was the icing. In keeping with the cupcake spirit, we all agreed that we wanted a thick, sturdy icing like the kind that comes out of the grocery-store bakery, but we also agreed that an icing that tasted of real butter, not shortening, would be better. The solution was a confectioners' sugar buttercream—basically, butter and confectioners' sugar whipped together until light and fluffy. Sometimes a little egg yolk or milk is added for a silkier texture, but we found that a bit of heavy cream was even better.

What's more is that a simple buttercream is a canvas for a vast array of variations: Vanilla and chocolate were compulsory offerings, but we also developed coffee and peppermint buttercreams, and each had ardent fans. Underneath it all, however, was a heavenly, super-chocolaty chocolate cupcake that was not much more difficult to assemble and bake than a boxed cake mix.

WHAT WE LEARNED: For tender cupcakes, use the easy melted-butter method: Whisk together the eggs and sugar, then add the melted butter and chocolate. A combination of cocoa powder and bittersweet chocolate delivers deep chocolate flavor. The addition of sour cream makes a rich, moist cupcake that's not greasy. A combination of baking powder and baking soda provides just the right amount of lift. And an easy-to-prepare confectioners' sugar buttercream, enriched with heavy cream, makes a thick, fluffy frosting.

DARK CHOCOLATE CUPCAKES

Makes 12 cupcakes

This recipe does not double very well. Cupcakes made from a doubled batch and baked side by side in the oven yield a slightly compromised rise. It's best to make two separate batches and bake each separately. Store leftover cupcakes (frosted or unfrosted) in the refrigerator, but let them come to room temperature before serving.

8	tablespoons unsalted butter, cut into 4 pieces
2	ounces bittersweet chocolate, chopped
½	cup (1½ ounces) Dutch-processed cocoa powder
¾	cup (3¾ ounces) unbleached all-purpose flour
½	teaspoon baking soda
¾	teaspoon baking powder
2	large eggs
¾	cup (5¼ ounces) sugar
1	teaspoon vanilla extract
½	teaspoon salt
½	cup (4 ounces) sour cream

1. Adjust an oven rack to the lower-middle position and heat the oven to 350 degrees. Line a standard-sized muffin tin (cups that have ½-cup capacity) with baking cup liners.

2. Combine the butter, chocolate, and cocoa in a medium heatproof bowl. Set the bowl over a saucepan containing barely simmering water; heat the mixture until the butter and chocolate are melted and whisk until smooth and fully combined. Set aside to cool until just warm to the touch.

3. Whisk the flour, baking soda, and baking powder in a small bowl to combine.

4. Whisk the eggs in a second medium bowl to combine; add the sugar, vanilla, and salt and whisk until fully incorporated. Add the cooled chocolate mixture and whisk until combined. Sift about one-third of the flour mixture over the chocolate mixture and whisk until combined; whisk in the sour cream until combined, then sift the remaining flour mixture over the batter and whisk until homogenous and thick.

5. Divide the batter evenly among the muffin tin cups. Bake until a skewer inserted into the center of the cupcakes comes out clean, 18 to 20 minutes.

6. Cool the cupcakes in the tin on a wire rack until cool enough to handle, about 15 minutes. Carefully lift each cupcake from the muffin tin and set on a wire rack. Cool to room temperature before icing, about 30 minutes. (To frost: Mound about 2 tablespoons of icing on the center of each cupcake. Using a small icing spatula or butter knife, spread the icing to the edge of the cupcake, leaving a slight mound in the center.)

EASY VANILLA BEAN BUTTERCREAM
Makes about 1½ cups, enough to frost 12 cupcakes
If you prefer to skip the vanilla bean, increase the extract to 1½ teaspoons. Any of the buttercream frostings can be made ahead and refrigerated; if refrigerated, however, the frosting must stand at room temperature to soften before use. If using a handheld mixer, increase mixing times significantly (by at least 50 percent).

10 tablespoons unsalted butter, softened
½ vanilla bean, halved lengthwise
1¼ cups (5 ounces) confectioners' sugar
Pinch salt
½ teaspoon vanilla extract
1 tablespoon heavy cream

In a standing mixer fitted with the whisk attachment, beat the butter at medium-high speed until smooth, about 20 seconds. Using a paring knife, scrape the seeds from the vanilla bean into the butter and beat the mixture at medium-high speed to combine, about 15 seconds. Add the confectioners' sugar and salt and beat at medium-low speed until most of the sugar is moistened, about 45 seconds. Scrape down the bowl and beat at medium speed until the mixture is fully combined, about 15 seconds. Scrape down the bowl, add the vanilla extract and heavy cream, and beat at medium speed until incorporated, about 10 seconds, then increase the speed to medium-high and beat until light and fluffy, about 4 minutes, scraping down the bowl once or twice.

VARIATIONS
EASY CHOCOLATE BUTTERCREAM
Follow the recipe for Easy Vanilla Bean Buttercream, omitting the vanilla bean and heavy cream and reducing the sugar to 1 cup. After beating in the vanilla extract, reduce the speed to low and gradually beat in 4 ounces melted and cooled semisweet or bittersweet chocolate.

EASY COFFEE BUTTERCREAM
Follow the recipe for Easy Vanilla Bean Buttercream, omitting the vanilla bean and dissolving 1½ teaspoons instant espresso in the vanilla extract and heavy cream.

EASY PEPPERMINT BUTTERCREAM
Follow the recipe for Easy Vanilla Bean Buttercream, omitting the vanilla bean, reducing the vanilla extract to ¼ teaspoon, and adding ¾ teaspoon peppermint extract along with the vanilla extract.

EQUIPMENT CORNER: Muffin Tins

WE DON'T RECOMMEND SUPERMARKET MIXES FOR cupcakes, but what about supermarket cupcake pans? Are they good enough, or do kitchen shops offer something better (and more expensive)? To find out, we rounded up six muffin tins, aka cupcake pans, which ranged in price from $3 to $21.

As has been our experience with other bakeware, we found that darker, nonstick muffin tins were better heat conductors than shiny uncoated tins and yielded cupcakes and muffins with more color—and more flavor. Cupcakes baked in dark tins also rose better and sported nicely domed tops. The pallid cupcakes baked in shiny pans had flat tops.

All four of the nonstick tins in our lineup were deemed acceptable, but beware of pans with excessive weight. The Calphalon Commercial ($20.99) and Anolon SureGrip ($19.95) muffin tins tipped the scale at more than 2 pounds (no one-handed lifting of these pans). Baker's Secret ($5.69), the supermarket staple, performed well and finished in a respectable second place. But Wilton Ultra-Bake ($7.99) was the clear winner, in part because of its generous 2-inch lip.

BEST MUFFIN TIN

Among pricier competition, the inexpensive Wilton Ultra-Bake ($7.99) turned out ideal cupcakes and muffins and boasts the thoughtful (and rare) addition of handles.

TASTING LAB: Dark Chocolates

DARK CHOCOLATE SOUNDS SIMPLE ENOUGH, DOESN'T IT? In reality, though, dark chocolate is anything but simple. Located somewhere between milk chocolate and unsweetened chocolate, dark chocolates are made mostly from two basic ingredients: chocolate liquor (also called cocoa mass or abbreviated to just cocoa on labels; it is the result of grinding roasted cacao beans) and sugar.

Although the term "dark" has no official meaning, it generally refers to chocolates labeled sweet, semisweet, or bittersweet. The only regulation from the U.S. Food and Drug Administration (FDA) that concerns these dark chocolates is that they must contain at least 35 percent chocolate liquor, although most contain more than 55 percent and on rare occasions go as high as 99 percent. The rest consists of sugar and, depending on the manufacturer, emulsifiers, flavorings, extra cocoa butter (for fluidity and smoothness; some cocoa butter exists naturally in the chocolate liquor), and milk fat (if present, in small amounts only).

To complicate matters, many companies sell more than one line of dark chocolate, the difference being in their percentage of chocolate liquor. The consumer is readily stymied by the fact that these percentages are not always printed on the label. As a result, many labels offer little reliable indication of what the chocolate inside tastes like, leaving us all, as it were, in the dark.

Hoping to make some sense of this confusing array of dark chocolate choices, we organized a tasting. We included nine samples chosen to mirror the widely divergent choices that every consumer faces, tasting each chocolate raw, in chocolate sauce, and in flourless chocolate cake.

Prepared to assess the various chocolates in the tasting as we would fine wines (the flavor descriptors typically used to describe chocolate include fruit, apple, smoke, tobacco, cherry, raspberry, and tannin), we ended up judging them on a much simpler scale. We found, to our great surprise, that one factor had more influence on the success or failure of a chocolate than any other: sugar.

If sugar content is that important, we reasoned, it should be readily identifiable on labels. For that matter, we assumed, sugar content should be regulated. Wrong, on both counts. The government-mandated nutritional information printed on the back of the labels includes sugar by number of grams but not in percentage terms. Not even the terms "semisweet" and "bittersweet" are surefire indicators of a chocolate's sweetness. (Some brands of bittersweet contain more sugar than some brands of semisweet. Callebaut Dark "Bittersweet," for example, contains more sugar than Scharffen Berger's semisweet.) The FDA draws no official distinction between the two.

To figure out total sugar content (a number that includes added sugar as well as sugars that occur naturally in the chocolate liquor), you must divide the number of sugar grams by the number of grams in the serving size (both listed on all labels) and then multiply by 100. Our top three finishers—Ghirardelli, Callebaut, and Hershey's—had sugar contents of 44 percent, 44 percent, and 49 percent, respectively.

The four high-cocoa (remember, that's chocolate liquor) chocolates tasted—the expensive brands revered by pastry chefs—had sugar contents that ranged from 28 percent to 35 percent, about 10 percent lower than the sweeter chocolates at the top of the ratings. While they did earn ardent support from a vocal minority of tasters, they ended up in the lower half of the ratings overall because most tasters were put off by their lack of sweetness and challenging flavor profiles.

If the really bitter dark chocolates did not score well in our tasting, what, then, is their appeal? Technical advisors from the Belgian chocolate company Barry Callebaut put it this way. "Sugar," they said, "interferes with the perception of chocolate flavor nuances in the product." The experts argue that high-cocoa chocolates have a more robust and nuanced flavor, and our tasters' comments supported this assertion.

In descriptions of the cake and the sauce made with these chocolates, the words "bitter," "sour," and "sharp" appeared again and again, but a few tasters picked up on distinct flavors they didn't notice in the sweeter chocolates. In the Lindt, people noticed coffee, tobacco, smoke, and tannin; in the El Rey it was a roasted quality, smoke, cherry, and fruit; the Valrhona evoked toast, raspberry, sour apple, and vegetable; and in the Scharffen Berger it was cherry, wine, raisins, flowers, and fruit. These lower-sugar chocolates have flavor profiles that are more complex than those of our winners, but they are not necessarily more likable.

What, then, to buy? Unless you have a rarefied palate (at least when it comes to chocolate), you don't have to shell out a lot of money or search gourmet shops to find a winning brand. Our top choices included the pricey Callebaut Dark "Bittersweet" Chocolate 835, but also the inexpensive Hershey's Special Dark and our overall winner, Ghirardelli Bittersweet.

Rating Dark Chocolates

TWENTY MEMBERS OF THE AMERICA'S TEST Kitchen staff tasted nine different dark chocolates in three formats: raw, in chocolate sauce, and baked into flourless chocolate cake. The chocolates are categorized as "sweet" or "distinct and bitter" based on tasters' perceptions and total sugar content, rounded to the nearest whole number. Within each category, the chocolates are listed in order of preference based on their combined scores from the three tastings.

BEST OVERALL DARK CHOCOLATE

Ghirardelli Bittersweet Chocolate Premium Baking Bar

$2.69 for 4 ounces; 44% sugar

With its high percentage of sugar, this California chocolate was considered the most balanced, neither too bitter nor too sweet. Its smooth, creamy texture also won points. Tasters noted both "flavor bursts" and its range of flavors with comments such as "starts sweet and finishes bitter," which explains why this chocolate stood out and was our overall favorite.

SWEETER DARK CHOCOLATES

RECOMMENDED

Callebaut Dark "Bittersweet" Chocolate, 835

$58 for 11 pounds; 44% sugar

The merits of this Belgian chocolate were a creamy texture, gentle bitterness, and interesting nutty and tropical "coconut" notes.

RECOMMENDED

Hershey's Special Dark Mildly Sweet Chocolate

$1.59 for 7 ounces; 49% sugar

The sweetest sample and appreciated for it. Numerous tasters remarked on its "milky" qualities. A slight waxy texture was noted when sampled raw, but both the sauce and the cake were considered "very creamy and smooth."

RECOMMENDED WITH RESERVATIONS

Baker's Bittersweet Baking Chocolate Squares

$2.29 for 6 ounces; 36% sugar

Tasters preferred true-to-its-name Baker's (made by Kraft) when cooked. Without much bitterness, "nutty," "roasty," and "coffee" flavor notes came through in the sauce and cake, but raw Baker's scored poorly because the texture was considered "gritty" and "chalky."

RECOMMENDED WITH RESERVATIONS

Perugina Bittersweet Chocolate

$2.25 for 3.5 ounces; 36% sugar

With high ratings in the cake test, tasters considered Perugina "balanced" and "subtle." The "silky, creamy" texture was well received in all tests, but the flavor was too mild for some when eaten plain or in the sauce, and a few tasters picked up "artificial" and "plastic" flavor notes.

DISTINCT AND BITTER DARK CHOCOLATES

RECOMMENDED WITH RESERVATIONS

Lindt Excellence Dark Chocolate, 70% cocoa

$2.75 for 3.5 ounces; 28% sugar

While Lindt was rated fairly smooth, complex, and creamy across the board, it was better received raw and in the sauce. In the cake many tasters thought it was not sweet enough.

RECOMMENDED WITH RESERVATIONS

El Rey Gran Saman Dark Chocolate Carenero Superior 70%

$2.95 for 2.8 ounces; 35% sugar

Considered to be aggressively bitter, this Venezuelan chocolate was also rated as one of the most complex. Tasters frequently repeated the adjectives "roasted," "nutty," and "smoky," and rarely mentioned the word "sweet."

RECOMMENDED WITH RESERVATIONS

Valrhona Guanaja 70% Cacao Dark Bitter Chocolate

$3.50 for 2.62 ounces; 35% sugar

This "very bitter and fruity" French chocolate had unique flavor characteristics. Tasters found "cherry," "wine," and even a mild vegetal flavor akin to olive oil. The texture was described as dry and firm.

RECOMMENDED WITH RESERVATIONS

Scharffen Berger Bittersweet Pure Dark Chocolate, 70% Cacao

$7.99 for 9.7 ounces; 33% sugar

A complex Californian, Scharffen Berger scored very high when eaten raw, with tasters noticing flavors from "acidic" to "cherry" and "earthy," but not sweet. It fared poorly, however, in the sauce and cake, in which it was considered "too bitter" and "astringent."

A cake stand makes it easy for Erika to frost our Old-Fashioned Chocolate Layer Cake. But if you don't have a stand, improvise by setting the cake on a Lazy Susan.

OLD-FASHIONED
chocolate cake

Remember old-fashioned chocolate layer cake—the kind moms everywhere baked? Each towering slice had a tender, airy, open crumb and was frosted with silky-smooth wisps of chocolate heaven. These homespun cakes were tall, sweet, and chocolaty, not dense, dark, and bitter, and they were eaten with an ice-cold glass of milk, not a demitasse of espresso.

Admittedly, many of those birthday party chocolate cakes were made with a boxed mix. While those mixes deliver a pleasantly spongy, moist texture and guaranteed height, they were also full of artificial flavors—which, as kids, we did not find objectionable. But, as adults with grown-up palates, we wanted real chocolate flavor in our cake. Therefore our goals were twofold: create an old-fashioned chocolate layer cake with the same moist, tender crumb we so fondly remember and infuse this cake with true chocolate flavor—chocolaty enough to please adults, but not so dense that it might scare away the kids at the table.

OLD-FASHIONED CHOCOLATE LAYER CAKE

WHAT WE WANTED: The towering layer cake of childhood, moist and chocolaty and slathered with thick, billowy frosting.

While almost everything has been super-sized in recent years, chocolate cakes have moved in the opposite direction, becoming denser, richer, and squatter. Many contemporary chocolate cakes are so intense that just a few forkfuls are satisfying. These cakes are delicious, but sometimes we'd rather have a real piece of cake, not a confection. The cake we had in mind would have a spongy but moist texture that offered a nice contrast with its thick coating of frosting.

We knew that the mixing method would be key to getting the right texture. Creaming, beating butter with sugar before whipping in the eggs and flour, is the most popular method for many home-baked cakes. The sugar crystals help whip air into the softened butter, which helps the cake rise in the oven. While this method is fine for yellow cake, the addition of so much melted unsweetened chocolate undoes the effects of creaming, and we found that the resulting cakes were fairly dense as well as a bit tough and dry. We tried various ways to lighten the load (more leavening, more eggs), but eventually we came to suspect that this method would never produce a fluffy, tender chocolate cake.

Next up on our list of mixing methods was "reverse creaming," which has come into vogue in recent years. Proponents tout reverse creaming as the best way to deliver maximum tenderness, and, in fact, this method has become the test kitchen's preferred way to prepare a yellow cake. By mixing very soft butter with flour before adding any liquids, less gluten (the source of cake structure) can develop, yielding a tender and fluffy cake. When we tested reverse creaming with chocolate cake, the results were tender and fluffy, as promised, but the cake was too fragile to stand up to a thick heap of frosting. We suspected that the additional moisture and fat provided by the chocolate were getting in the way.

How could we get volume, structure, and tenderness in the same cake? Stumped, we reconsidered a method that had been previously dismissed—ribboning, a process of whipping eggs with sugar until they double in volume, then adding the butter, dry ingredients, and milk. The term refers to the ribbon-like strands that form (between the whisk and the batter) when the eggs and sugar are whipped. The technique is often the first step in making a French-style sponge cake, or génoise. Interestingly, many of the American cake recipes we had pulled from late nineteenth-century cookbooks relied on this technique. That's because chemical leaveners (baking soda and baking powder) were not yet widely used. The egg foam was responsible for aerating the cake. While we were planning on using a leavener for extra security, maybe this technique would deliver both the height and the structure we wanted.

We followed the basic génoise procedure of whipping eggs with sugar until light and fluffy, then adding the melted chocolate and butter, followed by the dry ingredients and milk. The cake was a bit too dry and not quite chocolaty enough, but ribboning had yielded a better combination of structure and tenderness than any of the other methods we had tried. Clearly, achieving volume with eggs and sugar right at the beginning of mixing was key. And when we increased the liquid side of things by adding a full cup of buttermilk, we had a fairly moist cake with good structure and spongy volume. Adding some cocoa powder to the flour mixture improved the chocolate flavor. Not perfect yet (the cake could still be more moist and chocolaty), but getting closer.

The solution to the moisture problem finally presented itself as we combed yet again through the stack of old chocolate cake recipes. Although some called for simply melting the unsweetened chocolate and mixing it into the batter, we came across a few references to chocolate "pudding" or "custard." This wasn't pudding or custard in the classic sense (chocolate, milk, eggs, sugar, cornstarch) but a simpler concoction of chocolate, water, and sugar. Probably taken

up to keep the chocolate from burning, this technique was popular in the early 1900s. We found recipes using this technique in *The Settlement Cookbook* (1901), one of the most important American cookbooks of its era, and in the first edition of *Joy of Cooking* (1931). Although we could find few modern references to this method, we were reminded of the supermarket cake mixes used by our mothers. They also had included powdered "pudding" for extra moisture. We'd always assumed this was just a gimmick, but maybe these cake-mix makers were onto something.

To test this theory, we made another cake using our working recipe, this time melting unsweetened chocolate and cocoa powder in hot water over a double boiler, then stirring in sugar until it dissolved. What came from the oven was the moistest chocolate cake yet, with a pronounced yet subtle chocolate flavor and a rich brown color. It was gloriously tall, and the crumb was open and spongy yet also tender and moist. Here was the cake we had been searching for!

We wanted a silky, voluminous frosting with good chocolate flavor to pair up with our tender, well-structured cake. We imagined the finished cake sitting on a cake stand on the counter of an old-time diner, barely fitting under its high glass dome. Frostings fall into three basic categories: meringue, buttercream, and ganache. Meringue and buttercream easily produce a frosting with great volume, but the emphasis is never really on the chocolate. We found that the beaten egg whites and sugar in a meringue frosting and

the pound of butter in most buttercreams overwhelmed the chocolate flavor. Ganache is all about chocolate—it can be as simple as heated cream poured over chopped sweetened chocolate—but its texture is usually quite dense. Could we make a ganache that was soft and billowy?

Our first thought was to whip butter into the ganache once it had cooled. The frosting left a nice trail of peaks behind a spatula, but it wasn't as silky and glossy as we wanted—and it had a tendency to break into a clumpy mess. As the frosting set, it became too hard, forming a helmet-like shell around our cake. Adding some corn syrup and sugar made the frosting more pliable and shiny, but the emulsion was still breaking. After a week of experimenting with various temperatures, times, and ingredients, the solution turned out to be a simple reversal of the conventional ganache procedure: We poured cold (rather than heated) cream into warm melted (rather than room-temperature) chocolate, waited until the mixture reached room temperature, then whipped it until fluffy. Success! Our chocolate frosting was now creamy, billowy, and—most important—stable.

Our cake was all that we had imagined. The moist, tender, and airy cake layers were perfectly balanced by the light yet creamy frosting.

WHAT WE LEARNED: For a tall cake with a tender crumb, use the ribboning method to mix the batter. This method is used for French-style sponge cakes and consists of whipping the eggs and sugar until the mixture doubles in volume, forming "ribbons" when the beaters are lifted. For full chocolate flavor, melt unsweetened chocolate with hot water and cocoa powder. The water "blooms" the chocolate and deepens its flavor, and the mixture, called a "pudding," also gives the cake a rich moistness. For a creamy, lush frosting with great chocolate flavor, a ganache-style frosting is preferred. To ensure creaminess and stability, reverse the mixing procedure by pouring cold (instead of heated) cream into warm melted (instead of room-temperature) chocolate. Cool down the mixture to room temperature and then whip until fluffy.

OLD-FASHIONED CHOCOLATE LAYER CAKE

Serves 10 to 12

Do not substitute semisweet chocolate chips for the chopped semisweet chocolate in the frosting—chocolate chips contain less cocoa butter than bar chocolate and will not melt as readily. For best results, don't make the frosting until the cakes are cooled, and use the frosting as soon as it is ready. If the frosting gets too cold and stiff to spread easily, wrap the mixer bowl with a towel soaked in hot water and mix on low speed until the frosting appears creamy and smooth. Refrigerated leftover cake should sit at room temperature before serving until the frosting softens.

cake

12	tablespoons unsalted butter, very soft, plus extra for greasing the pans
1¾	cups (8¾ ounces) unbleached all-purpose flour, plus extra for dusting the pans
4	ounces unsweetened chocolate, coarsely chopped
¼	cup (¾ ounce) Dutch-processed cocoa powder
½	cup hot water
1¾	cups (12¼ ounces) sugar
1½	teaspoons baking soda
1	teaspoon salt
1	cup buttermilk
2	teaspoons vanilla extract
4	large eggs, plus 2 large egg yolks

frosting

16	ounces semisweet chocolate, finely chopped (see note)
8	tablespoons unsalted butter
⅓	cup sugar
2	tablespoons corn syrup
2	teaspoons vanilla extract
¼	teaspoon salt
1¼	cups cold heavy cream

1. FOR THE CAKE: Adjust an oven rack to the middle position and heat the oven to 350 degrees. Grease two 9-inch-round by 2-inch-high cake pans with softened butter; dust the pans with flour and knock out the excess. Combine the chocolate, cocoa powder, and hot water in a medium heatproof bowl; set the bowl over a saucepan containing 1 inch of simmering water and stir with a heatproof rubber spatula until the chocolate is melted, about 2 minutes. Add ½ cup of the sugar to the chocolate mixture and stir until thick and glossy, 1 to 2 minutes. Remove the bowl from the heat and set aside to cool.

2. Whisk the flour, baking soda, and salt in a medium bowl. Combine the buttermilk and vanilla in a small bowl. In the bowl of a standing mixer fitted with the whisk attachment,

---

TESTING NOTES:
Two Styles of Chocolate Cake

Thoroughly Modern
Modern chocolate cakes, like this one, are rich, dense, and squat and often are covered with a truffle-like frosting.

Unabashedly Old-Fashioned
Old-style chocolate layer cakes, like ours, stand much taller and are crowned by soft, billowy frosting.

whisk the eggs and yolks on medium-low speed until combined, about 10 seconds. Add the remaining 1¼ cups sugar, increase the speed to high, and whisk until fluffy and lightened in color, 2 to 3 minutes. Replace the whisk with the paddle attachment. Add the cooled chocolate mixture to the egg-sugar mixture and mix on medium speed until thoroughly incorporated, 30 to 45 seconds, pausing to scrape down the sides of the bowl with a rubber spatula as needed. Add the softened butter one tablespoon at a time, mixing about 10 seconds after each addition. Add about one-third of the flour mixture followed by half of the buttermilk mixture, mixing until incorporated after each addition (about 15 seconds). Repeat using half of the remaining flour mixture and all of the remaining buttermilk mixture (the batter may appear separated). Scrape down the sides of the bowl and add the remaining flour mixture; mix at medium-low speed until the batter is thoroughly combined, about 15 seconds. Remove the bowl from the mixer and fold the batter once or twice with a rubber spatula to incorporate any remaining flour. Divide the batter evenly between the prepared cake pans; smooth the batter to the edges of the pan with a spatula.

3. Bake the cakes until a toothpick inserted into the center comes out with a few crumbs attached, 25 to 30 minutes. Cool the cakes in the pans for 15 minutes, then invert onto a wire rack. Cool the cakes to room temperature before frosting, 45 to 60 minutes.

4. TO MAKE THE FROSTING: Melt the chocolate in a heatproof bowl set over a saucepan containing 1 inch of barely simmering water, stirring occasionally until smooth. Remove from the heat and set aside. Meanwhile, heat the butter in a small saucepan over medium-low heat until melted. Increase the heat to medium; add the sugar, corn syrup, vanilla, and salt and stir with a heatproof rubber spatula until the sugar is dissolved, 4 to 5 minutes. Add the melted chocolate, butter mixture, and cream to the clean bowl of a standing mixer and stir to thoroughly combine.

5. Place the mixer bowl over an ice bath and stir the mixture constantly with a rubber spatula until the frosting is thick and just beginning to harden against the sides of the bowl, 1 to 2 minutes (the frosting should be at 70 degrees). Place the bowl on a standing mixer fitted with the paddle

attachment and beat on medium-high speed until the frosting is light and fluffy, 1 to 2 minutes. Stir with a rubber spatula until completely smooth.

6. TO FROST THE CAKE: Spread a dab of frosting in the center of a cardboard round cut slightly larger than the cake. Place one cake layer on the cardboard round. Spread 1½ cups frosting evenly across the top of the cake with a spatula. Place the second cake layer on top, then spread the remaining frosting evenly over the top and sides of the cake. Cut into slices and serve.

trial and error, we discovered that cooking a mixture of melted unsweetened chocolate, cocoa powder, hot water, and sugar—what many older cookbooks call a chocolate "pudding"—improved the cake's flavor considerably.

At least one aspect of this phenomenon we had seen before. While developing other chocolate dessert recipes, we've found that adding hot water to cocoa solids before incorporating them into the recipe causes a "blooming" effect, enhancing the chocolate flavor in the final dish. Here, too, when the unsweetened chocolate and cocoa powder were combined with hot water, they formed an emulsion, tiny droplets of cocoa solids and cocoa butter dispersed in water. The result? A noticeably more chocolaty cake.

When we took the additional step of adding ½ cup of sugar to the mix, however, the flavor enhancement was even more dramatic. What was going on? Research revealed that sugar's strong affinity for water was key. As soon as we dissolved the sugar in the pudding mixture, the sugar molecules bonded tightly with the water molecules, leaving the flavorful cocoa solids free to dissolve in the cocoa butter (the fat)—a better medium than water for conveying chocolate flavor. (Chocolate flavor molecules are more soluble in fat than in water.) Skip the pudding step and you'll have a cake that's diminished in chocolate flavor.

SCIENCE DESK:
Enhancing Chocolate Flavor

UNSWEETENED CHOCOLATE CONTAINS COCOA SOLIDS and cocoa butter, while cocoa powder contains mostly solids. We found that a combination of melted unsweetened chocolate and cocoa powder produced a cake with the best chocolate flavor. But the way we combined them proved key to our recipe's success.

Some recipes add the cocoa powder with the flour and other dry ingredients, but we found that this produced a cake with fairly weak chocolate flavor. After much

Add Water
Blooming chocolate and cocoa powder in hot water gave us a cake with good chocolate flavor.

Stir In Sugar
Adding sugar to the mix created a chocolate "pudding," resulting in even greater chocolate flavor.

TECHNIQUE: Frosting a Layer Cake

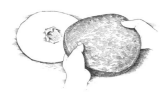   

1. To anchor the cake, spread a dab of frosting in the center of a cardboard round cut slightly larger than the cake. Center the first layer of cake bottom-side down on the cardboard round. Set the cardboard round with the cake on the stand.

2. Place a blob of frosting in the center of the cake and spread it to the edges with an icing spatula. Don't worry if crumbs are visible; the filling will be sandwiched between layers.

3. To level the frosting and remove any excess, hold the spatula at a 45-degree angle to the cake and, starting at the edge farthest away from you, gently drag the spatula toward you. Turn the cake slightly and repeat. It will take a few sweeps to level the frosting.

4. Using a second cardboard round, slide the second cake layer, crust-side up, on top of the frosted bottom layer, making sure that the layers are aligned. Press the cake firmly into place.

5. A thin base coat of frosting helps seal in crumbs. To coat the top, place a blob of frost-ing in the center of the cake and spread it out to the edges, letting any excess hang over the edge. Don't worry if it is imperfect. Smooth the frosting as in step 3.

6. Scoop a large dab of frosting on the spatula's tip. Holding the spatula perpendicular to the cake, spread the frosting on the side of the cake with short side-to-side strokes. Repeat until the entire side is covered with a thin coat of frosting. Refrigerate the cake until the frosting sets, about 10 minutes.

7. Apply a thick final coat of frosting to the top and sides, following steps 5 and 6. When icing the sides, apply a coat thick enough to cover and con-ceal the cardboard round.

8. If you don't own a rotating cake stand, you can perform steps 1 through 7 on a Lazy Susan. Just set the cardboard round on the Lazy Susan and spin slowly.

EQUIPMENT CORNER:
Revolving Cake Stands

THE TRUTH IS THAT A CAKE FROSTING STAND IS NOT AN essential piece of baking equipment. Certainly you can frost a layer cake on a plate or cardboard cake round, but a stand makes the task easier. These stands elevate the cake, giving the baker a better view and making it possible to hold the spatula steady while rotating the stand—improving the likelihood of seamless frosting. We tested five models. All but one, the flat Wilton Trim 'n Turn, worked well. Because the Wilton Trim 'n Turn is flat, it doesn't elevate the cake at all, making it an impractical choice. The ultimate stand (made by Ateco) consists of a metal table over an enameled cast-iron base. It costs $62.99—too much for the occasional birthday cake. A plastic version of the same stand is $43 cheaper and makes cake decorating just as easy.

BEST CAKE STANDS

The Ateco Professional Icing Turntable ($62.99), at left, is a metal stand and is the best choice for pros. The Ateco Revolving Cake Stand ($19.95), at right, is plastic, but does the job at a much more reasonable price.

TASTING LAB: Chocolate Chips

NOT SO LONG AGO, MOST MARKETS HAD ONE—AND ONLY one—brand of chocolate chips, Nestlé Toll House Morsels. (Ruth Wakefield made the very first chocolate chip cookies at the Toll House Inn in Whitman, Mass., in 1930 and eventually sold the recipe to Nestlé.) Seventy-five years later, she would be amazed at the dozens of chips available in numerous flavors (raspberry, peanut butter, butterscotch) and shapes (mini, regular, and chunks). Are any of these chips better than the original? We tasted nine popular brands of semisweet chips, plain and in a chocolate chip cookie, to find out.

Chocolate chips contain less cocoa butter than bar chocolate. The lower fat content means that chips don't melt as readily, which is a good thing—they hold their shape better. Among the brands tested, the fat content hovered in a narrow range of 27 to 30 percent, and we found that the fat percentage did not correlate with tasters' preferences. Our tasters did pick up big differences in creaminess, awarding extra points to brands that were especially smooth melters. Smoothness is more a function of conching (the beating process used to turn unsweetened baking chocolate into eating chocolate) than of cocoa butter content.

Chocolate chips contain more sugar than bar chocolate—in some cases too much, according to our tasters. In general, the sweetest chips landed at the bottom of the rankings. Overall, our tasters said the most important factor separating decent chips from great chips was chocolate flavor. Our top-rated chips were praised for their "intense" chocolate flavor; tasters complained about the "unremarkable" chocolate flavor in several low-rated brands.

So what's the chip of choice? According to our tasters, two relative newcomers. Guittard Classic Chips and Nestlé Toll House Chunks won points for their good chocolate flavor and moderate sweetness. The original Toll House morsels finished in a respectable third place.

Rating Chocolate Chips

TWENTY-TWO MEMBERS OF THE AMERICA'S TEST KITCHEN STAFF TASTED NINE DIFFERENT CHOCOLATE CHIPS RAW STRAIGHT out of the package and baked in chocolate chip cookies. The chocolate chips are listed in order of preference based on their combined scores from the two tastings. The chocolate chips can be purchased nationwide.

RECOMMENDED

Guittard Classic Semi-Sweet Dark Chocolate Chips

$2.79 for 12-ounce bag

Tasters loved the "buttery," "mellow chocolate flavor" and "lovely silky texture" of these chips. Though widely available throughout most of the country, availability in the Northeast is limited. See www.guittard.com for mail-order sources.

RECOMMENDED

Nestlé Toll House Semi-Sweet Chocolate Chunks

$2.50 for 11.5-ounce bag

Though their unorthodox "rough-cut," "square" shape divided tasters, the "good chocolate flavor" and "nice blend of chocolate and sweet" helped these chips share top honors.

RECOMMENDED

Nestlé Toll House Semi-Sweet Chocolate Morsels

$2.50 for 12-ounce bag

These familiar chips were praised for their "intense" chocolate flavor and "great creaminess," though some found them "almost too sweet," "like marshmallows."

RECOMMENDED

Guittard Super Cookie Chips

$2.79 for 10-ounce bag

Fans of these "big" chips praised the "good bitter/sweet balance" and "great chocolate flavor," though others found them "a little bland" and "more like milk chocolate."

RECOMMENDED

Baker's Semi-Sweet Chocolate Chunks

$2.85 for 12-ounce bag

"These aren't chips," complained one taster of these "solid" chunks that nonetheless won some fans with their "good balance" and "smooth" texture.

RECOMMENDED

Hershey's Semi-Sweet Chocolate Chips

$2.29 for 12-ounce bag

These chips have a "rich, distinct flavor" that several detractors found "not very chocolaty" and "too sweet."

RECOMMENDED WITH RESERVATIONS

Ghirardelli Semi-Sweet Chocolate Chips

$2.69 for 12-ounce bag

Many tasters liked the "rich flavor" of these chips, but some panned the "saccharine sweetness" that made them taste like a "caramel confection."

RECOMMENDED WITH RESERVATIONS

Hershey's Special Dark Chocolate Chips

$2.29 for 12-ounce bag

These new "dark" chips from Hershey's were criticized as "too sweet," with "unremarkable" chocolate flavor.

RECOMMENDED WITH RESERVATIONS

Mrs. Field's Semi-Sweet Chocolate Chips

$2.59 for 12-ounce bag

While some praised the "strong flavor" and "nice creaminess" of these chips, several tasters noted an odd "nutty" flavor. Most tasters deemed them "too sweet."

For a not-too-sweet apple dessert, pair a tart apple such as Granny Smith with a sweet apple like Golden Delicious or McIntosh, as we did in Skillet Apple Brown Betty and Easy Apple Strudel.

EASY APPLE
desserts

When it comes to apple desserts, apple pie may be the most popular, but it's also the most involved. When you don't want to fuss with pie, but you still want that warm and comforting combination of apple and pastry, there are other options.

Take apple brown betty—apples, sugar, and buttered bread crumbs. This baked fruit dish is decidedly humble, but delicious nonetheless—especially when served warm with a scoop of vanilla ice cream. But this often-overlooked dessert needs a serious makeover—too many versions are a soggy mess with muddied flavors.

Classic apple strudel, a European specialty, consists of lightly sweetened apples, raisins, and nuts wrapped in paper-thin pastry. Traditional recipes involve hours of preparation, rolling and pulling the pastry dough until it is so thin you can read a newspaper through it. We reasoned that there must be an easier (and quicker) way. Determined to find out, we set about streamlining this sophisticated dessert, without compromising its flaky texture and sophisticated flavors.

Join us as we resurrect one humble apple dessert and streamline another.

APPLE BROWN BETTY

WHAT WE WANTED: An exemplary version of the simple baked apple dessert—tender pieces of sweetened, lightly spiced chunks of apple topped with buttery toasted bread crumbs.

No doubt the creation of Colonial forebears reluctant to let anything go to waste, apple brown betty is a simple baked fruit dessert traditionally made with apples and leftover bread. Butter and sugar were added to enrich and sweeten the mixture, but the original recipe was plain by design. Although apple brown betty recipes abound in both old and new American cookbooks, rarely does the dish make it off the page and into the kitchen. Modern cooks instead choose cobblers and crisps. Charmed by the dessert's simplicity in an era of complicated culinary creations, we set out to rejuvenate this rustic classic.

In its most basic form, apple brown betty contains only four ingredients: apples, bread crumbs, sugar, and butter. There are numerous variations on this theme, however, so to begin our testing we made a range of recipes. Some were basic (buttered bread crumbs on top of sweetened pieces of apple). Others were more complicated (one recipe had 14 ingredients). To our dismay, tasters were neither comforted by the simple versions nor impressed by the elaborate ones. Each had soggy, mushy bread crumbs. Most were overly seasoned with spices, while others tasted bland and flat.

At this point, we made a few decisions. First, we would stick with the traditional (and short) ingredient list. Modern recipes with lots of add-ons seemed antithetical to this basic recipe. Second, we would try to coax as much flavor as possible from these core ingredients. Last, we had to do something about the texture: Soggy and mushy just would not cut it with the test kitchen.

Because betties get much of their flavor from the crumbs, we figured we would start there. We tried a wide range of homemade bread crumbs—processed from white and wheat sandwich bread, English muffins, cinnamon-raisin bread, brioche, pound cake, angel food cake, sourdough, and baguettes—as well as store-bought dried bread crumbs. Crumbs made from cake and rich breads were out of place in this simple dessert, and sourdough crumbs were too strongly flavored. Store-bought crumbs were highly seasoned and too finely processed. In keeping with the straightforward nature of the dish, tasters preferred white sandwich bread pulsed in the food processor until coarsely ground. We used Pepperidge Farm Sandwich White, but any supermarket loaf with a sturdy, fairly dense crumb will work.

Although we had concluded that crumbs made from sandwich bread were the most authentic, most convenient, and therefore best choice, they were awfully plain. Toasting the bread crumbs in a skillet with some butter seemed like a good way to enrich their flavor and improve their texture. One test cook suggested adding some of the sugar, which is usually tossed with the apples. This not only sweetened the crumbs but caused them to crisp and slightly caramelize. Mixing the bread slices—crusts attached—with 3 tablespoons butter and 2 tablespoons sugar in the food processor was easy enough, and the lot could then be added to a cold skillet and cooked over medium heat until deep golden brown. We then spread the mixture on a paper towel–lined plate to cool. The paper towels absorbed excess butter and kept the crumbs crisp, with a slight chew.

With the flavor and texture of the crumbs greatly improved, it was time to start testing apples. We decided to limit our tests to varieties widely available throughout the year in major supermarkets: Granny Smith, McIntosh, Gala, Golden Delicious, and Braeburn, as well as various combinations thereof. We ultimately determined that a blend of two apples was better than one in terms of both texture and flavor. In the end, tasters preferred a combination of Granny Smith and Golden Delicious, with the sweeter flavor of the Goldens complementing the tartness of the Grannies. Tasters preferred apples cut roughly into ½-inch cubes, which gave them a forkful of apples and crumbs with each bite. Apple slices were too large and, as one taster said, a smaller dice made the betty look too much like stuffing.

In a nod to tradition, we baked the apples, butter, sugar, and bread crumbs together in a foil-covered dish; the results were varied, but none were very good. By sprinkling some of our tasty crumbs into the apple mixture (to thicken the juices) and reserving the rest to sprinkle over the apples just before serving, we were able to keep the topping crisp. But tasters complained (fairly loudly) that the apples were still bland. We could add spices to the mix, but first we wanted to coax more flavor from the apples, butter, and sugar. Eyeing the empty skillet we had used to toast the crumbs, we wondered could we caramelize the apples and sugar on top of the stove in a hot skillet slicked with butter?

Our first attempt at preparing a "skillet" brown betty was not wholly successful. Although we were able to fit all of the apples in the pan, they did not cook evenly; those crowded together on the bottom of the skillet cooked faster than the others. We solved this problem by quickly cooking the apples in two batches. After the second batch of apples was done, we returned the first batch to the skillet and finished the dish by sprinkling the rest of the crumbs over the top. This method was much preferred. The apples cooked uniformly and turned an even golden brown. At this point we also tested different kinds and combinations of sugar and found that light brown sugar worked best with both the apples and the crumbs.

Cooking the apples in the skillet had improved their flavor greatly. They tasted richer, deeper, and slightly caramelized—something baked betties could never achieve. We still had two problems, however. The apples were just a tad too firm, and the dessert was a bit dry. The crumbs were more like stuffing and needed some juices to help them meld with the apples. We had come a long way from soggy and mushy; we had actually made a betty that was too dry and crunchy!

After much testing, we discovered that the solution was to add cider to the pan with the sautéed apples and then reduce it by half, a process that took just a few minutes. In addition to making the finished dessert saucier, the extra liquid helped to cook the apples until they were soft but still firm enough to hold their shape—exactly the texture we were looking for. The cider also deglazed the bottom and sides of the pan, picking up every bit of caramelized flavor and returning it to the dish. Finally, the sugars in the cider gave the dish a syrupy consistency and a deep apple flavor.

We stirred in ½ cup of the buttered, sugared, and toasted crumbs to thicken the betty and then sprinkled the rest on top to keep them crisp. We tweaked the flavor by adding just ¼ teaspoon each of ground cinnamon and ginger (along with the sugar at the outset of the sautéing process) and by adjusting the sweet/tart balance with a little lemon juice just before serving. This betty's makeover was now complete. It came together even more quickly than the original and, in the opinion of the test kitchen, was much improved as well. The soggy bread crumbs had been replaced by a crisp topping, and the apples had gone from bland and pedestrian to lightly spiced and caramelized, with their flavor enhanced by the reduced cider. Now we had a simple apple dessert that was both frugal and delicious.

WHAT WE LEARNED: For a lightly sweetened, crisp crumb topping, toast white sandwich bread crumbs with butter and a bit of sugar. The sweet/tart combination of Granny Smith and Golden Delicious apples makes a not-too-sweet apple filling. Instead of baking the dessert, prepare it in a skillet on the stovetop, which allows you better control, and cook the apples in two batches to ensure even cooking. After preparing the bread crumbs, remove them from the pan and caramelize the apples. Add brown sugar to the apples along with ginger and cinnamon for a deepened, lightly spiced flavor. The addition of apple cider to the fruit adds welcome moisture and a further dimension of apple flavor, and a bit of lemon juice brightens the filling. Thicken the filling with a portion of the toasted bread crumbs and reserve the remainder for sprinkling over the top.

SKILLET APPLE BROWN BETTY

Serves 6 to 8

If your apples are especially tart, omit the lemon juice. If, on the other hand, your apples are exceptionally sweet, use the full amount. Leftovers can be refrigerated in an airtight container; topped with vanilla yogurt, they make an excellent breakfast.

bread crumbs

4   ounces sliced white sandwich bread (3 to 4 slices), torn into 1-inch pieces
2   tablespoons packed light brown sugar
3   tablespoons unsalted butter, cut into 4 pieces

apples

¼   cup packed (1¾ ounces) light brown sugar
¼   teaspoon ground ginger
¼   teaspoon ground cinnamon
    Pinch salt
3   tablespoons unsalted butter
1½ pounds Granny Smith apples (about 3 medium), peeled, cored, and cut into ½-inch cubes (about 4 cups)
1½ pounds Golden Delicious apples (about 3 medium), peeled, cored, and cut into ½-inch cubes (about 4 cups)
1¼ cups apple cider
1–3 teaspoons juice from 1 lemon (see note)

1. FOR THE BREAD CRUMBS: Pulse the bread, sugar, and butter in a food processor until coarsely ground, about four 1-second pulses. Transfer the crumbs to a 12-inch skillet; toast over medium heat, stirring constantly, until the crumbs are deep golden brown, 8 to 10 minutes. Transfer to a paper towel–lined plate; wipe out the skillet.

2. FOR THE APPLES: Combine the sugar, spices, and salt in a small bowl. Heat 1½ tablespoons of the butter in the now-empty skillet over high heat; when the foaming subsides, stir in the Granny Smith apples and half of the

sugar mixture. Distribute the apples in an even layer and cook, stirring two or three times, until medium brown, about 5 minutes; transfer to a medium bowl. Repeat with the remaining butter, the Golden Delicious apples, and sugar mixture, returning the first batch of apples to the skillet when second batch is done.

3. Add the apple cider and scrape the bottom and sides of the skillet with a wooden spoon to loosen the browned bits; cook until the apples are tender but not mushy and the liquid has reduced and is just beginning to thicken, 2 to 4 minutes.

4. Remove the skillet from the heat; stir in the lemon juice, if using, and ⅓ cup of the toasted bread crumbs. Using a wooden spoon, lightly flatten the apples into an even layer in the skillet and evenly sprinkle with the remaining toasted bread crumbs. Spoon the warm betty into individual bowls and serve with vanilla ice cream, if desired.

VARIATIONS

SKILLET APPLE BROWN BETTY WITH PECANS AND DRIED CRANBERRIES

Tart cranberries enliven the sweet filling.

Follow the recipe for Skillet Apple Brown Betty, adding ½ cup pecans to the food processor along with the bread, sugar, and butter and processing as instructed, then adding ½ cup dried cranberries to the apple mixture with the cider.

SKILLET APPLE BROWN BETTY WITH GOLDEN RAISINS AND CALVADOS

Any applejack, or even brandy, can be used in place of the Calvados.

Follow the recipe for Skillet Apple Brown Betty, substituting ¼ cup Calvados or brandy for an equal amount of the apple cider and adding ½ cup golden raisins to the apples along with the cider-Calvados mixture.

TASTING LAB: Vanilla Ice Cream

WHILE SOME SUPERMARKET VANILLA ICE CREAMS ATTEMPT to get by on just the basics—"all natural" blends of cream, sugar, vanilla, and little else—many cartons sport labels that read like highlights from a chemistry textbook. Some manufacturers substitute imitation vanilla extract for the real stuff, while others bet on visual appeal, using ground-up vanilla-bean specks to give the illusion of full flavor.

Does any of this hocus-pocus deliver a better product? To find out, we tasted 18 varieties, including 10 French-style (with egg yolks) and 8 regular (yolkless) vanilla ice creams.

The side-by-side comparison was striking. Some were fluffy and light; others were dense and rich. A few had assertive vanilla notes that reminded tasters of "frozen, boozy eggnog." Several ice creams, on the other hand, seemed to be lacking in vanilla flavor altogether.

Contrary to expectations, the French vanilla ice creams—prized for the rich flavor and creamy texture that comes from egg yolks—did not sweep the competition. In fact, regular-style Turkey Hill Vanilla Bean just edged out French-style Edy's Dreamery (the winner of our 2001 French vanilla tasting) for first place. Yes, the French-style ice creams (with 12.5 percent to 17.0 percent butterfat) took five of the six top spots, while leaner eggless vanilla ice creams (with 11.6 percent to 12.3 percent butterfat) took four of the five bottom places. But the top ranking of Turkey Hill Vanilla Bean (with just 12.1 percent butterfat) did not fit the neat pattern of more fat equals better quality.

Just as puzzling were tasters' comments about the texture of this yolkless winner. "What an amazingly gooey, creamy texture!" wrote one taster. "Nice eggy mouthfeel," said another. Double-checking the list of ingredients, we saw no evidence of any egg product. Even stranger, a quick skim through the rest of the comments revealed similar remarks about the "custardy" texture of a few of the other regular (yolkless) samples. Either our tasters were completely clueless, or there was something in these ice creams that was giving them (the ice creams) a faux-French demeanor.

We studied the labels and soon noticed a clear pattern. Every regular-style ice cream that had passed for French vanilla contained substances such as carob bean gum, carrageenan, guar gum, and mono- and diglycerides. Could these additives be mimicking the textural effect of egg yolks?

We were partly correct. Carob bean gum, carrageenan, and guar gum are all stabilizers, added to ice cream to help keep ice crystals from forming and wreaking havoc on texture. Mono- and diglycerides, on the other hand, are emulsifiers, added to ice cream to keep the fat from separating—which, in turn, contributes a luscious, silky texture. Egg yolks, which naturally contain the emulsifier lecithin, serve this same function in French-style ice creams. So it was the mono- and diglycerides that had fooled our panelists into praising the "custardy" texture of the eggless ice creams.

A much clearer picture was emerging: High fat content and egg yolks can give ice cream a rich, creamy texture, but the judicious use of stabilizers and emulsifiers goes a long way toward making up for the absence of either one. The ice creams in our lineup that got the lowest scores for texture have low fat content and no egg yolks, stabilizers, or emulsifiers (that is, the "natural" regular-style ice creams). Our winning ice cream, Turkey Hill Vanilla Bean, contains emulsifiers as well as two stabilizers. And runner-up Edy's Dreamery has egg yolks, stabilizers, and a high fat content. No wonder it received the highest score for texture in the entire lineup.

Of course, ice cream is more than just creamy. Some of the best-textured contenders fumbled when it came to flavor. Although the occasional ice cream lost points for too-potent vanilla notes (especially "artificial" or "boozy" flavors), by the end of the tasting it was clear why "vanilla" is often synonymous with "plain." In fact, weak vanilla flavor was the reason cited most often by panelists for awarding an ice cream a low score.

There are three forms of vanilla found in supermarket vanilla ice creams. Natural vanilla extract is made by steeping ground vanilla beans in a solution of alcohol and water to extract more than 240 flavorful compounds, the most dominant of which is called vanillin. Imitation vanilla extract is made by synthesizing vanillin from either eugenol (found in clove oil) or lignin (a by-product of the paper industry). The third form is vanilla beans themselves.

Only two of the ice creams—Blue Bunny regular and Blue Bell French—contained imitation vanilla extract. One failed to make it out of the elimination round, and the other landed in next-to-last place in the main tasting. Clearly, natural vanilla is a key component in good ice cream. But how much is enough?

To answer this question, we had our lab examine all 18 samples for vanillin content and found that more vanillin generally translated to higher ratings from our tasters. The differences were fairly dramatic. On the low end, several ice creams contained only 2 milligrams of vanillin (per kilogram), and many of these were eliminated early on for weak vanilla flavor (including Breyers Natural and Turkey Hill French). Other ice creams contained nearly 10 times as much. In the end, our winning Turkey Hill Vanilla Bean (4 milligrams) and second-place Edy's Dreamery (10

milligrams) represented the extremes of what our tasters considered the right amount of vanilla flavor. Ice creams with more than 10 milligrams tended to lose points for "extract overkill," while those with fewer than 4 milligrams had tasters asking, "Where's the flavor?"

So where did we come out? Turns out it is possible to pull one over on Mother Nature—and, when it comes to vanilla ice cream, some strategic engineering is actually a desirable thing. Our tasters liked both French-style ice creams with stabilizers and regular (yolkless) ice creams with stabilizers and emulsifiers. If you prefer your ice cream smooth, subtle, and balanced, Turkey Hill Vanilla Bean is our top choice, while those who like vanilla that packs more of a punch might opt for the second-place Edy's Dreamery.

SCIENCE DESK: Overrun and Ice Cream

ALL ICE CREAMS ARE AERATED TO MAKE THEIR TEXTURE lighter and softer. Federal regulations allow ice cream manufacturers to increase the volume of their ice cream by up to 100 percent. The amount of air added to the ice cream is called overrun. Premium brands with a dense texture (often sold in pint containers) have less overrun than fluffy brands (often sold in big containers).

Brands with low overrun (between 21 percent and 24 percent) took most of the top spots in our tasting (including second, third, and fourth), while brands with high overrun (between 78 percent and 97 percent) landed in the last four spots. But there was one brand that did not fit this neat pattern. Our taste-test winner, Turkey Hill Vanilla Bean, has 94 percent overrun (the second-highest in our tasting). It achieved better texture through better engineering (see Tasting Lab on page 295 for details). So what does this mean practically? A 10-ounce serving of Turkey Hill will tower over a regular sugar cone. A 10-ounce serving of second-place Dreamery (with 21 percent overrun) looks pretty skimpy by comparison.

Rating Vanilla Ice Creams

TWENTY MEMBERS OF THE AMERICA'S TEST KITCHEN STAFF TASTED 18 VANILLA ICE CREAMS—10 FRENCH-STYLE BRANDS (made with egg yolks) and 8 regular brands (made without egg yolks). (Eight brands were eliminated after scoring low in preliminary rounds.) The two styles were tasted separately in preliminary rounds; the top five of each group advanced to a final round, the results of which are given below. The ice creams are listed in order of preference based on their scores in this tasting and can be purchased nationwide.

HIGHLY RECOMMENDED
Turkey Hill All Natural Flavor Vanilla Bean (regular)

Mono- and Diglycerides, Guar Gum, and Carrageenan; Estimated Overrun: 94%; $4.99 for 1.75 quarts

"Exactly what vanilla ice cream should taste like," said one panelist about the only yolkless contender in our top six.

HIGHLY RECOMMENDED
Edy's Dreamery Vanilla (French-style)

Carob Bean Gum, Guar Gum, and Carrageenan; Estimated Overrun: 21%; $3.69 for 1 pint

Tasters gave Dreamery the top score for texture, clearly enhanced by three stabilizers and egg yolks, and praised its strong vanilla flavor. This brand is called Dreyer's on the West Coast.

RECOMMENDED
Häagen-Dazs Vanilla (French-style)

No Stabilizers or Emulsifiers; Estimated Overrun: 21%; $3.79 for 1 pint

Rich, creamy, and "buttery," this high-fat brand was some tasters' favorite, but others found the vanilla flavor much too strong.

RECOMMENDED
Häagen-Dazs Vanilla Bean (French-style)

No Stabilizers or Emulsifiers; Estimated Overrun: 21%; $3.79 for 1 pint

"So many vanilla specks it looks like Cookies 'n' Cream," said one taster. The strong, boozy flavor called to mind "rum steeped with vanilla."

RECOMMENDED WITH RESERVATIONS
Ben & Jerry's Vanilla (French-style)

Guar Gum and Carrageenan; Estimated Overrun: 24%; $3.49 for 1 pint

Creamy, rich, and subtly flavored, but some found it too subtle in vanilla intensity. "Fatty but flavorless," complained one taster.

RECOMMENDED WITH RESERVATIONS
Blue Bunny Premium Natural Vanilla Bean (French-style)

No Stabilizers or Emulsifiers; Estimated Overrun: 78%; $3.24 for 1.75 quarts

High vanillin and modest fat content were a recipe for major vanilla intensity. Texture was icy.

RECOMMENDED WITH RESERVATIONS
Turkey Hill Philadelphia Style All Natural Vanilla Bean (regular)

No Stabilizers or Emulsifiers; Estimated Overrun: 88%; $4.99 for 1.75 quarts

Lost points for a "lean and icy" consistency that its sibling (our winner) solved with stabilizers and emulsifiers.

RECOMMENDED WITH RESERVATIONS
Breyers Extra Creamy Vanilla (regular)

Carob Bean Gum and Guar Gum; Estimated Overrun: 85%; $4.99 for 1.75 quarts

This yolkless ice cream simply didn't have enough vanilla flavor.

RECOMMENDED WITH RESERVATIONS
Blue Bunny Premium Vanilla (regular)

Carob Bean Gum, Guar Gum, Mono- and Diglycerides, and Carrageenan; Estimated Overrun: 88%; $3.24 for 1.75 quarts

One of two ice creams that used synthetic vanilla, this brand confounded tasters with its additive-addled texture—"velvety" to some, "gummy" to others.

RECOMMENDED WITH RESERVATIONS
Edy's Grand Vanilla Bean (regular)

Cellulose Gum, Mono- and Diglycerides, Guar Gum, and Carrageenan; Estimated Overrun: 97%; $4.79 for 1.75 quarts

Tasters decried the "frozen marshmallow fluff" texture, and the abundance of vanilla specks belied the low vanillin content. This brand is called Dreyer's on the West Coast.

QUICK APPLE STRUDEL

WHAT WE WANTED: A streamlined method for preparing this typically time-consuming European apple dessert, without sacrificing its full apple flavor or crisp, flaky crust.

Apple strudel, lightly spiced apples in a thin, flaky pastry, is meant to be savored by the forkful, preferably with a strong cup of coffee. We wanted all the flavor and charm of this apple dessert, but we didn't want to bother with the hours of preparation the paper-thin dough requires. So, chucking the notion of homemade strudel dough, we started with a simpler option—store-bought phyllo dough—and set out to dramatically simplify this classic dessert while keeping the rich apple filling and as much of the crisp, flaky texture as possible.

A classic apple strudel contains apples, bread crumbs, sugar, cinnamon, raisins, and sometimes walnuts. Although this combination sounds appealing, the strudel recipes we tested initially were in a sad state: dry, bready fillings overpowered by the flavor of the spices and leathery, bland crusts that separated from the filling as soon as a fork came near. We wanted the filling and pastry in our strudel to come together as a unified whole. The crust must be crisp and flaky yet still hold its shape. The filling should be moist but not wet, and the flavor of apple should shine through.

Our first strudels threatened to shatter to bits if we so much as looked at them askance. Butter is usually brushed between the layers of phyllo dough to help keep them crisp and flaky, so we thought that by eliminating the butter we might get a more cohesive crust. But the phyllo crust without butter was still crisp, only now it was also dry and unappealing. We tried adding a bit of milk to the butter, in the hope that the added moisture might help, but that strudel was simply soggy. Then a test cook recalled a method she used while working as a pastry chef. For crisp, cohesive Napoleon layers that retained a bit of chew, she sprinkled sugar on each layer of phyllo with the butter. The melted sugar acted as glue between the layers and added flavor to an otherwise bland dough. The results weren't perfect, but we knew we were on the right track.

Working with phyllo requires constant attention. Left alone, the layers dry out and crack almost instantly. We were careful to keep damp towels over the unused phyllo while layering the sheets, but then we were sending our strudel into a hot oven for upward of 40 minutes, totally unprotected. With sugar between the layers, the strudel held its shape better, but as it cooled on the rack, the outer layers curled and flaked like a bad sunburn. We thought the long time in the oven might be drying out the phyllo, so we tried baking the strudel at very high heat—475 degrees—for just 15 minutes. This crust was perfect: toothsome yet slightly yielding, with a deeply caramelized exterior. And it could be cut into clean, solid slices. There was only one problem: The apples were still raw.

Up until this point, we had been using sliced Granny Smiths, figuring that a firm, tart apple would be best. The quick blast of heat was perfect for the phyllo, but the apples never had a chance to cook and soften. We tried slicing the apples thinner, about 1/8 inch. Still too firm. In the past, the test kitchen has found that a combination of apples works well in pies, so we applied the combination to strudel. Our half-McIntosh, half-Golden Delicious strudel was a success, the former adding body and apple flavor, the latter a pleasant texture.

Lemon juice replaced some of the tartness that had departed with the Granny Smiths. A scant 1/4 teaspoon of cinnamon made the filling sweet and well rounded. After testing various combinations of brown and granulated sugars, we discovered that less was more—just 1/4 cup of granulated sugar added a clean sweetness that tasters liked.

Almost every recipe we'd seen called for raisins of some kind, and tasters preferred milder golden raisins to dark ones. Added straight to the apples, the raisins were a bit dry and chewy, but we found that simmering the raisins in liquid plumped them up in no time. For the liquid, we

tried Calvados (apple brandy), which added a great layer of sweet apple flavor that everyone liked. Knowing that not many houses stock Calvados and that some cooks might not want to use alcohol, we looked for an alternative. Readily available apple cider proved to be the best substitute for Calvados.

Tasters were split on whether they liked chopped nuts in the filling. We decided to make the nuts optional. We knew the bread crumbs, a classic component of strudel, were there to absorb the juices from the apples and prevent a damp crust, but we weren't completely convinced they were necessary. We were wrong. Strudel made without bread crumbs was soggy and loose. But the ½ to ¾ cup of bread crumbs most recipes called for resulted in a strudel that stuck to the roof of the mouth. We settled on ¼ cup of fresh bread crumbs, which gave us a strudel that was moist without being too wet. The flavor, however, was still bready. We browned the crumbs in butter, and tasters loved the results. The filling was now buttery and rich, moist but solid.

WHAT WE LEARNED: Replacing homemade strudel dough with purchased phyllo dough makes for a crust with crisp, flaky layers in a fraction of the time. Brush the phyllo sheets with melted butter, then sprinkle them with sugar. The butter and sugar stabilize the layers (so they don't shatter) and add necessary flavor. A combination of Golden Delicious and McIntosh apples, sliced ⅛ inch thick, makes a filling with layered apple flavor and just the right texture. Just ¼ cup fresh bread crumbs, browned in butter, thickens the filling without weighing it down. Golden raisins, plumped in the microwave with Calvados (apple brandy), add a sophisticated, fruity dimension to the apple filling, and fresh lemon juice adds some welcome brightness.

EASY APPLE STRUDEL

Serves 6 to 8

Note that Athens phyllo, the most commonly available brand (as well as our preferred brand), is sold in two sizes. Both are 1-pound packages, with the larger size containing 20 sheets measuring 18 by 14 inches and the smaller size containing 40 sheets measuring 14 by 9 inches—exactly half the size of the larger sheets. We prefer the larger sheets in our strudel, but if all you can find are the smaller sheets, divide the filling evenly and make two smaller strudels.

The best ways to defrost the phyllo are in the refrigerator overnight or at room temperature for three to four hours; it doesn't defrost well in the microwave. Make sure that the phyllo sheets you use for the strudel are not badly torn. If they have small cuts or tears in the same location (sometimes an entire package sustains cuts in the same spot), when forming the strudel, flip alternating layers so that the cuts will not line up, thereby creating a weak spot that can cause the strudel to burst during baking. Serve the strudel warm with lightly sweetened crème fraîche (recipe follows) or whipped cream; if you choose to make the crème fraîche, make it before starting the strudel because it must stand at room temperature for about 1½ hours before serving.

½	cup golden raisins
2	tablespoons Calvados or apple cider
6	tablespoons (¾ stick) unsalted butter
¼	cup fresh white bread crumbs
2	small Golden Delicious apples (about 10 ounces), peeled, cored, and cut lengthwise into ⅛-inch-thick slices
2	medium McIntosh apples (about 13 ounces), peeled, cored, and cut lengthwise into ⅛-inch-thick slices
¼	cup (1¾ ounces) plus 2 tablespoons granulated sugar
⅓	cup finely chopped walnuts (optional), toasted in a small dry skillet over medium heat until lightly browned and fragrant, about 4 minutes

¼ teaspoon ground cinnamon
⅛ teaspoon salt
1 teaspoon juice from 1 lemon
5 sheets defrosted phyllo (see note)
1½ teaspoons confectioners' sugar

1. Adjust an oven rack to the lower-middle position and heat the oven to 475 degrees. Heat the raisins and Calvados in a small saucepan over medium heat (or in the microwave, covered with plastic wrap) until simmering. Cover, remove from the heat, and let stand until needed.

2. Melt 1 tablespoon of the butter in a small skillet over medium heat; when the foaming subsides, stir in the bread crumbs and cook, stirring frequently, until golden brown, about 2 minutes. Transfer the bread crumbs to a small bowl and set aside.

3. Drain off and discard any remaining liquid from the raisins. Toss the apples, raisins, bread crumbs, ¼ cup of the sugar, the walnuts (if using), cinnamon, salt, and lemon juice in a large bowl to combine.

4. Melt the remaining 5 tablespoons of butter. Place a large sheet of parchment paper horizontally on a work surface. Following the illustrations on page 301, fill and roll the strudel. Place the strudel, seam side down, on an ungreased baking sheet; brush with the remaining butter and sprinkle with the remaining sugar. Cut four 1-inch crosswise vents into the top of the strudel and bake until golden brown, 15 minutes. Cool on the baking sheet on a wire rack until warm, about 40 minutes.

5. Sieve the confectioners' sugar over the strudel. Using 2 large metal spatulas, transfer the strudel to a platter or cutting board, and cut into slices with a serrated knife. Serve with Lightly Sweetened "Crème Fraîche" or whipped cream.

TESTING NOTES:
Why Strudel Shatters
We found that the phyllo on most strudels, including this one, curled and shattered as it cooled. Sprinkling sugar between the layers of phyllo "glues" them together in the oven and prevents this problem.

LIGHTLY SWEETENED "CRÈME FRAÎCHE"
Makes about 1 cup
Adding sour cream to whipped cream mimics the pleasantly tart flavor of the rich French-style whipped cream, crème fraîche—a classic accompaniment to sweet desserts.

½ cup (4 ounces) sour cream
½ cup (4 ounces) heavy cream
⅛ teaspoon vanilla extract
⅛ teaspoon salt
2 teaspoons sugar

Whisk the sour cream and heavy cream in a bowl; set aside at room temperature until thickened to the consistency of yogurt, about 1½ hours. Just before serving, stir in the vanilla, salt, and sugar.

BEST PHYLLO DOUGH

We tried an expensive organic brand of phyllo, but Athens phyllo dough, which is widely available in supermarkets nationwide, yielded the crispiest crust. Note that this phyllo comes in two sizes (see recipe note for using the smaller size).

TECHNIQUE: Assembling Strudel

1. Place a large sheet of parchment or waxed paper on a large work surface, long side toward you. Place I sheet of phyllo on the parchment paper, brush liberally with melted butter, and sprinkle with I teaspoon sugar. Repeat with the remaining 4 sheets of phyllo.

2. Place the apple filling in a 3-inch strip about 2½ inches from the bottom of the phyllo, leaving about 2 inches on either short side.

3. Fold the short ends of the phyllo over the apples.

4. Fold the end closest to you over the apples and continue rolling loosely, using the parchment paper as a guide. Don't roll too tight, as this can cause tearing during baking.

5. Place the finished strudel, seam side down, on an ungreased baking sheet. Brush the strudel with the remaining butter and sprinkle with the remaining I teaspoon sugar.

6. Cut four I-inch vents into the top of the strudel for steam to escape.

EQUIPMENT CORNER: Pastry Brushes

WHEN SILICONE PASTRY BRUSHES FIRST EMERGED, HEAT-resistance (up to 600 degrees) and durability (bristles that don't break off) were their sole selling points. Their performance was poor. More egg wash and melted butter dropped onto the counter than got swabbed onto the food, thanks to thick, sparsely distributed bristles. But recently overhauled designs had us basting chickens, stirring hot sugar syrup, and brushing dough with butter and egg wash to see if the new models could match our favorite natural boar's hair brush, made by Oxo ($5.99).

The Henckels ($11.95), Le Creuset ($9.95), and MIU France ($7.99) brushes were as chunky bristled and non-absorbent as ever. The other models faced the absorbency problem head on. Suction components (resembling bulb basters) provided impressive absorption but poor delivery: Baster-style brushes by Orka ($9.95) and Cuisipro ($10.95) spewed rather than gently swabbed. Decreasing bristle diameter was more effective. The Oxo Good Grips ($6.99), iSi Basics ($7.99), Progressive International ($11.99 for a set), and Williams-Sonoma ($16) models sported sleek 1-millimeter-thick bristles—the losers' bristles were twice as thick—giving them superior absorption. Only the Oxo rivaled our natural-bristled winner (its new sibling), thanks to an ingenious innovation: a row of perforated flaps hidden among the bristles. The flaps trap liquid until the brush hits the food, working in much the same way as the plastic wand included in a child's bubble-blowing kit. Oxo's natural-bristle brush has the slightest edge in absorbency, but superior heat-resistance, easier cleaning, and the promise of never again plucking stray boar's hairs out of pastry dough break the tie in the silicone's favor.

BEST PASTRY BRUSH
The perforated flaps of Oxo's silicone brush trap liquid nicely and clean up easily.

Toasted coconut, sprinkled over the top of our creamy Key Lime Bars, gives the bars an added dimension of flavor and pleasant textural contrast.

FAVORITE CITRUS
CHAPTER 25 *desserts*

Even after the heartiest meal, we find the bracing bite of a citrus dessert welcome. Lemon Bundt cake, glazed with a snowy white icing, is a simple, elegant dessert. But time and again, we are disappointed in its often elusive lemon flavor. Some recipes soak the cake in a sugar syrup flavored with lemon, but we find this makes the cake soggy, ruining its springy fine crumb. We wanted to find a way to infuse Bundt cake with the assertive tang of lemon without marring its texture.

Key lime pie is another favorite citrus dessert, but transporting this pie, which has a delicate, wobbly filling, can be difficult. We wanted to find a way to transform this pie into a bar cookie. Not only would a Key lime bar be more portable, it could also be eaten out of hand, making it a far easier dessert to serve—and eat.

Join us as we infuse one citrus dessert with bright lemony flavor and make another dessert easier than ever to enjoy.

LEMON BUNDT CAKE

WHAT WE WANTED: A moist, lemon Bundt cake with serious citrus flavor.

Bundt cakes have a unique design that allows them to stand on their own, exclusive of fancy fillings or embellishments. This unfussy quality makes them perfect vehicles for showcasing simple flavors, whether rich chocolate or fragrant vanilla.

Lemon Bundt cakes are a different story: Whereas other flavoring agents can simply be increased to heighten their intensity, lemon flavor in cake is fleeting at best. Normally an assertive flavoring agent, lemon juice is drastically muted when exposed to the heat of the oven. And to complicate matters further, this highly acidic juice (few items in the kitchen compare) can wreak havoc on the delicate nature of baked goods.

A sampling of lemon Bundt cakes revealed the various ploys used to compensate for these problems. Some recipes simply drape a cloak of sweet, gloppy frosting over the cake. Others saturate it with a syrupy soak that makes for an overly sweet and sodden cake. Some manage to get a pungent flavor inside the cake by means of lemon extracts and oils, but these products can leave behind unpleasant, artificial aftertastes if used indiscriminately. Flavor issues aside, we were also determined to come up with a cake that stayed true to proper Bundt cake texture: Unlike a light and fluffy layer cake (which is safely anchored by frosting), a Bundt cake must be firm enough to hold its own when sliced and served. At the same time, it should be less rich and compact than the typical pound cake. Could we strike this textural balance yet still achieve pure, vibrant lemon flavor?

Many baking recipes are based on simple formulas, mnemonic tools used to pass down recipes through the generations. Bundt cakes commonly fall into the 1-2-3-4 cake category: 1 cup butter, 2 cups sugar, 3 cups flour, 4 eggs (plus 1 cup milk, a liquid component that sets both layer and Bundt cakes apart from pound cake). Almost two-thirds of the recipes we tried took advantage of this conveniently proportioned formula, which produced just the right volume but also made for a dry, uninspired texture—too crumbly and too coarse.

So began our battery of tests, starting with decreasing the flour and increasing the milk (to moisten) and eggs (for structure), all of which produced dense and gummy cakes. We had more luck increasing the butter, but 2½ sticks (tasters' favorite for richness and tenderness) left behind a greasy residue. We settled for an increase of just 2 tablespoons. Finally, replacing the milk with buttermilk yielded a lighter, more tender crumb and a nice, mild tang.

Most Bundt cakes follow the standard mixing technique of creaming butter and sugar, adding eggs, then alternating flour and liquid until combined. Could we streamline these steps? We tried several variations on the ultra-easy dump-and-stir method. But as soon as we bit into the rubbery, dense cakes, we knew that creaming was indeed necessary to achieve a light and even crumb. The whipping action aerates the batter, contributing lightness to the final cake.

We were now ready to give this cake a hefty boost of flavor. Our instincts still told us that if we used enough lemon juice in the batter, at least some flavor would survive the 45 or 50 minutes in the oven. But after a generous ½ cup of potent lemon juice transformed the cake's texture into a fragile and crumbly mess, we were reminded that playing with acid is no casual affair. (Lemon juice has a pH of about 2.3, even stronger than vinegar.) Acids interfere with the formation of gluten, the protein that's so vital to a cake's structure. The more acidic the batter, the less structure in the cake, and the cakes we were now making were literally fall-apart tender. Fragile was not what we were going for. But we wondered if we could harness acid's gluten-weakening tendency to produce a slightly more delicate crumb. A modest 3 tablespoons of lemon juice did the trick.

Such a paltry amount had absolutely no effect on the

cake's lemon flavor, however. So we turned to our next favorite part of the lemon, the zest (the yellow part of the peel; the white part, the pith, is very bitter and unpleasant). We noticed that most recipes called for a miniscule amount, using the zest from just one lemon to flavor a whole cake. Hoping the zest wouldn't affect texture in the way the juice had, we increased it steadily until tasters cried "Pledge!" We settled for three lemons' worth of zest for a floral, perfumed lemon flavor that was not reminiscent of furniture polish.

We had one final adjustment to make. We had been removing the zest from the lemons using a Microplane rasp grater (which the test kitchen prefers to a box grater or traditional hand-held zester), but the fine strands of zest were showing up in the cake as yellow, fibrous specks. First, we tried mincing the strands with a chef's knife (reducing the zest to tiny flecks). Better, but not perfect; the flecks were still fibrous. The solution was a brief soak in the lemon juice after mincing, which softened the flecks nicely. After all, we wanted the taste of the zest, not the texture.

Now that we'd used as much lemon juice and zest in the cake itself as was palatable, we regrouped and concentrated on the exterior. Many recipes overdid it on the glazing or soaking front; we thought that a minimalist approach might do the trick. Using only basic ingredients—lemon juice and confectioners' sugar—we whisked together a simple glaze. Just the opposite of sweet and cloying, this glaze was too sour and overwhelmed the delicate flavor

of the cake. We tried adding zest (too floral here), butter (too muting), and, finally, buttermilk, as it was already on hand. Supplementing some of the sour juice with the more mild yet tangy buttermilk smoothed out the flavor without dulling the brightness. But this now thick and gooey glaze felt heavy on top of such a tender cake. Thinning the glaze with more juice and buttermilk merely caused it to run off the top and sides, pooling underneath the cake rather than clinging to it. If the cake was still warm, however, the thick glaze melted into the cake and then dried into a thin, mottled shellac. To improve on the presentation, we reserved half of the glaze for use once the cake had cooled; now a more moderate amount of thick, white glaze stood out against the golden crust of the cake.

WHAT WE LEARNED: Buttermilk (rather than milk) is our dairy of choice for lemon Bundt cake. It gives the cake a light, tender crumb. Three tablespoons of lemon juice further ensures a tender texture. For bright lemon flavor, use a generous 3 lemons' worth of grated lemon zest. But to prevent tough strands of zest from marring the texture of the finished cake, mince the grated zest, then soften it in lemon juice. A simple confectioners' sugar icing thinned with lemon juice and buttermilk provides just the right amount of sweetness and smooth, citrusy tang. For best flavor and presentation, brush some of the glaze on the warm cake and reserve the rest to brush on the cake once it's cooled.

LEMON BUNDT CAKE

Serves 12 to 14

You will need between 5 and 6 tablespoons of lemon juice for this recipe. Because the amount of juice can vary from lemon to lemon, we suggest you first measure the juice from the three lemons you have zested, then juice a fourth lemon if necessary. The cake has a light, fluffy texture when eaten the day it is baked, but if well wrapped and held at room temperature overnight its texture becomes more dense—like that of pound cake—the following day.

cake

Grated zest plus 3 tablespoons juice from
3 lemons (see note)

- 3 cups (15 ounces) unbleached all-purpose flour
- 1 teaspoon baking powder
- ½ teaspoon baking soda
- 1 teaspoon salt
- 1 teaspoon vanilla extract
- ¾ cup buttermilk, preferably low-fat
- 3 large eggs plus 1 large yolk, at room temperature
- 18 tablespoons (2¼ sticks) unsalted butter, at room temperature
- 2 cups (14 ounces) sugar

glaze

- 2–3 tablespoons lemon juice (see note)
- 1 tablespoon buttermilk
- 2 cups (8 ounces) confectioners' sugar

1. FOR THE CAKE: Adjust an oven rack to the lower-middle position and heat the oven to 350 degrees. Spray a 12-cup Bundt pan with nonstick baking spray with flour (alternatively, brush the pan with a mixture of 1 tablespoon flour and 1 tablespoon melted butter). Mince the lemon zest to a fine paste (you should have about 2 tablespoons). Combine the zest and lemon juice in a small bowl; set aside to soften, 10 to 15 minutes.

2. Whisk the flour, baking powder, baking soda, and salt in a large bowl. Combine the lemon juice mixture, vanilla, and buttermilk in a medium bowl. In a small bowl, gently whisk the eggs and yolk to combine. In a standing mixer fitted with a flat beater, cream the butter and sugar at medium-high speed until pale and fluffy, about 3 minutes; scrape down the sides of the bowl with a rubber spatula. Reduce to medium speed and add half of the eggs, mixing until incorporated, about 15 seconds. Repeat with the remaining eggs; scrape down the bowl again. Reduce to low speed; add about one-third of the flour mixture, followed by half of the buttermilk mixture, mixing until just incorporated after each addition (about 5 seconds). Repeat using half of the remaining flour mixture and all of the remaining buttermilk mixture. Scrape down the bowl and add the remaining flour mixture; mix at medium-low speed until the batter is thoroughly combined, about 15 seconds. Remove the bowl from the mixer and fold the batter once or twice with a rubber spatula to incorporate any remaining flour. Scrape into the prepared pan.

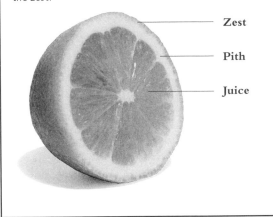
3. Bake until the top is golden brown and a wooden skewer or toothpick inserted into the center comes out with no crumbs attached, 45 to 50 minutes.

4. FOR THE GLAZE: While the cake is baking, whisk 2 tablespoons of the lemon juice, buttermilk, and confectioners' sugar until smooth, adding more lemon juice gradually as needed until the glaze is thick but still pourable (the mixture should leave a faint trail across the bottom of the mixing bowl when drizzled from a whisk). Cool the cake in the pan on a wire rack set over a baking sheet for 10 minutes, then invert the cake directly onto the rack. Pour half of the glaze over the warm cake and let cool for 1 hour; pour the remaining glaze evenly over the top of the cake and continue to cool to room temperature, at least 2 hours. Cut into slices and serve.

KEY LIME BARS

WHAT WE WANTED: The tangy richness and bright citrusy flavor of Key lime pie, made portable in a bar cookie.

Key lime pie is a brilliant pairing of rich and refreshing, sweet and tart, all in a buttery, crisp crumb crust. But what this classic dessert offers in elegance and simplicity it lacks in portability: We wanted a Key lime bar—all the appealing qualities of Key lime pie but without the need for a fork. Turning a round pie into square cookies shouldn't be too hard, right?

To get our footing, we started out with two recipes: one for Key lime bars made with cream cheese (typical of many recipes), the other for Key lime pie. The bars with cream cheese were heavy and dense, like a lime cheesecake. (Not quite what we had in mind.) As for the pie, we transformed it into bars by baking it in a square baking dish. Naturally, they set the flavor standard, but for a cookie, the filling was too soft and supple, the crust too thick, dry, and crumbly. Clearly, some fine-tuning would be required to get this transformation to come out right.

First things first: the crust. A graham cracker crust is traditional for a Key lime pie, so it was the obvious choice. But we were not enamored of the graham crust. Its flavor was too assertive (especially given the amount we needed to make a bar we could hold in our hands), and it didn't really complement the filling. We swapped in animal cracker crumbs, the test kitchen's crust of choice for coconut cream pie. Their more neutral flavor placed the lime flavor squarely in the limelight. Whereas a pie crust can be tender and delicate, the crust for the bars needed sturdiness; this meant increasing the butter, but not so much that the crust would become greasy. Brown sugar outdid granulated because it gave the crust a slightly richer, rounder flavor. As with all crumb crusts, this one required prebaking to firm it up, and 325 degrees proved the best temperature for producing an evenly browned crust.

With the crust firmly in place, we focused on the filling. Key lime pie filling is an easy mixture of sweetened condensed milk, lime juice, lime zest, and, more often than not, eggs. We already knew that the test kitchen's Key lime pie filling didn't have a texture firm enough for bar cookies, but we were determined to make it work with some minor retooling. Leaving the condensed milk and lime juice in place, we tried everything that we thought might set the texture. The filling called for four egg yolks; we decreased the yolks, we added more, we omitted the yolks altogether. We tried whole eggs, no eggs, then a few egg whites, then several whites. That soft, pudding-like texture seemed inescapable. Next, we reached for the flour canister, thinking that some starch might help set things up. What the filling then had was a pasty, granular texture.

We took a moment to regroup. Then came the epiphany. We recalled the cheesecake lime bars that we'd made at the outset. The filling had neither eggs nor starch, yet it was sturdy—rigid, even. We made batches of lime bars with 8, 6, and 4 ounces of cream cheese incorporated into the filling. These were all thick and gluey, but we were onto

something. We took the cream cheese down to 3, then 2 ounces. And there they were: lime bars with a firm, creamy, rich, finger-food-friendly filling. One whole 14-ounce can of sweetened condensed milk provided all the sweetness the filling needed. We tried various amounts of lime juice, but ½ cup was best. It was enough to make the lime flavor sparkle without scaring away those with low tartness thresholds and without thinning the filling. Concerning lime juice, fresh-squeezed Key lime juice, with its heady fragrance and pleasant acidity, was the favorite by a narrow margin; still, regular fresh lime juice held its own, favored by some for standing up to the buttery crust and rich, creamy filling. A tablespoon of grated lime zest added lime essence; we minced it to keep its texture from being an annoyance. As for mixing the filling, it was easily accomplished by hand. Some bar recipes include some sort of streusel or crunchy topping. A streusel didn't make sense, but we took a cue from the tropics and experimented with a toasted-coconut topping, which added a subtle textural contrast and more depth of flavor. The test kitchen was split over whether this topping was an improvement, so we left it optional. Finally, we had distilled the essence of a billowy slice of Key lime pie into a tidy, portable bar. Who said it's not cool to be square?

WHAT WE LEARNED: For a not-too-sweet cookie crust that stands up to the citrus filling without overwhelming it, use animal cracker crumbs (instead of the typical graham cracker crumbs), and enrich the crumbs with butter and brown sugar for rich, rounded flavor and sturdy texture. To prevent a too-wobbly filling, fortify the mixture with tangy cream cheese. For a filling with fresh citrus flavor, use a combination of fresh-squeezed Key lime juice (although regular lime juice can be substituted) along with grated lime zest. Be sure to mince the grated zest, to prevent strands from marring the smooth texture of the filling. And, if desired, sweetened shredded coconut, toasted to deepen its flavor, can be sprinkled on top of the bars for an added dimension of flavor and textural contrast.

KEY LIME BARS

Makes sixteen 2-inch bars

If you cannot find fresh Key limes, use regular (Persian) limes. Do not use bottled lime juice. Grate the zest from the limes before juicing them, avoiding the bitter white pith that lies just beneath the outermost skin. The optional coconut garnish adds textural interest and tames the lime flavor for those who find it too intense. The recipe can be doubled and baked in a 13 by 9-inch baking pan; you will need a double layer of extra-wide foil for the pan (each sheet about 20 inches in length) and should increase the baking times by a minute or two.

crust

5	ounces animal crackers
3	tablespoons packed brown sugar (light or dark)
	Pinch salt
4	tablespoons unsalted butter, melted and cooled slightly

filling

2	ounces cream cheese, at room temperature
1	tablespoon grated lime zest, minced
	Pinch salt
1	(14-ounce) can sweetened condensed milk
1	egg yolk
½	cup fresh lime juice, from about 20 Key limes or about 3 Persian limes

garnish (optional)

¾	cup sweetened shredded coconut, toasted until golden and crisp

1. Adjust an oven rack to the middle position and heat the oven to 325 degrees. Cut about a 12-inch length of extra-wide heavy-duty foil; fold the cut edges back to form a 7½-inch width. With the folded sides facing down, fit the foil securely into the bottom and up the sides of an 8-inch-square baking pan, allowing the excess to overhang the pan sides. Spray the foil with nonstick cooking spray.

2. TO MAKE THE CRUST: In the workbowl of a food processor, pulse the animal crackers until broken down, about ten 1-second pulses; process the crumbs until evenly fine, about 10 seconds (you should have about 1¼ cups crumbs). Add the brown sugar and salt; process to combine, ten to twelve 1-second pulses (if large sugar lumps remain, break them apart with your fingers). Drizzle the butter over the crumbs and pulse until the crumbs are evenly moistened with the butter, about ten 1-second pulses. Press the crumbs evenly and firmly into the bottom of the prepared pan. Bake until deep golden brown, 18 to 20 minutes. Cool on a wire rack while making the filling. Do not turn off the oven.

3. TO MAKE THE FILLING: While the crust cools, in medium bowl, stir the cream cheese, zest, and salt with a rubber spatula until softened, creamy, and thoroughly combined. Add the sweetened condensed milk and whisk vigorously until incorporated and no lumps of cream cheese remain; whisk in the egg yolk. Add the lime juice and whisk gently until incorporated (the mixture will thicken slightly).

4. TO ASSEMBLE AND BAKE: Pour the filling into the crust; spread to the corners and smooth the surface with a rubber spatula. Bake until set and the edges begin to pull away slightly from the sides, 15 to 20 minutes. Cool on a wire rack to room temperature, 1 to 1½ hours. Cover with foil and refrigerate until thoroughly chilled, at least 2 hours.

5. Loosen the edges with a paring knife and lift the bars from the baking pan using the foil extensions; cut the bars into 16 squares. Sprinkle with the toasted coconut, if using, and serve. (Leftovers can be refrigerated up to 2 days; the crust will soften slightly. Let the bars stand at room temperature about 15 minutes before serving.)

VARIATION

TRIPLE CITRUS BARS

Using three types of citrus (orange, lemon, and lime) gives these bars a slightly more complex, floral flavor.

Follow the recipe for Key Lime Bars, substituting 1½ teaspoons each grated lime zest, lemon zest, and orange zest (mince zest after measuring) for the lime zest, and using 6 tablespoons lime juice, 1 tablespoon lemon juice, and 1 tablespoon orange juice in place of all lime juice.

TASTING LAB: Lime Juice

KEY LIMES ARE A TINY, YELLOWISH VARIETY THAT GROWS only in tropical locales (like the Florida Keys, from which they got their name). Key lime aficionados herald the fruit's "distinctive" flavor and fragrance compared with conventional Persian limes, but we wondered if our tasters could tell the difference in a blind taste test.

Sampled plain, the Key lime juice tasted slightly less tart than its Persian counterpart, and a quick lab test confirmed that impression (the juice from the conventional limes had a lower pH than the Key lime juice, indicating higher acidity). When we made Key lime bars with both varieties, once again the Persian-lime version tasted a bit more tart, though tasters were split over which variety made the better bar. The deciding factor may be the amount of work involved: To get the half cup of lime juice called for in our bar recipe, we had to squeeze three Persian limes. With the Key limes, it took almost 20!

Both Key lime juice and regular lime juice are sold presqueezed in shelf-stable bottles, and we wondered whether these would do in a pinch. The short answer? No way. The four brands we tried were at best "bracingly bitter," and, in some cases, "just plain rancid."

Key Limes
Subtle tartness,
skimpy yield

Regular Limes
Bracing tartness,
generous yield

SCIENCE DESK: The "Magic" of Sweetened Condensed Milk

THESE DAYS, CONVENIENCE FOOD PRODUCTS ARE everywhere, but the trend is hardly new. Back in 1856, American home cooks began taking advantage of sweetened condensed milk, a shelf-stable dairy product based on discoveries made centuries earlier by cooks in India and Latin America. Packed with calories and nutrients, this "magical" product has been credited with everything from reducing the infant mortality rate to nourishing Civil War soldiers. But today it's mostly about dessert-making convenience: Instead of reducing milk and sugar, you can just pop open a can—and there's no expiration date.

Sweetened condensed milk is made commercially by flash-heating fresh milk and evaporating it, using a specialized vacuum drier (that's the "condensed" part). Once granulated sugar is added, the preservation process begins. The water-hungry granulated sugar and the natural sugar in the milk (lactose) pull in moisture from bacteria, killing them off in the process. The result is milk thickened to a gooey syrup—an ideal consistency for many desserts.

In our Key lime bar recipe, sweetened condensed milk offers an additional advantage: it keeps the filling from curdling. Curdling occurs when an acid (like lime juice) comes in contact with milk's protein strands and causes them to unwind and become entangled. In sweetened condensed milk, the sugar molecules coat these protein strands, which keeps them from entangling. If we'd used fresh milk instead, the creamy texture of the filling would have been compromised.

TESTING NOTES: Does Fat Content in Sweetened Condensed Milk Make a Difference?

In our recipe for Key Lime Bars, sweetened condensed milk plays a key role in keeping the filling creamy and sweet. Because condensed milk comes in full-fat, low-fat, and fat-free varieties, we wondered if the fat, or lack of, would make a difference in our bars.

Reduced-fat and nonfat sweetened condensed milk are made with low-fat or nonfat milk, with the exception of one brand, which contains soybean oil. We prepared Key lime bars with full-fat condensed milk and pitted them against bars made with the reduced and nonfat condensed milk. Surely our tasters would detect the difference in the lower-fat products, right? To our surprise, tasters were just as happy eating desserts fattened up with soybean oil and reduced-fat products, although they did notice a more assertive lime flavor in the latter. In the end, any of these sweetened condensed milk products will do. Our advice? Stick with the whole milk option for maximum creaminess, but the leaner options won't lower the bar.

Tasters liked Key Lime Bars made with low-fat and nonfat sweetened condensed milk (left and center), but for maximum creaminess choose whole sweetened condensed milk (right).

Julia enjoys a slice of light cheesecake that has a rich flavor and creamy texture reminiscent of the full-fat original.

LIGHTER
CHAPTER 26
desserts

While a crisp apple or bowl of juicy berries makes an admirable end to a meal, there's an allure to baked desserts that is hard to resist. But many desserts have a lot of fat and calories; for most of us, they should be more the occasional indulgence than regular weeknight fare. We wanted to come up with recipes for two classic desserts, carrot cake and cheesecake, that would make them both light enough and good enough to enjoy most any day of the week.

Many light carrot cakes look like the real thing, but one bite quickly dispels the notion. Not only dry but also heavy and dense, these cakes may be "light" when it comes to fat and calories but not when it comes to texture. We wanted tender cake, sweet and lightly spiced. And we wanted our cake to be slathered in a thick, creamy frosting.

The recipes we tested for light cheesecake were no better than the carrot cakes—in fact, they were worse. Most were plagued by a rubbery texture and pasty, Spackle-like consistency. And in place of the lightly sweetened, tangy flavor of a full-fat cheesecake, these lightened cheesecakes were tinged with off, artificial flavors. We would have to do some serious testing to come up with a lightened cheesecake that would pass muster among tasters. Join us as we uncover the secrets to low-fat desserts that you'll really want to eat.

LIGHT CARROT CAKE

WHAT WE WANTED: A lightened version of moist, lightly spiced carrot cake—complete with a thick slather of sweet cream cheese frosting.

A relic of the health food craze, carrot cake was once heralded for its use of vegetable oil in place of butter and use of carrots as a natural sweetener. But was it ever a healthy cake? With most tipping the scales at 500 calories and 31 grams of fat per slice, carrot cake seemed ripe for a test kitchen makeover. We wanted to create a truly great carrot cake, one where the natural sweetness of the carrots takes center stage. Most important, it had to be moist and rich without being soggy and greasy from an overabundance of fat.

Working with a basic carrot cake recipe, our first mission was to find a way to reduce the amount of fat. After some initial testing, it was obvious that tasters preferred oil rather than butter for its cleaner, subtler presence in the cake. But most typical versions of carrot cake contain around 1½ cups oil—not our idea of low fat. To find out how much oil we could remove without compromising the flavor or structure of the cake, we gradually reduced the oil ¼ cup at a time. Surprisingly, we found that the cake made with only ½ cup of oil was as moist, tender, and flavorful as some of the full-fat versions containing three times as much oil. Most carrot cake recipes also called for four to five eggs per cake, but we found that three eggs gave the cake a slight spring and a tender crumb without adding unnecessary fat.

Next we focused on the sugar. The cake clearly benefited from both granulated and light brown sugar, the former giving the cake clean sweetness and the latter bringing out the warmth of the spices. After trying different ratios of the two sugars, we settled on 1 cup of granulated sugar and 1 cup of brown sugar. This 50/50 ratio is very different from traditional carrot cake recipes, which use, at most, a third as

much brown sugar as granulated. We found, however, that the additional brown sugar guaranteed that the cake would stay moist, even with the drastic reduction in oil.

Now that we had significantly reduced the amount of fat and calories, we could turn our attention to the other key ingredients. We knew we wanted our cake to contain enough carrots to confirm at first glance that it was indeed carrot cake. We flatly rejected any idea of first boiling, steaming, or pureeing the carrots, as was called for in some recipes. It was just too much work, and we thought that this should be a simple recipe. Grating the carrots was clearly the way to go; the carrots steam and soften in the cake as it bakes so that no annoying, stringy bits mar the cake's finished texture. It took a few failed efforts before we realized that just the right amount of carrots was paramount, because their high moisture content could determine whether the cake was perfectly moist or downright soggy. After baking cakes with as few as 1 cup grated carrots (no carrot presence) and as many as 5 cups (soaking wet cake), we found that 3 cups (1 pound of carrots) was the perfect amount to give the cake a pleasantly moist texture and just enough carrot flavor.

For the dry ingredients, all-purpose flour worked better than cake flour (the latter proved too delicate for this sturdy American classic), and we used 2½ cups as the base for our tests. We quickly found that this cake would need healthy amounts of baking soda and baking powder, 1 teaspoon and 1¼ teaspoons, respectively (nearly twice the amount found in many recipes), to give it sufficient lift and a beautiful brown color. While many recipes use handfuls of every baking spice in the pantry, we found that a conservative touch with cinnamon, along with a little help from nutmeg and cloves, won the approval of tasters.

It was time to perfect our mixing technique. Just as we would with a butter-based cake, we tried creaming the oil into the sugar and then beating in the eggs with an electric mixer before adding the dry ingredients and carrots. The cake tasted good, but the bottom of the cake was much too dense and wet. We then wondered if we could use a food processor to mix the cake, and tried processing the eggs and

oil together with the sugar, before stirring in the flour and carrots. This was better; however, the texture of the cake was still a bit too heavy and leaden. Moving back to the electric mixer, we wondered if beating some air into the eggs before adding the oil, flour, and carrots would have any impact on the cake. You bet it did—no more soggy bottom, no more heavy texture. Because we had whipped air into the batter by way of the eggs, the cake now had a moist, delicate crumb and a very nice rise.

Our cake was now good enough to eat on its own, but there was no way we were going to pass up the frosting. Traditional cream cheese frostings consist of cream cheese, butter, and confectioners' sugar—extremely tasty, but hardly healthy. We were able to reduce some fat by replacing the full-fat cream cheese with Neufchâtel reduced-fat cream cheese (other lower-fat substitutions such as nonfat and light cream cheese made the frosting runny and gummy). We added the requisite butter and confectioners' sugar and whirred the mixture together in a food processor. We wanted to lower the fat further, so we tried removing the butter from the frosting, but its absence made the frosting too loose. The solution turned out to be the mixing method. Instead of mixing the cream cheese and sugar in the food processor, which overworked the mixture into a soupy mess, we mixed it by hand. This decidedly low-tech method allowed us to control the consistency and end up with a frosting that was spreadable. The result? Even with the addition of our cream cheese frosting, this carrot cake has significantly less fat and calories than the original cake alone. Add to that a healthy dose of carrots, and this is one dessert we can feel good about.

WHAT WE LEARNED: To cut the fat in the cake, reduce the oil from 1½ cups to just ½ cup and reduce the eggs from five to three. It's necessary to whip air into the eggs to keep the cake from being too dense and leaden. For the frosting, replacing the cream cheese and butter with Neufchâtel reduced-fat cream cheese and mixing it by hand gave us a thick and creamy frosting with less fat.

LIGHT CARROT CAKE WITH LIGHT CREAM CHEESE FROSTING

Serves 16

You can either use the large holes of a box grater or the large-holed shredding disk in a food processor for grating the carrots. Use a metal cake pan, not a glass or Pyrex pan, for best results. This cake is terrific with a dusting of confectioners' sugar, or for a special treat try it with our Light Cream Cheese Frosting (recipe follows).

	Vegetable oil spray
2½	cups (12½ ounces) unbleached all-purpose flour
1¼	teaspoons baking powder
1	teaspoon baking soda
1¼	teaspoons ground cinnamon
½	teaspoon ground nutmeg
⅛	teaspoon ground cloves
½	teaspoon salt
3	large eggs
1	cup packed (7 ounces) light brown sugar
1	cup (7 ounces) granulated sugar
½	cup vegetable oil
1	pound carrots (about 6 medium), peeled and grated (about 3 cups)
	Light Cream Cheese Frosting (recipe follows)

1. Adjust an oven rack to the middle position and heat the oven to 350 degrees. Lightly coat a 13 by 9-inch metal baking pan with vegetable oil spray, then line the bottom with parchment paper.

2. Whisk the flour, baking powder, baking soda, spices, and salt together in a medium bowl; set aside. Using an electric mixer, beat the eggs and sugars together in a medium bowl until they turn thick and creamy, 1 to 3 minutes. Turn the mixer to low and slowly whip in the oil until thoroughly combined and emulsified, 30 to 60 seconds. Sift half the flour mixture over the batter and gently mix in. Repeat once more with the remaining flour mixture and continue

to whisk the batter gently until most of the lumps are gone (do not overmix). Using a rubber spatula, gently stir in the carrots.

3. Pour the batter into the prepared pan and smooth the top. Bake until a toothpick inserted into the center of the cake comes out with a few moist crumbs attached, 35 to 40 minutes, rotating the pan halfway through baking (do not overbake). Cool the cake in the pan for 10 minutes, then invert the cake onto a wire rack and remove the parchment paper. Flip the cake right-side up, and cool completely on a wire rack, about 2 hours, before frosting (if desired) and serving.

LIGHT CREAM CHEESE FROSTING

Makes about 2 cups

Be sure to mix the frosting by hand—an electric mixer or food processor will turn the frosting soupy.

12	ounces Neufchâtel (⅓ less fat) cream cheese, softened but still cool
1	teaspoon vanilla extract
1½	cups (6 ounces) confectioners' sugar

Mix the cream cheese and vanilla together in a large bowl with a rubber spatula. Add the confectioners' sugar and stir until thoroughly combined and smooth.

NEW YORK-STYLE CHEESECAKE

WHAT WE WANTED: A lighter cheesecake that could stand up to the full-fat version—rich and creamy. And this light cheesecake would need to be so good, we'd want to make it again and again.

Of all the desserts that people long for in a low-fat form, cheesecake is probably the most popular—but it's also the most difficult to lighten. Since just one modest slice has more fat than most people should consume in a day, never mind in one dessert, cheesecake would require a serious makeover, and we had our doubts that it would be a successful one.

Low-fat recipes in hand, we headed into the kitchen to get a handle on the landscape of low-fat alternatives. Just about every low-fat cookbook has tried to create some version of a reduced-fat cheesecake. The result is usually a rubbery, gummy mess, chock-full of artificial and off-flavors. And it's no wonder: Cheesecake is pretty much 100 percent fat in a graham cracker crust. Removing the fat would take away everything we love about the ideal New York cheesecake: its thick, smooth, satiny, creamy core, a velvety exterior, and sweet and tangy richness throughout. Or would it?

A standard New York cheesecake contains 580 calories and 43 grams of fat per slice. These jaw-dropping numbers mostly come from the whopping 2½ pounds of cream cheese that make up the base. In order to trim some fat it was obvious we were going to have to find an alternative to the cream cheese. We had hoped that we could simply substitute nonfat cream cheese for the full-fat cheese, but we quickly realized this was not the case. Cheesecakes made this way had an unsettling gummy consistency and a dry, chalky texture. Using all Neufchâtel reduced-fat cream cheese still gave us a cheesecake with a high amount of fat. Light cream cheese was a better alternative but the flavor was still off. Instead, we knew we'd need to cut one of these lower-fat cream cheeses with something else. We tried tofu, ricotta, and low-fat mayonnaise. In each case the cakes were beyond

disappointing. Either they tasted terrible or they had a texture that bore a striking resemblance to linoleum. That was until we tried cottage cheese.

We had seen several recipes with cottage cheese, but had dismissed this ingredient because we were concerned it would make the filling grainy. But then we wondered, what would happen if we processed the cottage cheese? We put a pound of 1 percent milk fat cottage cheese in the food processor and let it run until it was perfectly smooth. The processed cottage cheese with a pound of light cream cheese was a great combination. The filling was smooth and rich with just the right density. There was one drawback, however. It was a little loose from the liquid in the cottage cheese. We simply spooned the cottage cheese into a bowl lined with paper towels and allowed them to draw off some of the moisture while we prepared the other ingredients in the cheesecake. This worked perfectly, wicking away the majority of the moisture.

With the cottage cheese–light cream cheese combo we had an ideal base and knew we were on a roll, but we also knew it was missing that trademark tang that is essential to any great New York cheesecake. Most cheesecakes use sour cream to provide this tang, but when we tried to substitute no-fat and low-fat sour cream we found that the cakes had a tacky texture and odd aftertaste. We then tried yogurt, and while it certainly provided the tang we sought, the yogurt was too watery and made a cake that was too runny. Someone in the test kitchen then suggested yogurt cheese, also called labne, which is essentially plain yogurt drained of its whey. It was the perfect solution. It offered a touch of tartness and helped give the cheesecake a smoother, creamier texture without making it too wet. We decided to make our own yogurt cheese using low-fat plain yogurt (see page 319).

Eggs help bind a cheesecake, giving it structure and a creamy texture; they also contribute a fair amount of fat. While some cheesecakes use a combination of whole egg

and yolks, we decided to stick with just whole eggs in order to get the most structure with the least fat. We tried as few as one and as many as six whole eggs, and found that three eggs were the right number. Three eggs helped build a firm, rigid structure and gave our cheesecake the requisite dense, velvety texture without adding an excessive amount of fat.

Our cheesecake was now on its way and suddenly there was renewed interest among the once-doubtful test kitchen staff: Volunteer tasters were beginning to crawl out of the woodwork. Perfecting the flavor of the cheesecake was easy. Lemon juice is an ingredient commonly found in New York cheesecake and we liked the way it brightened the other flavors in our cheesecake, but found it clashed slightly with the already tangy filling. For us, lemon zest was a better route. It provided a floral note and subtle tang without being too aggressive. Just a bit of salt (cream cheese already contains a good dose of sodium) and a couple teaspoons of vanilla extract rounded out the flavors. Simple was decidedly better—everyone in the test kitchen appreciated this minimalist approach.

With the filling behind us we could now turn our attention to the all-important graham cracker crust. In order to keep fat and calories to a minimum we considered a simple dusting of crumbs on the bottom of the cheesecake, but tasters were unanimous in their protest. They wanted a crust with more presence. We tried making a thicker crust with low-fat graham crackers, a tablespoon of butter, and no sugar. But this crust was very wet. We tried brushing the crust with egg whites in order to form a protective barrier, but this gave the crust an odd, spongy texture. It was obvious we needed the butter to provide a moisture barrier, and we would have to use more of it. We increased the butter a tablespoon at a time, and settled on 4 tablespoons of butter. This amount gave the crust a rich, toasty flavor and crisp texture. Although this was more fat than we ideally wanted in the crust, we would rather have a little bit more fat than a soggy bottom.

When it came to baking the cheesecake we preferred the standard New York method—500 degrees for about 10 minutes, then 200 degrees for about an hour and a half. This method yielded the nut-brown surface that is a distinguishing mark of an exemplary New York cheesecake. It also produced a lovely graded texture, soft and creamy at the center and firm and dry at the periphery. To ensure a properly baked cheesecake, we found it best to bake the cake to an internal temperature of 150 degrees. Although it may seem unnecessary, an instant-read thermometer inserted into the cake is the most reliable means of judging the doneness of the cheesecake. After the cheesecake had chilled, we knew we had achieved perfection. It sliced into a neat slab with a cleanly set center texture—not a wet, sloppy one. Each slice kept its shape, and each bite felt satiny on the tongue—cheesecake heaven. And where did we end up in terms of fat and calories? We trimmed 180 calories from the original to end up with 400 (340 without topping) calories per slice and slashed the fat by 30 grams, for a total of 13 grams! Not bad at all.

WHAT WE LEARNED: To cut the fat, replace full-fat cream cheese and sour cream with a combination of light cream cheese, low-fat cottage cheese, and an unusual ingredient—low-fat yogurt cheese (yogurt that has been drained of its whey). Lighten the cake further by using fewer whole eggs instead of the typical combination of whole eggs and yolks. Lemon zest (not lemon juice) brightens the creamy filling. Pureeing the filling in a food processor gives the cheesecake an ultra-smooth texture. For a crisp crust with great buttery flavor, combine graham cracker crumbs and sugar with just 4 tablespoons of melted butter. To accurately determine doneness, use an instant-read thermometer and remove the cheesecake once the temperature reads 150 degrees.

LIGHT NEW YORK-STYLE CHEESECAKE

Serves 12

Be sure to use light cream cheese in this recipe; it is most commonly sold in tubs, not blocks. You can buy low-fat yogurt cheese (also called labne) or make your own with low-fat yogurt—allow about 12 hours for the yogurt to drain (see below right for instructions). For a more lemony flavor, use the increased amount of lemon zest.

crust

- 9 whole graham crackers (5 ounces), broken into rough pieces and processed in a food processor to fine, even crumbs (about 1¼ cups)
- 4 tablespoons unsalted butter, melted
- 1 tablespoon sugar

filling

- 1 pound 1 percent cottage cheese
- 1 pound light cream cheese, at room temperature
- 8 ounces (1 cup) low-fat yogurt cheese (see note)
- 1½ cups (10½ ounces) sugar
- ¼ teaspoon salt
- ½–1 teaspoon grated zest from 1 lemon
- 1 tablespoon vanilla extract
- 3 large eggs, at room temperature
  Vegetable oil spray
  Fresh Strawberry Topping (optional), recipe follows

1. FOR THE CRUST: Adjust an oven rack to the middle position and heat the oven to 325 degrees. In a medium bowl, stir together the graham cracker crumbs, melted butter, and sugar until combined. Transfer the mixture to a 9-inch springform pan and press evenly into the pan bottom. Bake the crust until fragrant and beginning to brown, 10 to 15 minutes. Cool on a wire rack. Increase the temperature to 500 degrees.

2. FOR THE FILLING: Meanwhile, line a medium bowl with a clean dish towel or several layers of paper towels. Spoon the cottage cheese into the bowl and let drain for 30 minutes.

3. Process the drained cottage cheese in a food processor until smooth and no visible lumps remain, about 1 minute, scraping down the workbowl as needed. Add the cream cheese and yogurt cheese and continue to process until smooth, 1 to 2 minutes, scraping down the sides of the bowl as needed. Add the sugar, salt, lemon zest, and vanilla and continue to process until smooth, about 1 minute, scraping down the sides of the bowl as needed. With the processor running, add the eggs one at a time and continue to process until smooth.

4. Being careful not to disturb the baked crust, spray the insides of the springform pan with vegetable oil spray. Set

---

TECHNIQUE: Making Yogurt Cheese

Line a fine-mesh strainer set over a deep container with 3 paper coffee filters or a double layer of cheesecloth. Spoon 2 cups plain low-fat yogurt into the lined strainer, cover, and refrigerate. After 10 to 12 hours, about 1 cup of the liquid will have drained and the yogurt will have a creamy, cream cheese–like consistency. Transfer the yogurt cheese to a covered container and refrigerate—it will keep for about 1 week.

the springform pan on a rimmed baking sheet. Pour the processed cheese mixture into the cooled crust.

5. Bake for 10 minutes. Without opening the oven door, reduce the oven temperature to 200 degrees and continue to bake until an instant-read thermometer inserted into the center of the cheesecake reads 150 degrees, about 1½ hours.

6. Transfer the cake to a wire rack and run a paring knife around the edge of the cake to loosen. Cool the cake at room temperature until barely warm, 2½ to 3 hours, running a paring knife around the edge of the cake every hour or so. Wrap the pan tightly in plastic wrap and refrigerate until cold, at least 3 hours.

7. To unmold the cheesecake, wrap a hot kitchen towel around the springform pan and let stand for 10 minutes. Remove the sides of the pan and blot any excess moisture from the top of the cheesecake with paper towels. Let the cheesecake stand at room temperature about 30 minutes before slicing.

FRESH STRAWBERRY TOPPING

Makes about 3 cups

A ruby-colored, glazed strawberry topping is the classic accompaniment to New York cheesecake. This topping is best served the same day it is made.

1	pound strawberries, washed, hulled, and cut lengthwise into ¼- to ⅜-inch wedges
¼	cup sugar
	Pinch salt
½	cup strawberry jam
1	tablespoon juice from 1 lemon

1. Toss the berries, sugar, and salt in a medium bowl and let stand until the berries have released some juice and the sugar has dissolved, about 30 minutes, tossing occasionally to combine.

2. Process the jam in a food processor until smooth, about 8 seconds. Transfer the jam to a small saucepan and bring to a simmer over medium-high heat. Simmer, stirring frequently, until dark and no longer frothy, about 3 minutes. Stir in the lemon juice, then gently stir the warm jam into the strawberries. Cover with plastic wrap and refrigerate until cold, at least 2 hours or up to 12. To serve, spoon a portion of the topping over individual slices of cheesecake.

TASTING LAB:
Supermarket Whole Bean Coffee

IT'S EASIER THAN EVER TO GET A DECENT CUP OF COFFEE made with fresh-roasted beans; just go to your local coffeehouse—there seems to be one, such as Starbucks, on almost every street corner these days. And, conveniently, you can also buy whole beans at many of these same coffeehouses for at-home brewing. But that convenience comes with a price, so when we noticed whole bean coffee at the supermarket, we wondered if it would measure up, with perhaps

were striking. Some coffees were strong and smoky, others tasted light and "chocolaty," still others boasted hints of caramel or molasses. For a few of the brands, the tasting sheets overflowed with invective decrying bitter, rancid, or harsh qualities. Most surprising, Starbucks came in not first but fifth out of the eight samples. "Burnt, with a bitter aftertaste," said one taster. "Like gnawing on charcoal," said another. Top honors went instead to Green Mountain Roasters and Eight O'Clock, which tasters found complex and well-balanced.

Those of us who are Starbucks regulars were puzzled by the brand's poor performance. And we weren't convinced that we'd been blithely sucking down "burnt coffee" twice a day. So we devised one more test—a tasting of coffee with milk. Why? An informal poll revealed that more than two-thirds of the test kitchen's staff add milk to their coffee, and it seemed only fair to try the brands that way, too. So we brewed up eight more pots, added ¾ cup warmed whole milk to each, and summoned 25 (chart says 20 staffers) soon-to-be-jittery tasters into the test kitchen for another tour.

Sure enough, preferences changed. This time, Green Mountain and Eight O'Clock, the plain-coffee champs, ended up in the lower ranks—bland and insipid, according to tasters. In contrast, Starbucks landed near the top, along with Millstone and Seattle's Best, two other fairly assertive coffees. The bitter, burnt notes that had menaced tasters in the first round were suddenly "robust" and "complex" when tempered by the milk. Simply watered down? Not quite. Additional research revealed that the proteins in milk (and cream) bind some of the bitter-tasting phenolic compounds, reducing the bitterness and intensity of the coffee flavor.

So far we had based our analysis on tasters' subjective descriptions. But there was a better way. In general, the longer a coffee bean roasts, the darker and more strongly flavored it becomes. Although it's possible to make a rough comparison of roast darkness by eyeballing alone, experts use an instrument called an Agtron to measure exactly how

some change to spare. Our trip to the supermarket had us staring down an aisle boasting several brands of whole bean coffee. Some even hailed from coffeehouses like Starbucks and others were straight-ahead supermarket brands, priced per pound at less than what you might pay for a single cup of coffeehouse coffee.

For our tasting, we bought eight whole bean coffees and for each brand we chose the "house blend," or whatever medium roast was widely available. Test kitchen staffers tried the coffees brewed regular strength. The differences much light the beans reflect. The higher the Agtron reading (that is, the more light the beans reflect), the lighter the roast: An Agtron reading of 85 would indicate an ultra-light, almost tea-like coffee; the darkest French roast out there would be closer to 15.

To find out how roast darkness lined up with taster preference, we sent the samples to a lab that specializes in coffee analysis. The Agtron readings differed markedly. From darkest to lightest: Starbucks (34.9), Millstone (36.5), Seattle's Best (40.0), Chock Full o' Nuts (40.3), Green Mountain (48.0), Folgers (48.9), Eight O'Clock (51.4), and Dunkin' Donuts (59.9).

From these data, we made two important discoveries. First, according to coffee-industry standards, the four darkest coffees in our lineup (Starbucks through Chock Full o' Nuts) are considered "dark" roasts, while the remaining four (Green Mountain through Dunkin' Donuts) are "medium." Second, roast darkness correlated with our tasting-room experience: Green Mountain and Eight O'Clock, both lighter roasts, triumphed in the plain tasting yet proved too mild in the milk round. By contrast, the three darkest roasts (Starbucks, Millstone, and Seattle's Best) were the milk-round champs.

Still troubling was how to explain Chock Full o' Nuts, Folgers, and Dunkin' Donuts—three brands that stubbornly refused to play by the light-roast/dark-roast rules.

Luckily, some of the best discoveries happen by accident. The lab we hired to measure roast darkness had included several other tests for the same fee. Most of the data seemed better suited for a coffee dissertation than a cookbook: "package integrity" scores, moisture levels, and so forth. When we reached the last line, however, we noticed an odd-sounding measurement: "6 quakers," read one report; "1 quaker," read another. We had no idea what a quaker was, but given that the three problem coffees—Chock Full o' Nuts (7), Folgers (8), and Dunkin' Donuts (9)—had the most, we were determined to find out.

Turns out, a quaker is coffee-industry jargon for an underdeveloped coffee bean that fails to get sorted out before the roasting stage. Less dense than a regular, mature bean, quakers can wreak havoc on the coffee's flavor profile, imparting a spoiled taste to the brew. So desirable is quaker-free coffee that beans are graded based on quaker count, and buyers are willing to pay a premium for beans that come up clean in spot tests.

The lab had found quaker counts in our coffees ranging from 0 to 9—based on a 100-gram sample (just over a cup). Do those numbers really matter to the casual coffee drinker? In a word, yes. In a 1-pound (455-gram) bag of Millstone coffee, you would expect to find just 4½ quakers total, while in a 1-pound bag of Dunkin' Donuts coffee there might be 40.

So where did we come out? Turns out it is possible to get good whole bean coffee at the supermarket, but you may have to spend close to coffeehouse prices. Millstone ($7.99 for 11 ounces) and Starbucks ($9.39 for 12 ounces) were our favorite darker roasts, while Green Mountain Roasters ($7.49 for 12 ounces) and Eight O'Clock (a cheap $4.99 for 13 ounces) were the best for light-roast fans and those that drink their coffee black.

TESTING NOTES:
Watch Out for Quakers

The beans on the left may come from the dark side, but it's the pale ones on the right that visit evil upon a good brew. Quakers—light-colored, underdeveloped beans found in most commercial coffees—impart a rancid, "spoiled peanut" taste to the entire pot. In the tasting room, we had better luck with low-quaker-count brands.

Good Beans   **Quakers**

Rating Supermarket Whole Bean Coffees

TWENTY MEMBERS OF THE AMERICA'S TEST KITCHEN STAFF TASTED EIGHT DIFFERENT WHOLE BEAN COFFEES FROM THE supermarket (in all cases, the medium roast or "house" blend) at regular brew strength plain and with ¾ cup whole milk (per 12-cup pot). The coffees were analyzed by Coffee Lab International of Waterbury, Vermont, for roast darkness and "quakers," underdeveloped beans that affect the flavor profile of a batch (experts use quaker counts to grade coffee). The coffees are listed below in two groups—lighter roast and darker roast—in order of preference based on their scores in this tasting. The coffee beans are available nationwide.

LIGHTER-ROAST COFFEES

RECOMMENDED
Green Mountain Coffee Roasters Our Blend
$7.49 for 12 ounces
Agtron: 48.0; Quakers: 6
Soft, balanced, and pleasantly acidic, this was a lighter roast even the dark-roast camp could get on board with. Hints of caramel and fruit.

RECOMMENDED
Eight O'Clock Coffee Original
$4.99 for 13 ounces
Agtron: 51.4; Quakers: 6
We liked this inexpensive brand's smooth body, its nutty, almost chocolaty flavor, and its "toasty aroma," especially in the plain tasting.

RECOMMENDED WITH RESERVATIONS
Folgers Classic Supreme
$3.99 for 12 ounces
Agtron: 48.9; Quakers: 8
"Yuck—from my dad's old thermos," recalled one taster. "Reminds me of bad truckstop coffee," said another. The strong astringency was fine with milk but bothered tasters in the plain round.

NOT RECOMMENDED
Dunkin' Donuts Original Blend
$8.49 for 16 ounces
Agtron: 59.9; Quakers: 9
The lightest roast of the group failed to impress our tasters. ("Chocolaty but thin—is there coffee in here?") Unpleasant "molasses" off-notes, a bitter aftertaste, and the highest quaker count in our lineup.

DARKER-ROAST COFFEES

RECOMMENDED
Millstone Colombian Supremo
$7.99 for 11 ounces
Agtron: 36.5; Quakers: 1
This West Coast brand was neck-and-neck with Starbucks for winning over our own dark-roast enthusiasts. The deep, smoky, "chocolaty" flavor profile with a slightly bitter finish proved a good foil for milk, but some of our light-roast camp found it "harsh."

RECOMMENDED
Starbucks Coffee House Blend
$9.39 for 12 ounces
Agtron: 34.9; Quakers: 1
This self-proclaimed "light roast" from Starbucks was still darker than any of the other coffees in our lineup. Fans praised the rich, "almost chocolaty" flavors and deep, smoky aroma, but others found it burnt.

RECOMMENDED WITH RESERVATIONS
Seattle's Best Coffee Seattle's Best Blend
$7.69 for 12 ounces
Agtron: 40.0; Quakers: 0
Not a quaker to mar the flavor profile, but tasters still weren't that impressed. Dark and smoky, yet this brand lacked the complexity to round out such strong flavors. "Smells like tar."

NOT RECOMMENDED
Chock Full o' Nuts Soho Morning Roast
$5.79 for 12 ounces
Agtron: 40.3; Quakers: 7
The three bags we sent to the lab had three different roast darknesses. (The company says it was aiming for about 40.) Every version our panel tasted was plagued by metallic off-notes, "bracing acidity," and a "cardboard" aftertaste.

CONVERSIONS

A NOTE ON CONVERSIONS

SOME SAY COOKING IS BOTH A SCIENCE AND AN ART. We would say that geography has a hand in it, too. Flour milled in the United Kingdom and elsewhere will feel and taste different from flour milled in the United States. So we cannot promise that the loaf of bread you bake in Canada or England will taste the same as a loaf baked in the States, but we can offer guidelines for converting weights and measures. We also recommend that you rely on instincts when making our recipes. Refer to the visual cues provided. If the bread dough hasn't "come together in a ball," as described, you may need to add more flour—even if the recipe doesn't tell you so. You be the judge. For more information on conversions and ingredient equivalents, visit our Web site at www. cooksillustrated.com and type "conversion chart" in the search box.

The recipes in this book were developed using standard U.S. measures following U.S. government guidelines. The charts below offer equivalents for U.S., metric, and Imperial (U.K.) measures. All conversions are approximate and have been rounded up or down to the nearest whole number. For example:

1 teaspoon = 4.9292 milliliters, rounded up to 5 milliliters
1 ounce = 28.3495 grams, rounded down to 28 grams

Volume Conversions

U.S.	METRIC
1 teaspoon	5 milliliters
2 teaspoons	10 milliliters
1 tablespoon	15 milliliters
2 tablespoons	30 milliliters
¼ cup	59 milliliters
½ cup	118 milliliters
¾ cup	177 milliliters
1 cup	237 milliliters
1¼ cups	296 milliliters
1½ cups	355 milliliters
2 cups	473 milliliters
2½ cups	592 milliliters
3 cups	710 milliliters
4 cups (1 quart)	0.946 liter
1.06 quarts	1 liter
4 quarts (1 gallon)	3.8 liters

Weight Conversions

OUNCES	GRAMS
½	14
¾	21
1	28
1½	43
2	57
2½	71
3	85
3½	99
4	113
4½	128
5	142
6	170
7	198
8	227
9	255
10	283
12	340
16 (1 pound)	454

Conversions for Ingredients Commonly Used in Baking

Baking is an exacting science. Because measuring by weight is far more accurate than measuring by volume, and thus more likely to achieve reliable results, in our recipes we provide ounce measures in addition to cup measures for many ingredients. Refer to the chart below to convert these measures into grams.

INGREDIENT	OUNCES	GRAMS
I cup all-purpose flour*	5	142
I cup whole-wheat flour	5½	156
I cup granulated (white) sugar	7	198
I cup packed brown sugar (light or dark)	7	198
I cup confectioners' sugar	4	113
I cup cocoa powder	3	85
Butter†		
4 tablespoons (½ stick, or ¼ cup)	2	57
8 tablespoons (I stick, or ½ cup)	4	113
16 tablespoons (2 sticks, or I cup)	8	227

*U.S. all-purpose flour, the most frequently used flour in this book, does not contain leaveners, as some European flours do. These leavened flours are called self-rising or self-raising. If you are using self-rising flour, take this into consideration before adding leavening to a recipe.

†In the United States, butter is sold both salted and unsalted. We generally recommend unsalted butter. If you are using salted butter, take this into consideration before adding salt to a recipe.

Oven Temperatures

FAHRENHEIT	CELSIUS	GAS MARK (IMPERIAL)
225	105	¼
250	120	½
275	130	I
300	150	2
325	165	3
350	180	4
375	190	5
400	200	6
425	220	7
450	230	8
475	245	9

Converting Temperatures from an Instant-Read Thermometer

We include doneness temperatures in many of our recipes, such as those for poultry, meat, and bread. We recommend an instant-read thermometer for the job. Refer to the table at left to convert Fahrenheit degrees to Celsius. Or, for temperatures not represented in the chart, use this simple formula:

Subtract 32 degrees from the Fahrenheit reading, then divide the result by 1.8 to find the Celsius reading.

EXAMPLE:
"Roast until the juices run clear when the chicken is cut with a paring knife or the thickest part of the breast registers 160 degrees on an instant-read thermometer." To convert:

$160°F - 32 = 128°$
$128° \div 1.8 = 71°C$ (rounded down from 71.11)

INDEX

INDEX